*For fellow musicals fiends Rita Abrams, Morris Bobrow,
Mary McGeachy, Kathy Philis, and Randy Poe,
and in sunny memory of Ray Golden*

"What care I who makes the laws of a nation?
Let those who will, take care of its rights and wrongs.
What care I who cares for the world's affairs
As long as I can sing its popular songs."

—IRVING BERLIN

CONTENTS

INTRODUCTION

✦ *Tuning Up* ✦

When Robert Preston shouted "Ya got trouble!" in River City . . . when Carol Channing, all in red, glided down a gilded staircase while waiters at the Harmonia Gardens serenaded her with "Hello, Dolly!" . . . when Barbra Streisand defied us to rain on her parade in *Funny Girl* . . . when Joel Grey bid us *willkommen* and invited us into his seedy club—audiences were instantly enchanted. After such indelible moments, musicals were not the same, and neither were we.

Showstoppers! is about many of Broadway musicals' most unforgettable numbers—why they were so effective, how they were created, and what makes them still resonate—told wherever possible through the eyes of the performers, songwriters, directors, and choreographers who first built these explosive numbers. Their reminiscences are set against as much backstage lore as I could gather along the way, so though the book is primarily about the songs, it's also about the shows surrounding them.

Just what constitutes a "showstopper" requires a little translating and is sure to lead to arguments and ugly scenes. Musicals fanatics take this stuff seriously. Showstoppers are the key to every musical, often defining the show. They are the numbers that knocked us out when we first heard them and bring us back again and again. Ben Brantley, the *New York Times* theater critic, wrote, "A showstopper is a moment of performance so rousingly expert and energizing that the audience response—usually rapturous applause and noises that sound like 'bravo!'—freezes the show in a moment of loud, pagan worship." That pretty much covers it—the bare bones, anyway.

Shows of course are not truly stopped anymore, as they were in musicals' early days, when a performer would take a bow after a number or maybe do an encore or two. A showstopper, for our purposes, is just a generic catchall term for any big number that either provokes a rousing response or deeply moves an audience—any song that lights you up, makes you grin, or stirs you in some way. They're songs that gladden the spirit and leap out of the show, if not almost off the stage, that you want to see all over again—right *now*. Think of the exuberant title song of *Anything Goes*, which ended act 1 of Kathleen Marshall's spectacular, eye-popping 2011 revival of the Cole Porter classic. The number kept topping itself with each exhilarating new chorus and lasted about fifteen minutes.

But what exactly is a showstopper—or better yet, *why* is it a showstopper? This is an admittedly fuzzy area; stopping shows is a highly inexact science. Not everyone agrees what stops a show. A showstopper is the number that you recall whenever the show is mentioned—"Big Spender" in *Sweet Charity*, "I Am What I Am" in *La Cage aux Folles*, "Doin' What Comes Natur'lly" in *Annie Get Your Gun*, "The Ladies Who Lunch" and "You Could Drive a Person Crazy" in *Company*, "All That Jazz" in *Chicago*, "Tomorrow" in *Annie*, "Broadway Baby" in *Follies*, "Popular" in *Wicked*, "Springtime for Hitler" in *The Producers*.

Showstoppers are not merely impressive numbers but the engines that propel the shows, often straight into legend, and help keep the musical they're in alive and steadily performed. Beyond that, they've often become a vital part of Americana, firmly lodged in the country's collective memory. No matter your age, they refuse to be forgotten; even Alzheimer's patients can still sing them.

It's impossible to watch a classic showstopper like "I Cain't Say No," "You're the Top," "America," "One," or "Some People" and not be delighted anew, like the audiences who first witnessed them. A showstopper restores faith in the form, recharges passions, and fires up the protective instincts of the musical theater faithful, hoisting our flickering torch. The beleaguered musical is forever expiring and being reborn despite every known hazard— insane production costs, criminal ticket prices, aging audiences, a ban on movie musicals, and zero airplay on radio and TV. The great show tunes, when they were played on radio, once helped link Americans.

How are such eye-popping illusions created and crafted? I've tried to answer that question—one that has rarely even been asked before, or at least has not been investigated in much depth. *Showstoppers!* explores the songs' origins and explains why the songs still matter to us, not just among those lucky or old enough to recall historical original performances but right up to this season's Broadway hits and revivals. Later performers may vary in talent, but the numbers nearly always pay off. Most showstoppers are close to performer-proof, constructed of sturdy, timeless, trend-defying theatrical materials. Cabaret singer Wesla Whitfield, who lives off show tunes, observes, "These really great songs are deceptive: they appear simple but there's amazing craft going on underneath. 'I'm wild again, beguiled again, a simpering, whimpering child again'—that's brilliant! Not just the fun of it, but the way it keeps the internal rhythm going so that the song is not a lecture but a story."

My idea was to learn how classic showstoppers were built, in some cases line by line, step by step, to figure out why the numbers work so well, what makes them tick like precision watches and go off onstage like time bombs. When a number ignites, such as "One" from *A Chorus Line* or "The Rain in Spain" from *My Fair Lady* or "Gee, Officer Krupke" from *West Side Story*, there is nothing like it in any other art form. It's lovely if you were there to witness it originally (often I was), but in every case the showstopper outlived the star who first laid down the blueprint of how the number should be done: Robert Preston prancing lightly through "The-Sadder-but-Wiser-Girl" and "Marian the Librarian," Joel Grey oozing salacious decadence in "If You Could See Her," Celeste Holm confessing her unrepressed inhibitions in "I Cain't Say No."

Showstoppers! isn't just a fond exercise in nostalgia. The book is also a first-hand report from the trenches, including eyewitness accounts by the original creators, still alive and in many cases still kicking. It's a long journey, eighty years, from "Manhattan," the smash hit from 1925, to *Jersey Boys* in 2005.

Showstoppers, almost by definition, tend to be big splashy razzmatazz numbers, but a roll call of blockbusters might wear everyone out. So to guard against that monotony I'm including several "silent showstoppers"—heart-stoppers. These eloquent ballads, quiet songs, and moving moments don't leave crowds cheering but create their own powerful impression: "Send in the Clowns," "Some Enchanted Evening," "People," "Ohio," "If He Walked into My Life." A showstopper may be the essential key to a show—"Cabaret," "Ya Got Trouble," "Springtime for Hitler." Or it may come out of nowhere and delight us but leave no dent whatever on the plot—"Get Me to the Church on Time," "Sing for Your Supper," "Brush Up Your Shakespeare," "Let's Do It." Sensational songs all, but not really crucial to the story they pop out of; they were added to a show just for kicks.

To further muddy the theatrical waters, should finales and first-act closers be considered legitimate showstoppers? And what about show *starters*—great openers, which earn their own chapter here? With one exception (*Garrick Gaieties*), revues are off-limits, as are off-Broadway shows, jukebox musicals that are collections of old hits (again, with a major exception, *Jersey Boys*, for good reasons), and re-creations or reiterations of old shows (*42nd Street*, *My One and Only*, *Crazy for You*), however wonderful or packed with show-stopping standards.

Since Rodgers and Hammerstein, Broadway holy writ has decreed that songs must always advance the plot. Says who? Songs that break that rigid rule are often the best numbers in the show. People love musicals for the songs (and dances), not the plot, or "book." And anyway, a sturdy story can survive a great song that's just out to have fun. Nobody is going to stomp up the aisle and demand a refund if a number fails to advance the plot. It's hard to dislike shows like *Babes in Arms*, *Anything Goes*, or *Grease*, which have half a dozen great songs propping up a lame libretto (or "book"). Many showstoppers were created as pure star turns or unapologetic crowd-pleasers, and they earn their place in sheer joy.

Critic Robert Benchley wrote, "If you're going in for books, you might as well stay home and tell stories every evening." Walter Kerr added, "What Benchley knew, and what all the rest of us knew, was that the essential purpose of a musical-comedy book was to be interrupted. The question was not whether you had a 'strong' book, but whether you had a flexible book, one that could easily accommodate all the treasures a composer and a choreographer could cook up." Kerr also lamented the disappearance from modern musicals of humor, mainly inspired stage clowns. He asked, "Why can't there be foolish, as well as wise, musicals? Must all librettos be sane, and all their songs sworn to allegiance?" A great crowd-pleasing number—just a notch below a showstopper—is its own excuse.

My working definition of a major crowd-pleaser is "I Don't Need Anything but You," which skips along late in act 2 of *Annie*, sung by Annie and Daddy Warbucks. It occurs after Annie has moved into Warbucks's mansion and been newly outfitted in her trademark Little Orphan Annie outfit, itself a major crowd-pleasing coup de théâtre: suddenly the ragamuffin orphan emerges as the familiar comic-strip Annie in her red dress with a Peter Pan collar, Mary Janes, and orange ringlets. Annie enters via a staircase—her "Hello, Dolly!" moment—and she and Warbucks slip into their ecstatic number.

The moment works its disarming spell no matter how often you've seen it, and here's why: Annie finally has found a home *and* a father. The song is another of Broadway's welcome-home songs, and watching it leaves you feeling stupidly happy; it's a song full of cheery, almost teary feeling. You root for Annie and even for the formerly hard-boiled plutocrat Warbucks, who has found an adorable daughter on his doorstep. Pure schmaltz? Yes, indeed, like the show itself, but even as you realize that you're drowning in schmaltz, you don't feel cheaply manipulated—or maybe you do and just don't care. As musicals buff Mark Steyn writes, "Audiences don't reason it out like that; we just eat it up."

Annie earns our goodwill (and heart) because it's so neatly knit together by Thomas Meehan's book, by Charles Strouse and Martin Charnin's infectious score, by Charnin's canny staging, and, to be sure, by the engaging performances of Andrea McArdle and Reid Shelton in the original production. The spirit of the song dilutes the sentimentality and turns it into a tasty theatrical moment (a near showstopper) that sends the show over the top (a show topper?), your classic 11 o'clock number, the old term for a rousing number toward the end of the show calculated to send you home happy. Great musicals are packed with just such blatant crowd-pleasers: "Be a Performer" from *Little Me*; "Zip" from *Pal Joey*; "Gooch's Song" from *Mame*; and "I'm Past My Prime," "Jubilation T. Cornpone," and "The Country's in the Very Best of Hands," all from *Li'l Abner*—just a few of the great songs I didn't have room for.

Showstoppers are very much about performance—all performers dream of stopping the show—which of course is what we love about musicals as much as the music itself, so I've zeroed in on the performers who first created these milestone moments. The thrill of seeing a great number performed in front of you, live, by an irresistible entertainer is nothing like watching that same number on a movie or TV screen, or hearing it on a cast album. In a theater, you share the elation not only with the artist—the pure joy of his or her performance—but also with everyone in the house. You feel it's being sung that night just for you. And of course it is; it's as if everyone else in the audience is just a bystander.

Certain performers have been known to abuse the occasion. Zero Mostel's Tevye added nightclub shtick to *Fiddler on the Roof*. Once the rave reviews were safely in, Mostel felt free to futz around onstage, performing belly rolls and mugging outrageously. The show turned into *Zero Fiddling on the Roof*. In *Two by Two*, when Danny Kaye broke a leg during the run of the 1970 Richard Rodgers–Martin Charnin musical about Noah's ark, Noah suddenly turned into a Catskill comic. Kaye whirled around the stage in a wheelchair, using the injury as an excuse to cut up. Audiences loved it—the show wasn't exactly knocking them out—and Kaye's high jinks kept it running while the writers and director writhed.

Those are prize examples of not just stopping a show but stepping on it. Performers like Mostel, Kaye, Ethel Merman, Carol Channing, and Barbra Streisand were often out to polish their diva credentials, turning shows into one-person circuses (especially on tour, where directors can't get at them), singing to the audience instead of the characters. Certain performers can stop a show just by how they enter, cannily cuing applause by scanning the house to announce their arrival. They're well-oiled applause machines.

Performers have sly tricks to trigger an encore, such as Pearl Bailey milking the title song in *Hello, Dolly!* When the crowd demanded "More!," Bailey would shake her head no a few times, then look at the conductor, who would point to his watch, only to finally shrug and relent, as if unable to resist the audience begging Bailey to repeat the number. So Bailey would kick off her shoes, hike up her girdle, and sing "Hello, Dolly!" again, with all those galloping waiters dispatched to the wings so that she had the stage all to herself. But it was all calculated.

"It's a great word, *showstopper*," says Tommy Tune, a master of the genre, both as performer and choreographer. "I will tell you what I learned about showstoppers, and I learned it from Michael Bennett. Michael's theory—he was my mentor, even though he was younger than me—was that showstoppers endure because it's the one chance for the audience to take the show away from the performers. 'We will not let you go on with the show—it is our turn to celebrate!' It is kind of a selfish thing, like, 'We are going to clap until we decide we don't want to clap anymore.' They don't consciously know that. It's a collective thing, like a revolution or a riot. It just sort of happens."

Tune adds: "I don't think initially any directors ever set out to do showstoppers. We set out to put the numbers on as they came and that served the show, but once we found there was such a thing as a showstopper, everybody wanted to have one of those in their show. So the audience could say: 'That was a good show, but that number was a real showstopper.' When you say showstopper, I go right to what I think is my favorite, which is the 'Hello, Dolly!' number. That's the ultimate showstopper, the showstopper of showstoppers. That's the best-constructed showstopper I ever saw."

Tune costarred in and cochoreographed *My One and Only*, the 1983 smash musical created around Gershwin songs, which he starred in opposite the unlikely but fetching Twiggy. "There was a showstopper in *My One and Only* done by two people, Charles 'Honi' Coles and myself, to the title song. Now that was the big showstopper in that show, and it was just the two of us. If we had done that in the first scene it wouldn't have had the same impact. It was a very quiet soft-shoe, and because of where it came in the show—everything else in the show was so boisterous and energized—we did a very quiet number and it stopped the show—to the point, as in vaudeville, that we would have to do it again. That happened every night."

Tune recalls the first time it happened: "We did it, and when we finished it the audience took the show away from us, and I didn't know what to do. Honi Coles, being my senior, he was seventy-two years old at the time, I whispered to him, 'What should we do?' We could not go on with the show. He said, 'Let's do it again.' So I just gulped and I walked down to the edge of the stage. This is opening night and the critics were in place and this is a legitimate musical, but I broke the fourth wall. I leaned down to our conductor and I said, 'Take it again from the top.' He looked up at me and said, 'What?' And I said, 'Take it again from the top of the dance.' They turned their sheet music pages back and we did it again."

Of contemporary shows—*Hairspray, Newsies, Wicked, The Book of Mormon, Hamilton*—where every number is cranked up to showstopper level, Tune says, "I think those shows are all overcrowded. When it starts on that high level, what happens to me is that, after twenty minutes, the show gets more and more desperate with each coming number because they have to keep it up at that level. I find them exhausting. They are not artful. After twenty minutes I have gotten my fill. I need a palate cleanser, a quiet moment. Sometimes you have to stand and just look at a painting in a museum."

The composer Burton Lane (*Finian's Rainbow, On a Clear Day You Can See Forever*) said that writing a showstopper was a no-brainer for veteran songwriters. "Jerry Herman did it with 'Hello, Dolly!'—the number is pure vaudeville. So is 'Mame.' Banjos plunking, music building, changes of tempo. Anyone who's ever had any vaudeville experience knows that when you want to stop the show, musically, there are certain things you do with the beat and stop-time. When you get the right song to go with those tricks, it's an unbeatable combination!"

Ken Bloom, the musicals historian, says, "I think showstoppers are more about energy. Do you really like the song, or is it the voice or the orchestration? I don't think people know why they are reacting to a showstopper. When you have a kick line, people react to it, especially if it looks really hard." He adds, "We don't really have showstoppers anymore—very few. It's because the older songwriters knew how to write for specific people, like Ethel Merman. They knew what she could do. I am sure 'Defying Gravity' stops *Wicked* every performance, but if you had a recording of every woman who had played Elphaba and had to name who is singing, you couldn't do it because they're all so similar. 'Defying Gravity' is a showstopper because of the stagecraft—just like 'Memory.'"

Whether it's a big toe-tapping showstopper or a small heartrending ballad, these are the so-called take-home tunes, the moments we most cherish, that often sell the entire show to us, push it over the top and ultimately carve out a niche in the Broadway pantheon. A friend once told me, "Musicals are a series of small miracles." Such miracles don't happen by accident; they just look spontaneous when effortlessly performed. Said miracles are the result of not only creative sparks but also savvy stagecraft and sweaty grunt work, much of it revealed here. People love the idea of artistic inspiration, that a great number springs fully formed from a songwriter's brow, like in the movies, but far more often it's the result of hard labor, detailed thought, and long nights bent over a keyboard or a clipboard.

Most of these songs have become a beloved, vital part of theatrical history, if not American folklore, and some have even found a home in the language—"There Is Nothin' Like a Dame," "Diamonds Are a Girl's Best Friend," "What I Did for Love," "The Impossible Dream (The Quest)," "You'll Never Walk Alone," "Doin' What Comes Natur'lly." Once a song title appears in a headline, you know it's made it through callbacks into posterity ("Monica Was Just a Girl Who Couldn't Say No," "His Impossible Dream Is Realized," "Three Cops Who Will Never Walk Alone").

In studying first-night reviews of famous musicals, I was astonished how little mention was made of many shows' knockout songs. Milestone musicals often got ho-hum reviews as critics regularly failed to notice works of genius under their noses. In Brooks Atkinson's opening-night *New York Times* review of *Gentlemen Prefer Blondes*, he mentions one song, and it wasn't "Diamonds Are a Girl's Best Friend"; he fails to name even one number in his *Music Man* review, and his review of *My Fair Lady* only refers to a couple of songs in passing, with no details. In his notice for *Can-Can*, a show he dismissed as "not one of Cole Porter's best works," he astonishingly neglects to mention "Allez-Vous-En," "C'est Magnifique," "It's All Right with Me," and "I Love Paris." In many old reviews, critics spent more time discussing sets and costumes than songs—the beating heart of musicals. It's like reporting a great baseball game and neglecting to mention four grand slams. Critics still tend to take a score's best songs for granted, seeming almost unaware of their impact on a show and the audience. Even now, critics rarely discuss the actual songs with much interest or detail. It all seems quite strange.

I've tried to flesh out my discussions of the songs with whatever colorful, intriguing, or lurid backstage stories I could pry out of people who were there at the creation—stars, directors, songwriters, choreographers, stage managers, chorus members, critics, archivists, musical mavens, publicists, bystanders . . . whoever had anything pertinent or, better yet, impertinent to say. *Showstoppers!* tries to shed a new light on the dynamic between performers and audiences, the fragile art of enchanting a crowd of strangers, but also tries to zoom in on the gritty backstage day-to-day reality; the bloody creative battles and injured feelings; the threats, temperaments, and testy exchanges; the clash of creative egos at work. Prior to December 19, 1957, "Ya Got Trouble" was just words and dots on paper until it was brought to life by Robert Preston and company at the Majestic Theatre.

———

Showstoppers! is a personal, idiosyncratic, highly selective survey but also a journalistic journey into landmark musicals, America's major contribution to world culture (along with more-revered jazz).

Musicals are a totally American experience. Their optimism, energy, inventiveness, sentimentality, and infectious showbiz spirit reflect the country in many ways. They're a mix of kitsch and schmaltz, satire and sentiment—whatever is in the air. Some shows are musical time capsules: 1950's *Guys and Dolls* could not have happened in 1985, nor could 1957's *West Side Story* have happened in 1950; *How to Succeed in Business Without Really Trying* is clearly of 1961, a musical whose score includes both a prescient "A Secretary Is Not a Toy" and a prefeminist "Happy to Keep His Dinner Warm." *Wicked* is a darker, snarkier 2003 response to 1939's upbeat, bouncy *Wizard of Oz.* Many shows are historical documents—*Show Boat, Anything Goes, Hair, Company, Rent.*

Showstoppers! is a celebration of musicals but also a critical love letter, full of affection and prejudices, stage crushes, and a few crushing disappointments—a remembrance of theatrical flings past. In his memoir *Ghost Light,* former *New York Times* theater critic Frank Rich recalls how, as a boy, he scoured trash baskets in Times Square, scooping up discarded *Playbills*— buried treasure. I have my own collection of vivid memories, *Playbills* of the mind, of performers I saw in shows fifty years ago. You may forget what you ate for lunch yesterday, but a great showstopper stays with you to the grave. One friend told me, "When I saw my first musicals as a little girl I thought this was how life was supposed to be." Maybe we like them because they're not at all like life. The great ones never fail to make us happy. A college pal told me when I mentioned my idea to write this book, "It's time to view the showstopper as Shakespeare viewed the sonnet."

Everyone (well, everyone you'd care to know) loves musicals, but I get a sense that they're too often considered just amusing diversions when, in fact, many shows become personal touchstones, with compelling, transcendent powers. Why do these classic moments endure? What accounts for the compulsiveness of the more fanatical among us who go to any lengths, trekking to remote playhouses, to catch a beloved, rarely performed musical, such as *She Loves Me* or *Dames at Sea*?

Even after a century of dazzling marvels, musicals have never enjoyed the elite cultural cachet of opera, ballet, classical music, or even jazz. But Mel Brooks says, "The Broadway musical distinguishes America from every other country in the world." Why did America create and perfect the musical? It's a unique mutant gene in our national DNA. America has produced few great operas, but we've created 99 percent of the world's great musicals, America's true operas—"the closest thing America has to classical music," in musicals curator Philip Furia's words.

Opera demands lush music and great voices, but a landmark musical needs all of that *plus* incisive lyrics and astonishing dancing. Opera has rarely felt the slightest need for dancing, or for lyricists equal to its composers. Opera has no Lorenz Hart, Oscar Hammerstein, Stephen Sondheim, Ira Gershwin, Fred Ebb, Cole Porter, Jerry Herman, or Irving Berlin. I'll happily put "People Will Say We're in Love" or "Make Believe" up against *La forza del destino*. Opera lovers have advised me to read the libretto beforehand or to listen to the album, the worst imaginable case for art. Homework! Musicals are instantly comprehensible if they're any good. You may get more out of a show upon later visits, but you needn't study the score or pore over the plot of *The King and I* or *Company* or *Gypsy* to love it immediately.

This is, as has often been true in their lifespan, a precarious time for musicals. If theater is the "fabulous invalid," musicals remain in a chronic unstable condition. They're our most restless form, shooting off in all sorts of new, radical, bizarre, often troubling directions. Revivals of *Company* and *Merrily We Roll Along*, staged by stuntmaster John Doyle, had the cast doubling as the pit band. Puppets have invaded the form. Are tap-dancing robots waiting in the wings? *Hamilton*, the rage of 2015, surprises audiences by utilizing hip-hopping rapping Founding Fathers to relate "a story about America then, told by America now," as creator, writer, and star Lin-Manuel Miranda explains.

Showstoppers! celebrates a rich, exciting, sensuous art form. Old musicals are too often treated like rare coins, not vital, living events. These are my notes from hundreds of shows I've seen and covered—not just those on the lavish stages of Broadway and the West End but also musicals found in chilly church basements, cramped black boxes, dusty barns, drab school auditoriums, and makeshift theaters in far-flung communities I've eagerly visited in quest of a rarely done musical—*The Boys from Syracuse, Rags, Bells Are Ringing, Call Me Madam, Little Mary Sunshine.*

Since I began the book more than a decade ago, several of the legendary people I talked to who created the great shows have, alas, passed on (Marvin Hamlisch, Celeste Holm, John Raitt, Betty Garrett, Cy Coleman, Fred Ebb, Onna White, Adolph Green, Betty Comden, Jerry Orbach, Edie Adams), but many are still here, and I got to a lot of them. My prize catches: Patricia Morison, the original Kate in *Kiss Me, Kate*, ninety-eight when we talked; lyricist Sheldon Harnick, then eighty-eight; composer John Kander and producer-director Harold Prince, each eighty-four; performers Marge Champion, ninety-four, and Dick Van Dyke, eighty-eight. All of them spoke candidly and eagerly. Their recollections are invaluable, so I moved quickly, fearing it might be the last chance some of these crucial theater veterans would have to talk about the landmark moments they had a major hand in shaping.

(Note: In most cases I was granted permission to quote lyrics, but a few songwriters' estates and music publishers denied permission, for all sorts of reasons, some understandable—when I had harsh things to say about a show like *Wicked* or a song like "Sherry"—but other times the denials were inexplicable or seemingly arbitrary; in the case of *Les Misérables*, one word condemned me—I called the movie version *disappointing*. Sometimes the publisher or estate requested that I correct a word or fix a fact, which I did eagerly, but in a few instances [*Damn Yankees*, say], I was denied permission anyway. Go figure. The world of song permissions is dark, labyrinthine, and Kafkaesque. For lyrics I was sadly not allowed to quote, I have done my best to paraphrase them. It's not nearly as satisfying as quoting the actual lines, many of which are brilliant ["A Little Brains—a Little Talent" and "Popular," to name just two I love], but the lyrics for all the songs in the book are readily available online, and in many cases performances of the songs can be found on YouTube, and I urge readers to look them up.)

My own introduction to the art of the showstopper came in 1953, at my first Broadway musical, *Can-Can*, which opened me to everything a great musical can be. It was at the Shubert Theatre in fabled Shubert Alley. My rich cousin Sade provided tickets to a matinee, which struck me as an odd time to see a live show. I didn't realize Broadway shows were performed in daylight, like movies. It seemed to me then, and still does, that a musical, to work its wiles, really should disrobe in the dark.

Can-Can stirred and seduced me, with all the most potent elements of musical theater packed into one delectable package, everything performed with high energy, great skill, personality, and style. And yet the songs' greatest appeal, the beauty of any great musical number, is how each one felt fresh and tossed off, polished but playful, unlabored, extemporaneous, utterly of the moment. Your first musical is as unforgettable as a first kiss, maybe more so. I was knocked out by the frisky dances and by the sexy, frilly dance-hall hostesses onstage. With my father alongside me, I was both embarrassed and turned on by the can-can girls leaping high in the air, skirts lifted to reveal lacy petticoats, garters, and pink panties, before landing in perfectly executed splits—a highly erotic experience for a callow lad of fifteen from Oakland, California. As Will Parker reports in *Oklahoma!* after he's seen a "dandy burleekew" in Kansas City, "They'd gone about as fur as they could go!"

Those naughty can-can dancers had my eyes bulging and adolescent sap bubbling. I'd never glimpsed anything so sexy outside of *Esquire* Vargas girl calendars tucked in my bedroom drawer. But each of the girls on the Shubert stage was alive and smiling and only yards away, jumping, kicking, and whirling as they sang the showstopping title song.

Can-Can sizzled with carnal sex, not just the chorus girls or even Gwen Verdon slithering across the stage as the snake in a soft-core "Garden of Eden" ballet but also Cole Porter's risqué lyrics, full of leering songs like "Never Give Anything Away," "Come Along with Me," and the show's big hit, "It's All Right with Me." The song's illicit theme—that it's OK to be attracted to a woman who's not your wife or girlfriend—startled the romantic innocent in me who had never considered so scandalous a concept.

Easily the most dazzling number was the brilliant, showstopping title song, which exhaustively lists all the people, creatures, even machines, that can can-can. Like the chorus girls, Porter's astonishing, cartwheeling double and triple rhymes in a typical list song left me agog at his fertile mind and lyric facility: "If an ass in Astrakhan can / If a bass in the Saskatchewan can / Baby, you can can-can, too." Wow. There are better, deeper musicals than *Can-Can*, but for me it defines a certain kind of musical, now nearly extinct: a musical with a light tread, a sassy twinkle, snappy lyrics, and innate theatrical know-how. When it arrived in 1953, nobody suspected it might be among the last of its kind. Four years later, *West Side Story* arrived with a menacing bound, packing a different kind of heat.

A musical like *Can-Can* makes a promise, a bargain, when an orchestra strikes up the overture (in the days when musicals had tantalizing overtures) that in the next two hours there will be a glorious moment, maybe even two or three, when you will be swept away with a number that can make you gasp. *Showstoppers!* hopes to reveal how these exiting historical moments happened and explain why they still caper fondly and glitter brightly in our memories many decades later.

Hold on. I just heard the orchestra tuning up. Let's meet back here right after the show.

PART I
JUST FOR OPENERS

It's hard to think of a great musical that doesn't start with a stunning opening number that doesn't just set the scene but establishes the theme, style, and tone. The opener may make all the difference. It's the song that says hello, creates a crucial first impression, and, ideally, allows the audience to relax and look forward to a musical that they have paid dearly to see.

An opener is the number that shouts *Listen up!* and invites us to look forward to all that is about to follow. It tells us: *Stop worrying, you're in good hands.* A not-so-great opener can confuse an audience or get a musical off on a leaden left foot. Two not-yet-hit shows—*Fiddler on the Roof* and *A Funny Thing Happened on the Way to the Forum*—were famously in trouble in their first weeks because the openers didn't do their job. They neglected to communicate what was coming up. The rewritten openers—"Tradition" and "Comedy Tonight"—got each show off to a robust start, set the evening's agenda, grabbed the audience's attention, and gave each score just the rollicking shove it needed to send it rolling on to triumph. Both shows might have succeeded anyway, but their rewritten knockout opening numbers put the audience in a receptive state and booted the shows into high gear.

A great opening is an audio preview of coming attractions. A just OK opener puts the audience on alert. Musicals scholar Mark Steyn claims, "What's wrong with most [bad] musicals can usually be traced to something in the first ten minutes." *Gypsy* opens with a bunch of little girls bleating out a banal kiddie song, "May We Entertain You," in a tacky vaudeville act, but the show is swiftly kickstarted when the stage mother from hell Rose Hovick (Ethel Merman originally), strides down the aisle bellowing, "Sing out, Louise!"—a phrase now firmly embedded in showbiz lore. That moment warns us, *Watch out for this woman—she sounds formidable.* Rose's unsung first line is the show's true opener.

Marvin Hamlisch explained that the opening number in *A Chorus Line*—"I Hope I Get It"—is as significant as any number in the show. It tells the audience what's at stake and why they should care. "You need to tell an audience what the show is about." He pointed to another great near opener, "The Telephone Hour" in *Bye Bye Birdie*: "It's not just the music and lyrics—look at that set!" marveled

Hamlisch, indicating a stage chocked with teenagers in a honeycomb of cubicles babbling on telephones in their bedrooms. "There are so many things that go into that first song." Mark Steyn notes, "In a musical, the first number has to be more than just the number which comes first."

Openers are far more vital now than they used to be, when shows had overtures to help set the mood before the curtain went up. In those days they also had curtains, which have since been abandoned for no discernible reason. Most musicals now open cold, with nothing to help warm up an audience. So the heavy burden of setting the right mood falls entirely on that first number. In the days of overtures and a curtain that masked the opening scene, the audience had a chance to settle back in their seats and get set for something presumably wonderful about to occur. Today's openers are out there on their own.

Nobody knows just why or when it was determined that musicals don't need overtures. A few shows still use them, mainly revivals written during the overture era, which often trim them to only two minutes. Were audiences squirming in their seats and growing restless if forced to sit through a four-minute musical teaser? The overture was suddenly regarded as a time-wasting drag, when in fact it's just the opposite. It provided an opening jolt of electricity that charged up an audience. Big musical movies like *Funny Girl* (and even nonmusical films, like *Doctor Zhivago* and *Around the World in 80 Days*) had overtures, sometimes even intermissions, signifying it was not just a movie but an event. Somehow the overture degenerated into background music for yakkers. Audiences, now used to movies, treat overtures as a kind of live Muzak. Today the overture has been replaced by a utilitarian announcement commanding you to turn off your cell phone and all electronic devices, unwrap your damn candy, take no photos, and basically shape up. Not a welcoming, let alone exciting note to begin on—a totally antitheatrical, mood-destroying moment that has all the charm of an airport terminal announcement.

The overture was invented to provide a melodic, mood-enhancing climate, an emotional transition between opening your program and opening your senses to the show about to start. There are few more thrilling moments in theater than the overture to *Gypsy*, with that slide whistle and cymbal crash denoting we are about to enter the tinny world of vaudeville, or the drum major's whistle that leads off the overture to *The Music Man*—a signal that a marching band may soon be heading your way.

Of course, a great overture sets up such high expectations that it requires an exciting opening number to top it. These days the opener has to do the work of the rudely abandoned overture. Here are a few electrical openers that can make the hair on your arms stand up and perhaps cause your heart to flutter a few beats faster.

GUYS AND DOLLS

◆ 1950 ◆

"Fugue for Tinhorns"

You could tell *Guys and Dolls* would be a winning thoroughbred from the first bugle blast of **"Fugue for Tinhorns,"** maybe the most identifiable opening notes in Broadway history. Its electrifying fanfare calls the horses—and the audience—to the starting gate, and opening-night playgoers were off and grinning at the 46th Street Theatre the night of November 24, 1950.

Instantly, the Frank Loesser song piques your interest, perks up your ears, establishes the scene and characters in slangy racetrack lingo, and alerts you to the musical about to follow. The raffishly attired trio lets us know we're on foreign but friendly ground—underground Broadway, home to bizarre denizens who look and sound like cartoon characters and yet seem totally authentic. The musical, subtitled "A Fable of Broadway," is based on tales by Damon Runyon, the street's most astute and amusing chronicler.

The rousing opener lifts our spirits with a song of overlapping three-part harmony as each guy in the trio, clutching a tip sheet, argues why his horse is the best bet. The charged number's very first line, sung by gambler Nicely-Nicely Johnson, grabs your ear: "I got the horse right here / The name is Paul Revere, / And here's a guy that says if the weather's clear, / Can do, can do"; it's that Runyonland racetrack speak, "can do, can do," that tips us to the show's insider savvy, assuring us we're on solid turf. Even the wry title, "Fugue for Tinhorns," alerts us that this is no ordinary musical.

Nicely-Nicely (played first by the beloved and amusing Stubby Kaye; meet him again on YouTube) insists his nag is a sure thing: "I tell you, Paul Revere, now this is no bum steer, / It's from a handicapper that's real sincere"; and his pal Benny Southstreet argues, "But look at Epitaph, / He wins by a half, / According to this here in the Telegraph."

The opener is a roundelay of racing terms, tout chatter, and the nags' names. In three minutes, we have the setting, the flavor of the show, and the cast of characters. Just concocting a classic fugue for three gamblers is itself a happy, wonderfully innovative touch. We're rooting them all on before anyone utters a spoken word as the gamblers announce their day's picks. Even though the show is about craps players, not horse players, it's clear the show was written by a guy who knew his way around the track.

The original book was written by Jo Swerling, but it didn't capture Runyon's ragtag Times Square world, so Loesser called on his pal Abe Burrows, who wrote the hit radio show *Duffy's Tavern*, which was peopled with

Racetrack touts, Stubby Kaye at right, declaring their picks in *Guys and Dolls*.

Runyonesque characters. (Trivia note: Burrows's son James, a chip off the old tavern bar, cocreated *Cheers*.) By the time Burrows was hired, Loesser had written the entire score, so Burrows had to imagine all the scenes around Loesser's songs, the exact reverse of how musicals are normally written, which may explain why the scenes so neatly fit the songs that emerge from them.

But in early rehearsals, "Fugue for Tinhorns" was an orphan that didn't fit in anywhere in the show. Coproducer Ernie Martin had a good idea (occasionally producers have one). "It had nothing to do with the plot," recalled Martin's partner Cy Feuer. "We had a great piece of material, and we're struggling to find a spot for it, and then Ernie finally said, 'If you've got no place to put it, why don't you stick it up front, as a genre piece, where it's not about anything but it opens the show and sets the whole thing going?' Which is where it went and did exactly what Frank [Loesser] thought it would do."

In Susan Loesser's biography of her father Frank, Carin Burrows, Abe's widow, recalled her opening-night memory after "Fugue for Tinhorns": "There was such a reaction from the audience. That's when we knew we had an enormous hit. There's an electricity in the audience that is palpable. You know it right away." Or to swipe the title of Cy Feuer's memoir, I got the show right here.

THE MUSIC MAN

◆ 1957 ◆

"Rock Island"

The hypnotic sing-song opener of *The Music Man* isn't even a song; it's a chant, without music or lyrics that rhyme. **"Rock Island"** is a 1950s white man's Middle West rap that breaks out aboard a trainload full of Iowa traveling men in straw hats, chattering about a stranger in their midst about whom they've heard dark rumors.

First nighters at the Majestic Theatre on December 19, 1957, who had come to see a new show called *The Music Man* must have been perplexed by an opening song about a music man without any music. Even more daringly, the opener takes place in a railroad car in which all the men are babbling in some strange dialect. They're going on about "noggins" and "piggins" and "firkins" that sound like made-up terms, but they're real items. What the heck is a "hogshead" or a "demijohn"?

After a few bars, though, we catch the drift, but even if we don't quite absorb every word, the staging of the opening scene is so skilled (originally the work of director Morton DaCosta and choreographer Onna White), and the jiggling salesmen's chanted conversation is so infectious, that we listen even harder. Early *Music Man* audiences must have wondered, *What sort of weird musical journey are we on exactly?*

In fact, the show's exposition is neatly set up in the men's babble, which tells us the era, the locale, and the salesmen's plight; finally, on the very last note, Harold Hill himself is revealed. It's all disclosed in a few brief bursts of jabber.

Eventually one guy gets down to cases: "Ever met a fella by the name a'f Hill? . . . He's a mu-u-sic man. / And he sells clarinets to the kids in the town with the big trombones and the rat-tat-tat drums . . . with uniforms too, / With the shiny gold braid on the coat and a big red stripe."

Meredith Willson's language instantly pulls us back to 1912 Iowa. The archaic phrasing and terminology, the precise period details of the lyric, sets us down in a specific place and time and starts the show with a sense of great authenticity. Wherever we're headed, we've got a reliable guide to take us there. Right off, we're intrigued, involved, and on our way.

Willson's bantering song lacks music or rhyme but is hitched to a hypnotic rhythm that mimics the beat of a train chugging through the Iowa cornfields as the salesmen bounce in their seats shouting a call-and-response to the cadence of a clickety-clack railroad rhythm: "CASH for the merchandise," cries one; "CASH for the buttonhooks," the other salesmen reply. "Whadayatalk, whadayatalk, whadayatalk." Critic Walter Kerr called it a "syncopated conversation." He wrote that the man behind it all, Meredith Willson, "is impatient with dialogue."

Willson turned dialogue into prose music. When he was the host of CBS Radio's *Sparkle Time* (later *The Ford Music Room*), he wrote pieces in unison for a vocal quartet called the Talking People, as well as a Jell-O commercial in "speak-song," all warm-ups for *The Music Man*. Willson used the technique throughout *The Music Man*, in contrapuntal songs like "Piano Lesson," which begins with Marian instructing her pupil Amaryllis in dialogue, which is then overlaid with her mother's hectoring spoken song, "If You Don't Mind My Saying So."

As the opening scene develops, *chug, chug, chug, chug* goes the train as

Troubled traveling salesmen aboard the Rock Island railroad confront the shady guy named Harold Hill who peddles uniforms for a boys' band.
JERRY OHLINGER'S MOVIE MATERIALS

it gathers steam, accompanying the chanting salesmen gripping their sample cases and hanging on to the overhead straps of a herky-jerky locomotive. Steam billows alongside the train as it pulls out of the station and gathers speed while the conductor bellows, "River City junction, next stop! Board! All aboart! . . . We're 'cross the state line into Iowa. River City! Population twenty-two hundred and twelve. Seegarettes illegal in this state. Booard!"

This is just the first of several numbers in Willson's inspired score whose tunes subtly emerge from ambient sounds, an ingenious device that Willson told me was coincidental; he even seemed surprised when I mentioned it in an interview. Hard to believe a man of Meredith Willson's wide musical background failed to detect his own technique. One song after another is triggered by the homey sounds of River City life, using the natural rhythms where the song is set:

- "Marian the Librarian," in which Hill pleads with the librarian to give him a tumble, opens with Marian stamping books being checked out of the Madison Public Library—"Mar-r-r-rian" [thump], "Madame Libar-r-r-ian" [thump], "I love you madly madly, madame librarian" [thump, thump, thump], and so on. Hill sings the number in hushed stage-whispered tones, so as not to disturb the library patrons, who eventually join in his plea and wind up as a chorus dancing ever so quietly amid the stacks.

- "Gary, Indiana," sung by Marian's lisping kid brother, Winthrop (in the original script he was spastic), is a kind of speech lesson that gives him confidence to speak. It's a song with few *s*'s, allowing him to confidently repeat "Gary, Indiana" again and again.
- "Lida Rose" and "Will I Ever Tell You," intertwined nostalgic reveries crooned by the Buffalo Bills quartet, are affectionate echoes of barbershop songs. Hill instructs the quartet how to sing, revealing he actually does know a few things about music despite his con game. "Singing," he tells the foursome, "is just sustained talking," and after a few lessons (teaching them to start by crooning "ice cre-e-e-am") the four members of the sudden barbershop quartet are harmonizing beautifully. They pop up throughout the show, as backup singers serenading whatever needs to be serenaded. "Ladies, from now on," promises Hill, "you will never see one of these men without the other three!"
- "Pick-a-Little" is a musical cacophony, a patchwork ditty sewn together from pecking noises that mock the gossiping hens in town who suspect something may be up between Marian Paroo and Harold Hill. It's a spoken sound effect of phrases that mimic biddies nattering to each other ("talk-a-little, pick-a-little, talk-a-lot, pick-a-little"). It's another singsong recitative that's both accurate and funny. Throughout his idiosyncratic score, Willson infuses the number's syncopation into the Music Man himself; Hill speaks in a melodic metronomic beat.
- "Wells Fargo Wagon," also warbled by Winthrop, is a Willsonesque list song of goods on their way to the excited townspeople ("I got a box of maple sugar on my birthday / In March I got a gray mackinaw / And once I got some grapefruit from Tampa / Montgom'ry Ward sent me a bathtub and a cross-cut saw"), all recited by townspeople, repeated in a solo by Winthrop, to the clippety-clop rhythm of wagon wheels he hopes are bringing the promised instruments and uniforms to River City. It's a salute to the Costco of its day.
- "Piano Lesson" is a catchy little tune that segues seamlessly out of scales plunked on a keyboard by Amaryllis, Marian's pupil. The song begins as a practice piece that becomes another unrhymed dialogue between Marian and her mother, nagging her about being too fussy about men after Marian tells her mother that the "music professor" in town has followed her home. Marian instructs her pupil, "Now, don't dawdle, Amaryllis. . . . So do la ti mi / A lit-tle slow-er and please / keep the fing-ers curved as nice / And as high as you poss-ib-ly can." Mrs. Paroo cuts in, in her

thick Irish brogue, "If ya don't mind me sayin' so / It wouldn't have hurt you / To find out what the gentleman wanted." Marian: "I know what the gentleman wanted." Mrs. Paroo: "What, dear?" Marian: "You'll find it in Bal-l-lzac." Willson repeats the keyboard scales ploy at the beginning of "Goodnight, My Someone," sung by Marian. The lullaby begins simply, with Amaryllis at the piano, then gently swells into a lush, fully orchestrated ballad (and what a perfect turn-of-the-twentieth-century name—Amaryllis).

Willson himself began by tootling a piccolo in John Philip Sousa's marching band at nineteen, then became a flutist in Broadway pit orchestras, a radio music director, and an occasional comedy foil on comedy and variety shows. On radio's last extravaganza, *The Big Show*, he was both conductor and straight man to baritone-voiced hostess Tallulah Bankhead, whom he always addressed as "Miss Bankhead, sir." He wrote the show's closing theme, "May the Good Lord Bless and Keep You," a later hit.

Willson's song bag was full of tricks, and in *The Music Man* he uses them all. It's a show that's been steadily revived for close to sixty years and remains as fresh, amusing, and incredibly listenable and likable as the night it opened. The score bursts with melodic invention. Willson's follow-up shows, *The Unsinkable Molly Brown* and *Here's Love* (based on *Miracle on 34th Street*), are conventional musicals that reveal little of the innovative brilliance that makes *The Music Man* a singular work of genius.

In eight years and several revisions (with help from coscriptwriter Franklin Lacey), Willson poured all of his talents into the musical, which said all he had to say. It's a memoir of his boyhood, a romantic scrapbook of a place and time that comes out of Willson's gut. As *New York Times* critic Brooks Atkinson said in his review, "Mr. Willson has a fresh slant on Americana. Although he does not take it seriously, he loves it with the pawkiness [a dry wit] of a liberated native." It may still be the most unabashedly all-American of all American musicals.

One of the show's ballads, "Till There Was You," carved out a unique niche in pop history—the only song from a Broadway musical ever recorded by the Beatles. Willson loathed rock 'n' roll, which he called "garbage . . . a creeping paralysis . . . a plague . . . a scaly corruptor of taste and a babbling destroyer of craftsmanship." He must have been chagrined when the major rock group of all time paid him the compliment of recording one of his songs.

The official title of the show's opening song is "Rock Island," the name of the famous railroad line the salesmen are traveling on (the same "mighty fine line" Johnny Cash sang about that same year), but the number is usually identified by its central theme—"But he doesn't know the territory!," the men's complaint about the outsider they've heard of, name of Harold Hill, seated right in their midst. One of the men on board says Hill threatens to muscle in on their sacred territory. For a traveling man, territory is everything. Ask Willy Loman, a traveling man whose tragic downward trajectory in *Death of a Salesman* began when he was transferred out of New England to a territory he didn't know and, worse, where nobody knew him.

All the salesmen aboard the Rock Island train are cronies, highly suspicious of a possible usurper of their territory and clientele. Traveling men in those days were a tight community on wheels that stuck together and warned their brethren of any impending crisis, like the outlier they've heard about selling boys' band uniforms, of all things. He can't be up to any good, they rightly figure.

"Rock Island" is a triumphant opener that swiftly captures the Norman Rockwell flavor of River City, not just the characters but the small-town attitudes and language. The show is peppered with lovely forgotten phrases like "brazen overtures," "libertine men and scarlet women," "the sadder-but-wiser girl," "You watch your phraseology, young lady!" and "shipoopi," a 1912 endearment Willson turns into an entire song about old-time courtship habits ("A woman who'll kiss on the very first date / Is usually a hussy, / And a woman who'll kiss on the second time out / Is anything but fussy").

In *The Music Man*, Willson invented a kind of sung speech (in classical music called "Sprechgesang" by Engelbert Humperdinck, or "Sprechstimme" by Arnold Schoenberg—pretty fast company for a Mason City piccolo player). It's defined as "speaking rhythm," first heard in European opera and years later made famous on Broadway in *My Fair Lady* by nonsinger Rex Harrison's recitatives "Why Can't the English?," "I'm an Ordinary Man," and "I've Grown Accustomed to Her Face."

Willson had devised the method long before *The Music Man*, when he came up with a vocal quartet for his CBS Radio show, with commercials spoken like a Greek chorus. Bobby McFerrin's so-called "voicestra" is a descendant of Willson's concoction.

Willson's concept was to give ordinary people a musical voice, to turn the vocally challenged into singers of a sort. He explained, "Shouldn't they also have a way to release their musical feelings, like everybody else who can sing?" He said, "I wanted to write the dang songs as dialogue. Without rhymes. People don't talk in rhyme." Producers Feurer and Martin, who turned down a chance to present *The Music Man*, had tried to talk him out of his crazy notion, explaining that audiences accepted characters who broke into song with lyrics that rhyme. But the songwriter stuck to his lyrical guns. "I was determined to bridge dialogue and song," said Iowa-stubborn Meredith Willson.

GYPSY

♦ 1959 ♦

"Some People"

"Some People" from *Gypsy* arrives after a cutesy-pie vaudeville ditty, "May We Entertain You," sung by Mama Rose's daughters Baby June and Louise, but it's really the show's tingling opener.

The song establishes the steamroller tone for the show's indomitable lead character, who reveals her worldview and determined take-me-or-leave-me attitude. "Some People" is what musicals scholars call a classic "I want" song, establishing Rose's purpose and goals. Rose defiantly lays out what she's all about and how she's different from everyone else and why she likes it that way.

Librettist Arthur Laurents told lyricist Stephen Sondheim, "We need a song where she tells the old man, 'I'm leaving this goddamn place. I'm getting out, I need 88 dollars. I had a dream last night . . .'" Sondheim then asked composer Jule Styne, "You know that percussive thing? Give me a long strain for 'Some People,' something slow." Styne and Sondheim were creatively in tune, with no collaborative envy or ego, despite Sondheim's original wish to also write the music.

"When you write with him," Styne said of Sondheim, "you actually feel good as a composer. He places value on the music. What kind of word fits each note. When you soar musically, he knows he must say something as important as the notes. He never asks for extra notes. And he doesn't put the full value on the rhyme, like most lyricists. The thought is the main thing with Steve. The music must set the character as well as the words." Sondheim, for his part, told Styne's biographer, "The only thing annoying about Jule's

Ethel Merman blasting "Some People" in *Gypsy*.

working habits is how fertile he is. He teems with ideas. Jule doesn't allow you to get discouraged. I prefer to get discouraged [so] it was a good change for me. If he's hurt when you don't like something, he doesn't show it."

"Some People" pulsates with Styne's inspiring, driving tune, which exactly fits Sondheim's gutsy lyrics. The song seems like it was written by one person, like all great collaborations. It spells out Rose's plan, setting the musical in motion. We learn who she is and that she refuses to knuckle under to anyone. Right away, we see her bravado manner, evident in her opening line in the show as she strides down the aisle toward the stage, braying, "Sing out, Louise—sing out!," a phrase now one of musicals' most quoted lines; it's the stage mother's mantra, even the title of a book of anecdotes about musicals.

"Some People" is set up with an impassioned speech Rose makes to her disapproving father, explaining why she needs to borrow eighty-eight dollars to pay her rent or buy a train ticket, which triggers the song that expresses her life credo. The first draft included a verse in which Rose tells her father to go to hell, but Merman balked, fearful it would make the audience dislike her, which is most stars' first concern. As Sondheim writes, "Rose didn't care what people thought of her; Merman did."

In the song, Rose doesn't quite tell her dad to go to hell, but she pretty much tells everyone else to. Unlike other get-outta-my-way musical heroines (Dolly, Mame, Fanny Brice, Molly Brown), Rose doesn't try to charm anyone except Mr. Goldstone the producer, but only because he can help her.

The speech launches Rose's tough-talking opening stanza: "Some people can get a thrill / Knitting sweaters and sitting still— / That's okay for some people / Who don't know they're alive." There it is, ladies and gentlemen, Mama Rose's entire character—intrepid, insulting, intriguing—spelled out in four embattled lines. The lyric later continues with one of Sondheim's masterful triple inner rhymes: "Some people can be content, / Playing bingo and paying rent— / That's peachy for some people, / For some humdrum people to be, / But some people ain't me!"

You can compare the character's style in a YouTube bouquet of various Roses—Merman, Patti LuPone, Judy Garland, Bernadette Peters, Tyne Daly, Liza Minnelli, Linda Lavin, Betty Buckley, Bette Midler. It's a little like an audition, but you can't hear enough to decide; though Peters makes a vivid impression, she's very un–Mama Rose–like in a jiggly strapless gown.

It's a great song, mocking—in fact, downright disdainful of—how the other half lives (or doesn't live), while telling us about her delusional dreams, her past, and her hoped-for future in the dynamic release as she cries: "Good-by-y-ye / To blueberry pie!" Then, in stubborn defiance of tradition and defeatism, she shouts: "Some people sit on their butts, / Got the dream, yeah, but not the guts! / That's living for some people, / For some humdrum people, I suppose / Well, they can stay and rot— / But not Rose!" Sondheim couldn't resist repeating his "some humdrum people" rhyme, and who can fault him?

He excuses it this way: "I suspect that the profusion of inner rhymes here is due less to character than to the exuberance I felt at being released from two years of *West Side Story*'s 'right / night / fight' rhyming." That was OK for some people, but not him.

MAME

◆ 1966 ◆

"It's Today"

The official opening number in *Mame* is a little hymn sung by young Patrick called "St. Bridget" that delivers crucial dramatic exposition. But **"It's Today,"** the show's true opener, follows "St. Bridget" and jump-starts the show. It's a classic Jerry Herman picker-upper that proclaims the glory of leaping out of bed and welcoming the morning with a joyous whoop.

Herman found *Mame* the easiest of all his musicals to write. "It was everything that I understand and believe in," he told me, "the joy of life and the characters." In the show's most quoted line, Mame proclaims, "Life is a banquet, and most poor sons of bitches are starving to death!" (In the movie version, SOBs was changed to "suckers"—such innocent times.) Mame declares it, but Herman puts her philosophy into ecstatic practice in "It's Today," a phrase Herman took from his mother's life credo. As a child, he'd come home from school one day to find the house festooned with balloons and confetti. He asked her what holiday it was, and she said, "It's today!" Ruth Herman believed in celebrating every day like a holiday. Her son very much concurs.

That seize-the-day theme is echoed in many a gleeful Herman number. In writing "It's Today," Herman stole the idea not just from his mother but from himself, recycling a tune used in two earlier off-Broadway revues, *Nightcap* and *Parade*, titled "Showtune in 2/4" ("There is no tune as exciting / As a show tune . . .").

"It's Today" has an ebullient theme—live for today—that starts *Mame* off on an irrepressible note. It's a classic "I am" song that tells us what Mame Dennis is all about, a declaration of merriment sung from the top of a staircase, the composer's favorite design element. The tune accelerates, then puts the brakes on, then speeds up again, and slows down. As it nears the end, it becomes more than just a bubbly opener in a reference to the party "gift" Mame has just been given—her young nephew Patrick. A line in the lyric advises, "There's a 'thank you,' you can give life / If you live life all the way."

The song is reprised in the show and even in the clunky film version starring Lucille Ball, but Lucy was unlovable in the film, lacking the zip, warmth, and appeal of Angela Lansbury, who imbued the character with the required savoir faire. Lucille Ball had plenty of appealing traits, but *savoir faire* was never a term ascribed to her. Ball was embarrassingly miscast in the hope of capitalizing on her fading sitcom charisma (one critic called the show a great vehicle for over-the-hill performers), but the musical falls to pieces without a vivid Mame. Herman, like nearly everyone, thought Lucille Ball was monumentally wrong for the movie. His review: "She could not sing and she could not dance. She was just not the right person. It should have been Judy Garland."

In "It's Today," Mame proclaims, "Light the candles, / Get the ice out, / Roll the rug up, / It's today! / Though it may not be anyone's birthday, / And though it's far from the first of the year, / I know that this very minute has history in it, we're here!" Then, "Tune the grand up, / Dance your shoes off, / Strike the band up, / It's today!" Just reading the lyrics might not cause you to roll up the rug and break open the champagne, but Herman's bright, celebratory tune is so irrepressibly fizzy that your spirits are sure to be lifted and your toes set a-tapping. It's guaranteed to put you in exactly the right mood for the two-hour party about to start.

All that optimism has overshadowed, if not hidden, Herman's inventive but underrated musicianship. "If he hadn't become a fine lyricist, he'd still be regarded as a great theater composer," says singer and archivist Michael Feinstein. "To be simple without being cliché is nearly impossible." Herman walks that treacherously thin line, daring to be direct but not banal—also Irving Berlin's great skill.

Composer Charles Strouse (*Annie, Bye Bye Birdie*) pinpoints Herman's signature device: "A song of his always states a theme and it keeps sequentially building on itself, without a release." Herman makes sure that you're infused with the melody, shamelessly repeating it until—as in "It's Today," "Before the Parade Passes By" (*Hello, Dolly!*), or "The Best of Times" (*La Cage aux Folles*)—it explodes with joy. The one Herman musical that featured a depressive big lady, *Dear World*, a show about an obsessed old woman trying to rescue the planet from evil polluters (based on Giraudoux's *The Madwoman of Chaillot*) was a resounding flop, yet it's one of Herman's most innovative if least jolly scores, in which he reveals a tougher, darker, sardonic side. He never tried that again, backpedaling to musicals with rosier themes. But even in *Dear World*, he managed four positive songs—"Kiss Her Now," "Tomorrow Morning," "One Person," and the title song, a plea to the planet to heal itself, which few liked, but it's infused with Herman's never-say-die spirit.

CABARET
◆ 1966 ◆

"Willkommen"

E ven if **"Willkommen,"** the dynamic opener that beckons us into *Cabaret* with a deadly welcoming smirk, arrived halfway through act 1, it would easily stop everything. The song's famous vamp gets its hooks into us before one word is sung. Like all great vamps, it nudges the audience and says, *Get set for something sensational.*

Beyond its seductively sinister instrumentation, "Willkommen" gets right down to business by handling several nuts-and-bolts theatrical functions with crisp efficiency; it's a model for all openers. "Willkommen" introduces us not only to the show but also to one of its central characters, the preening pansexual Emcee (originated by Joel Grey), our hedonistic host, who comes on like Dracula, inviting us into his dank castle with a menacing "Goot e-e-evening, frands!" The Emcee displays his supposedly tantalizing harem of moth-eaten showgirls in ripped stockings and with greased faces. They do their best to look lascivious but look more like parodies of debauchery.

The song also welcomes us into the shadowy Kit Kat Klub, where "in here life ess beautiful!" The sneering Emcee and his seamy chorus line establish the depraved sexual and moral atmosphere of the show to follow, pointing the way to the creepy world we will inhabit for the next two hours, a metaphor for the rancid German political climate lurking just outside the Kit Kat Klub's doors.

So the song not only kicks off the musical with a threatening, irresistible opening number but also serves as plot device, characterization, show starter, and mood setter. By the time the number ends, we're up to our necks in pure lechery and a climate of Nazi wretchedness. Not bad for one tune, which composer John Kander says "took maybe half an hour to write."

In *Broadway Babies Say Goodnight*, Mark Steyn notes, "At first glance it seems for *Cabaret* the most obvious and old-fashioned opening you could come up with: 'Welcome to the show.' But Joel Grey is seducing us . . . into the club as a retreat from the troubles of the world—whereas what happens in the cabaret is . . . a comment and mirror on what's going on in the wider world. . . . In 'Cabaret' the cabaret is the main character, and it's set up perfectly."

The gaunt, nasty nightclub Emcee, in garish whiteface, crimson lips, and spidery eyelashes, sings "Willkommen" to the tinny sound of a tacky but bravely peppy onstage ensemble. The noxious number corners us before segueing into a scene on a train with an American writer traveling to Berlin on the eve of Nazism. We're passengers on the same railroad car and then, suddenly, seated at a table next to him at that Berlin dive you don't want to be seen at but might just want to take a quick peek inside.

Joel Grey salaciously ogling a Kit Kat Girl in *Cabaret*.

The tawdry Emcee and Kander and Fred Ebb's insistent score grab you by the lapels and drag you into the show. Grey is like a barker, buttonholing wary but willing passersby to enter a sleazy, sweaty peep show that reeks of political and personal corruption. Walter Kerr in the *New York Herald Tribune* described how Grey "bursts from the darkness like a tracer bullet. . . . Mr. Grey is cheerfully charming, soulless and conspiratorially wicked. In a pink vest, with sunburst eyes gleaming out of a cold-cream face. He is the silencer of bad dreams, the gleeful puppet of pretended joy, sin on a string. No matter what happens during the evening, he can make gaiety out of the macabre."

"Willkommen" also first woke up most audiences to the work—and to the gritty/glitzy world—of songwriters John Kander and Fred Ebb. Plus of course we got to meet Joel Grey, whose devious Emcee became an indelible character in musical history. Grey embodied the part so thoroughly that it's been almost impossible to match his leering mask, snarl, and sneaky moves. Many have tried. Not even Alan Cumming's raunchy Emcee in Sam Mendes's acclaimed but over-the-top 1993 London and 1998 and 2014 Broadway revivals could make you forget Grey; it almost made you treasure Grey's subtler version. Gillian Lynne's 1986 London revival was labeled by Mark Steyn as "swastikas a-go-go, with a scene even 'Springtime for Hitler' might balk at." (YouTube lets you watch both Grey and Cumming performing the song together at a Kander and Ebb tribute; Grey clearly outperforms Cumming with his stylish moves and braying voice.) Most people had never heard of Joel Grey before he slithered into the spotlight singing, indeed sneeering, "Veel-ko-men, biahn-venue, velcome"; afterward, nobody could forget him, and the song became a calling card; his recent memoir is titled *Master of Ceremonies*.

·············· BACKSTAGE DISH ···············

+ Here's a semibizarre footnote: Sandy Wilson, who wrote the perky, innocent 1920s musical parody *The Boy Friend*, had first dibs to write the score for a musical version of John Van Druten's play *I Am a Camera*, based on Christopher Isherwood's bleak stories that first set a musical version in motion. Wilson's title was *Goodbye to Berlin*, but the producer let the musical rights lapse, and Hal Prince snapped them up. Joe Masteroff, who eventually wrote the *Cabaret* book, said that Wilson's songs all sounded like *The Boy Friend* with a German accent—charming but without guts.
+ Wilson wanted Julie Andrews for the lead because of her triumph in *The Boy Friend*, but her manager said no; Julie Andrews as Sally Bowles might have sent her career in a radically different direction. Kander and Ebb wanted their pal Liza Minnelli to star in the stage version, but Hal Prince nixed it. "[She] wasn't British—I'm not sure why that was important to me—and she sang too well. I still think that was a flaw in the film."
+ Prince initially was turned off by the idea of musicalizing *I Am a Camera*, mainly because the idea then was to make it a vehicle for emerging stars Gwen Verdon or Tammy Grimes. Prince felt a show about a loose girl who sings racy songs in a Berlin dive wasn't enough. He didn't get interested until he came up with the idea to set her story against political unrest in Germany.

♦ For the movie version of *Cabaret*, four numbers were deleted from the stage show, including "Meeskite" and "It Couldn't Please Me More," and three new songs were added—"Money," "Mein Herr," and "Maybe This Time," which later became a Liza Minnelli blockbuster.

In the film, Bob Fosse took out all the songs involving Cliff's landlady and her Jewish boyfriend and kept only the "real" songs performed in the Kit Kat Klub. Fosse felt that young moviegoers no longer accepted the musical's defining convention—that a character could suddenly burst into song with full orchestral accompaniment.

♦ Originally, Kander and Ebb wrote several vaudeville-style songs that were to be sung by various characters in *Cabaret*, but in the end they decided to have all of them sung by one character, the Emcee. "Willkommen" itself was originally a song cycle called "Welcome to Berlin," to introduce the audience to 1930s Berlin. Harold Prince's early plan was to make the Emcee a cheesy, pathetic performer who does impressions of various well-known performers in Weimar Germany.

♦ Prince bristled at critics who claimed he was influenced by Bertolt Brecht in *Cabaret* and later *Evita*. "I'm tired to death of reading about how influenced by Brecht I am," he told Allan Wallach of *Newsday*. "I am not influenced by Brecht. I don't like Brecht that much. That whole alienation thing."

♦ When "If You Could See Her"—in which the Emcee dances with a tutu-clad gorilla he claims to adore (the grotesque image began as a dream Fred Ebb had)—was first performed in previews, the song's vile anti-Semitic tagline, "If you could see her through my eyes . . . she wouldn't look Jewish at all," was instantly, unsurprisingly controversial. Jewish groups that had bought blocks of tickets to the show heard about the number, protested, and threatened to cancel their bookings; rabbis wrote Prince asking him to remove the line. He heard people arguing about it in the lobby after the show.

Swallowing hard, because he loved the number and its devastating tagline, Prince told the writers that the producer half of him was overruling the director and that—to help keep the show running and not alienate a large portion of its potential audience—he was taking the line out of the show. The line was always greeted with a gasp and stunned silence, just as Ebb intended. Prince suspects Ebb never forgave him for cutting the line, but he said, "I was where the buck stopped, and I said, 'I am not going to jeopardize this show over this line. If it's cowardly of me, it's cowardly of me, but the show is too important.' It was a pragmatic decision on my part, and I've never regretted that I did it."

Ebb remarked years later, "It might have killed [Hal's] career. He needed that hit as much as we did. He was the producer, and a producer depends on theater parties, especially at the beginning of the run. We were all so desperate that we did things we never would today. Coming up with another punch line was one of the most difficult tasks that I've ever had to face in the theater." The new line was, "She isn't a *meeskite* at all!" *Meeskite*—"ugly" in Yiddish—refers back to a charming earlier song in the show, "Meeskite," sung by Herr Schultz (Jack Gilford) to his gentile lady friend, Fräulein Schneider (Lotte Lenya).

After *Cabaret* got rave reviews and was safely up and running, Grey snuck the line back into the song whenever anyone important was in the house. "I would!" he impishly admits. Taken to task by the stage manager after the show, Grey would always claim, "It just slipped out." By the time the movie came out, six years later, *Cabaret* was such a hit show that it was deemed safe to use the line in the film, and it has since been restored in one of the two licensed stage versions. Fred Ebb revealed that in the movie the offending line is spoken in a whisper, without musical accompaniment, so that if it was later deemed too offensive for distribution Fosse could cut the line without having to bring back all the musicians. "They were still afraid," said Ebb.

◆ Kander explains how he and Ebb collaborated, often in the kitchen at Ebb's place: "We worked in the same room at the same time and we improvised. Fred might have a line or I might have a rhythm, but he would never hand me a lyric and I would never hand him a melody. So neither of us ever presenting the other with a problem, saying, 'Here's something I really like, now go solve it.' We screw it up together." This is very different than most classic songwriting teams' methodology, writing music and lyrics separately before meeting to hash it out. After Ebb's death in 2004, when Kander collaborated with Rupert Holmes to finish *Curtains*, a show begun with Ebb, he said, "Writing it, I felt I was cheating on him."

He so admired his late partner's instincts that he told arts reporter Jesse Green in 2006, "My feeling was that I was the untalented member of the duo. . . . I felt inadequate. Fred could improvise in meter and rhyme like a Shakespearean actor from the original Globe. A lot of what people mean when they say they recognize a Kander and Ebb song, came from him. The anger, that's Fred's." He credits himself for bringing to the team "a lyricism or a more reflective tone." He added, "For Fred the perfect score would be one with no ballads. He thought I was too sentimental." Yet Kander says, "People think Fred was the vulgar one, but many of the dirtiest lines in our songs are mine."

On NPR's *Fresh Air* in 2012, Kander elaborated on the team's MO: "We could say anything to each other, though we both have thin skins. A third creature, called 'Kandernebb,' came out of our partnership. We worked very fast and we wrote a lot of crap, but we never didn't have a good time in forty years." They wrote their dark *Cabaret* ballad "I Don't Care Much" as a party stunt between dinner and dessert.

• •

Joel Grey, still wiry and vital at eighty-one when we spoke in 2014 at a noisy lower Manhattan bar and grill near his home, is nearly fifty years away from the landmark musical he helped make into a legendary show. Grey had been performing for twenty-four years when *Cabaret* came along and transformed his life. Grey did many shows after *Cabaret*—*George M!*, *The Grand Tour*, *Chicago*, *Wicked*—but no role ever defined him like the nasty master of scaremonies.

How were you chosen by Hal Prince for the bizarre Emcee role?
Hal saw me in *Stop the World—I Want to Get Off* [he replaced Anthony Newley], so that might have had an influence, you know—the whiteface mime-ish character. It was the first thing I ever got that I didn't have to audition for. I had doubts about doing it. I thought, this is a show in which I'm making my Broadway debut, in a role that I'm creating, and there's *no* dialogue! But I thought the score was sensational.

I was concerned as an actor that it was just going to be a song-and-dance turn. I almost said no. My work was cut out for me to make it seem like that character was pervading all the proceedings—the spirit of the show. A lot of people who saw the show thought I had dialogue. So that was my job, my challenge [to create a flesh-and-blood character without any dialogue]. The pedigree [Prince, Kander, Ebb] was so great, and they were friends of mine, so I said I didn't know how I was gonna do this, but I'm gonna try. I just thought, *These are great songs!* I was astonished. And when I heard the gorilla song ["If You Could See Her"], I was sold.

Did "Willkommen" grab those first audiences?
I remember in Boston nobody thought opening night that the show was going to be a success—because of the subject matter. So there was not a lot of

expectations. After the opening number, the show stopped, just *stopped!* The audience could not stop cheering. It was almost like we had to do it again, but we didn't. That was reassuring.

How did you go about creating the Emcee character?
It was Hal's and my creation. He had seen somebody like that in Germany [during the war]—a midget, I think. So it was a collaboration—we talked about it all the time. But it seemed, in its bare state, too tame. I thought he needed to be darker. My theater background kicked in, and my self-preservation.

What did you think of Alan Cumming as the Emcee in the 1998 Broadway revival?
I thought it was very different. He's a good actor, very gifted, but it was a very different approach. That whole show was totally different from what Hal envisioned. It began sort of where our show finished. It was immediately wild and crazy and scary with Nazis. It was nothing that made you say, "Oh, my God!" It didn't build. It didn't fool people [as Prince's version did]. A dubious Fred Ebb, having heard about Cumming's portrayal before the Sam Mendes revival opened, commented, "They all say, 'Oh, but you should have seen his Hamlet!' Fine. Let him stick to Hamlet."

Was it a valid version?
No, in my opinion. It was just so opposed to what the original intent was—that is, to shock people more gradually, later in the show.

What did you think of the movie version with Liza Minnelli?
Well, everything was changed. Bob Fosse redid every single dance, every number. He made it his own, and that was amazing. I thought the original staging was perfect. So I was concerned, but then I saw that he found a new way to do it that was equally dark and equally exciting and equally good, I appreciated that.

Did you feel, like Hal Prince, that Minnelli was too good a singer for the role?
[*Smiles, then says diplomatically*] Who's to say that she [Sally] couldn't have been a good singer? But [it's clear] she's not gonna succeed.

A few days after I talked to Grey, John Kander met with me to discuss the show in the composer's three-story townhouse, with a steep winding staircase leading to an attic-like study, where he sat next to a piano and a roll-top desk. Kander is low-key, polite, and soft-spoken, responding to questions slowly and carefully. Fred Ebb, his late longtime partner, was very much his opposite, a chatty, garrulous guy who laughed a lot, with a more caustic New York personality than Kander's mellow Kansas City demeanor.

Which was the first song you wrote for *Cabaret*?
[*He plays a few bars of* "Willkommen" *on the piano, a kick to hear coming from the fingers of the very man who composed it.*] "Willkommen" was the first song we wrote for it. We would almost always try to write the first song of a show first. We became almost superstitious about it. It was more than superstition. Very often the first song we would write would inform the style of the rest of the show.

[They ended up writing some forty-seven songs for the show, of which only fifteen were used. The very first thing they wrote for "Willkommen" was the now world-famous vamp—"those little musical figures that, when they work, really kick-start a song," as Kander put it. One critic calls him "the champ of the vamp"—among them his famed vamp for "New York, New York."

Ebb told critic Mark Steyn, "The reasons you give for writing the opening song last are exactly the reason why we do it first—to define the show before you begin writing it. It's like a court of law: first you get up and say, I'm going to prove to you this man is guilty, and then you proceed to do so. But you state your case up front. When you find something you like it tells you the direction you want to go in. You have to trust your unconscious."]

Did *Cabaret* change much during rehearsals?
We had originally written a lot of what we thought of as Berlin songs to be sung *between* scenes. Then it evolved to where we thought we could have just one person do that. Joel was working separately, in another room from the rest of the company, so they didn't see him. Hal [Prince] had been pressuring Joel to show us what he was going to do. He had been working on it, but we had not been able to see it. That afternoon when we saw the Emcee for the first time it was very exciting. It was good-bye to Joel, and out came the Emcee! And then, when we went out of town with the show, we continued to work

on that character. At the first previews he discovered that the audience was repelled by him, and it came as a shock to him. He took that and kept playing with it. Then he realized he had to *not* be too menacing. So that is something that evolved.

Can you think of a song in *Cabaret* that worked better during previews or out of town, in one place or another?

When we came to New York, it was suggested to Hal, but none of us agreed with this, that since "Cabaret" was a strong song, was a hit song, we should put it in the first act when Sally Bowles first appears, and that a song called "I Don't Care Much," a very melancholy piece, should be where "Cabaret" was [but the switch was never made]. [In the team's dual memoir, *Colored Lights*, Kander reveals that "Cabaret" was almost cut by Prince, who didn't want two "welcoming" songs in the show—he felt both numbers said "welcome to the cabaret," but choreographer Ron Field loved the song and talked Prince into using it anyway.]

When you were writing *Cabaret* did you study German music from that era?

I certainly did. I had sort of known the music before, but I bought every old German vaudeville song. All of *Cabaret* is vaudeville. There was a collection of these songs, and I just listened and then I forgot about them. You don't want to imitate a song, but there is a feeling, a certain style. The only German composer I didn't listen to, purposely, was Kurt Weill.

Because you didn't want to consciously imitate him? Did anybody make that suggestion?

There were some. I said before we opened that some critics might feel that Weill was what I was doing so I was very carefully avoiding that. Lotte Lenya [Weill's widow] said before we opened, "No, no, darling, it is not Weill. When I walk out on that stage I'm in Berlin." I thought, if *she* feels that way then I don't really give a shit what anybody else thinks.

How did you feel about Bob Fosse's movie version of *Cabaret*?

Two ways. We were not very involved with it. We wrote the music and then we were done. When we first saw it at a private screening, we felt awful because we didn't like it, because it was so far away from the original staging. The story was different, Sally was different, the Lotte Lenya part was changed. So our first reaction was we didn't like it. Then we went to see the movie in the theater, and, having had that experience—knowing we should not expect a Broadway show—we looked at it again and thought it was a masterpiece.

What was it like working with Bob Fosse, known for being hardheaded and uncompromising?
That was interesting. During the writing process we had a really good time. Then we went into rehearsal and he had his heart attack, and when we went back into rehearsal he was much darker, much more difficult to deal with. It was harder, and he was particularly hard on Fred.

Why was he so hard on him?
Because they were the collaborators on the book. Fred was very unhappy.

———

Cabaret producer-director Harold Prince was, surprisingly, given his stature on Broadway, totally accessible. He was more eager to chat than some lesser-grade theater personages. Prince, then eighty-four, was a lively conversationalist. It was easy to see how his energy and enthusiasm helped fuel so many great Broadway shows in addition to *Cabaret*—*Fiddler on the Roof*, *She Loves Me*, *Company*, *Follies*, *Evita*.

Did Joel Grey have "Willkommen" in hand from the start, and how much did you help him shape it?
In so far as I helped shape it, I said, "We are on the wrong track with the Sally Bowles musical. It really should not be about Sally Bowles [Jill Haworth on Broadway and Liza Minnelli on screen]. It should not be about a girl dancing on the tables who drinks too much and has an abortion. It should really be about Germany." So I said we should write another character in, the Emcee. I knew the character because when I was in the army I saw this emcee in 1951 in Stuttgart and never forgot him.

[Prince recalls that specific Stuttgart emcee in detail in his memoir *Contradictions*: "There was a nightclub called Maxim's in the rubble of an old church basement. I hung out in Maxim's. There was a dwarf Emcee, hair parted in the middle and lacquered down with brilliantine, his mouth made into a bright red cupid's bow who wore heavy false eyelashes, sang, danced, goosed, tickled and pawed four lumpen Valkyries waving diaphanous butterfly wings."]

"Willkommen" perfectly sets the tone for the whole show.
Oscar Hammerstein said that in the first three to five minutes of a show you

must tell the audience what to expect for the rest of the evening. If you don't follow that with what they are expecting for the rest of the evening, you are in terrible trouble. If you do, then you are home free.

You said *Cabaret* was the show that set you free to experiment in other shows. How important was that one song "Cabaret" to the entire show?
It was very important. Bob Fosse used it in a different way in the movie. He used it as a pop song and Liza sang it at the end of the show. I used it differently. I used it sensibly in the plot because Sally Bowles gets pregnant and she is working in this club and she is performing for people and then suddenly she moves out of the club, a silver shredded drop curtain comes down, she parts it, and comes down in the audience and works in limbo, where Joel Grey worked all night long, which was the area of the stage where we commented on things political and personal. She sings, "I used to have a girlfriend name of Elsie" and so on. While she sings "Cabaret" she is deciding to have an abortion. That's very important. Bobby [Fosse] didn't deal with that at all, and the public was very happy. That's fine. The movie, which I thought was really swell, was not the show.

It was different in many ways, but with few improvements on the stage show.
The Emcee made no trajectory in the course of the movie. He did not start as representing Germany in the depression, flat on its back, as a tragic, pathetic, bad-taste entertainer, as in John Osborne's play *The Entertainer*, which was my image. What happens is, that by the end of the show this little entertainer has become Nazi Germany. That was a trajectory that was very important. When I saw the movie, I thought, terrific movie, but I wish he had not totally disregarded that aspect of the Emcee's character.

Would you agree Liza Minnelli seemed far too good a singer for that character? Sally Bowles is supposed to be a mediocre singer we meet in this crummy little joint. The kind of performers you would see there are not Liza Minnelli.
Totally! You got it. The idea is that Sally is *not* a great professional singer. Jill Haworth [the original, more modestly talented Sally Bowles] was this little English girl who sang nicely but slightly amateurishly and really was just charming. There was a thin thread of hysteria in the character about this little girl about to make a mess of her life, and she does. Jill was terrific and wonderful in that part. By the way, so was Judi Dench in the London version; she was brilliant in it.

CHICAGO

◆ 1975 ◆

"All That Jazz"

L ike any mesmerizing opener, **"All That Jazz"** defines its show, *Chicago*; plus we meet one of its enticing lead convicts, Velma Kelly—such a tantalizing name, as if emblazoned in neon. After this bewitching opener the score would seem to have nowhere to go but down, yet the wonder of *Chicago* is that it maintains that same level of sizzle to the very last song—"Keep It Hot."

Gwen Verdon and Chita Rivera kept things hot all evening in the original 1975 Bob Fosse production, and Bebe Neuwirth and Ann Reinking relit the torch in the even more torrid 1996 revival—first produced in a short run for the New York City Center's Encores! series and still running as of 2016. All four slinky seductresses conned their way into our hearts, or anyway our groins. One of Fosse's credos, on full sensuous display in "All That Jazz," was, "Make love to the audience."

The number not only establishes the show's mood and style but also ended up defining the life of its eventually burned-out spirit, director-choreographer Fosse. Not for nothing was his movie biography called *All That Jazz*, set during rehearsals for *Chicago*, when Fosse was felled with a heart attack, the focus of the film. The phrase originated in the 1950s, if not earlier, a hipster term meaning "etcetera"—the '50s version of "whatever." Lyricist Fred Ebb got the title from a Time-Life book series on the twentieth century, whose headline ALL THAT JAZZ: BLACK AMERICA'S GIFT TO THE WORLD deals with the Jazz Age, when the show is set. It's a musical about the tawdry anything-goes 1920s, America's favorite, or at least most storied and flashy, decade. *Chicago* is all about the glories of flash and trash.

"All That Jazz" was Fosse at his Fosse-est, a number meant to show off Fosse and Velma/Verdon, one of the two sexy villains, in a dance full of signature Fosse moves that have by now been so imitated they're almost clichés. The sizzling number was seared into recent memory by Bebe Neuwirth in the '95 revival, who began as a dancer and has a slim, flat ballerina's body. She's not built like a sex bomb, like Verdon and Rivera, but Neuwirth has so many slinky, insinuating moves, gestures, and come-hither looks that it might as well be Marilyn Monroe up there wriggling through "All That Jazz." Neuwirth radiates her own serious carnality; even as the sardonic, repressed feminist Lilith on TV's *Cheers* (and the spinoff *Fraser*) she gave off steamy (and funny) vibes, as she first did in a memorable 1982 revue *Upstairs at O'Neals'*, her breakout show.

Neuwirth performed "All That Jazz" with delicious lust, though critic Ben Brantley called her "a slightly robotic performer, almost too technically proficient," but he added, "That chilliness feeds right into the show's sensibility." The moment she stepped onstage, in her lacy fishnet black temptress uniform, with a teasing smirk, Velma/Neuwirth is saying, "Here I am—come and get me." As Neuwirth told Eddie Shapiro in his book *Nothing Like a Dame*, a performer's first impression is crucial. "When people come onstage there's something you get for free," she said—the performer's attitude, what we feel about them before they even move a muscle or open their mouth. Shapiro sketches in Neuwirth's appeal in *Chicago*: "She's positively feline: still, but acutely alert, and ready to pounce." Purring or hissing, Velma can put *Cats* out of business with a tossed head and an arched leg. ("I'm gonna rouge my knees / And roll my stockings down / And all that jazz.")

Chita Rivera was responsible for Bebe Neuwirth winding up on Broadway in *Chicago* when Neuwirth went to see Rivera's one-woman show and ventured backstage to meet the legend. When Neuwirth, uncertain about her next career move, told Rivera she was thinking of auditioning to understudy Juliet Prowse and Ann Reinking in a Long Beach revival of *Chicago*, Rivera said, "Do it!"

She did it. Recalls Neuwirth, "She really encouraged me to make the call." Neuwirth phoned the producer and almost pleaded to do the role. "I said I want to offer my services. You don't even have to pay me. I just want to learn the parts and understudy. I could be an understudy for free. It was crazy." The producer said, "Funny you should call. Let me call you back about that." Ten minutes later he called and offered her the part of Velma, which Reinking wasn't eager to play, happy just to choreograph the show.

———

Bebe Neuwirth talked to me about "All That Jazz," the show itself, Bob Fosse, audiences, the movie *Chicago*, and critics.

"All That Jazz" is the number people remember most. Like all the numbers in the *Chicago* revival for Encores!, Ann Reinking based the dances on the original 1975 Fosse production, but how was the opener actually put together?

What I did was to improvise from a certain vocabulary in other Fosse shows. They are in my body and ready to go. I had done other Fosse shows, so I have

Bebe Neuwirth discussing the fine points of "All That Jazz" in Chicago.

a vocabulary within me to draw from. I maybe tweaked them a little bit, but it ended up being pretty much what I fooled around with. I did not take choreography from the original show.

You said his dances spoke to you in some way. He meant something to you early in your career.

It was actually before I had a career. I was thirteen when I saw *Pippin*, and all the dancers onstage—not only their excellence but the choreography—resonated very deeply with me. It was a visceral response. I felt I had that choreography within me, and it resonated with me. I did not know who Bob Fosse was and I didn't know musical theater, but I knew what I was watching onstage; it was like recognizing myself in a way. It was an egoless thing. It was not, "I can do that." It was just right. I wanted to be a professional ballet dancer, but I did not have the strength or technique to be a ballet dancer at thirteen. I was heartbroken I was not going to be a professional ballet dancer. So I was a dancer, but where was I going to go? When I saw *Pippin* I recognized that I could be a dancer. It gave me the confidence.

You're quoted as saying, "People think that if you slide around and do some hip bumps, people think that it is Fosse, but I can tell you this is not Fosse." So what *is* Fosse?
I can tell you a few things that it is not and a few things that it is. I can tell you that it is not vulgar. It is not garish. It is certainly sensual and understated. It is specific and clean. It is recognizable. There are certain trademarks and a certain angle of the head. It encompasses irony and a lot of eccentricity and humor. It is physical, in that you get pulled up, but there is also something where you hunch down a bit as well. Also, it is very much "show time," as they say in "All That Jazz." But there is something [in his style] very much turned inward. Ann Reinking says Bob said his dancers have a secret. It is very deep. When you see somebody performing in a Fosse show and they are grinning at the audience, that grin is not a happy grin for the folks. It is very ironic, inwardly focused, something else is going on. He was a very complicated man. It is not shallow work. It is something deeply engaging about the style.

Some people say he was often working out his demons. Do you see that in his choreography?
People are nasty critters. They want to know what he was doing backstage. I choose not to participate. Look at what he was doing *on* stage. Who did he sleep with? I could not care less. All artists have their personal life. If I know someone is a terrible person, it does affect my appreciation. But I knew Bob well enough to tell you he was not a monster. He tried to be a good man. There was no evil in him.

When you look back at the first production at Encores!, what are your memories of being in that show, of the rehearsals?

We realized that the show was greater than the sum of its parts. All the dancers were handpicked by Ann Reinking. It is not just his style, it is a whole mind-set—embracing the irony of the darkness and finding the joy in that. Another unusual thing—it was an older cast. The ensemble was not your everyday, average ensemble of a Broadway show. These were seasoned, extraordinary artists. Nobody auditioned. Everyone was at least in their thirties. Only one who was in her late twenties. Some were in their forties, one guy in his fifties. Almost everybody knew each other. Some were best friends. Some were husbands and wives. There were some ex-affairs. Other people had been through tragedies.

So every performer was handpicked by Fosse?
There was a fantastic galvanizing feeling in the group. We did not say, *Look at us.* We just were who we were and stared down the audience, like in the beginning of "All That Jazz" everybody stares straight forward and is very still and walks very slowly toward the audience.

How did you prepare? How did you see the Velma Kelly character?
I look at what Velma says and does. I look at what other people say about her. What she wants and what she is there for is pretty clear, but it's also finding what is funny in the role and making sure it's played truthfully. Finding the truth so it's funny without *telling* people it is funny. What is funny about Velma is that she is a ham. I did not approach Velma as a sexy murderess. She is a woman who wants to be in vaudeville. That is why it's funny. If you just go out and play a sexy murderess (and I don't know how you play sexy; you either are or you're not), a murderess is not funny. It *is* funny that she killed her husband and sister with an ice pick and wants to be in vaudeville. She loses her temper because her husband is having sex with her sister. But she is not a dangerous murderess.

***Chicago* was an instantaneous smash in 1996.**
The audience response was incredible. We were blowing the roof off the theater. They loved the show and the music so much. We could not really believe it until we saw it. Every once in a while there is something that goes beyond everything else. It's almost spiritual; it is happening on another level. I thought it would run eleven months. I thought it was too good to last. Our *New York Times* review was on the front page. That's a rare thing. And still I thought, *It's too good to last.* But years later they're still selling out. What

made it sweet was knowing how good the piece was. I felt like, *The show is the toast of Broadway—and it* should *be the toast of Broadway.* There were people camped outside the theater at three and four in the morning.

What is it about the show that has grabbed audiences and made it run almost twenty-five years?

One thing I think audiences responded to at first was that nothing came between them and the show. The pendulum on Broadway [in 1996] had swung all the way over to big effects, scenery, moving videos, things falling out of the sky, rising to the heavens. All this *stuff* was going on—special effects just for the special effects. *Chicago* was pared down to the pure material. Singers and dancers were there dancing and singing their songs. There were no special effects. The special effects was the material. So nothing got between the material and the audience. The show is a pure theatrical experience. The audience responded to it then and are still responding to it now. I also think that when *Chicago* first opened in '75, it was ahead of its time. It was a response to Watergate and the media circus. Fosse was always ahead of his time, everything he did. Some people were not quite ready for it in 1975. We opened in '96 after the O. J. Simpson trial, so people knew what they were watching. There was no mistaking what we were doing. It's an evening of vaudeville making a special commentary. As Billy Flynn [the defense lawyer] says, "It is all showbiz, kid," and to fully develop that idea, they got the cross-dressing singer, they got the girl chorus number, they got the ventriloquist act, they got everything. There is one act after another. The conductor and others introduce each act. It is a brilliant concept. Whether you interact with it intellectually or not, it is wildly entertaining. It is sexy and dark and smart. And the music is beautiful. The musicians are right there on the deck [over the stage].

What did you think of the movie version?

I did not see it. I have my own experience with *Chicago*, and I don't want to get outside of that. I want to keep my head in the sand. It might be a mistake, but I am a fearful person and I don't read reviews. There are a few shows that I don't want to see again because certain memories are so special and precious to me so I want to keep them.

PART II

THEY STOPPED THE SHOW

As detailed in this book's introduction, all the songs in this section lift us out of our seats and almost viscerally transport us. I might have chosen sixty others, equally vibrant, on my waiting list, but the numbers I finally singled out demanded to be included and saluted. Each song has earned its way into the Broadway pantheon. Some are obvious, unavoidable choices ("Hello, Dolly!," "Seventy-Six Trombones," "There's No Business Like Show Business"); others may be less obvious ("Ohio," "An Old-Fashioned Wedding," "We Both Reached for the Gun"). What they all have in common is craftsmanship, style, wit, warmth, and joy. Each number uses every tool of the theatrical trade. When you hear the song, it seems the absolutely perfect crystallization of a moment, of a specific mood in the show. The song expresses what dialogue and dance cannot. The song emotionally—or even literally—stops the show, always with good reasons. Here are just a few.

The actor Joseph Bova once said, "The whole theater is bigger than life anyway, but a musical is even bigger than that." And a showstopper is bigger still. The entertainment historian and critic Leonard Maltin, in his narration for the *Top Hat* DVD, said of musicals generally: "We live in such a cynical time that it may be hard for some people—younger people—to really appreciate what these musicals did for audiences then—and still do. Because they lift your spirits, some people dismiss them as escapism, as mere fluff. I don't think there's anything 'mere' about it. It's art of the highest quality."

And finally a friend, Randy Poe, waxes ecstatic: "Theater songs offer greater emotional range than any other art I know. I believe fully in the philosophy of good lyrics and the power of strong tunes. I never question a good lyric's philosophy the way I do poems and books and plays. Good lyrics are like little commandments for me. They can bring totally unsolicited tears to my eyes. Plays, great or classic as they may be, are just not in the same league as musicals. It's a crazy chemistry. Novels are one guy against the word. Movies are directors, largely. Dramas are acting and story. But the musical is a complex contraption that needs these little miracles—called showstoppers—to occur constantly."

GARRICK GAIETIES

◆ 1925 ◆

"Manhattan," "Mountain Greenery"

One of the oldest showstoppers still sung (the oldest in this book anyway), and one that engages us ninety years after it was written, **"Manhattan"** popped out of a musical revue, *Garrick Gaieties*. It wasn't a book musical, but why let that keep us from celebrating it? Not only was the song the hit of the show, and later a huge popular favorite outside the show, but it also put Richard Rodgers and Lorenz Hart on the Broadway map for keeps after six years of knocking around, well, Manhattan. (When they first wrote it for their unproduced show *Winkle Town*, Rodgers was a mere nineteen.)

Garrick Gaieties was a fundraiser meant for only a two-night run, to raise money to buy tapestries for the cash-strapped Theatre Guild at the Garrick Theatre (the opener is titled "Gilding the Guild" a.k.a. "Soliciting Subscriptions"), but the show proved so popular that it ran 211 performances and gave rise to two more editions. It also rescued Rodgers from a career in the babywear business, a potentially more lucrative career for him then than songwriting, which had been a dead end for him until then.

The *Gaieties* was the Theatre Guild's first musical show, so successful that it forced the Guild to close a long-run hit called *The Guardsman*, with megastars Alfred Lunt and Lynn Fontanne. When artistic director Theresa Helburn asked Rodgers, "What would you have us do?" to keep *Garrick Gaieties* running, without hesitation the cocky young composer replied, "Pack up the Lunts!"; he told Helburn his revue would make more money. The irreverent show actually satirized *The Guardsman* and other Broadway plays. The *Gaieties* was a hip show for theater insiders, the *Forbidden Broadway* of its day. A second (and then a third) *Garrick Gaieties* followed, featuring one of the team's other major long-lasting hits, "Mountain Greenery."

The 1925 *Garrick Gaieties* was a real-life *Babes in Arms* put on by a group of young Guild actors called the Junior Players, bursting with young performers and written by two songwriters in their twenties. The cast featured a pre–torch singing Libby Holman and three giant theatrical gurus-to-be—Lee Strasberg, Harold Clurman, and Sanford Meisner. The revue was alive with catchy melodies, smart lyrics, and a youthful spirit that epitomized Rodgers and Hart, who epitomized the restless, exuberant Jazz Age '20s. According to his biographer, Hart didn't much want to write a revue, interested only in book musicals, but his canny, ever-pragmatic younger partner talked him into it, realizing the show would be seen by the Broadway cognoscenti—producers, music publishers, and showbiz reporters.

"Manhattan" got a standing ovation, rare in those days. "Everyone was standing," Rodgers, who was conducting the orchestra, recalls in his memoirs. "They were not just standing, either. Standing and clapping, cheering, stomping, waving and whistling. I turned back to the orchestra and had the boys strike up 'Manhattan.' The cast sang it. The musicians sang it. Even the audience sang it." Ten curtain calls later, the audience reluctantly went home. Critics fell hard for the revue, with eleven Rodgers and Hart numbers. Critic and humorist Robert Benchley called it "by miles . . . the most civilized show in town."

Even so, reviews in New York newspapers like *The Tribune* failed to mention "Manhattan" and noted, with a stifled yawn, "The music by Richard Rodgers is pleasant and the lyrics by Lorenz Hart are serviceable, if frequently obvious."

"Manhattan" is not just the first but the definitive Rodgers and Hart hit—fresh and frisky, with an irresistible, gently swaying, laid-back tune that doesn't overwhelm the clever lines, jokes, and rhymes that announced the arrival of a great new songwriting team. Rodgers and Hart went on to write twenty-six shows—until Hart's sorry death at forty-eight in 1943. He lived just long enough to attend the opening of *Oklahoma!*, which Rodgers wrote with Oscar Hammerstein II when Hart became too much of a wreck to work.

A dwarfish (under five feet) alcoholic and conflicted, closeted gay man, Hart got drunk opening night of a 1943 revival of *A Connecticut Yankee*, had to be taken from the theater when he began babbling aloud, then wandered the streets in mid-November until he was found on a curb outside a bar on Eighth Avenue, coatless and chilled. He was taken to Doctors Hospital, where he died of pneumonia and, many felt, heartbreak. A troubled soul—but not in 1925, when he was a laughing, boozing, boisterous, frenetic, cigar-puffing, check-grabbing, tiny bon vivant and lyric genius.

"Manhattan"—maybe the best New York song ever written—captures the flavor, sights, sounds, and even scents of the city's streets it both celebrates and gently kids. George M. Cohan gave the city its first heartfelt toast in "Give My Regards to Broadway." John Kander and Fred Ebb's "New York, New York" is a rousing, even grand, patriotic anthem played after New York Yankee wins, and the original "New York, New York" by Leonard Bernstein, Betty Comden, and Adolph Green is also a playful salute to "a wonderful town." Charles Strouse and Martin Charnin's spirited "N.Y.C." from *Annie* and Stephen Sondheim's "Another Hundred People" are vital New York numbers.

All are stirring New York songs, but they lack the touchstones of the Rodgers and Hart song that make it so intimate—"We'll go to Coney / And eat baloney / On a roll. / In Central Park we'll stroll, / Where our first kiss we stole, / Soul to soul . . ." A lovely, evocative line, with that endearing Hart-felt "soul to soul," a typical throwaway Larry Hart grace note, succinct and perfect. Only a born and bred New Yorker would refer just to "Coney" instead of "Coney Island" and would memorialize dining on baloney on a roll, a feast for newlyweds on the town in the song. "Manhattan" also staked out Rodgers and Hart's claim on New York as their private musical preserve (until Cole Porter showed up). Hart's lyrics almost single-handedly raised the level of Broadway songwriting; before him, the gold standard was P. G. Wodehouse, whose lyrics were witty but lacked Hart's emotional fervor and insights.

This is a special New York number because it speaks in the city's native language, in sassy conversational phrases that make it sound extemporaneous. It's a boy-girl duet that is a comic love song to Manhattan as well as a lighthearted ballad crooned by lovers extolling the simple everyday glories of this most exotic isle right at their feet. Rodgers's laid-back melody—someone likened it to a stroll—fondly complements the lyrics.

Rodgers told the *New York Herald* in 1926 that Hart wrote the lyrics "on a dirty envelope in four minutes and 12 seconds," but later he commented, "Larry says he really worked on the song." So which was it—a last-minute burst of inspiration or pure perspiration? Hart, a chronic procrastinator, may have dashed off the lyrics, as he was wont to do, but this may be Rodgers fondly embellishing a songwriting legend. Hart was also a craftsman, so he likely sweated over every word.

In any case, the song was sung by June Cochrane and a young Sterling Holloway, the tall, lanky character actor with a loopy voice and a mop of unruly red hair who popped up in a hundred films (including lending his voice to Disney cartoons *Winnie the Pooh*, *The Aristocats*, and *The Jungle Book*). The song was originally sung "in one"—that is, in front of a plain curtain, sans scenery, while a set was changed behind them.

Yet even on a bare stage, the song's lyrics sketched in a Manhattan setting. Rodgers says in his memoirs that "Manhattan" got two encores opening night and easily could have gotten more if they'd written more choruses. He adds, "If one song can be said to have 'made' Rodgers and Hart, it surely was 'Manhattan.'" The song became an instant perky dance band request in New York nightclubs.

"Manhattan" was in fact written years before *Garrick Gaieties* for their first unproduced show, *Winkle Town*, which Max Dreyfus, powerful head of Harms Music, brusquely turned down in 1922. After *Garrick Gaieties* was a smash, an annoyed Dreyfus asked Rodgers why he hadn't offered their songs to him. Rodgers said he had, after which he said the producer declared, "There is nothing of value here. I don't hear any music. I think you'd be making a great mistake [to be a composer]." Dreyfus never apologized but efficiently signed them up.

Rodgers recalled that when Dreyfus dismissed "Manhattan" and some other songs, "I was so stunned I couldn't say a word. Nothing of value? He didn't hear any music? With two sentences, the verdict was being handed down that I had no talent." Others in music publishing told Rodgers the song was too clever (or to quote another Hart lyric, "too good for the average man"). Even Oscar Hammerstein II, part of their theatrical circle, told the boys that "Manhattan" was too clever to grab audiences. Producer Theresa Helburn was far more prescient than Dreyfus when Rodgers played a few songs for her. As she later wrote, "Sitting on the empty stage of the Garrick, Dick Rodgers played the songs, and Larry Hart, a slight frail youth, not over five feet in spite of his elevator shoes," sang it for her. "When they came to the song 'Manhattan,' I sat up in delight. These lads had ability, wit, and a flair for a light sophisticated song." The lads did indeed.

"Manhattan" is filled with all the earmarks of Larry Hart's wise-guy lyricism, starting with the verse that lays out the story line of a couple forced to honeymoon in Manhattan: "Summer journeys / To Niag'ra / And to other places / Aggra- / Vate all our cares. / We'll save our fares! / I've a cozy little flat in / What is known as old Manhattan. / We'll settle down / Right here in town!" Already, two sublime interior rhymes—"Niag'ra / Aggra-vate," followed by "flat in / Manhattan." Then yet a third great rhyme in the opening stanza: "We'll have Manhattan, / The Bronx and Staten / Island too."

Instantly he's got our attention, as his subway travelogue unfolds: "It's very fancy / On old Delancey / Street, you know. / The subway charms us so / When balmy breezes blow / To and fro." Nobody had ever praised the everyday sites of Manhattan that were/are the usual targets for abuse, casually embracing New Yorkers' love-hate relationship with the city. He turns the humid, smelly subway into a gentle tram ride in Switzerland. Then as we get off on the Lower East Side, he asks, "And tell me what street / Compares with Mott Street / In July? / Sweet pushcarts gently gliding by." Are we in Kiev, Hong Kong, or New York? The next few lines sound forced, Hart showing off his verbal acrobatics: "We'll go to Greenwich / Where modern men itch / To be free." At one point he dares rhyme "onyx" with "Bronnix," as old Bronx natives pronounced it.

His follow-up stanza depicts a truer snapshot: "We'll go to Yonkers / Where true love conquers / In the wilds. / And starve together, dear, / In Childs'" (a favorite local chain restaurant). And then the song's sweetest couplet, "The city's clamor can never spoil / The dreams of a

In the original 1925 *Garrick Gaieties*, Sterling Holloway and June Cochrane, as boy and "goil," lead a guided tour of "Manhattan," Rodgers and Hart's first hit in their first produced musical.

IRA D. SCHWARTZ/MUSEUM OF THE CITY OF NEW YORK

boy and goil." Finally we reach the end of Hart's musical guided tour—"But Civic Virtue cannot destroy / The dreams of a girl and boy. / We'll turn Manhattan / Into an isle of joy!" Exactly what the song says, it does for listeners. Hart was surprised the song caught on, with huge sheet music sales, because of its tricky lyrics: "The song hit of a show is usually a very simple one with monosyllabic words," he said. But a pop song could go viral in 1925 even without YouTube, thanks to radio airplay, records, hotel bands, and sheet music. (A likely facsimile of how the number looked when first staged in 1925 can be found on YouTube in a rare 1929 film clip of an unidentified couple crooning the number, probably very close to how it originally sounded and was performed in 1925's *Garrick Gaieties*.)

In 1939, for a show called *Too Many Girls* (most famous for discovering a Cuban conga drum player named Desi Arnaz), Rodgers and Hart wrote an antirhapsodic song about New York, "Give It Back to the Indians," almost as successful as "Manhattan" ("Broadway's turning into Coney, / Champagne Charlie's drinkin' gin, / Old New York is new and phony, / Give it back to the Indians!"

"Manhattan"—and specifically Hart's sophisticated lyrics—is credited with almost single-handedly elevating Broadway songwriting, long mired in either starchy, gooey European operettas by Rudolf Friml, Sigmund Romberg, and Victor Herbert or the moon-June doggerel of Tin Pan Alley hacks. As "Manhattan" reveals, Hart was capable of writing playfully about real subjects, real people, and real locales. He could devise clever, unpredictable rhymes for songs and write with equal feeling about adult romance, triumphant or tragic, or pushcarts and baloney sandwiches. Apart from Brits William S. Gilbert and P. G. Wodehouse, there had been nobody quite like Hart, who could do it all with such facility and regularity in show after show—and in the American vernacular. Even the great Gilbert, stuck in comic-opera mode with partner Arthur Sullivan, rarely wrote moody ballads like Hart.

Hart turned down an opportunity to work with Rodgers on *Oklahoma!,* claiming it wasn't his kind of show, a folk tale set on the prairie. Rodgers, realizing his lifelong partner was on a self-destructive binge, efficiently pivoted to Oscar Hammerstein II, very much an outdoorsy guy, with a farm in Doylestown, Pennsylvania, where Rodgers and Hammerstein often conferenced beneath sprawling shade trees (and where the teenage Stephen Sondheim often visited).

Mark Steyn wrote that when Rodgers began writing with Hammerstein, after Hart's demise, it was as if he had moved to the suburbs. Mary Cleere Haran, the late cabaret singer, said, "There's an old saying on Broadway that when Richard Rodgers wrote with Oscar Hammerstein they wrote for all America. But when he wrote with Lorenz Hart they were writing for five guys sitting at the bar at Sardi's."

The country wasn't the urban and urbane Larry Hart's most comfortable turf, nor was it Rodgers's (both grew up in handsome Harlem brownstones), but they were pros and could fake it beautifully for a show—and in **"Mountain Greenery"** they did precisely that. The song, a showstopper from the second *Garrick Gaieties* in 1926, is a paean to rural life that neither Rodgers nor Hart had real feeling for. But Hart rhapsodized about it as breezily as he does in "Manhattan," as did the actor singing it—again, the gawky but charming Sterling Holloway, who first crooned it in the revue. Hart, drawing on his days as a counselor and songwriting prodigy at Brant Lake summer camp, wrote one of his most endearing lyrics:

"In a mountain greenery, / Where God paints the scenery / Just two crazy people together. / While you love your love, let / blue skies be your coverlet, / When it rains we'll laugh at the weather. / And if you're good, I'll search for wood / So you can cook . . . while I stand looking. / Beans could get no keener re- / Ception in a beanery. / Bless our mountain greenery home!" Those two sly interior rhymes—"lover / let / coverlet" and "keener re-ception in a bean-ery"—are what people love about Larry Hart, not just the fancy wordplay but the cozy imagery that takes him beyond mere Broadway songsmithing, details like "search for wood" and "coverlet" and slang like "beanery." These sound like real people, not just singers in a cute number.

For lyric masters, overrhyming is an occupational hazard. At times, yes, Hart rhymes for rhyme's sake, but we excuse him his excesses because of the unforgettable and unexpected images he comes up with that make his songs impossible to resist. Listen to his lyrics in "There's a Small Hotel," a similar song about a couple's snug hideaway (Rodgers's melody suggests hand-holding lovers), in which he describes the hotel in such detail you can see it. You've slept here. "There's a wishing well," and "one room, bright and neat," with "a distant steeple, / Not a sign of people. / Who wants people?" Hart goes on to mention chintz curtains and prints of Grant and Grover Cleveland. His "chintz/prints" rhyme may tickle the ear, but it's really the intimate imagery that draws us into his songs, like the last line, as the bedroom light clicks off: "We'll creep into our little shell / And we will thank the small hotel / Together." G'night.

A CONNECTICUT YANKEE

◆ 1927 ◆

"Thou Swell," "To Keep My Love Alive"

In every way except their ability to write unforgettable songs, there was never a more dysfunctional partnership than that of Richard Rodgers and Lorenz Hart. Rodgers, a methodical workaholic, family man, and reliable, stern, no-nonsense fellow, was the temperamental opposite of Hart, who hated to work and was often locked in a room by Rodgers to force him to write a lyric. Hart lived a flamboyant life of drinking, partying, and indulging in ill-fated homosexual affairs. For all that, they stayed together a quarter century and produced twenty-seven musicals and close to forty songs that remain not just standards but the gold standard for Broadway show tunes.

Several of their musicals have multiple hits, like *A Connecticut Yankee*, which produced "Thou Swell" and "To Keep My Love Alive," and *The Boys from Syracuse* (1938), with a score that includes "This Can't Be Love" and "Falling in Love with Love," plus "Sing for Your Supper," "Dear Old Syracuse," "He and She," and "Oh, Diogenes!"—lesser known songs but each one a head-spinning showstopper.

Their single most prolific show, *Babes in Arms*, was a virtual hit parade— "My Funny Valentine," "Where or When," "Johnny One-Note," "The Lady Is a Tramp," "I Wish I Were in Love Again," and the robust title song, plus two clever ditties, "Way Out West" and "You Are So Fair," that reveal Hart's dazzling wordplay and Rodgers's rarely praised facility at fashioning great novelty tunes. These are just the blockbusters, but this remarkable team produced an equal number of heart-stoppers—"Spring Is Here," "Little Girl Blue," "You Are Too Beautiful," "It Never Entered My Mind," "You Took Advantage of Me," "Nobody's Heart," "I Didn't Know What Time It Was," "Blue Moon," "Ten Cents a Dance," "Isn't It Romantic," "Bewitched, Bothered and Bewildered," and dozens more. I could write a book (to toss in another standard, from *Pal Joey*). For *this* book, though, let's just zero in on two still-sung Rodgers and Hart showstoppers from a show maybe too loosely based on Mark Twain's *A Connecticut Yankee in King Arthur's Court*.

In **"Thou Swell,"** Hart lays out the idea in his inspired title—a love song that mixes '20s slang with ye olde English, stylishly, wittily, winningly. The joyous lyric trips off the couple's tongues as if Elizabethan English is their native language. Hart's lines effortlessly mesh the show's bizarre time-travel plot: a man is conked on the head by his fiancée, when she learns he still loves an old lover who turns up at a bachelor party, and lands in King Arthur's court in 528.

It's a primitive, less witty *Spamalot*, saved by three great songs that make it worth enduring a labored plot you don't want to know more about. In 1927, musicals were still mainly excuses to churn out great songs. That same year, the anything-goes party ended when *Show Boat* docked on Broadway and something new happened—a theatrical sea change. Plot mattered. But rarely mentioned is that after *Show Boat* most musicals went back to their usual goofy plots.

A DVD of the original *Connecticut Yankee* is available, a 1955 TV version produced and directed by Max Liebman, with Eddie Albert (in the part originated by William Gaxton), Janet Blair, and Gale Sherwood. It's creaky and grainy but worth watching just to get an idea of the Broadway show and a rare chance to see Boris Karloff singing, as King Arthur. Let's just say he won't make you forget Richard Burton in *Camelot*. There were two *Connecticut Yankee* movies, a nonmusical version with Will Rogers in 1931 and an embarrassing 1947 musical with Bing Crosby wearing a beard, with awful songs by (it's hard to imagine) Johnny Burke and Jimmy Van Heusen.

In *Words and Music*, the catchy but dubious 1948 biopic about Rodgers and Hart, the ever-swell June Allyson sings "Thou Swell" to a pair of hoofing knights in armor. The song was an example of Rodgers's attempt to swing, and jazz musicians quickly picked up on it. In the '40s it became a jazz staple, recorded by Bix Beiderbecke, Sarah Vaughan, Fats Waller, Joe Williams, and Nat King Cole. Because of its zippy, danceable syncopation, musicologist Alec Wilder felt "Thou Swell" might have been written with Fred Astaire in mind.

Rodgers's "Thou Swell" melody is beyond catchy—he never wrote a more irresistibly singable tune—and Hart's words ride on the composer's music so easily that, as in most of their songs, it sounds as if it's the product of one mind. The introductory verse is Hart at his most Hart-like, as the guy sings, "Babe, we are well met, / As in a spell met, / I lift my helmet." Once the refrain arrives, the number switches into high gear: "Thou swell, thou witty, thou sweet, thou grand! / Wouldst kiss me pretty? / Wouldst hold my hand?" "Wouldst kiss me pretty" is such a tender phrase you easily fall in love with the song. Then, "Both thine eyes are cute, too; / What they do to me. / Hear me holler I choose a sweet lollapaloosa in thee." It's pretty safe to say that nobody but Larry Hart would toss "lollapaloosa" so casually into a lyric, but here is the perfect place for it, beautifully juxtaposed with "in thee." Hart deftly tucks it into a rhyme with "choose a" and then matches "holler" with "lolla-paloosa." It must be one of the few five-syllable words in love song history, surely the least likely.

The lyric continues, "I'd feel so rich in a hut for two; / Two rooms and a kitchen I'm sure would do; / Give me just a plot of, / Not a lot of land, / And thou swell! Thou witty! Thou grand!" I've heard the song a thousand times, but not till this moment did I catch the interior rhyme "rich in" and "kitchen." The hut-for-two setting recalls Hart's snug "There's a Small Hotel" and "Mountain Greenery." A lavish collection of Hart's lyrics and life, edited by his sister-in-law Dorothy Hart, is titled *Thou Swell, Thou Witty*.

About the best you'll ever see "Thou Swell" performed can be found in a YouTube excerpt from a 2002 Rodgers and Hart concert tribute at Lincoln Center, with Rebecca Luker. It's irresistible, charming, even sexy; Luker rolls her big blue eyes and melts your heart (mine anyway), and her delivery is impeccable. She is quite swell and witty. "Thou Swell" became a jazz as well as a pop standard, and Peter Martins includes it in a 2003 ballet of Rodgers and Hart tunes. Listen carefully and you can catch "Thou Swell" playing ironically in the background of *All About Eve* at the party where Bette Davis warns, "Fasten your seat belts, everybody—it's going to be a bumpy night!"

The showiest number in *A Connecticut Yankee*, **"To Keep My Love Alive,"** is the last lyric Lorenz Hart wrote, for the 1943 revival of his and Rodgers's 1927 show, revived in part to keep Hart's career alive as his life was falling apart; Rodgers put up $100,000 of his own money. Hart was a mess by then, but you'd never guess it to hear the song's verbal cartwheels that helped it achieve showstopper status. A witty song, even performed simply but with

Vivienne Segal in *A Connecticut Yankee* explaining how she kept her loves, if not her lovers, alive.

Vivienne Segal's own sassy sardonic spin, it's irresistible even seven decades later. In "To Keep My Love Alive," Hart went out in a blaze of lyric glory. The song invariably triggers an ovation, perhaps less for its performance than for Hart's sheer versifying virtuosity. It's an inspired idea that Hart fulfills by executing the lyrics with astonishing dexterity.

"To Keep My Love Alive" is a gleefully ghoulish list number in which the female lead (originally sung by Vivienne Segal, whom the sexually confused Hart once proposed to) blithely reveals how she murdered all her husbands— mercy killings, as she sees them, to help keep her love for them constant. It's a long song, with four wordy stanzas, but rich in classic Hart verbal acrobatics and comic imagery. In his hands, much like Alfred Hitchcock, he makes murder sound oh-so merry.

Throwing herself on the mercy of the court, the murderess matter-of-factly explains her MO in the opening verse, setting up the song with the phrase, "Till death do us part." The first stanza continues, "I married many men, a ton of them, / And yet I was untrue to none of them, / Because I bumped off ev'ry one of them / To keep my love alive." Her first confession: "Sir Paul was frail; he looked a wreck to me. / At night he was a horse's neck to me, / So I performed an appendectomy / To keep my love alive." A stunning triple rhyme, unforced. There follow fourteen more killings, each as artfully stated as the first, until this penultimate line: "Sir Marmaduke was awf'lly tall; he didn't fit in bed. / I solved that problem easily; I just removed his head." No tricky rhymes here, just vivid imagery, two of a dozen equally inventive schemes for bumping off husbands in the ten-minute number. Rhymey? Sure, but that's the fun, even the whole point of the song. We get to indulge a great lyricist at work and revel in his wordplay as much as he does.

•••••••••••••••• BACKSTAGE DISH ••••••••••••••••

✦ As merrily mordant as "To Keep My Love Alive" is, its backstory is grimly and ironically sad. Rodgers recalls that Hart was sober during their creative period, maybe out of respect for Segal. But once rehearsals ended, Hart crashed. In another binge, he left his hat and coat in a bar one night and wandered into the snow outside, where he was later found soaked and shivering. He was taken to Doctors Hospital, where he died of pneumonia on November 22, 1943. Five days before, Hart got so drunk on the opening night of *A Connecticut Yankee* that he began jabbering to the actors from his seat and Rodgers had him escorted outside and home.

✦ Rodgers, writes his biographer Meryle Secrest, wanted Segal to end each chorus with an increasingly lower D. Songwriter Hugh Martin recalled that she snapped, "If I sing that low note eight nights a week, I'll develop balls." To which Rodgers, a bit of a homophobe, allegedly countered, "If you do you'll be the only one in the show who has them." One critic wrote of Segal's performance, "Her delivery of 'To Keep My Love Alive,' a song with the arsenic-and-old-lace style of . . . humor, had the audience arching its back and purring for more."

✦ In the original 1927 *Connecticut Yankee*, "Thou Swell" saved the show, Rodgers says in his memoir. He expected "My Heart Stood Still" was the song that "would really grab them," but opening night the number was only "greeted cordially," he said, disappointedly. Not until William Gaxton began "Thou Swell" a little later in the act did Rodgers experience a tingling he compared to the feeling he got during "Manhattan" in their first show, *Garrick Gaieties*. Writes Rodgers, "The audience reaction was so strong that it was like an actual blow. Though there were no audible sounds, I could feel the people loving Gaxton, adoring Constance Carpenter [opposite him in their duet] and going wild over the song. The applause at the end of the number was deafening, and Billy and Connie returned to give several encores. That did it; from then on, the show was in. Nothing, I knew, could stop it from being a smash."

In rehearsals, the company was split over the number, some worrying the lyrics were "too complicated for the audience to understand," reports a Hart biographer (e.g., "Babe, we are well met— / I lift my helmet"). In fact, the audience not only instantly grasped the lyrics but embraced them, reveling in Hart's wry, unlikely mix of old English and new slang.

● ●

PARIS

❖ 1928 ❖

"Let's Do It (Let's Fall in Love)"

Arguably, and fittingly, Cole Porter's first hit song, **"Let's Do It (Let's Fall in Love),"** or sometimes just "Let's Do It," is a risqué showstopper from his initial 1928 Broadway smash *Paris*, introduced by Arthur Margetson and French star Irene Bordoni (she of the famous eyes that pop up later in "You're the Top"), who beguiled audiences.

Critics raved about the song, and a reviewer in Chicago referred to "this joyously tuned and worded anthem with which Bordoni rang 12 bells." It's hard to say for sure if it stopped the show back in '28, but the sexy innuendoes surely stopped audiences in their tracks. As one historian writes, "Porter taught audiences to listen to lyrics." Philip Furia and Michael Lasser write in *America's Songs*, "Bordoni breathed into Porter's innocent title phrase so much suggestiveness that it had to be subtitled, 'Let's Do It (Let's Fall in Love)' to get it past censors." The song jolted audiences, became a huge hit, put Porter on the map at last, and was a turning point in musicals—and maybe sex— in American pop songs.

"Let's Do It" is the definitive Porter list song, full of topical pop culture references, and Porter's trademark double entendres. As David Schiff wrote in *The Atlantic*, "Musicological archaeologists of the distant future will be able to reconstuct much of our musical culture . . . out of just [Porter's] songbook."

During rehearsals, "Let's Do It" replaced the equally suggestive "Let's Misbehave," a 1927 Porter song that turned up in a 1962 revival of *Anything Goes* (of which maybe the sexiest version is a striptease by Christopher Walken in the movie *Pennies from Heaven*). The song is a witty, jubilant jumble of all the creatures, even machines, that might conceivably do "it," such as, unsurpassably, "Lithuanians and Letts do it." It is almost as if Porter devised the phrase "let's do it" just so he could write a deliciously naughty song with five refrains rich in innuendo—the first about ethnic groups, the second about birds, the third marine life, the fourth insects, and the last devoted to nonhuman mammals. Noël Coward added his own saucy lines when *he* did it, such as, "Even Liberace, we assume, does it."

There was little question what "it" meant, especially after British author Elinor Glyn's famous story—published a year before Porter's song, in a collection called *"It" and Other Stories*—defined "it," which gave rise to *it*'s most famous spokeswoman, Clara Bow, the movies' It Girl. In Glyn's story, the protagonist was male, but Hollywood changed it to a shopgirl out to seduce her boss. "It" in the Glyn story didn't refer just to sex but to magnetism, appeal, and self-confidence. When Hollywood adapted the story in 1927, the studio simply boiled *it* down to plain old sex appeal (or "s.a." as it was sometimes then coyly called).

Hoping to distract blue noses and radio censors, Porter added that parenthetical "(Let's Fall in Love)" to the title, a sly ruse that failed to throw censors off the scent but gave the song a thin veil of decency. It might have been the first song to openly confess that, yes, sex happens, is actually fun, and ought to be sung about. The number seems almost to have been an accompaniment to the liberated Jazz Age, a veritable flapper theme song. Porter was nervous that the song might be banned in England, but when he met the United Kingdom's chief censor, the Lord Chamberlain, at a party, he congratulated Porter on his witty lyrics.

So "Let's Do It" pretty much introduced it-ness—that is, adult sex—to pop music, indeed to musicals. If it wasn't the first suggestive pop song ever written, it was undeniably the raciest (and partly racist), with a couple of funny but raunchy lines unfit for radio consumption, such as, "Moths in your rugs do it, / What's the use of moth balls?" and "I've heard that lizards and frogs do it / Layin' on a rock / They say that roosters do it / With a doodle and cock." Porter was not just pushing the envelope in 1928, he was pushing it under the covers.

The wicked couplet was later altered to "Penguins in flocks, on the rocks do it, / Even little cuckoos in their clocks do it," a cleaner and cleverer line. If you think moth balls and cocks were racy, the original opening chorus went, "Chinks do it, Japs do it, / Up in Lapland little Lapps do it." The offensive lines were blithely sung on 1928 recordings by Bing Crosby and Rudy Vallee and, in 1941, by the usually discreet Mary Martin. Porter eventually changed the first two phrases to the opening line everyone knows: "Birds do it, bees do it, Even educated fleas do it."

The song just might have been inspired—or at least given a pop boost—by Margaret Mead's scandalous 1928 bestseller *Coming of Age in Samoa*, in which the anthropologist daringly revealed that sweet young Samoan women actually did it—indulged in casual sex before marriage. Yet Porter doesn't include Samoan girls in his global roundup of people who do it—Finns, Lapps, Siamese, Argentines, the Dutch, indeed just about everyone *but* Samoans: "The Dutch in Old Amsterdam do it / Not to mention the Finns, / Folks in Siam do it—think of Siamese twins / Some Argentines, without means, do it, / People say, in Boston, even beans do it / . . . Mos-qui-tos, heaven forbid, do it, / So does every katydid do it."

A few other steamy "do" songs worth noting—the Gershwins' "Do, Do, Do" ("what you've done, done, done / Before, baby"), from *Oh, Kay!*, and George Gershwin and Buddy DeSylva's even more suggestive "Do It Again" ("Oh, oh, oh, do it again!," maybe inspired by Molly Bloom's orgasmic "Yes!"es in *Ulysses*), which Irene Bordoni got famous singing in depraved New York City. It became her signature song and may well have inspired Porter to write "Let's Do It." "Do, Do, Do" didn't bring down the censors' wrath in 1926, maybe because Ira Gershwin's risqué lyrics are set to such a perky tune and it's sung so innocently in the show by girl- and boy-next-door types that the notion of actual sex seems beyond the realm of possibility: "Do, do, do / What I do, do, do / Adore, baby. / Let's try again, / Sigh again, / Fly again to heaven. / Baby, see, it's A, B, C— / I love you and you love me." Surely that can't be about sex—it's not even about love. It's almost a nursery rhyme ("Baby, see, it's A, B, C"), recalling another classic patty-cake ditty, "Tea for Two."

Maybe the earliest "doing it" song was by Mr. Clean, Irving Berlin, a 1911 hit titled "Everybody's Doin' It Now," but in this case the "it" was a nonexistent dance that Berlin thought up, hoping to cash in on dance crazes like the

Turkey Trot, which is mentioned in the song ("Everybody's doing it / Doin' what? / The Turkey Trot"—maybe the derivation of "hot to trot"?).

After several false starts in failed shows, "Let's Do It" finds Porter happily in his element, mixing outlandish rhymes, sexy asides, and exotic references in a lyrical romp. Just to pick a few refrains at random: "Penguins, in flocks, on the rocks, do it" and "Why ask if shad do it? / Waiter, bring me shad roe."

You could almost make a case that Porter's "anything goes" era in American pop culture began in earnest with "Let's Do It."

GIRL CRAZY

• 1930 •

"I Got Rhythm"

Strangely, it's hard to find Gershwin songs that decisively stopped shows. The Gershwins wrote scores of enduring songs but surprisingly few all-out showstoppers. Their songs tended to be plush ballads ("Someone to Watch Over Me," "Embraceable You," "But Not for Me"), ingratiating charmers ("Funny Face," "I've Got a Crush on You," "Bidin' My Time"), or rhythmic jazz songs ("Fascinating Rhythm," "Clap Yo' Hands," "Fidgety Feet"), but few were numbers that brought down the house. In a way, the Gershwins were beyond bringing down houses. They built them, as Wilfrid Sheed writes in *The House that George Built*, his lively, loving book about the great Broadway composers.

A few of George and Ira's potential showstopper candidates—"'S Wonderful," "Lady, Be Good!," "Of Thee I Sing," "Strike Up the Band"—don't quite make the cut here. Perhaps it's because the Gershwins' stage shows were in the 1920s (or '30), before the era of the showstopper-obsessed choreographer, when unadorned singing was plenty. "Swanee," Gershwin's first and biggest money-maker in 1919 (lyrics by Irving Caesar), was not in a musical but in a revue that opened a new movie house; the song was a flop until Al Jolson saw it and sang it in his new show *Sinbad* to frenzied applause. Most of the brothers' biggest songs were in movies. One of their hit-filled stage shows was *Oh, Kay!*, with a libretto by Guy Bolton and P. G. Wodehouse (who in his pre-Jeeves days was a prominent lyricist on early Jerome Kern shows like *Very*

Good Eddie), which featured five charmers—"Dear Little Girl," "Do, Do, Do," "Clap Yo' Hands," "Fidgety Feet," and "Someone to Watch Over Me"—but no real roof raisers.

Two of the earliest Gershwin shows, both of which starred Fred and Adele Astaire, were *Lady, Be Good!* (1924) and *Funny Face* (1927), both top-heavy with standards-to-be ("'S Wonderful," "How Long Has This Been Going On?," "Fascinating Rhythm," "Funny Face") and stylish dances by the Astaires but no true showstopper—except Adele Astaire herself, a performer whose fetching personality infatuated audiences. Meanwhile, Adele's self-effacing little brother danced in her shadow until she ran off to marry the Duke of Devonshire and retired—Fred's big break.

In 1930, the Gershwins packed *Girl Crazy* with three infectious songs that became classics—"Embraceable You," "Bidin' My Time," "But Not for Me"—and two comedy songs—"Could You Use Me?" and "Treat Me Rough," showstopper also-rans. But the one surefire showstopper was **"I Got Rhythm,"** mainly because it was belted out of the park by a newcomer named Ethel Merman in her Broadway debut. The show—and the song—made an immediate star of Merman. (Another new face, Ginger Rogers, was the featured star, singing "Embraceable You.") The musical was later notable for its orchestra, which included young pit musicians named Glenn Miller, Gene Krupa, Jimmy Dorsey, and Benny Goodman. Some pit.

Because of its hairpin rhythmic changes and melodic bursts, Ira realized a traditional rhyme scheme for "I Got Rhythm" was absurd. He wrote in his chatty handbook, *Lyrics on Several Occasions*, that heavy rhyming "seemed at best to give a pleasant and jingly Mother Goose quality to a tune which should throw its weight around more." Ira did his best. He decided not to rhyme most lines. "This approach felt stronger, and I finally arrived at the present refrain, with 'more-door' and 'mind him–find him' the only rhymes." He said the scheme "was a bit daring for me, who usually depended on rhyme insurance."

Broadway lore has it that after he heard Merman sing "I Got Rhythm," George Gershwin counseled her never to take a singing lesson. Unthinkable—she never had and never would. The twenty-two-year-old ex-stenographer from Astoria, Queens, sang effortlessly in a lower chest voice with the volume turned to high. Even Pavarotti liked Merman, once telling her he admired her natural *passagio*, a word she had to look up; it's the ability to shift from a chest to a head voice. It's amazing that such a brief number with almost nothing to say could be turned by Merman into a showstopper by the sheer force of her voice and personality: "I got rhythm, / I got music, / I got my man, / Who could ask for anything more? / I got daisies / In green pastures, / I got my man." The lyric has nothing to do with rhythm; the theme is all in the music. It's as if Ira gave up trying to devise a real idea, said to hell with it, and just tossed in a dummy lyric.

Merman later recalled her breakthrough moment: "I held a C note for 16 bars, an entire chorus, while the orchestra played the melodic line—a big tooty thing—against the note. By the time I held that note for four bars the audience was applauding. I did several encores. It seemed to do something to them. Not because it was sweet or beautiful, but because it was exciting. Few people have the ability to project a big note and hold it. It's not just a matter of breath; it's a matter of power in the diaphragm. I'd never trained my diaphragm, but I must have a strong one. When I finished the song, a star had been born. Me."

In "I Got Rhythm," Merman held the note while the orchestra played the melody of the first refrain and then she held the same note for a second refrain; one report testifies that "the house went mad." The swing tune quickly became a jazz standard, but Ira found it the hardest of all Gershwin's zigzag melodies to write words for, fragmented tunes that Wilfrid Sheed described as "moving targets for Ira to throw lyrics at if he could."

Ira hated how Merman held that C forever, but it helped turn her into a star overnight and helped turn *Girl Crazy* into a craze. Holding notes became a Merman trademark, and other singers tried to imitate the trick whenever they sang the song. Ira may have flinched, but his edgier brother loved it, claiming it gave the song even more feverish excitement.

"She stopped the show cold with her singing, and the audience demanded many encores," writes singer Michael Feinstein, an expert on all things Gershwin who got his start as Ira's assistant, in his detailed inside book *The Gershwins and Me*. (Ira might have winced at the title's grammar, or maybe hailed its colloquial honesty.) The *New York Times* reported that Merman appealed "to the vast delight last evening of the people who go places and watch things being done," as if the critic regarded her as a faddish curiosity. Feinstein says that after Merman sang for the Gershwins, George told her that if there was anything she didn't like about their songs, he'd be happy to change them, and Merman replied, maybe half-jokingly, "They'll do very nicely." When Feinstein wondered if George would really have changed a song for her, Ira said, "He was just being polite," but added that if she had requested a B-flat in the sixth bar, not a B, he might have fixed it for her. Ira was not a Merman fan, unlike George. "He thought her singing was too brash, too 'in your face,'" writes Feinstein, and because she was crass, a little vulgar, and unworldly, "it was unlikely she'd be appealing to someone as circumspect and decorous as Ira, who may have been the least vulgar person who ever lived."

Director Greg MacKellan says "I Got Rhythm" "is wedded to Merman becoming a star with that song. She did something vocally people had never heard—they'd never heard belting like that before. So you have this propulsive song, and Merman and the music are so in sync. You have that happy thing where the song and the lyric and a perfect performance come together, and the perfect performer is doing something new. It was just this sensation." Shows, let alone solos, rarely create overnight stars on today's Broadway. Can anyone name the stars from *The Lion King, Hairspray, Jersey Boys, The Book of Mormon, Newsies,* or *Matilda*?

Another Ethel, Ethel Waters, helped solidify the song's place as a pop standard and gave the number what archivist Dwight Blocker Bowers calls its "revivalist fervor." Louis Armstrong instantly seized on the song and recorded it in 1931, lending the number his regal imprimatur. It has since been recorded by countless jazz artists—"the song with the largest number of variations on its chords" maintains a distinctive stat provided by Bowers. "I Got Rhythm" was such a hit that Gershwin came up with a kind of sequel, "I Got Rhythm Variations," which he played on a 1934 concert tour but which was rarely heard thereafter.

Ira constantly policed singers to keep them from singing "*I've* got rhythm." He preferred the more common slangy "I got." Ira repeated the phrase "Who could ask for anything more?" four times in the song but didn't use it as a title—"Somehow the first line of the refrain sounded more arresting and provocative." But he loved the line "Who could ask for anything more?" so much that he used it in two other Gershwin songs—"Nice Work If You Can Get It" and "I'm About to Be a Mother" from *Of Thee I Sing.* In a rewritten version of *Girl Crazy, Crazy for You* in 1992, "I Got Rhythm" was sung by Jodi Benson and choreographed by Susan Stroman to within an inch of its life. The show made Stroman Broadway's most inventive, most-wanted choreographer.

The original *Girl Crazy* is rarely revived but lives on in the peppy MGM version with Mickey Rooney and Judy Garland belting out a zippy "I Got Rhythm" in front of Tommy Dorsey's orchestra. You can watch Merman herself sock it out in a YouTube clip from a 1956 TV show. There's also a rare, grainy black-and-white YouTube clip of Garland in what looks like a '50s TV production of *Girl Crazy.* Maybe the world's least likely singer to perform it, Karen Carpenter, is very much worth hearing in an audio-only YouTube cut in which she slows the song way down and sings it with her usual warmth and actual feeling. I'd never heard "I Got Rhythm" slowed down, but she almost turns it into a ballad.

Michael Feinstein explains why "I got" is "punchier" than "I've got": "'I got' allows for the equal separation of each word in the phrase and fits the staccato notes far better than 'I've got.' 'I've got rhythm' is much too formal. Also, if the singer had to enunciate 'I've' the words would meld into each other, the spacing would be lost, and the impact would be muted."

The Gershwins' other big "rhythm" hit, "Fascinating Rhythm," was from 1924's *Lady Be Good!*, and the two songs, along with other syncopated numbers by the team, gave jazz, then considered déclassé, a respectable place on Broadway. "Fascinating Rhythm" sounds like it was written with showstopping in mind, first performed by the Astaires and a novelty star of the day, Cliff Edwards, a.k.a. "Ukulele Ike" and Walt Disney's Jiminy Cricket. The song had nothing to do with the plot, such as it was, but was devised as a stand-alone "specialty" number for the Astaires and Edwards. The lyrics—as in "I Got Rhythm" and "Fidgety Feet"—are just hamburger helper, footwork filler in which the singer/dancer is helplessly possessed by rhythm ("Each morning I get up with the sun— / Start a-hopping, / Never stopping— / To find at night no work has been done . . . Oh, how I long to be the man I used to be! / Fascinating rhythm, / Oh, won't you stop picking on me!"). The number became the big moment in *Lady Be Good!* It seems odd, though, for a guy who loved to use (and invent) colloquialisms, that Ira didn't title the loose-limbed song "Fascinatin' Rhythm," deleting the apostrophe as he had in "I Got Rhythm." Fascinating.

ANYTHING GOES

◆ 1934 ◆

"You're the Top"

Of all the great list songs from musicals, **"You're the Top"** resides securely at the top of the list—a 1934 number from *Anything Goes* that, throughout its many verses, keeps effortlessly topping itself. Most comedy songs run out of gas a third of the way in, then simply repeat the main joke several ways. Porter does that too—it's the nature of the list song—yet his fertile, restless brain was able to bat out clever, unexpected new verses and deft rhymes with ease. Even on the four hundredth hearing, his lyric ingenuity and unexpected rhymes still impress you.

When the song was new to *Anything Goes* audiences, they demanded as many encores as Ethel Merman and costar William Gaxton could manage, so Porter was forced to keep cranking out new stanzas to keep playgoers amused. At one performance, Merman all but pleaded with the audience to let the show continue as planned. "There are no more lyrics!" she shouted in despair after singing the seventh and last refrain: "You're the top! / You're the tower of Babel. / You're the top! / You're the Whitney stable. / By the river Rhine, / You're a sturdy stein of beer. / You're a dress from Saks, / You're next year's taxes, / You're stratosphere." In his opening-night review, Brooks Atkinson of the *New York Times* singled out the song for modest praise, calling it "one of the most congenial songs Mr. Porter has written." Congenial?

As in so many opening-night reviews of shows now considered landmark musicals, there is scant mention of the great Porter songs; critics spent more time discussing the performers and sets or dutifully describing the show's elaborate, inane plot. In the *New York Herald Tribune*, the show was labeled both a "revue" and "a comic opera" by critic Percy Hammond, a little unsure exactly what he was watching.

"You're the Top" was such a seemingly random yet perfect list of people, places, and things—topical and classical, highbrow and low—that even Noël Coward couldn't resist adding to it, in homage. The song is so solidly constructed, musically, that almost anybody can mimic it, in the master's spirit if not in his inventive vein. People used to send the songwriter their own versions of the song, many of them ribald.

Porter once described his methodology: "First I think of an idea for a song and then I fit it to a title. Then I go to work on a melody, spotting the title at certain moments in the melody. Then I write the lyric—the end first—that way it has a strong finish. . . . I do the lyrics the way I'd do a crossword puzzle. I try to give myself a meter which will make the lyrics as easy as possible to write, but without being banal. . . . I try to pick for my rhyme words of which there is a long list with the same ending."

So let's start, like Porter, with the idea behind "You're the Top"—a duet of lavish praise sung by a man and woman flattering each other outrageously, two people telling each other how terrific they are. That romantic premise is almost forgotten as you listen to the unlikely pairings and playful rhymes, caught up in Porter's roster of the world's A-list items. It becomes a kind of game, and in fact at parties in the 1930s people would sit around devising their own versions. The fun comes in anticipating the next juxtaposed famous names and rhymes, each couplet trying to outdo the last. No matter how often you've heard the lyrics you still relish the bizarre matchups, smiling not so much at the familiar jokes as at Porter's seemingly inexhaustible ingenuity. When he ran out of rhymes for "top" he devised a few of his own—"blop," "G.O.P." (i.e., "gop").

One writer calls list songs "lyrical exhibitionism," and indeed few lyricists can resist the opportunity to show off their verbal dexterity, from Lorenz Hart's "To Keep My Love Alive" and "Zip" to Stephen Sondheim's "A Little Priest" and "I'm Still Here." Even the unflashy Oscar Hammerstein II was unable to ignore the temptation, writing two list songs in *The Sound of Music*—"My Favorite Things" and "Do-Re-Mi." But Porter remains easily the acknowledged king of the list song—"Always True to You in My Fashion," "Brush Up Your Shakespeare," "Let's Do It," "Nobody's Chasing Me," "The Physician," "Can-Can." It's a long list.

Porter could write exquisitely touching songs, but apart from his lists he is most remembered for his, well, touch songs. Nobody but Lorenz Hart dared mention the sex act with equal parts passion and playfulness, as in risqué Porter classics like "Let's Do It," "I've Got You Under My Skin," "All of You," "Love for Sale," "Let's Misbehave," "Never Give Anything Away," "Too Darn Hot," and "But in the Morning, No"—the latter as close to X-rated as he got. Porter rarely mentioned the word *sex* but neatly eluded censors most of the time by pretending that his songs were all about falling in love, not falling into bed. In "All of You" you can almost hear heavy panting ("[I love] the east, west, north and the south of you").

In the teasing introductory verse to "You're the Top," justifying what follows, the master coyly apologizes for his inarticulateness with a wink of false modesty: "At words poetic, I'm so pathetic / That I always have found it best, / Instead of getting 'em off my chest, / To let 'em rest, unexpressed. / I hate parading my serenading / As I'll probably miss a bar, / But if this ditty is not so pretty, / At least it'll tell you how great you are."

The song's jaunty melody, one of his most irresistible tunes but overshadowed by Porter's effortless wordplay, keeps the number from turning tiresome. Anyone can hum it instantly. Musicologist Gerald Mast points out how, on successive mentions of the title, Porter's lines "leap up, to its top note, on every repetition of the word 'top.'" He also observes how far less effective the song would be if it were titled "You're the Tops."

Mark Steyn, in his sharp, irreverent book on musicals, *Broadway Babies Say Goodnight*, astutely comments, "Invariably praised for their slick rhymes, Porter's best laundry lists work because of their music—'If old **hymns** you like / If bare **limbs** you like / If Mae **West** you like / Or me un**dressed** you like . . .' [from "Anything Goes"]. You don't notice the device because the words and music are so indivisible, but in this song—the release of 'Anything Goes'—Porter keeps the 'you like's set on repeated notes but then, on the emphasized rhyme words, the melody changes, stepping up the scales chromatically. That's what gives the song forward propulsion; that's why it seems to be getting *funnier*."

In the song, Porter zips about the globe, zigzagging from the Mona Lisa and Tower of Pisa to "Inferno's Dante and the nose on the great Durante." (Note that Dante is just Dante, but Durante gets bigger billing as "the *great* Durante.") He links a melody by Strauss to Mickey Mouse and a turkey dinner to a Derby winner, implying that they're equally sensational. To Porter, there is no pop hierarchy. In his world, and in this song particularly, anything does indeed go. In *Easy to Remember*, a book on his favorite songs, William Zinsser says "You're the Top" was his teenage introduction to sophistication, though he had never heard of Napoleon brandy or Camembert, singled out in the song for their topness; "I wasn't up on my brandies and cheeses," he says. So for Zinsser and others, the song—and many others like it—are teachable moments. "In this one song," wrote a *New Yorker* critic, "he has summarized American civilization better than any symposium of national thinkers have ever been able to do."

How the title came about is up for grabs. According to Robert Kimball's book of Porter lyrics, "You're the Top" was inspired by a cruise down the Rhine that Porter took in 1934, on which he asked some of the passengers to name the favorite things they had ever seen or done; Kimball says Porter later used a few of the items in his song. Perhaps, but it sounds a little too neat. You can't imagine Porter needing any help coming up with celebrity names, place names, and brand names. A profile in the *New Yorker* reported that Porter wrote the song in Paris after a dinner where he and a wealthy guest "entertained themselves by making up a list of superlatives that rhymed." Porter referred to the song as "just a trick," and he worried people would soon be bored by it. Ethel Merman felt it might not go over because it was such an odd comic love song, and essentially it *is* a love song.

Anything Goes—and specifically "You're the Top"—established Merman as a voice, a Broadway force to be reckoned with. Her friendship with Porter

Ethel Merman demonstrating how "Anything Goes" aboard ship in *Anything* Goes.

began with this show and its show-stopping score, which, lest we forget, also includes the belter's anthem "Blow, Gabriel, Blow," which Merman instantly owned after introducing it, along with "You're the Top." Brooks Atkinson observed that Merman's authority made "every line sound like a masterpiece of wit."

Merman thenceforth became Porter's favorite female singer (also Irving Berlin's), partly because every line was loudly and precisely articulated by her and could be heard in the back row of the balcony, if not out on the sidewalk. Merman wasn't a great actress, but she forced you to pay attention. She made a mighty noise. Porter told her she "sounded like a brass band going by," and Berlin famously said she forced him to write good lyrics "because the audience will hear every word." More than that, she was faithful to each quarter note and syllable. "I never change a word," she said. "I don't tamper with the melodies or rhythms." Music to any songwriter's ears. She did, however, refuse to sing "Kate the Great," which was cut from the show when even the brazen, oft-crude Merman was offended by the lyrics: "She made the butler / She made the groom / She made the maid who made the room."

They were an odd couple, the earthy Merman and the elegant Porter, not unlike the comic couplings in "You're the Top." Merman wrote in her memoir *Don't Call Me Madam*, "What Cole had done was to analyze my voice and turn out songs which showed off its vitality. 'You're the Top' brought audiences to their feet because it was a new kind of love song. There had never been a song like it before. A complete original. So I wasn't surprised that at the peak of its popularity Cole received 300 parodies a month."

Porter said he custom-made tunes for her range, ending songs on what he called her best note, A-natural. He admired her diction, especially her precise consonants, like the letter *D*, or the way Merman could flatten a note for comic effect—also how she could create "clinkers," for laughs. It was her sharp instinct, belting "I Get a Kick Out of You," to elongate "if" in the line— "It would bore me terr-*ifff*-ically, too." In her memoir, Merman admires her own handiwork: "I took liberties with that word. I paused in the song after the syllable 'rif.' It was just a way of phrasing, of breaking a word, but for some reason that pause killed the people. I'm not enough of a musician to know why." She remarks that, whereas Porter and Gershwin wrote career-making songs for her iron-clad stage persona, "it was Irving Berlin who made a lady out of me" with gentle ballads.

Merman is still the top, instantly verifiable on a YouTube clip from the otherwise lame 1936 movie *Anything Goes*, where she tells Bing Crosby *he's* the top even as he clowns it up in a bizarre beard; Merman is surprisingly cute. She and Frank Sinatra do a YouTube duet on *The Colgate Comedy Hour*, Streisand vamps the song singing dumb revised lyrics, and there's audio of Allan Sherman croaking out a parody version at a party ("so if baby, I'm a schmendrick, you're the top").

In revivals of *Anything Goes*, the fourth-longest-running show of the 1930s, with more Porter standards than any of his other scores, theater programs often provide a glossary of now-obscure names in "You're the Top," such as film actress Irene Bordoni, crooner (of "Let's Do It" renown) Rudy Vallee, "a Nathan panning" (by brutal theater critic George Jean Nathan), composer Vincent Youmans, or references to a Bendel bonnet (ritzy female milliner) and the Zuider Zee (inlet on the North Sea), but mostly Porter chose names and places everyone is still familiar with. A few stanzas include now-arcane brands—Phenolax (a popular laxative) and Drumstick Lipstick (a chic brand).

Porter's delayed success in 1934 finally came about because, as the literary mantra dictates, he wrote about what he knew best—the sophisticated world he traveled in. Porter loved the cultivated life he kidded as only someone could who felt so at home among the well born, among ninetieth-floor penthouses, Park Casino oysters, Waldorf salads, Lady Astor, and Ritz hot toddies. Just like the 1912 Iowa of Meredith Willson's *The Music Man*, his fellow midwesterner Cole Porter (from Peru, Indiana) knew the territory.

Porter's "You're the Top" list, apart from being amusing, is a cross-section of what Americans considered valuable in the 1930s. As Gerald Mast notes, "'You're the Top' is a catalog of cultural values of 1934." The song travels well. In *Dancing at Lughnasa*, Brian Friel's 1990 play set in the '30s, the song is used as an atmospheric device when the five lonely, morose Irish sisters in the play listen to "You're the Top" on their battered phonograph to cheer themselves up. Heinz once rewrote the song for a ketchup commercial that Porter would have loved.

Interestingly, because it's meant as a kind of love song, the lyrics have none of Porter's trademark double entendres, but he was long thought to be the author of a ribald parody, more recently attributed by archivist Robert Kimball to Irving Berlin, of all people, whose raunchy version may startle admirers of his romantic ballads. If it is indeed by Berlin, the parody reveals a shocking side of a guy considered a buttoned-up conservative. It's almost as if he's telling Porter, *Anything you can do, I can do bawdier*:

"You're the top! / You're Miss Pinkham's tonic. / You're the top! / You're a high colonic. / You're the burning heat of a bridal suite in use, / You're the breast of Venus, / You're King Kong's penis. / You're self-abuse. / You're an arch / In the Rome collection. / You're the starch in a groom's erection / I'm a eunuch who / Has just been through an op, / But if baby, I'm the bottom / You're the top." Berlin maybe missed a chance to exit laughing by neglecting to switch the final phrase to "You're on top."

Porter's favorite couplet in his own song, one biographer claims, was "You're romance. / You're the steppes of Russia, / You're the pants on a Roxy usher." My own favorite is a silky internal rhyme: "You're the nimble tread / Of the feet of Fred / Astaire." P. G. Wodehouse, Porter's favorite lyricist, provided a few new references for the song's British version, including this controversial line, later deleted: "You're the top, / You're the great Houdini. / You're the top, / You're Mussolini."

"You're the Top" was hardly the first great list song (the first and foremost model would have to be Gilbert and Sullivan's showstopper from *The Mikado*, "I've Got a Little List"), but Porter's song, eighty years later, remains the most definitive textbook example, the gold standard by which all other list songs are still measured.

············ BACKSTAGE DISH ··············

+ The rollicking title song of "Anything Goes" (which accidentally gave the hodgepodge show its name) was not Porter's phrase. The show's coauthor Russel Crouse, in his memoir, says it was blurted out by the show's costar William Gaxton one day during frenzied rehearsals when the director asked the actor if he would mind entering right after the curtain was raised. Gaxton shrugged, "In this kind of a spot, anything goes!" Porter obliged with one of his punchiest songs, giving an urgently needed meaning to the marquee. The show's equally vague working title had been "Hard to Get."

+ The musical was indeed a hurried slapdash affair—and it plays like it, with a wacky plot about a wimpy guy who smuggles himself aboard a luxury liner to win a girl and ends up mistakenly fingered as most-wanted bootlegger, even though the bootleg and flapper craze was pretty much over by then. The first act was knocked out in ten days, and the second act was finished while the cast was still rehearsing the first act. The plot had to be hastily rewritten when a real ocean liner, the SS *Morro Castle*, went down in flames off the New Jersey coast, killing 134 passengers. The original book by P. G. Wodehouse and Guy Bolton was thrown overboard and a new script hurriedly batted out by Howard Lindsay and Russel Crouse, the famous team's first collaboration. Lindsay and Crouse were allegedly so worried about the plot that they tried to talk friends out of seeing the show—until Merman's "I Get a Kick Out of You" convinced them it just might be a hit after all. The book was rewritten yet again for the 1987 Patti LuPone revival by Crouse's son Timothy and John Weidman, which included parts of four rewritten versions (1934, 1962, 1987, 2011), but it's still hopelessly silly, which director Jerry Zaks tried to wish away by calling it "serious silliness." The infectious songs easily keep the show afloat, an irresistibly tasty score that *New York Times* critic Ben Brantley called "a deluxe candy box of songs."

+ Like many of Porter's early musicals, his songs were simply dropped into scenes. Sometimes they fit the action or character, but often they didn't and were just tasty bonbons, like "Blow, Gabriel, Blow." The show's title succinctly sums up the patchwork story line. "Cole didn't care too much about the book," said the show's colibrettist Dorothy Fields. "He came to some rehearsals, but generally he just wrote songs, and he'd rewrite them, and then Herbie [her librettist brother] and I would have to fit them in."

Porter waited for each scene in *Anything Goes* to be delivered before writing a song to fit it, forcing him to rummage through his trunk for discarded numbers cut from earlier shows, such as "I Get a Kick Out of You," originally meant for a show called *Star Dust*. Porter took such care with his songs that often the introductory verse is a virtual song within a song, like the ornate opening to "I Get a Kick Out of You": "My story is much too sad to be told, / But practically ev'rything leaves me totally cold. / The only exception I know is the case, / When I'm out on a quiet spree, / Fighting vainly the old ennui / And I suddenly turn and see / Your fabulous face." It starts off as a lament and then—pow!—the song kicks into high ecstatic gear: "I get no kick from champagne . . ."

+ If a song didn't quite work, Porter would eagerly write a new one rather than revise a lyric; "Rewriting ruins a song," he said. When William Gaxton couldn't hit the high notes in "Easy to Love," Porter replaced it with "All through the Night." No problem; standards written while you wait. His early idol wasn't W. S. Gilbert, as you might suppose, but Robert Browning. "I suppose Browning started me writing lyrics," he said. Porter's favorite Cole Porter song was "Begin the Beguine," and his favorite show *Kiss Me, Kate*.

+ *Anything Goes*'s ebullient title number is as cutting a social comment in its way as "You're the Top" and could have been written last week ("And good's bad today, / And black's white today / And day's night today . . ."). In 1924, the song had more social commentary in it that had to be dropped. Jerry Zaks, who staged the hit 1987 revival, said, "Cole Porter had a high stake in making it all look effortless, though in fact he worked like a bandit. Some people think of him as glib and supercilious. His lyrics acknowledge the dark side of life—they just don't dwell on it." It seems to us now a much merrier time, one of the main reasons the show still gives us such a kick—despite what Paul Simon told Mark Steyn, dismissing lines like "You're the top, / You're the Coliseum": "We don't define wit that way anymore." Or at all, judging from most rock and folk songs.

+ Hollywood had two chances to make *Anything Goes* and botched both of them—one in 1936 with Merman, Bing Crosby, and Charles Ruggles, and again in 1956, also with Crosby plus Mitzi Gaynor, Donald O'Connor, and a totally different plot, which didn't help. It's a hapless remake, with songs from other Cole Porter shows plus needless "additional songs" by Sammy Cahn and Jimmy Van Heusen.

With Hollywood's usual aplomb, the 1936 version used only four songs from the stage show—"You're the Top," "Anything Goes," "I Get a Kick out of You," and "There'll Always Be a Lady Fair"—all scrubbed clean for moviegoers by the movie industry's new Production Code two years after Will Hays began patrolling movies for traces of naughty behavior. Just for good measure, the movie also tossed out "Blow, Gabriel, Blow" and "All Through the Night." But maybe the most interesting thing about the 1956 *Anything Goes* film is that the original line in the title song—"Good authors, too, who once knew better words / Now only use four-letter words"—was actually changed to "three-letter words"! Even a passing reference to four-letter words was deemed too dirty for the 1956 moviegoing public. Porter wisely stuck to Broadway musicals, where anything went.

• •

BABES IN ARMS

• 1937 •

"Johnny One-Note," "I Wish I Were in Love Again"

*B*abes in Arms is the original (or anyway most famous) hey-let's-put-on-a-show-in-the-old-barn! musical. I've been tracking Rodgers and Hart shows for fifty years, and I've only seen it done twice, both by small San Francisco companies. It's rarely revived, mainly because it's a show about teenagers that requires sophisticated young talent to bring it off.

Besides the show's five big songs, it also boasts three little-known numbers that fill out an absurdly catchy score. "Way Out West" is a cowboy song parody with ingenious Hart lyrics ("Git along, little taxi, / You can keep the change, / I'm ridin' home to my kitchen range, / Way out west on West End Avenue"). "You Are So Fair" is equally inspired, as Hart plays with the word "fair/fare," sung by a guy who begins by praising his girl's looks and winds up deciding she's not so great, after all ("You're only fair"). Finally, there's that rousing title song, a march to end all marches; even march-mad Jerry Herman could never surpass it.

Given all these musical riches, it's still a wonder *Babes in Arms* isn't constantly revived. The original 1936 cast featured baby-faced stars-to-be: Dan Dailey, Alfred Drake, Ray Heatherton, Robert Rounseville, and the Nicholas Brothers—not a bad collection. The female lead was Mitzi Green, all of sixteen. The Judy Garland–Mickey Rooney movie version used only three songs from the original score (the title song, "Where or When," "The Lady Is a Tramp"), ditching all the other terrific songs with Hollywood's usual wisdom. "The Lady Is a Tramp" was deemed little better than background music.

The musical's four biggest songs include **"Johnny One-Note,"** a designer showstopper calculated to get a huge hand for a single elongated note: "Johnny could only sing one note, and the note he sang was this: *AHHHHHHH*!!" (a C actually). It's a belter's holiday, but it mocks belters and, many thought, Ethel Merman in particular. *Forbidden Broadway*, the New York revue that satirizes musicals, once did a number called "Ethel One-Note." Rodgers and Hart hated belters who steamrolled their songs. They also wrote the cranky "I Like to Recognize the Tune," in *Too Many Girls*, blasting jazz bands that mangled their songs. "Johnny One-Note" is a one-note joke that drowns out some of Hart's subtlest rhymes: "Poor Johnny One-Note / Sang out with **gusto** / And **just o**-verlorded the place," followed by "Poor Johnny One-Note / Yelled willy-**nilly** / **Un**ti**l he** was blue in the face." And a few lines later, "Poor Johnny One-Note / Got in *Aida* / **Indeed a** great chance to be brave."

The most deserved *Babes in Arms* showstopper is **"I Wish I Were in Love Again,"** a sardonic, ironic, irresistible Rodgers and Hart comic love/hate song that shows off Hart's dazzling wordplay as stunning as any lyric he wrote. Mickey Rooney sings it as well on screen as you could hope, displaying his manic energy at his all-time Rooneyest; the number is a showcase for his performing charm and frantic style. As Oscar Hammerstein II said of Hart, "I think of him as always skipping and bouncing. I never saw his face in repose. I never heard him chuckle quietly." He might well have been describing Rooney.

"I Wish I Were in Love Again" was cut from the movie *Babes in Arms* but salvaged in *Words and Music*, the 1948 Rodgers and Hart biopic that bears almost no resemblance to the team's actual characters or careers. But it's a joyous excuse to watch their songs performed, and Rooney captures Hart's frantic persona as well as can be expected for a pug-nosed boy next door, a girl-crazy Irishman playing a swarthy gay New York Jewish guy. (But both men were short, so they got that part right.) Rooney in no way suggests the real Lorenz Hart; he comes across more like Larry Hardy.

**A distraught Mickey Rooney confesses "I Wish I Were in Love Again"
to a dubious Judy Garland in the film *Words and Music*.**

Greg MacKellan, who directed *Babes in Arms* for his San Francisco company 42nd Street Moon, explains how he approached "I Wish I Were in Love Again": "These people are kind of pissed off and baiting each other, so you can't do it with them holding hands and some cute dance moves. I kept the girl dancing, but after every other move, I had her slap him. They trip one another. It ended up with them falling over each other on the ground and they kiss. It took the audience by surprise. And it got huge applause, and I'm not sure it would have as just a cute little number like Judy Garland and Mickey Rooney do it in the movie. That's really not what the lyrics are saying. I just knew it needed these little nasty touches. And then—boom!—it was a big showstopper."

"I Wish I Were in Love Again" (a Hart biographer points out the rare use of a subjunctive in a song title; others he cites: "If I Were a Rich Man" and "If Love Were All") is about the mixed blessings of being out of love, with an insightful setup verse: "You don't know that I felt good. / When we up and parted. / You don't know I knocked on wood, / Gladly broken-hearted. / Worrying is through, / I sleep all night, / Appetite and health restored, / You don't know how much I'm bored."

It's a perfect premise for a grown-up love song. The character realizes he'd rather be in love, despite all the misery, spelled out in a series of insightful lines and unexpected rhymes that capture the romantic angst of love, with precision and inspired imagery: "The sleepless nights, / The daily fights, / The quick toboggan when you reach the heights; / I miss the kisses and I miss the bites," he or she sings, then muses about "The broken dates, / The endless waits, / The lovely loving and the hateful hates, / The conversation with the flying plates." Has anyone ever managed to enumerate, as succinctly, the agonies of love's confusion? That "conversation with the flying plates" floors you. Nobody then had ever devised such blithe lines about real-life love.

Hart's lyrics have nuggets of romantic wisdom casually embedded: "The furtive sigh, the blackened eye, / The words 'I'll love you till the day I die,' / The self-deception that believes the lie. / I wish I were in love again." The tossed-off "self-deception that believes the lie" sums up romantic love in five words. Then we get "No more pain, / No more strain, / Now I'm sane but I would rather be gaga!" (again, Hart's exact use of slang). And then this lyrical coup de grace, one of the most memorable couplets in all of show tune boy-girl coupling: "When love congeals, it soon reveals / The faint aroma of performing seals, / The double-crossing of a pair of heels, / I wish I were in love again!" Only Larry Hart ever put into words the sweet smell of sweaty sex. Lyricist Fred Ebb (*Cabaret*, *Chicago*) once said, doffing his hat, "Larry Hart made all lyricists a little braver."

THE BOYS FROM SYRACUSE

◆ 1938 ◆

"Sing for Your Supper"

A fter a lifetime of musicals, a major landmark show for me remains the
1963 revival of *The Boys from Syracuse*, a jaw-droppingly great production that ran nearly twice as long as the original 1938 show. The Rodgers and Hart musical, at the little off-Broadway Theater Four, had more pure pleasure per quarter note than almost any musical I've seen in half a century since. Yes, you had to be there, but the cast recording makes a bright case for its unsurpassed theatrical riches. If you don't know *The Boys from Syracuse*, you must immediately fill that glaring gap—indeed, chasm.

A musical version of Shakespeare's *The Comedy of Errors*, the show is one of Broadway's most irrepressible, irresistible, and inventive musical comedies—a show of unquenchable, nonstop exuberance; a score of charm, literate wit, and enchanting tunes. Richard Rodgers's music sails from high to high, matched by Lorenz Hart's sparklingly ingenious verbal high-wire act.

An equally smitten critic, Walter Kerr, wrote in the *New York Herald Tribune* of the 1963 production, "It is like the gentle rain of heaven, that show." Richard Watts Jr. in the *New York Post* echoed Kerr's ecstasy: "There is a feast of melody in *The Boys from Syracuse*." Watts added, and rightly so, "*The Comedy of Errors* has always seemed an excruciatingly unfunny farce and *The Boys from Syracuse* shows what was wrong with it." In 1938, a New York critic predicted that the show would one day be known as "the greatest musical comedy of its time." It isn't so regarded, alas, or even known to many playgoers, but among the musical-comedy cognoscenti it's very much in the running, with at least half a dozen inspired songs and another half dozen merely sensational numbers.

Apart from its array of infectious songs—not a dud in the score—its '38 cast seemed handpicked for the 1963 sold-out revival that cost an outlandish $33,000 to mount. Nobody famous came out of the show, but the cast consisted of witty, ingratiating performers like Stuart Damon, Karen Morrow, Kathryn Damon, and Julienne Marie. Christopher Hewett's wily direction was overseen by the persnickety Richard Rodgers, so it closely mirrored the original version, written and staged by George Abbott, at the peak of his powers, as were Rodgers and Hart. The original show featured Eddie Albert, Teddy Hart (Larry's brother), Hart look-alike comic Jimmy Savo, Wynn Murray, Muriel Angelus, and Marcy Wescott; Burl Ives had a bit part as a tailor's apprentice.

The Boys from Syracuse is a near-perfect musical adaptation that includes but two lines from its original source, "The venom clamors of a jealous woman. Poisons more deadly than a mad dog's tooth," after which an actor pops his head out and pipes, "Shakespeare!" The mistaken-identity plot (so dreary in the original labored farce) is performed vaudeville-style by toga-clad hoofers, "cuties in the forum" to quote a lyric, and Greek characters delivering Marx Brothers gags: "Did you bring your harp?" "No." "Good, then you can pick on me." Silly? For sure, but magnificently silly. In liner notes to the Broadway Angel 1963 cast album, Marc Kirkeby writes that "the Marx Brothers or the Three Stooges seem to have been on George Abbott's mind."

In spirit, the show is a lot like the more famous, equally frantic but less inventive *A Funny Thing Happened on the Way to the Forum*, Stephen Sondheim, Larry Gelbart, and Burt Shevelove's 1962 musical based on the plays of Plautus. Rodgers and Hart got there first. After you see *The Boys from Syracuse*, and few have because it's so rarely revived (the plot requires two sets of look-alike actors as twin slaves and their twin masters), *A Funny Thing Happened* tastes like pretty thin soup.

One London critic called **"Sing for Your Supper"** "a suggestive ditty"— but all it suggests is that a winning woman will be wined, dined, and well taken care of: "Sing for your supper, / And you'll get breakfast, / Songbirds always eat / If their song is sweet to hear. / Sing for your luncheon / And you'll get dinner. / Dine with wine of choice, / If romance is in your voice. / I heard from a wise canary / Trilling makes a fellow willing, / So, little swallow, swallow now." One might speculate that "sing" is a code word for something more vertical. In Hart's introductory verse, he writes, "Hawks and crows do lots of things, / But the canary only sings. / She is a courtesan on wings— / So I've heard." There you go.

"Falling in Love with Love" and "This Can't Be Love" didn't stop the show, but they give an idea of the score's riches, which also include a cascade of inspired comedy numbers—besides "Sing for Your Supper" there's "Dear Old Syracuse," "What Can You Do with a Man?" (a shrug of wifely exasperation by a housemaid whose husband is a lousy lover), and a frenetic dance solo, "Oh, Diogenes," an electrifying number by a courtesan who can't find an honest man; the singles scene in ancient Greece sounds grim. The opening number features a tap-dancing Greek chorus wearing masks of comedy and tragedy. (Woody Allen may have stolen the idea for a scene in his underrated movie musical, *Everyone Says I Love You*.)

The jubilant high point of the show and its plot, which both parallels and parodies Shakespeare's play, is "Sing for Your Supper," performed by a female trio chirping about the benefits of being a songbird, trilled in jazzy close harmony, like imitation Boswell/Andrews Sisters. It is quite possibly the uppest up-tune ever written. YouTube has several zippy versions, one with Rebecca Luker, Audra McDonald, and Mary Testa; another with Luker, Debbie Shapiro Gravitte, and Christine Ebersole (maybe my favorite, with the trio clad in Andrews Sisters skirts and hats); and a funny but fuzzy video featuring Kaye Ballard, Roberta Peters, and Donna McKechnie. A critic called the number "a show-stopping demand for instant gratification." "You Could Drive a Person Crazy" from *Company* is suspiciously similar in style to Hugh Martin's original jazzy 1938 arrangement for "Sing for Your Supper." On the other hand, "Sing for Your Supper" is reminiscent of "Three Little Maids from School Are We" from *The Mikado*.

Songbirds Marcy Wescott, Wynn Murray, and Muriel Angelus explain how to "Sing for Your Supper" in *The Boys from Syracuse*.

In any case, the guy responsible for bringing the number to life was Martin, a young, enterprising singer/songwriter/arranger who took it upon himself to write to Rodgers, suggesting he hire him to do some vocal arranging. Rodgers was smart enough to take him up on the offer. Martin, in his nineties when we spoke, related the story in detail, explaining how this showstopper was created from the ground up.

He began, "I don't know what possessed me to write to him—it really was sort of fate—but one day I sat down in the lobby of the Edison Theatre and wrote Dick Rodgers a letter that changed my life forever. I told him this is going to sound like a very pretentious letter, and I don't mean it to sound that way because I adore your work—I think you're the top—but I said there's one thing I don't understand—why you and your colleagues never employ vocal arrangements to enhance your work."

In his letter, Martin said, "When I go to the movies I have more fun than when I go to a Broadway show—and it should not be that way because the music in the Broadway shows is much better than the movies—but I like the interesting things they do with the arrangements." He explained to me, "Shows then never had any vocal arrangements. They just sang a verse and two choruses. And that's what I said in the letter. I said, 'Please don't think I'm being critical, I just really would like to know the reason.'"

Martin went on: "Well, nothing happened for a couple of weeks, and then one day I got a phone call from a friend who turned out to be the rehearsal piano player on *The Boys from Syracuse*, and he said, 'Mr. Rodgers wants you to come to the Alvin Theatre right away—can you come now?' And I nearly fainted. I had no credits. I said I just hope my legs will hold me until I get there. When I got there, Dick Rodgers said, 'We're doing a new show, *The Boys from Syracuse*, and we're doing a number in the next-to-closing spot, and we thought it would be amusing if we had our three leading ladies sing it together. When I read your letter, I put two and two together and thought you would be somebody who could do it.'"

Martin told Rodgers he'd sure like to try. "Dick Rodgers didn't know a thing about me. I was a total unknown. He decided to take a chance because I guess the letter sounded articulate, and he figured, he sounds like he must know a little bit and so why not give him a shot at it? I've never been so flustered in my life. He gave me a copy of 'Sing for Your Supper' and said to fool around with it and 'see if you have any interesting ideas for our leading ladies,' and he introduced me to Marcy Wescott, Muriel Angelus, and Wynn Murray. They were all wonderful. So I went home, all fear and trembling, and sat at my piano and prayed to God that I would come up with something that would make the number even better than it was, because it's a delightful number as it was."

Martin continued: "I came in the next day and said, 'I've done it,' and Dick Rodgers said, 'Why don't you teach it to the girls instead of singing it to me, since it's three voices and you've only one head.' So I was very grateful for that, because I'm not a flashy demonstrator, but I knew that if the girls sang it he might be impressed. I hit a snag right away because Wynn Murray said, 'I can't learn harmony. I just can't do it, and that's the end of it.' Well, it took two or three days to convince her she *could* do it, and one day she came and just gritted her teeth and did it and we all got so excited we cheered Wynn. We sang it for Mr. Rodgers, and he said, 'That's exactly what I had in mind.' I guess I put the idea in his head. He admitted he didn't have a gift for vocal arranging. It's a special gift. The tempo and the style is exactly as Dick wrote it. He never said, 'This is great' or anything similar, simply a terse, business-like, 'This will work'"—Dick Rodgers at his most wildly complimentary.

Martin recalled, "He hardly paid me peanuts, but it put me on the map. I was credited in the very back of the program, next to 'Shoes by Capezio.'" After that, vocal arrangement credits began to appear in theater programs. Martin then was called by Josh Logan to do something similar for a show with Ethel Merman and Jimmy Durante, *Stars in Your Eyes*, for a song called "It's All Yours." "I had marvelous ammunition there. It became another showstopper." Did Merman heed his coaching? "No. One of the chorus girls told me Ethel said, 'You know that young upstart who thinks he's teaching me how to sing? I pretend I'm going to do it his way, but when I get onstage I do it my way.'"

Rodgers was so pleased with "Sing for Your Supper" that he hired Martin for his next show, *Too Many Girls*, to vocally arrange "I Like to Recognize the Tune"—also a showstopper, said Martin.

Director Greg MacKellan says, "The reason 'Sing for Your Supper' knocked everyone out in 1938 is the Hugh Martin arrangement. Nothing in the show prepares you for the fact that the three ladies in the show are going to sing this tight Andrews Sisters–type number. The *way* it's arranged is also amusing. It's not just amusing that they're singing this harmony but that the harmony itself is used for comedic effect. It's very smartly done." Martin insisted the idea was not to parody the Andrews Sisters. "I had never heard of the Andrews Sisters at that time. Dick said, 'They're like the Boswell Sisters' [an earlier close-harmony trio]."

As to the similarity in arrangements between "Sing for Your Supper" and Sondheim's "You Could Drive a Person Crazy," Martin said, "It's not very modest of me to admit it, but Steve is a fan of mine. He's written me fan letters. He said one of the reasons he went into show business is that he fell in love with my arrangements." Martin learned vocal arranging from singer Kay Thompson, Judy Garland's mentor, but he learned so well that Thompson felt he'd ripped her off. "In a way I did," he chuckled.

Martin loved the challenge of turning a good song into an irresistible one, if not a showstopper. "I knew nothing about musicals. I was working some-where else, acting in a show, and didn't even get to come to New Haven to see the opening night. But I got a telegram from them saying, 'Your number not only stopped the show, but they made them repeat it twice.' I never heard of an encore getting two encores. From then on it always got one encore."

He added, "If I'm not being terribly conceited, I don't think 'Sing for Your Supper' would've caused such a sensation or stopped the show if they'd just sung it. The arrangement brought it to life and brought out the humor of the three girls, and that made it click." Martin didn't design "Sing for Your Supper" to stop the show. "I've never really thought in those terms, like 'Let's knock their socks off.' I've always thought about the show first. I just wanted the show to be as good as possible."

"Sing for Your Supper" is the most obvious showstopper from *The Boys from Syracuse*, but "Dear Old Syracuse" is almost as gladsome, a parody of a hometown ode that begins, "This is a terrible city / The people are cattle and swine / There isn't a girl I'd call pretty / Or a friend that I'd call mine." Walter Kerr noted the song's "lyric pleasures to be wrought from compactness, from comic aptness, from the deft and daffy mating of the deadpan and the impertinent mind. Most lyrics nowadays [1963] perform the functions of slave labor. They are always pushing something—the plot, or character, or whatever else the authors have not been able to get into the dialogue." He relished the pure delight of an unapologetically witty lyric. "Almost never do we hear a lyric with a leap in its heart, with a slyness . . . or even with an unlikely phrase." And of Rodgers's music, Kerr wrote, "I don't know if anyone has ever written more melodic surprises into what was meant to be a conventional musical comedy."

"Sing for Your Supper"—indeed the entire score—brightly illuminates the demarcation between Rodgers and Hart and, five years later, the emergence of Rodgers and Hammerstein, whose five major shows all but obliterated the more lighthearted earlier work of Rodgers and Hart, who wrote nearly thirty shows in twenty-five years together. The overwhelming success of Rodgers and Hammerstein shows became the new Broadway gold standard in the 1940s. Their shows and songs were so influential that they virtually eradicated the purely entertaining, satirical, or whimsical musicals that came before. Not just *On Your Toes*, *The Boys from Syracuse*, and *A Connecticut Yankee*, but equally fanciful shows by the Gershwins, Cole Porter, and Howard Dietz and Arthur Schwartz, musicals rarely revived now.

Shows like *The Band Wagon*, *Of Thee I Sing*, and *Anything Goes* were suddenly declared passé by critics and perhaps playgoers whose appetites for serious and "significant" musicals were whetted by *Carousel*, *South Pacific*, and *The King and I*. Satire and whimsy were out, sincerity was in. Great as Rodgers and Hammerstein shows were, their success and influence squelched thirty-five years of an earlier, more ingratiating Broadway musical tradition.

What had been known as "musical comedy" now became the stately "musical play," as Rodgers and Hammerstein shows were labeled, to lend gravitas; "musical comedy" is now a dated term. Baby boomers who grew up with Rodgers and Hammerstein shows know almost nothing of the joyful musicals that were snuffed out overnight by R&H's massive fame, reputation, and commercial success, which made less serious shows seem trivial, not worth writing or barely even reviving. As William Zinsser writes in *Easy to Remember*, discussing show tunes of yore compared to today's scores, "What fundamentally changed was the audience. The love affair with language was over."

Brad Leithauser, in an insightful 2002 piece on Hart in the *New York Review of Books*, observed: "It grows harder, year by year, to accept that the songs of Rodgers and Hart are older, and theoretically more dated, than those of Rodgers and Hammerstein. How is it possible that Hammerstein succeeded Hart and not vice versa? Rodgers and Hart songs are far pricklier, more skeptical, more bittersweet—more contemporary—than Rodgers and Hammerstein. . . . While Rodgers and Hart did produce their share of corny songs, it's impossible to envision them introducing a musical with an upsurging, 'The hills are alive with the sound of music.'"

Rodgers and Hammerstein, he notes, are credited with perfecting the integrated musical of plot and score and creating the "mature" musical, but "each passing year sharpens a lively paradox: America's theater songs were often far more adult than before the musical went and grew up." Lyrics slowly became subservient to plot and theme. The play was now the thing, not the wordplay. Walter Kerr said it best, as he often did: "What we love about the show," he wrote in 1971, praising the frisky joys of *No, No, Nanette*, "and what we have been missing for so long, is its *playfulness*. It's like a puppy without a purpose. It's free and off and skipping. That seems strange to us now, and strangely appealing."

George Abbott wrote of the two team's differences in his autobiography: "Hart saw everything fancifully. His tongue was in his cheek, his poetry was light and airy. He saw love dancing on the ceiling, Oscar saw it across a crowded room. . . . The hits Rodgers wrote with Hammerstein were much bigger than those with Hart, and the financial reward was also much bigger. The solid meat is more popular than the soufflé."

Hart, a diminutive, deeply closeted gay man and severe alcoholic, was known for his dark side despite a cheery exterior, but once he hit middle age Rodgers became somber and even dour (in photos then he often has a sour expression). Rodgers was himself a secret drinker, womanizer, and depressive man despite his stolid demeanor and workaholic habits. In an interview I had with him in the mid-1960s for the *New York Post*, Rodgers came across as stern, brusque, forbidding, almost condescending—more like a financier than a composer; Hart always called him "the principal." Stephen Sondheim, who was first mentored by Hammerstein and later unhappily collaborated with Rodgers on *Do I Hear a Waltz?*, said of the men (while Rodgers was still alive), "Oscar had limited talent and unlimited soul, and Dick has unlimited talent and limited soul." You could say of Rodgers and Hart together that they had unlimited talent and unlimited soul.

· · · · · · · · · · · · · · BACKSTAGE DISH · · · · · · · · · · · · · · · ·

✦ Richard Rodgers recalled in 1964 how the show's idea was hatched. He and Hart were on a train to Atlantic City to work on *I Married an Angel* prior to its Broadway opening. "I idly said over the clacking wheels, 'Let's adapt a Shakespearean play into a musical.' I knew Larry would like the idea immediately. Anything novel or offbeat was always sure to interest him. Larry's eyes lit up, and I could almost see sparks coming out of his head. Instead of discussing the important problems facing us on *I Married an Angel*, we started tossing ideas back and forth about doing Shakespeare in song and dance. No one had ever done it before, and we had a pretty unlimited field."

They quickly thought of adapting *The Comedy of Errors* because it had a part for Hart's brother Teddy as one of the twin slave boys separated at birth (owned by twin masters also separated at birth), opposite a short, dark comic who resembled Teddy. "I know nepotism should be frowned on, but I also knew this was an inspired idea," Rodgers said. He and Hart planned to write the book themselves but turned the idea over to proven writer-director George Abbott, who had staged their 1935 show *Jumbo*. Abbott leaped at the idea and adapted, wrote, and directed the show. Said Rodgers, "The book he came up with was exactly what we wanted—bright, fast-moving but in its own wacky way very much in the bawdy Shakespearean tradition."

✦ It's astonishing that the show's score, among their greatest, was written while Hart was on drunken binges half the time. "Larry was drinking heavily," Abbott wrote, "and would be absent for days at a time. That didn't bother me because he was quick as lightning when he was there. If we needed a new verse, he'd pick up a pencil and paper, fidget himself into the next room for a few minutes, and come back with what we needed. I remember that's how he wrote the lyrics for 'Falling in Love with Love.' He scratched it on the back of an old piece of paper while Dick and I talked about something else."

• •

LADY IN THE DARK

◆ 1941 ◆

"Tchaikowsky (and Other Russians)"

The song that launched Danny Kaye's career, **"Tchaikowsky (and Other Russians),"** was a showstopper from *Lady in the Dark*, the 1941 Moss Hart libretto with music by Kurt Weill and Ira Gershwin about a fashion magazine editor's nervous breakdown. The show starred Gertrude Lawrence in a midlife crisis before it had a fashionable name, triggered by her character's inability to make up her mind between magazine covers—or men.

The dilemma became "The Saga of Jenny," an introspective number with some of Ira Gershwin's brightest lyrics. Hart had had just such a midlife crisis himself (about his sexuality, it was said) and put it onstage in this smart musical, one of the first with an introspective theme and a rare adult story (like "Pal Joey" just a year before).

The important songs, near standards, are "The Saga of Jenny" and the lovely "My Ship," but the number that brought the house down nightly occurs in a nightmare circus in which Kaye, who played Lawrence's fey photographer, does a tour de force triple-tongued number, rattling off forty-nine Russian composers in record time (thirty-nine seconds). Kaye tried to break his own record each performance, and on tour in Madrid, Ira Gershwin said, Kaye finally set a personal best when he was clocked in at thirty-one seconds.

In fact, several of the Russians Gershwin mentions are Russian Americans (such as Vladimir Dukelsky, later composer Vernon Duke), and three are Polish. Ira had first written the lyrics in 1924 as a light verse called "The Music Hour" for *Life* magazine, then a humor weekly, under the byline "Arthur Francis," the pseudonym he chose when he began collaborating with his brother, to avoid charges of nepotism.

"Tchaikowsky" had nothing to do with the plot and amounted to an old-fashioned "specialty" number from musical comedy's early days. It was shoehorned into the show when Kaye is a judge in Eliza's (the lady in the dark) nightmare. She hears a chorus sing a number and asks, "Who wrote that music?" Told who the composer was, Kaye cries, "Tchaikovsky? I *love* Russian composers!"—the cue for the inspired ex-Catskill performer to leap into the number, sung to Weill's wild sword-dance music. (Hassard Short, a theater veteran in charge of the show's physical production, took Weill aside at one point and warned him, "If you'll take my advice, you boys had better get two numbers ready in a hurry. You'll find that 'Jenny' and the Russian number won't make it.")

Gershwin ends the frenetic list of Russians with a fine flourish—"I really have to stop, the subject has been dwelt / Upon enough!"—before squeezing in two last composers, Gretchaninoff and Rachmaninoff, as a chorus sings, "He'd *better* stop because we feel we all / Have under- / Gone enough!" Philip Furia, in his Ira Gershwin biography, says the performance got "thunderous applause" from the audience, unprepared for a revue number in an otherwise somber psychological musical drama; the applause, Ira noted, "rocked the theater for at least a minute."

Kaye didn't actually sing the song but performed it a capella; he was way too fast for any orchestra to keep up with. Tom Lehrer, the legendary 1960s musical satirist, was so taken by the song as a boy that he later wrote his own version about a mathematician, "Lobachevsky" (a.k.a. "Plagiarize"), in which Lehrer rhymes several Russian mathematicians, an homage to Kaye and Gershwin but a great song on its own, a tribute to Nikolai Ivanovich Lobachevsky's plagiaristic habits.

Kaye later said he worried the song might be cut because it came just before Gertrude Lawrence's big solo, "The Saga of Jenny." She was unfazed, and Kaye's career as a specialist in rapid-fire lyrics was born. Lawrence knew how to cope with scene stealers like Kaye. Steven Bach describes the moment in his Moss Hart biography *Dazzler*: "During Kaye's number, Lawrence was onstage, sitting on a swing and passively watching him kidnap her audience. As the audience exploded with its approval of Kaye's tour de force, the lyricist [Ira] felt a hand clutch his arm and heard Moss's strangled croak, 'Christ, we've lost our star.' Moss remembered, 'They kept applauding and applauding, and in the back of the theater I was saying '*SHHhhh*,' trying to quiet them," knowing that the more they applauded the more likely the song would be cut.

Hart continued, "[Danny] kept bowing to Gertie as if to indicate she would sing next, and the more he bowed generously the more they applauded. Gertie just *looked* at him. And finally . . . she saluted and walked to the footlights and then sang 'Jenny' as she had never rehearsed it, with bumps and grinds, [like] a striptease, and completely topped him. The number allowed Liza to break through her former inhibited self to become a wildly carefree woman. Gershwin called Lawrence's performance 'a complete devastation of the audience,' and noted that the ovation for 'Jenny' lasted twice as long as the one for 'Tchaikowsky.' *Lady in the Dark* had been stopped twice in a matter of minutes, just as the show neared its climax."

OKLAHOMA!

◆ 1943 ◆

"I Cain't Say No"

Oscar Hammerstein isn't exactly acclaimed for his comedy lyrics, mostly for his touching ballads ("People Will Say We're in Love," "I Have Dreamed") and sermonettes ("Climb Ev'ry Mountain," "You'll Never Walk Alone"), but in fact he was capable of writing funny, even witty songs if the scene called for it—"There Is Nothin' Like a Dame," "Don't Marry Me," "The Gentleman Is a Dope," "Shall I Tell You What I Think of You?"

In Hammerstein's hands, comedy songs were always character songs, not just showy lyric displays of the sort that Lorenz Hart, Ira Gershwin, and Cole Porter tossed off with seeming ease. *Oklahoma!* famously changed the American musical, from gags and gams to something more real and meaningful. The show was lauded for integrating songs, story, and characters and for integrating social themes into a formerly frothy form. Even so, director George Abbott reports, "I did have the prescience to state that the show contained some of the best music that Dick [Rodgers] had ever done, but I certainly did not realize I had been watching an epochal production." The legend came later.

The critical cries of delight, and all of its groundbreaking elements—a fused score and story plus daring to open a musical not with a kick line of chorus girls but a cowpoke greeting a beautiful morning—assured everyone in 1943 that the show had a beautiful future after the title finale, which

Hammerstein added when producer Theresa Helburn mentioned in a cab ride home after a preview that she felt the show needed a more rousing finish—maybe a song about the land itself? Good idea. Hammerstein reworked a song in the show called "Oklahoma," added that triumphal *!*, moved it to the end, and turned a decent little musical into a groundbreaking epic. You can catch the first-rate 1999 revival with Hugh Jackman shown in a 2003 made-for-TV movie on PBS's *Great Performances*. There's also an exacting fresh-faced version on YouTube produced in 2011 by the University of North Carolina School of the Arts that replicates the 1943 original with what looks, sounds, and feels like great authenticity—proving it truly is an ageless show.

The musical's major showstopper was a comedy number that Porter or Hart might have written—**"I Cain't Say No,"** which reassured playgoers that, sincere and folksy and earthy as *Oklahoma!* was, it had not completely abandoned humor. "I Cain't Say No" is Hammerstein in a rare frisky mood, a lighthearted, lightly risqué lyric (for its time), one of three or four sly comedy songs in a score more lauded for its lush romantic moments. Apart from "I Cain't Say No," we get "Kansas City," "Pore Jud Is Daid," and "All er Nuthin'"—all comedy songs. But "I Cain't Say No," Ado Annie's heartfelt confessional, invariably stops the show, no matter how often you've heard it.

The number is sung by a robust farm girl who doesn't pretend to the innocent purity of her best pal Laurey, the virginal lead (Joan Roberts in the original cast, Shirley Jones in the 1955 movie). Annie has lustful appetites and is ready to admit to them, even if they embarrass her, which is what makes the song funny. She likes men and she likes sex—well, kissing anyway. There is no sex in *Oklahoma!* (except for Agnes de Mille's saucy French postcard dancing girls), but "I Cain't Say No" is as close to a suggestive moment as the show allows; and for 1906 territorial Oklahoma, it's about right.

Annie's song is especially potent because its sentiments run so contrary to the semicloying sweetness of the show. "I Cain't Say No" is a moment of honesty that plays against the goodness of all the other characters, both women and men—except, of course, for depraved unshaven Jud Fry, who lusts for Laurey in his lonely room, when, in fact, Annie is really the girl for him. She's ready and willing, even if she does have a quasi-relationship with Ali Hakim, a peddler on the make. He was a swarthy Syrian in the play that *Oklahoma!* is based on, *Green Grow the Lilacs*, portrayed in the musical by former Yiddish theater actor Joseph Buloff. (*Oklahoma!* was regarded as almost an "ethnic" show by some; one Arab on Broadway in 1943 could do that.) Ali undergoes a total conversion in the movie, in which the fast-talking Middle Eastern

**A more pristine Celeste Holm as Ado Annie before
she tells all in "I Cain't Say No" in *Oklahoma!***

peddler is played by fair-haired all-American boy Eddie Albert (who in fact
was Jewish, born Edward Heimberger).

"I Cain't Say No" is an aggrieved apology by a blunt, funny, oversexed
young farm girl who finds herself confronting her own out-of-control libid-
inous impulses. In 1906 America, such behavior—let alone public confession—was grounds for floozydom. Ado Annie, who paints herself as a Hester
Prynne of the prairie, admits she likes guys—in fact, *craves* them, and not just

in a romantic way. She's a late teenager with raging hormones before anyone even knew what a hormone was—in Oklahoma, anyway; and even those who knew would not have condoned a young girl discussing the subject in mixed company. But Ado Annie is eager for some action. Even her odd name sounds like rural slang for *slut* (for Ado read "I do," and "Annie" is an old nickname for a baseball groupie).

In any case, Annie is a bundle of teenage libido who feels a need to fess up. Her boyfriend Will Parker is just back from a Kansas City burlesque show with his own sex drive revved up, but then he's a guy so it's not naughty like "I Cain't Say No," which is sung right after Will tells us all about big-city sin. Forced to reveal her secret female longings, Annie begins with a reluctant admission, spoken in a contemplative drawl, slowly and hesitantly: "It ain't so much a question of not knowin' whut to do—I knowed whut's right and wrong since I been ten."

This is a touchy subject to talk about openly, but she tries, like Carrie divulging all on *Sex and the City*; but this is all about sex and the country. Annie tiptoes around the scandalous topic in Hammerstein's tantalizing verse that leads to the refrain that Celeste Holm first delivered with such comic aplomb at the Majestic Theatre in early 1943. What makes the song click, and clever, is that Annie is as much bothered as she is hot, and she's trying to explain her way out of it to herself. It's really less a confessional than a soliloquy as she puzzles out the answer while we listen in. For Annie, to kiss or not to kiss—that is her question. Of course "kiss" is a polite euphemism for something else, as it often was in songs of that era. Annie is a proper girl who tries to maintain her frontier decorum despite a churning sex drive.

Hammerstein's lyrics flirt suggestively with what's really on Annie's mind, as she asks, "Whut you goin' do when a feller gits flirty / And starts to talk purty," or muses, "S'posin' 'at he says yer lips are like cherries / Er roses, er cherries," and wonders further, "S'posin' 'at he says 'at you're sweeter'n cream? He's gotta have cream er die?" Dr. Freud might have something to say about allusions to "cherries" and "cream," but Annie squelches all such nasty thoughts by asking, "Whatcher gonna do? Spit in his eye?"

Annie takes us by surprise because of her proper gingham dress and parasol, looking more like Anne of Green Gables than a farm gal eager for a roll in the hay. Her funny, fevered admission sets the stage for the sexy dream to come in the de Mille ballet "Laurie Makes Up Her Mind," a sort of cowgirl can-can, a reply to Jud's porno pinups. The ballet was born when de Mille said to Hammerstein, "There's no sex in the first act. Let's do a ballet about what they've been talking about"—thinking about, anyway. "Laurey's been down in the smokehouse and she's seen the postcards. Don't think she isn't interested in them. They have a lurid appeal to her." When Hammerstein was shocked, the blunt de Mille asked, "Did you ever meet young girls? You have daughters, haven't you?" He had a couple. "Well, you don't know them. They're fascinated, believe me." Despite her sexy ballet, the columnist Walter Winchell, or some say Mike Todd, famously cabled his secretary at the show's out of town intermission, "No jokes, no legs, no chance"; the actual fabled telegram is said to have read, "No jokes, no tits, no chance."

What underscores the musical joke is that Annie can't help herself and yet is honest enough to proclaim her passion—sweetly, innocently. In "I Cain't Say No" and "Kansas City," Hammerstein depicts a red-blooded real-life couple that plays off the dreamy romantic yearnings of Curly and Laurey, whose sexuality never intrudes on their innocent ballads like "People Will Say We're in Love." At the time, only Cole Porter and Lorenz Hart dared intertwine in songs the two primal urges, love and sex. Hammerstein, though not known for his witty lyrics, was acutely aware whose shoes he was trying to slip into after Hart died, and he worked hard to keep people from saying, "Well, he's no Larry Hart." But Ado Annie's song, plus the score's two other comic numbers, "All er Nuthin'" and "Pore Jud Is Daid," measure up to them, all expressed in authentic western vernacular.

Director Josh Logan recalled Rodgers's worries about taking on Hammerstein. When Rodgers asked Logan how he felt about him and Hammerstein as a team, Logan told him, "Dick, you and Oscar would be unbeatable," but Rodgers worried, and asked, "Can he do comedy songs? Larry was always able to get big laughs. I don't know, I don't know." In musicals of the mid-'40s, sex was only discussed in comical terms. The idea that Laurey and Curly might desire each other is primly avoided. Curly, unlike Jud, is not permitted a lurid thought about Laurey. It isn't until Ado Annie's comic soliloquy that Hammerstein drags sex out into the open, as she sings of her thwarted feelings in a comic drawl, which stops the show.

"I Cain't Say No" is almost a critique of the show's wholesomeness, as when Annie sings, "I cain't be prissy and quaint / I ain't the type that c'n faint," which pretty much sums up Laurey and the show's other quaint characters—not counting ranch hand Will Parker's report on that burlesque show he saw in Kansas City, where one of the girls was "as round above as she was round below" and "she went about as fur as she could go!" Will is titillated but mildly shocked, but Annie is totally upfront about her urges. "But as soon as someone kisses me / I somehow sorta wanna kiss him back!," she reveals, and then she gets even racier: "Fer a while I ack refined and cool, / A settin' on the velveteen settee, / Nen I think of thet ol' Golden Rule, / And do for him what he would do fer me!" Hmm.

Susan Stroman choreographed a landmark British revival of *Oklahoma!* in 1998, with Trevor Nunn directing, which later moved to Broadway. Restaging an iconic musical like *Oklahoma!* calls for a combination of respect for the original production but a contemporary imprint, a delicate line Stroman has managed to walk in revivals of *Show Boat*, *The Music Man*, and *Crazy for You* (a rewrite of the Gershwins' 1930 *Girl Crazy*). Stroman unfixed audiences' hallowed memories by putting her own contemporary choreographic stamp on *Oklahoma!* without damaging the original in our heads.

"You have to treat it like a new show almost," she explained to me. "When Trevor Nunn and I did *Oklahoma!*, Trevor went back to the original play *Green Grow the Lilacs*, and I got permission from the estate to develop the music to support my choreography. I then sat with my pianist/arranger David Crane and we changed the dream ballet to my version of the dance. My choreography was more based on the idea of fighting for territory—in turn-of-the-century America you fought for territory—so the choreography was more fight oriented or had the theme of can you top this? The women were very much pioneer women, with dirt on their skirts. It's a lot less dreamy than the original, and also Laurey and Curly in our version were the original Laurey and Curly who dance the dream ballet [i.e., without balletic stand-ins, as in the original and film versions]. This *Oklahoma!* had a grittier feel. It's not geraniums in flower boxes and polka-dot dresses."

Zeroing in on "I Cain't Say No," Stroman says, "You have to listen to those lyrics. It's mostly just performance—the actors acting out those lyrics as if they were not singing at all but actually doing the scene with each other." The number that gave her the most trouble was "Kansas City." She recalls, "I really wanted Will Parker (Justin Bohon) to learn how to lasso. He was determined to learn, and he really did it. Then I was able to incorporate that lassoing with the other dancers, and it had a real-deal Oklahoma feel to it. It made the choreography richer because it had true elements of what an actual cowboy would do."

———

Ado Annie was first turned into flesh and blood by Celeste Holm, who embodied the character for all time in her finely tuned delivery. Nobody's ever performed it better (Gloria Grahame in the movie version wasn't as fresh, maybe because she had played too many troubled tramps on screen). Holm, who prior to *Oklahoma!* had not sung since high school, squeezed all the comic juices out of the song. The number made Holm a star and sent her to Hollywood, where she became known for playing smart, sharp-tongued characters with an edge, like the women Eve Arden portrayed on screen. Holm was the wisecracking romantic comic lead in films like *All About Eve* and *High Society*, getting off the sort of wisecracking lines she sings in "I Cain't Say No."

In films, Holm was always sophisticated, unlike Ado Annie, who may not know much but knows herself and can tell us exactly how confused she feels: "I heared a lot of stories and I reckon they are true / About how girls're put upon by men. / I know I mustn't fall into the pit / But when I'm with a feller, I fergit!" Has any sex manual ever laid out a teenage girl's dilemma more succinctly? One of the song's strengths is how it sounds like dialogue, like Annie talking to us more than singing lyrics, literally speaking her mind. Broadway chronicler Ethan Mordden notes that that was a new technique in 1943. "Songs tended to block the action, stop it dead. *Oklahoma!*'s songs convey it" in conversational numbers like "I Cain't Say No."

Holm told me her approach to the song was simple: "I was just trying to think how I should sing it. I realized the only way to make it funny was to make it a problem. For Annie it *was* a real problem. So I did it for real. I didn't try to be cute. Others try to do it cute. You may be cute in an ancillary way, but you'll ruin it." In 1998 Holm told an interviewer, "Invariably they get my part wrong. Ado Annie was very simple. She was cute, not corn-pone like everyone seems to play her." Holm just sang the number the way she felt it should be done, and that was that—no direction at all, she said, from director Rouben Mamoulian or the songwriters. After she first sang it, they told her, "That's it," satisfied with her instinctive version. "I'm an actress," she explained with a vocal shrug, as if to say, "No big deal."

Holm nailed the role when she did a hog call at her audition for Rodgers and Hammerstein that won them over. "They wanted to hear how big I could sing," she recalled. As she told it on NPR's *Fresh Air* in 1993, Rodgers asked her, "Could you sing a song as if you'd never had a lesson in your life?" She said, "Well, what does that sound like?" He said, "It's a bald, bold, unedited voice." Holm told me, "They wanted more of a noise, so I said I can call a hog. Our neighbors had hogs. We had a farm, but we didn't have animals." Rodgers wrote in his autobiography, "Knowing that she had a trained voice, I was surprised that she would want such a hoydenish role." When she finished, she related that Rodgers said, "'Well, that's loud enough, that's funny enough,' and that is how I got my job." She must have sung a real song at some point, but Holm always liked to retail the hog-calling story.

The show's creative team wasn't so sure at first that Holm was the girl for the part. Before she stopped the show in New Haven, a switchboard operator let her know that Rodgers and Hammerstein and Mamoulian were considering calling in Shirley Booth or Judy Canova, the hillbilly comedienne. When the show opened, Holm was fourth billed, earning $250 a week.

Holm says she never thought "I Cain't Say No" would stop the show. "*No-o-o-o.* You never think like that. You just learn it." Did it stop the show immediately? "Yes—and it startled the hell out of me. When you've been rehearsing you don't really think of that. I stood there numb." Hammerstein wrote an encore verse for her after the first performance stopped the show. "It's amazing how quickly you can learn an encore. I finally just stumbled off stage." Holm told Max Wilk in his book on *Oklahoma!*, "I'd never been in a musical before, so I didn't know what to do when the audience didn't stop applauding after I finished 'I Cain't Say No.' I kept trying to continue with the dialogue, but they wouldn't let me. It was embarrassing but it was glorious."

Hammerstein's encore verse is even wittier: "I'm jist a girl who cain't say 'No!' / Kissin's my favorite food! / With or without the mistletoe / I'm in a holiday mood! / Other girls are coy and hard to catch / But other girls ain't havin' any fun! / Ev'ry time I lose a wrestlin' match / I have a funny feelin' that I won!" Hammerstein's phrases—"kissin's my favorite food" and "I have a funny feelin' that I won!"—are not just clever but true to Ado Annie's wry character. Hammerstein was better than many male lyricists at understanding female sensibilities, in songs like "What's the Use of Wond'rin'?," "The Gentleman Is a Dope," and "(When I Marry) Mister Snow."

Holm was in her nineties when we spoke. Asked why the song works so well, she answered briskly, "It's a good song." Did she consider it at all risqué? "Sure it was risqué, but not that risqué." When I mentioned that other actresses do the role pretty much as she first did, she snapped, "I hope so!"

Director Greg MacKellan saw Holm perform the song when she was in her eighties. "Even when I saw her do it then she still knew exactly how to build the number," he recalls. "When she performed it she dropped fifty years. There was just this *command*. She knew how to put that number across, like nobody has put it across since—*certainly* not like Gloria Grahame in the movie. Plus it's such a clever lyric—you're halfway there any time you've got a clever lyric. It's a character we like from the moment she walks on." MacKellan says Hammerstein wrote Holm the encore verse backstage—not, as Holm maintained, after the first performance. "She went back out holding this sheet of paper, singing the encore lyrics Hammerstein had just written." Or maybe he had a verse in his coat pocket, just in case.

MacKellan recalls her performance in detail; "She was so—well, calculating is the wrong word. But she knew *just* when to lift her eyebrow, *just* when to let eyes pop a little bit, *just* when to do a little smirk. It was amazing. This is what being a theater star was for so many years and unfortunately no longer is. She had the audience in the palm of her hand. And this is a song so many people have heard a million times. I've seen the show a million times, and I've never had that number be as delightful as it was seeing her do it. She made it seem fresh to me. How she eased into it. It wasn't like 'I'm here to do this big show-stopping number,' but 'I've got a real problem here.' She communicated that."

Holm said she kept the song fresh by remembering that "the audience has never heard it before, so I put myself in their shoes." She claimed never to have seen anybody else do the role, including Gloria Grahame in the movie Holm said she was too upset to see, but got a consolation prize: "Before Gloria Grahame died, she wrote me a letter apologizing for having ruined the part in the film version. How do you like that?"

By 1955, when the movie came out, audiences would have had a hard time buying Holm as a virginal country gal after *All About Eve*, *Gentleman's Agreement*, and other urbane films. But she gave a much more interesting reason for not being cast in the movie: "I wouldn't sleep with Dick Rodgers," she revealed. He was insistent, but Holm refused, commenting over the phone, "Never when I gotta, only when I wanna." Ado Annie couldn't have put it any better.

ANNIE GET YOUR GUN

◆ 1946 ◆

"You Can't Get a Man with a Gun," "Doin' What Comes Natur'lly," "There's No Business Like Show Business," "An Old-Fashioned Wedding"

Except for *South Pacific* and *Babes in Arms*, no musical ever produced as many certified standards as *Annie Get Your Gun*. Irving Berlin was invited to write the show after Jerome Kern died, but Berlin felt it wasn't his cup of moonshine. He asked to try a few songs to see if he was up to the task—promptly turning out three or four later hits in a week. Berlin wound up writing eight lasting songs, including four surefire showstoppers.

Historian Ethan Mordden says that *Annie Get Your Gun*, along with *Kiss Me, Kate*, "was by far the most successful forties musical in global appeal"—clearly the all-time winner if measured by Hit Parade standards. It's easily the most revived of all Berlin shows. The songwriter until then hadn't given a whole lot of attention to scripts of his stage musicals (he felt more at home writing revue set pieces). Berlin's view was that if you wrote hit songs the shows would take care of themselves.

In this case, he wrote a hit show and the songs took care of themselves, even if the updated 1999 makeover by Peter Stone with Bernadette Peters isn't a great improvement over the original bland script that mainly serves to get us from showstopper to showstopper. Brad Leithauser wrote in a *New York Review of Books* piece on *Annie* redux, "The exposition is clumsy, most of the jokes are dopey, and the audience waits impatiently for the next song."

The idea for a musical about the 1880s sharpshooter Annie Oakley belongs to lyricist/librettist Dorothy Fields, who said she heard a story at the stage door canteen about a young sergeant with a row of sharpshooter medals at a shooting gallery on Coney Island who won all the prizes, which made her wonder how Annie Oakley might have done at a shooting gallery. Fields said it was the only brainstorm she ever had, though many of her lyrics would belie that. Fields's brother Joseph had devised a 1935 movie about Oakley that starred Barbara Stanwyck.

Dorothy Fields was set to write the score with her longtime partner Kern until he had a fatal stroke on Park Avenue while antique shopping in New York. Stunned and unable to imagine writing the score with anyone else, Fields decided against writing lyrics for the show, the only musical Rodgers and Hammerstein ever produced that they didn't write. Before *Annie Get Your Gun*, Irving Berlin knew he could write hit songs for revues and movies and sheet-music buyers, but he was unsure about writing what he called "situation songs"—that is, for dramatic scenes and characters.

"No single mind mastered as much of the popular American musical idiom, for so long, with such an unaffected wit and elegance, as Irving Berlin," Vincent Canby incisively wrote of him in 1999 in the *New York Times*. "Possibly because he felt himself to be an outsider, he saw and heard the world around him with a clarity denied the rest of us. The American experience was sunlight to his talent."

Berlin, who always had a keen eye fastened on the mass market, claimed he had rescued American popular song from its florid, overwrought European influences and turned it into something the average American could identify with. He did it in eighteen minutes, supposedly how long it took him to write "Alexander's Ragtime Band," the bestselling pop song in the country at that time; Berlin was twenty-three. At a Friar's Club roast in 1913, George M. Cohan, his idol, called Berlin's songs "music you don't have to dress up to listen to." In "Alexander's Ragtime Band," he wrote in a syncopated "ragged meter," explaining, "All the old rhythm is gone, and in its place is heard the hum of an engine, the whirr of wheels, the explosion of an exhaust."

Berlin was interpreting the sounds of 1920s New York City, setting them to music. "The new age demands new music," Jerome Kern told Alexander Woollcott in an early (1925) biography of the pop prodigy. "He honestly absorbs the vibrations emanating from people, manners, and the life of his time, and in turn gives these impressions back to the world—simplified, clarified, glorified."

Berlin heard songs in his head and, unable to play the piano, composed only in the key of F-sharp, using a lever under the keyboard to transpose his tunes into other keys. Berlin even hired assistants to suggest chords he might write in. He was a kind of musical idiot savant, and proud of it: "The fact that I only compose in F-sharp gave me certain harmonies that other writers missed, because they knew more about music." In 1915, he remarked, "In my ignorance of the laws of music, I have often broken all the laws." Berlin's credo: "'Easy to sing, easy to say, easy to remember, and applicable to everyday events' is a good rule for a phrase." Discussing *Annie Get Your Gun*, Stephen Sondheim observed, "Irving Berlin didn't write for smash finishes. He wrote gentle. He's very simple and straightforward. It was Merman who got the encores and the splash finishes."

Berlin was never shy about upholstering his growing legend, saying proudly, almost arrogantly, "The reason American composers have done nothing highly significant is because they won't write American music. They're as ashamed of it as if it were a country relative. So they write imitation European music which doesn't mean anything. Ignorant as I am, from their standpoints, I am doing something they all refuse to do: I'm writing American music."

The critic John Lahr says Berlin was the first composer to straddle Tin Pan Alley and Broadway. He wound up with 451 hit songs, eighty-two in the top ten and thirty-five that made it to number one. Or as Berlin wrote, feelingly, in the introduction to Al Jolson's theme song "Let Me Sing and I'm Happy,"

"What care I who makes the laws of a nation . . . as long as I can sing its pop-ular songs." He legislated through lyrics and music. As Walter Cronkite said at a televised one hundredth birthday celebration of Berlin, "He helped write the story of this country."

As much at home as Berlin was on ethnic turf, the Ozarks were foreign territory to the Russian-Jewish immigrant who didn't know from rifles, wild-west shows, and Indians. The box office bean counter in him also wondered if the show was a wise business decision. He said to Dorothy Fields, "I don't know if I'd want to do a show that isn't 'Irving Berlin's whatever.'" Berlin balked at writing the score, telling Oscar Hammerstein, "That hillbilly stuff, Oscar—it's not for me. I don't know the first thing about country music." Hammerstein calmly advised, "Just drop the 'g' off of words ending in 'ing'"—exactly as Hammerstein had done throughout the score of *Oklahoma!*

Berlin gave *Annie Get Your Gun* a shot, so to speak, and one weekend in a hotel room in Atlantic City (site of so many Broadway masterpieces) he pro-duced three songs, then two more the next week, every one of which eventu-ally became a standard: "There's No Business Like Show Business," "They Say It's Wonderful," "Doin' What Comes Natur'lly," "The Girl That I Marry," and "You Can't Get a Man with a Gun."

As essayist William Zinsser notes, "Most people wouldn't mind hav-ing written those songs in a lifetime, or even just *one* of them: 'There's No Business Like Show Business,'" the entertainment industry's anthem. Not to mention "I Got Lost in His Arms," "The Girl That I Marry," "They Say It's Wonderful," "I Got the Sun in the Morning," and "My Defenses Are Down." A couple of songs feel less organic to the show than his other buckskin-clad numbers. One song, "The Girl That I Marry," has been effectively retired for its gooey, chauvinist sentiments: "The girl that I marry will have to be / As soft and as pink as a nursery"—not exactly a description of Annie Oakley, let alone the brassy woman who first played her onstage, Ethel Merman.

Fields and her brother Herbert wrote the book for the 1946 show, but several of the lyrics had Dorothy's trademark female smarty-pants slant, ideal for the independent Annie Oakley character that the Fieldses created—out of whole cloth, mostly. The real Oakley, despite her calling, was not a rootin'-tootin' gal and in fact whiled away the time between shooting exhi-bitions sewing in her tent. Annie's real story was far more interesting than the Broadwayized version: She was born Phoebe Ann Mosey (Oakley was her grandmother's name) and grew up in Ohio, not the Ozarks. Her father froze to death when she was a girl. She had a fifty-year marriage to Frank Butler, her sharpshooter rival, but her major rifle rival was another woman, Lillian

Smith. Oakley was involved in charity work and womens' causes, such as advocating guns for women. Off-season the couple lived in wild and woolly Nutley, New Jersey. Oakley sued sixty newspapers for a false report in the Hearst newspapers that she stole money to support a cocaine habit; she won all but one case yet lost a fortune defending herself in court. After retiring—western movies made her passé—she even starred in a play.

So although *Annie Get Your Gun* might not be a compelling saga of Annie Oakley, indeed a pretty hokey version of her life, it remains a reliable, irresistible, relentlessly catchy Broadway show that, before the curtain fell, hit a dozen musical bull's eyes.

Making Annie seem even more fictitious, she was played by a star whose brash New York persona could not have been more unlike the authentic, modest Oakley; plus Merman was nearly forty when the show debuted and she played a love-struck country girl. A closer match might have been Judy Canova or even Mary Martin, who toured in the show. Betty Hutton in the screen version seemed truer to the theatrical character, if overly raucous and clownish; Hutton replaced Judy Garland, who was fired during one of her zonked-out periods. The much altered 1999 Broadway revival with Bernadette Peters shuffled songs and cut three, including, for politically correct reasons, "I'm an Indian Too"—a dumb song anyway. Reba McEntire, who replaced Peters, was to many critics the most authentic of Annies, with an innate down-home appeal that doesn't come naturally to homegrown Broadway belters.

Peters got the Tony, but McEntire got the raves and the tourists, rejuvenating the show's 2001 Broadway run. Create your own Annie Oakley on YouTube—Betty Hutton in the movie (funny and lively), Bernadette Peters in the 2001 revival (a cuddly fish out of water), or Reba McEntire (a refreshing unforced performance, if a tad twangy). There's a rare YouTube clip of Judy Garland doin' "Doin' What Comes Natur'lly" before she left the film. Her heart doesn't seem to be in it; she looks woefully miscast and uneasy as a mountain girl.

Merman never had any of the usual attributes of a Broadway baby. She wasn't quite pretty, nor sexy, cute, kittenish, or vulnerable, all the things that Broadway leading ladies of her era were supposed to be. She couldn't dance or even act all that well and had minimal comic chops. And yet when you hear her you're instantly, totally seduced. Her sheer vocal strength and authority are turn-ons of a different caliber. She rarely enacts a song, yet she's convincing, even singing a tender ballad like "I Got Lost in His Arms" or "Small World" from *Gypsy*.

Merman embodied all that a Broadway star should be. Her overpowering style, already larger than life, made her too "big" for the screen, so she never abandoned Broadway for Hollywood, like Julie Andrews, Barbra Streisand, and Bette Midler, likely Merman heirs. Streisand might have inherited Merman's crown had she not fled Broadway at the first opportunity for tinseled fame.

Merman always remained her own character, the ultimate saleswoman of song, without much nuance or subtlety. Gerald Boardman, the musicals historian, wrote, "There was always to be a touch of lowlife hardness in her roles." She played almost every role the same. Annie Oakley was just Mama Rose with a rifle, her Dolly Levi was Rose in a big hat. Merman once said, "Not to pat myself on the back, but when I do a show the whole show revolves around me. And if I don't show up, they can just forget it." You can count on one hand the number of performances she didn't show up for.

"I leave the songs the way they came out of the composer's head," she always said, which made her seem at times a robotic one-note performer, a player piano. She sang the bejesus out of a song but forget interpretation. It was all up front. What you heard was what you got. She made you believe every song was sensational. She had no persona beyond her stage self, an instinctive belter who had no idea how she did it. For Merman, singing was like breathing. "I just stand up and holler and hope the voice holds out." Merman still personifies Broadway. A year before she died, she said, "Broadway has been very good to me—but then I've been very good to Broadway."

Despite all these reasons, Merman was hardly an obvious choice to play Annie Oakley, but she and Dorothy Fields were pals, and when Fields visited Merman in the hospital, she asked her, "Merm, what would you think of yourself as Annie Oakley?" "I'll do it," said Merm. With her bravura presence and iron-lunged bellow, Long-Giland accent, and fullback figure Merman in a buckskin skirt made it look as if her head was poking through a carnival cutout of Annie Oakley. A backwoods Ethel Merman is a funny notion, but she got away with it. Merman could sell anything, even herself as a hillbilly from Queens. But if those two deeply entrenched New Yorkers, Berlin and Merman, were unlikely, even bizarre choices for a musical about a rifle-toting mountain gal, they attacked the score like Appalachian natives.

Berlin quickly slipped into the barefoot skin of rustic kinfolk, but he was used to writing in any dialect. As a hustling young songwriter, he had cranked out countless ditties of every ethnicity, starting with his first hit in 1907, "Marie from Sunny Italy." He wrote "Harlem on My Mind" and shameless "coon" songs plus numbers in every dialect, from Yiddish ("Sadie Salome

Go Home") to British ("My British Buddy"). He cut his Tin Pan Alley teeth writing vernacular songs, so Ozark lingo was just another dialect to Berlin, a fast study ("Folks are dumb where I come from / They ain't had any learnin'").

The one-dimensional nature of the Fieldses' Annie Oakley ideally suited Berlin's simple, direct style of songwriting—no tricky rhymes or subtle wordplay but plenty of little jokes plainly spelled out ("The gals with umbrellers are always out with fellers / In the rain or the blazin' sun, / But a man never trifles with gals who carry rifles"). Equally, the no-nonsense Oakley character somehow fit Merman's blunt, no-frills, straight-shooting style, but she was playing Ethel as much as Annie, and Berlin was writing for Merman, not Oakley.

Amazingly, the show was not greeted with a critical standing ovation, although Merman got her usual raves; the score was blithely

Ethel Merman jes' "Doin' What Comes Natur'lly" in *Annie Get Your Gun.*

dismissed by many. It's astonishing to realize many critics didn't even notice the brilliant songs right in front of them—maybe because it was an era when great show tunes were taken for granted. You would think the critics would be doing cartwheels—a few did, but many yawned. Lewis Nichols in the *New York Times* conceded, "It has a pleasant score," but he was sorry to report that there was not a "White Christmas" or "Easter Parade" in the entire show. *Time* labeled it "a great big, follow-the-formula, fetch-the-crowd musical. It bothers with nothing artistic or bizarre. . . . Irving Berlin has written more tuneful music in his time." Ward Morehouse of the *Sun* chimed in, "Irving Berlin's score is not a notable one, but his tunes are singable and pleasant." Louis Kronenberger, of *P.M.*, wrote: "Irving Berlin's score is musically not exciting—of the real songs [whatever that means] only one or two are tuneful." Kronenberger was only off by half a dozen standards. Almost alone among the New York press, Vernon Rice of the *Post* had the truest ear, saying it was "no use trying to pick out a hit tune because all the tunes are hits."

Berlin's score never condescends to the backwoods Oakley and, indeed, gives her terrific wisecracks in **"You Can't Get a Man with a Gun"**: "If I went to battle with someone's herd of cattle / You'd have steak when the job was done / But if I shot the herder, they'd holler bloody murder / And you can't get a hug from a mug with a slug / Oh, you can't get a man with a gun." The song is a sly favorite with the New York Gay Men's Chorus. Many of the numbers, for all their verve and charm, don't stick to the ribs like some of Berlin's great movie songs, with one exception, the universally appealing "I Got Lost in His Arms," Berlin at his warmest and most romantic ("I got lost / But look what I found").

In **"Doin' What Comes Natur'lly,"** Berlin shifts into full Dogpatch mode, a list song that describes Annie's ignorant but instinctive folkways: "You don't have to know how to read or write / When you're out with a feller in the pale moonlight. / You don't have to look in a book to find / What he thinks of the moon and what is on his mind. / That comes natur'lly."

Even if it's hard to buy Merman as Annie Oakley, "Doin' What Comes Natur'lly" nicely sums up Merman's approach to singing. Famously, she never had a singing lesson, just opening her mouth and doing what came naturally. Merman's "Doin' What Comes Natur'lly" includes one of her signature tricks—her so-called hiccup, sliding from one note to another or breaking a word like "gu-un" in half, which one writer compared to a cowboy yodel, and totally in character.

It's a great score even if stuck in a mediocre show with a script full of standard rural types and an unconvincing story about Annie and her early rival and later husband Frank Butler (Ray Middleton originally, Howard Keel on screen). The drab script is saved by its bright, bouncy songs, with only one second-rater, "I'm an Indian Too," a lame gag with Annie whooping it up like a heap-goofy redskin in *The Paleface* ("Just like Battle-Axe / Hatchet-Face, Eagle-Nose, / Like those Indians / I'm an Indian, too").

Not surprisingly, much backstage lore has attached itself to **"There's No Business Like Show Business,"** which originally was sung by Buffalo Bill and his cronies midway through act 1 to convince Annie to join their wild-west show. Musicals archivist Philip Furia observes that *Annie Get Your Gun* is less about Annie Oakley than it is about show business. John Heilpern wrote in the *New York Observer*, "To hear Merman sing 'There's no business like show business' is to *believe* her." She was showbiz's spokeswoman.

The song became such a runaway hit that, in the 1999 rewritten version, it was moved to the front of the show and insistently reprised twice more in the first act, unnecessarily hammering it home. Putting the song at the top of the show robs it of its later dramatic power. The revised *Annie* (one writer called it *Annie, Get Your Makeover*) is now played as a show within a show, as if we're watching the legend of Annie Oakley and Frank Butler, not seeing it play out in real time—to what purpose is hard to say.

Berlin tossed the song away after singing a new second chorus for Rodgers, Hammerstein, Dorothy and Herbert Fields, and Josh Logan. Berlin figured they hated the song. "I didn't like the way you all reacted this morning—it didn't register," said the easily discouraged Berlin. Logan relates in his memoirs, "It wasn't petulance"—Berlin seemed genuinely persuaded that his showbiz anthem was a loser.

Berlin was acutely sensitive to listeners' reactions. Logan recalled, "He sang it [the new chorus] right into our faces, draining us for reactions, as he had done before, and we said, 'Fine, fine.' Since we had gone quite crazy about the first chorus of 'Show Business,' it was hard to show greater enthusiasm for the second chorus." Berlin was depressed. "What's the matter?" he said. "Don't you like the song? Have you gone cold on it?" Logan tried to reassure him, but "Berlin was not mollified, as worried as a new bride suspecting her husband's lessening affections the day after the honeymoon." "Yes, yes," he told Logan, "but the way you looked, so skittish like."

In his Berlin biography, Laurence Bergreen writes, "Only by fixing his eyes on the listener could [he] sense if the song worked. If one blinked too often or one's eyes glazed for a second, Irving was apt to put the song away." For such a veteran of the showbiz wars, Berlin was chronically insecure, treating each song like his first. "Every time I start on a show," he said, "I wonder if this is the time I'll reach for it and it won't be there."

It was very much there. No song came more richly or intensely out of Berlin's gut, in phrases that capture his life in theater and showbiz mythology: "The opening when your heart beats like / A drum, / The closing when the customers / Won't come." Or, "You get word before the show has / Started / That your fav'rite uncle died at dawn. / Top of that your pa and ma have parted, / You're broken-hearted, but you go on." That's Showbiz 101.

One day, recounted Logan, he played the score for songwriter/arranger Hugh Martin ("The Trolley Song," "Have Yourself a Merry Little Christmas") but left out "There's No Business Like Show Business." Logan said, "Irving, you didn't sing 'Show Business.'" Berlin said, "No, no, that's out. I can take a hint. I've thrown it away." Logan cried, *What!* That's one of the greatest songs ever written!" Berlin said, again, sulkingly, "I didn't like the way you three reacted before." Logan again tried to explain, "We had heard the song before. We yelled our heads off the first time. We can't scream louder every time we hear it. You've got to play it for Hugh. He's got to hear it." Berlin said, "I don't think I could find it now. It's in a pile. My girl would need quite a while to dig it up." Berlin's secretary finally fished it out from under a telephone book.

Greg MacKellan, former artistic director of 42nd Street Moon, which revives neglected shows, notes, "What's interesting is that originally it was written for Buffalo Bill and two cronies. I don't think Irving Berlin sat down to write an anthem that was going to symbolize show business. He wrote a song for these guys trying to convince Annie to join the show—that show business is exciting but at the same time it has its foibles. It's a perfect number, but it's not a big production number. It's just got a great energy level."

By now the song has been so overexposed it's almost a patriotic march, so taken for granted by everybody that it's hard to hear it with fresh ears, but it sums up in a few lines showbiz guts and glory by a guy who knew the territory as well as anyone: "Yesterday they told you you would not go far . . . Next day on your dressing room they've hung a star." In nineteen words, it's the entire plot of *42nd Street* and every other backstage musical. And, "Nowhere could you get that happy feeling / When you are stealing that extra bow . . . The sawdust and the horses and the smell / The towel you've taken from the last hotel." The onetime teenage Lower East Side song hustler knew from stealing extra bows and hotel towels.

For the 1966 revival Merman, then fifty-eight, insisted on a new number for the occasion, which insiders called "Granny Get Your Gun." Berlin wrote the extra number upon demand by Merman, who, before she deigned to appear in a revival, insisted on a song that wasn't in the original score. He obediently turned out one more showstopper, **"An Old-Fashioned Wedding,"** a catchy countermelody with some of his smartest lyrics. It was his last great song, a challenge duet between Frank and Annie, who are on different matrimonial pages. She longs for a traditional wedding; he doesn't. John Lahr called it "Berlin's final flourish. It was also the final show-stopping fling of the traditional musical." Not quite but close.

Frank Butler croons, to a nostalgic melody, "We'll have an old-fashioned wedding / Blessed in the good old-fashioned way." To which Annie insists, in a snappy jazzed-up tempo: "I wanna wedding in a big church / With brides-maids and flower girls, / A lot of ushers in tailcoats, / Reporters, and pho-tographers / A ceremony by a bishop who will tie the knot and say / 'Do you agree to love and honor?' / Love and honor, yes, but not obey."

Then, further against Butler's wishes, Annie commands: "I wanna wed-ding like the Vanderbilts have, / Ev'rything big not small. / If I can't have that kind of a wedding I don't wanna get married at all." Berlin's lyrics echoed many a girl's fantasy. The spirited back-and-forth between bride and groom is laid down with comic precision in a wedding planner's worst nightmare.

Somehow Berlin managed to top even himself with "An Old-Fashioned Wedding" in a score that already had half a dozen money-makers in the bank, but he worried it hadn't stopped the show. When the '66 revival played Toronto prior to Broadway, Berlin called Merman after every performance to ask, "How did the new song go?" Merman would say, "It went great." "Did it stop the show?" "No, but they really liked it." This continued for a few days, until finally Merman said, "Irving, do you want the song to stop the show?" From that night forward, Merman made sure it did. Showstoppers on demand.

NPR's arts reporter Bob Mondello was there. He reported he had "never witnessed an actual number that stopped the show for an encore" until he saw this song, his first and only honest-to-god literal showstopper—Mer-man's duet with Bruce Yarnell singing "An Old-Fashioned Wedding." Mon-dello says Merman sang it six times, each time embellishing it with more shtick—pointing a finger at Yarnell, pounding his chest, dancing a jig—until the audience finally said enough already and the show resumed after half an hour. Yes, there is no business like show business, at least when Merman was running the show.

KISS ME, KATE

⋄ 1948 ⋄

"Brush Up Your Shakespeare," "Always True to You in My Fashion," "I Hate Men"

K iss Me, Kate was Cole Porter's 1948 return to runaway hit territory after a few flops. He was thought of as a used-up songwriter whose silly shows with funny songs had been overtaken by the new weighty musicals of Rodgers and Hammerstein. So the wild idea of a musical comedy taken from a Shakespearean play sounded far-fetched, a sure disaster. The show's producers, Arnold Saint-Subber and Lemuel Ayres, thought "it might be best to try someone else" to write the score rather than Porter, maybe even the same kid who had just written a Harvard Hasty Pudding show.

Patricia Morison, the original Kate, told me, "Everyone said, 'Who wants a musical based on Shakespeare? Cole Porter must have lost it!' But he persisted and it happened." She recalls the opening-night party. "Cole was at the top of the stairs, and the reviews came in, and he threw his cane away." Brooks Atkinson of the *New York Times* called the show a "terribly enjoyable humorous phantasmagoria of song." He wrote, "All his lyrics are literate as usual," but warned playgoers, "Some of them would shock the editorial staff of 'The Police Gazette.'"

So for Cole Porter—and for his aging collaborator Bill Shakespeare—*Kiss Me, Kate* was a colossal comeback. Even so, for all of its success, only one of the show's songs, "So in Love," was a major hit, perhaps because most of the songs are a bit too *Kiss Me, Kate*–specific.

The musical, a show within a show, about a troupe of traveling Shakespearean players and two backstage romances that mirror *The Taming of the Shrew*, is almost too clever and convoluted for its own good. The romantically linked squabbling lead characters, Fred Graham and Lilli Vanessi, played by Alfred Drake and Morison, were supposedly based on Alfred Lunt and Lynn Fontanne's backstage spats. Coproducer Saint Subber said he got the idea when he was a production assistant on the Lunts' 1940 tour of *The Taming of the Shrew*, but Bella Spewack claimed it was *her* idea after seeing *The Boys from Syracuse*, Rodgers and Hart's 1938 musicalization of *The Comedy of Errors*. Her first version of the book was written in pseudo Shakespearean prose, of which Alfred Drake said in 1998, "There's nothing worse than imitation Shakespeare, and hers was poverty stricken!" Drake slowly got her to include more Shakespeare and less Spewack. She later explained that the solution was not to adapt Shakespeare but to "contain him."

Early *Kiss Me, Kate* audiences must have wondered, *So who is actually singing this or that song—Petruccio or the star Fred? Kate or Lilli?* It's often unclear whether the Shakespearean actors are singing in the show within a show or in the original play. You need to keep untangling the twin plot lines (plus *Shrew* is complicated on its own), but the songs are so witty that it's worth the trouble.

Most of Porter's earlier shows had zany books (*Anything Goes, Something for the Boys, Nymph Errant, Du Barry Was a Lady, Jubilee*), flimsy wire coat hangers on which to hang his stylish songs, but *Kiss Me, Kate* had an original concept that challenged him and that he met with his smart lyrics, aided by theatrical craftsmanship. In his earlier shows, notes musical historian Mark Steyn, the songs are often interchangeable, but "I've Come to Wive It Wealthily in Padua" and "Brush Up Your Shakespeare" could only belong in *Kiss Me, Kate*. As Ethan Mordden points out, Porter wrote two sets of songs: "the quasi-operatic period spoofs for the *Shrew* scenes ["Wunderbar," "Were Thine That Special Face"] and character songs for the backstage scenes"—"We Open in Venice," "Another Openin', Another Show," "Why Can't You Behave?," "Always True to You in My Fashion."

Porter was so worried he couldn't write songs for such a complex plot (let alone one based on Shakespeare) that he kept devising reasons not to do the show. He insisted he wasn't that familiar with Shakespeare, but Bella Spewack talked him into it on her third try. Porter learned quickly on the job. Bella and her husband Sam would knock out a scene and send it to Porter, who would then write a song for it. This accounts for the show's choppiness. The show even has two competing openers, only three numbers apart—"Another Op'nin', Another Show" and "We Open in Venice"—both equally spirited. Overwhelmed by Porter's fertile pen, the Spewacks finally asked him to stop cranking out songs; the next day he sent them a showstopper, "Brush Up Your Shakespeare."

The score is a bulging song bag of classics that includes two semistandards ("So in Love," "Too Darn Hot") and four brilliant Porter riffs on Shakespeare—"Where Is the Life That Late I Led?," "I've Come to Wive it Wealthily in Padua," "Were Thine That Special Face," and "I Am Ashamed That Women Are So Simple" (each title plucked from Shakespeare's own libretto).

This isn't even counting "Where Is the Life That Late I Led?," "Why Can't You Behave?," and "Wunderbar," an operetta parody that sounds like an authentic waltz by Rudolf Friml (but in fact was written for an earlier unproduced Porter show and titled "Waltz Down the Aisle"). "Wunderbar" posed—still poses—a stylistic problem: it's meant to be a parody, but the music is so lush and the song is presented so romantically and robustly that audiences aren't sure how to take it. "By the time we got through the chorus," recalled Alfred Drake, "nobody wanted to laugh anymore."

Kiss Me, Kate has left such an indelible impression that it's impossible to watch *The Taming of the Shrew* without catching song cues in the dialogue and expecting another famous number. Nearly every other song in the score approaches a showstopper, but the two that halt the musical unfailingly are "Brush Up Your Shakespeare" and "Always True to You in My Fashion," with Porter's inspired wordplay wedded to irrepressible tunes.

Porter, unlike his slightly removed relationship to his earlier musicals, was hands-on in every facet of *Kiss Me, Kate*, no longer just the dapper celebrity songwriter who attended opening nights with friends as if seeing the shows for the first time. Morison vividly recalls, "He used to come to rehearsal and they would put a chair in the center aisle for him to watch. If he didn't hear a lyric, he had a little whistle around his neck, and he would blow it and say, 'I did not hear that last lyric.'" She can't recall that he ever blew the whistle on her.

The original performers of the show-stopping soft-shoe duet **"Brush Up Your Shakespeare"** (Harry Clark and Jack Diamond) are lost to history but happily exhumed on YouTube. People who know the delicious Cole Porter number from its 1953 movie version with Kathryn Grayson and Howard Keel (shot in 3-D, the only major 3-D musical) were knocked out by Keenan Wynn and James Whitmore's underworld mugs who warble an ode to the Bard in ersatz erudition. They're caught backstage and make like Shakespearian scholars, turned out in proper gangster garb—white ties, dark pinstripe suits, and fedoras, like gamblers from *Guys and Dolls* two years later.

It's an ebullient throwaway number that has nothing to do with the plot but endears you to the two merry mobsters who threaten to close the show to collect a gambling debt. The song is a textbook example of Porter's trademark list song, in which he rings endless changes on a theme, displaying the songwriter at his most literate, with references that flatter us for catching his in-jokes, double entendres, and purposely bad puns, groaners like rhyming "mussing" with "Much Ado About Nussing." The premise instantly grabs you—gangsters who can quote Shakespeare. But the joyous wordplay is its own reason (and reward) for existing. A great musical like *Kiss Me, Kate* is elastic enough to include an inspired song whether or not it's crucial to the plot.

"Brush Up Your Shakespeare" is neatly shoehorned into the second act when the gangsters who threaten Bill (Harold Lang, originally) to pay his gambling debt are caught onstage unexpectedly and hurriedly improvise a salute to Shakespeare, offering advice on how to seduce a woman with Elizabethan expertise. The lyrics reveal Porter at his most slyly risqué—"If she says your behavior is heinous / Kick her right in the Coriolanus," and the even more ribald, "When your baby is pleading for pleasure / Let her sample your 'Measure for Measure'" (that one may have gone over a few heads in 1946).

Jack Diamond and Harry Clark instructed audiences in how to "Brush Up Your Shakespeare" in *Kiss Me, Kate*.

The song finds Porter in an Ogden Nash mood, bending words to create nonsense rhymes. Wolcott Gibbs led off his *New Yorker* review, "Any man who will rhyme 'Cressida' with 'ambassador' is capable of practically anything, and that is exactly what Cole Porter has done in 'Kiss Me, Kate.'"

The number is such a guaranteed winner that Porter wrote in two curtain calls for the mobsters (the script was cut to make room). You never want to see these two guys leave the stage, and Porter might easily have banged out stanzas until he ran out of Shakespearean plays and plays on titles. Bella Spewack had an odd agreement with Porter that "there would be no songs for the gunmen"—for whatever reason—but response to the song easily overrode that rule. "We realized," she said, "it was a boffo number—a showstopper."

Its sing-song, almost childlike tempo adds to the song's fun, as the rogues execute a kind of toe dance while delivering ingenious R-rated lyrics. The simple cadence allows you to hear every pun and sexual reference, enunciated by mobsters with precise diction (again, echoed in *Guys and Dolls*). In the second reprise, Porter buttons up the idea of two hoods musing on Shakespeare by having them deliver their final words in British accents, shuffling off with "Forsooth!" and "Odds bodkins!"

It's hard to imagine a more perfect patter song than "Brush Up Your Shakespeare," but if you were to nominate a rival it might well be **"Always True to You in My Fashion."** And not just for its witty verbal dexterity but for the saucy liberated attitude of a female character, Lois Lane (originated by Lisa Kirk, played on screen by Ann Miller), who blithely boasts of a few casual flirtations to her boyfriend Bill, after asking him, in song, "Why Can't You Behave?" One Porter biographer observed that the song reflects Porter's homosexual affairs but emotional fidelity to his wife, heiress Linda Lee Thomas, who had her own flings. It's a welcome switch: a comedy number about a woman whose romantic misbehavior matches her boyfriend's.

Most of Porter's women were liberated well before Betty Friedan and Gloria Steinem. Think of his livewire heroine Nail O'Reilly Duquesne of *Red, Hot and Blue*, a former manicurist who tries to establish a national lottery to rehabitate ex-cons. Or the fearlessly bawdy courtesan Madame Du Barry in *Du Barry Was a Lady*. Or the patriotic Blossom Hart, a worker in the War Department in *Something for the Boys* who tries to convert a ranch house into a boardinghouse for soldiers' wives. Or the flamboyant revivalist minister Reno Sweeney in *Anything Goes*. Or the unrepressed La Mome Pistache, whose Montmartre club flaunts banned dancers in *Can-Can*. When *Kiss Me, Kate* was revived in 1999, with Marin Mazzie and Brian Stokes Mitchell, its producer Roger Berlind brushed away new feminist concerns, saying, "Well, that's Shakespeare. We're true to the sixteenth century." The thorniest political problem was whether to stage the famous scene where Petruchio spanks Kate, but Mazzie rationalized it, saying, a bit cryptically, "This isn't about a man taming a woman; it's more a matching up." Patricia Morison, asked if the show's message fit contemporary times, sighed, "That is a big bore. It's good flashy theater."

Both Kate in *Kiss Me, Kate* and her sister Bianca are feminists without portfolio who give their lecherous men as good as they get. "Always True to You in My Fashion" is a declaration of sexual independence. Porter says the song was inspired by a line in a poem by Ernest Dowson: "I have been faithful to thee . . . Cynara! In my fashion." It's hard to think of a song quite like it, in which a woman taunts her beau with a list of rich men she just may sleep with—albeit only for material gain—in a late forties prefeminist diamonds-are-a-girl's-best-friend era.

Tired of pleading with Bill to be faithful, Lois finally retorts with her own roll call of possible dalliances, tempering her temptations with an unpersuasive promise to remain faithful in her way—in brief, two can play this erotic game. Lois then flings open her own little black book of fantasies, singing, "If a custom-tailored vet / Asks me out for something wet, / When the vet begins to pet, I cry 'Hooray!,' / But I'm always true to you, darlin', in my fashion."

Patricia Morison, a dark beauty with an elegant air, hair smartly pulled back, was suggested to Porter by the show's director, John C. Wilson. She was Porter's first choice. He later recalled, "The moment I saw her, I thought, this is it, if she can sing." But she wasn't it quite yet, so Porter advised her, "Get someone to train your [speaking] voice." He suggested Morison work with elderly actress Constance Collier to learn how to play Shakespeare, specifically Kate, whom Collier had portrayed in England. "Collier had been a big star and was a grand dame," says Morison, who had only acted in B movies and in two B Broadway musicals.

Morison drove to Porter's home in Beverly Hills to audition. She figured someone else probably had the part—veterans Ruth Warwick, opera star Dorothy Kirsten, Lilli Palmer, Anita Colby, Mary Martin, and Ruth Chatterton were all considered—but she auditioned anyway, just for the experience (at the time she was committed to a potboiler TV series, *The Cases of Eddie Drake*). After hearing her, Porter told Bella Spewack, "Pat Morison is, to me, a much more interesting possibility. I feel strongly that this is our girl, so much so that I believe we might, overnight, create a new star. . . . Morison is the one." But Clifton Webb heard her at a party and told Porter, "That girl's voice won't carry in a theater." Now worried, Porter rented a large theater in Los Angeles and had Morison sing while he sat in the last row of the balcony, after which he decreed that Webb and all the other Morison doubters were "crazy." She played it two years on Broadway and a year in London. Among the near unanimous raves, *Variety* said, "Miss Morison is not only lovely to look at, but she can act and has a swell sense of comedy."

———

When we spoke by phone in 2014, Patricia Morison was an affable, quick, and chatty ninety-eight, easily able to recall all the details of her early years with *Kiss Me, Kate*, which changed her life—for a while, no other show she did could ever match it. As Porter predicted, it made her a star, but she had to be content with a modest post-*Kate* stage life—three years in *The King and I* on Broadway and in London, and other classic revival roles. Despite her stunning looks—she's still glamorous, black hair still pulled back as in *Kiss Me, Kate*—she never married ("not that I didn't come close").

When she tried out for *Kiss Me, Kate*, Morison "was doing very well in Hollywood, making a lot of money and all that. I was always the other woman or shooting somebody. I was making a film, *Song of the Thin Man*, the last in the series, when my agent took me out to sing for Cole Porter at his house on Rockingham Drive. They had a hard time raising money for the show. Everybody said, 'Who wants a musical about Shakespeare?' But I sang for him, and he called New York, and they said, 'Oh, no, she's not a singer.' They had an opera star in mind. But Cole persisted. He thought I was perfect. I was nervous, as anybody would be." She sang a Rodgers and Hammerstein song for Porter. After she got cast, she and Porter became close. "I have so many letters from him—we were very dear friends." She describes Porter as "a small, delicate, elegant man, very intelligent, very charming. I loved him."

Morison recalls, "We didn't know what we had until we opened in Philadelphia. We all rehearsed in separate rooms. We said to ourselves, if we all get good personal reviews, we'll be lucky. Actually, the Philadelphia opening was far more exciting than New York because we didn't expect such a reaction. We got this tremendous ovation, and then of course we realized we had a hit."

She says the numbers that drew the biggest responses included "Wunderbar" and her solo, "So in Love," but **"I Hate Men"** gave Morison her own showstopper. However, "in rehearsal nobody liked it except Cole. People came up to me and said, 'Oh, Pat, that song will make you look terrible, you shouldn't do it—why don't you get Cole to change it?' He wouldn't change anything. I used to go to Cole and say I'm worried. He said, 'Pat, I remember an operetta where this man sang, "I Want What I Want When I Want It" [Victor Herbert's *Mlle. Modiste*] and he banged a tankard on the table. So don't you worry, just bang that tankard.' The hard thing was to figure out how to stage the song. Everybody had ideas, and I had my own ideas. I had studied with Martha Graham and wanted to move around the stage like that." But she just banged her tankard and prayed.

"When we opened in Philadelphia I was petrified because everyone had doubts—the director didn't like the song, nobody liked it, people were concerned the song might offend men, including male critics—and then of course it stopped the show. It was a terrific surprise the opening night in Philadelphia. The reaction of the audience was wonderful." Brooks Atkinson in the *New York Times* called the song "the perfect musical sublimation of Shakespeare's evil-tempered Kate," when in fact it was an antimale rebuke.

There was equal concern over her entrance line. "My very first line in the play was 'You bastard!' I said to them, I could never say that line. So we tried 'You louse,' 'You jerk'—none of them worked. Opening night when I said, 'You bastard!,' the audience gasped." Morison had been in a few movies before *Kiss Me, Kate*, but she wasn't a film star and so of course didn't land the movie version, which is fairly faithful to the stage show. (Bob Fosse is one of the lead dancers.) Snub-nosed, vanilla-flavored Kathryn Grayson got the part, opposite Howard Keel. Morison says, "I didn't like the movie. It was nothing like the show. The leads didn't know how to perform the acting scenes, based on Lunt and Fontanne. It just turned into a regular MGM musical."

SOUTH PACIFIC

◆ 1949 ◆

"There Is Nothin' Like a Dame," "Some Enchanted Evening"

South Pacific officially cemented Rodgers and Hammerstein's Broadway dominance after *Carousel* in 1945 and their surprise blockbuster *Oklahoma!* two years earlier. *South Pacific* has so many songs that became classics, it's an embarrassment of riches: one sturdy standard after another, a veritable hit parade of the late forties that almost distracts from the plot; you almost forget there's an actual story going on here.

Seven of the first nine songs in the show are classics, some sort of Broadway record: "A Cockeyed Optimist," "Some Enchanted Evening," "There Is Nothin' Like a Dame," "Bali Ha'i," "I'm Gonna Wash That Man Right Outa My Hair," "I'm in Love with a Wonderful Guy," and "Younger Than Springtime." And that's just act 1. Nobody has ever topped that, and nobody ever will. *Annie Get Your Gun* comes close, with about eight standards. After Rodgers and Hammerstein's earlier show, the experimental failure *Allegro*, Rodgers was determined to write a score jammed with hits. He called *South Pacific* "failure-proof."

The show got unanimous rave reviews (one critic called it *South Terrific*), but a critic for the *New York Herald Tribune* was not so sure: "The Rodgers music is not his finest, but it fits the mood and pace of 'South Pacific' so felicitously that one does not miss a series of hit tunes." A mere nine. A London critic liked the music but called the show "a 42nd Street 'Madame Butterfly,' the weakest of all the Hammerstein-Rodgers musicals." In fact, Rodgers and Hammerstein had worried that *South Pacific* might be unfavorably compared to *Madame Butterfly*, but not many people linked the two. Only critic Kenneth Tynan recognized the show as "the first musical romance which was seriously involved in an adult subject" (somehow forgetting *Show Boat*).

Today, despite its score of nonstop milestone songs, the show has become an ethereal fairy tale that hasn't aged as well as the mythic *Carousel* or *Oklahoma!* because *South Pacific* is locked in a World War II time zone. Parts of the plot have become quaint, maybe even precious. The Polynesian natives are childlike, a few songs are a little cloying ("Happy Talk," "Honey Bun"), and the World War II drama seems plodding; it's the only major musical set during the war.

Even so, the show is still regularly revived by community theater companies everywhere—thousands of productions a year. The last Broadway revival in 2008, with Kelli O'Hara, got as ecstatic reviews as it did when it opened in 1949—maybe more so. Ben Brantley wrote in the *New York Times*, "I know we're not supposed to expect perfection in this imperfect world, but darned if I can find one serious flaw in this production." When it opened in '49, nobody knew it would still be a landmark musical more than half a century later; indeed, it's become a major American cultural touchstone.

South Pacific is thought of as Rodgers and Hammerstein's "problem show," with its focus on bigotry that gave it a semicontroversial reputation at the time: the plot hinges on the reluctance of Southern-born nurse Nellie Forbush to accept her lover Emile de Becque's two racially mixed children. Even more bluntly, there's the morality lesson sung by naval lieutenant Joe Cable (in love with teenage "Happy Talk" girl Liat), "You've Got to Be Carefully Taught."

Nothing happy about the talk in that number, which points out how racism is bred by bigoted relatives' ideas about "people whose eyes are oddly made" and whose "skin is a different shade" and how bigotry is "drummed in your dear little ear." The song jarred audiences when it suddenly emerged in act 2 from the musical's dreamy score set in an exotic South Pacific island paradise, where seldom was heard a discouraging word—except for imperialist Japan.

Audiences were used to escapist shows that didn't mention such unseemly matters as racism—not counting *Show Boat* eight years earlier, book and lyrics also by Oscar Hammerstein, based on Edna Ferber's novel about mixed-race lovers. Perhaps partly because of its daring theme, *South Pacific* won a Pulitzer Prize in 1950 and a Tony for Best Musical, plus a record that still stands—Tonys for each of its four leading actors: Mary Martin, Ezio Pinza, Myron McCormick (as Seabee Luther Billis), and Juanita Hall (Bloody Mary). In 1957, during the height of the Little Rock integration battle at Central High School, a revival of *South Pacific* at the Westbury Music Fair on Long Island was booed when Nellie mentioned she was from Little Rock (home of another Broadway little girl, Lorelei Lee of *Gentlemen Prefer Blondes*). Producers wanted to change Nellie's hometown, but director Josh Logan refused. Instead, a short speech before each performance requested the audience's—well, tolerance.

James Michener, author of *Tales of the South Pacific*, the short-story collection that inspired the musical, relates in his memoir that a group of New Englanders came to him after a New Haven performance and asked him to request Rodgers and Hammerstein please take "You've Got to Be Carefully Taught" out of the show. Hammerstein just laughed and said, "That's what the show is about!" Hammerstein also vowed to cancel a show in Wilmington, Delaware, if the seating was segregated; they obeyed his demand. Two Georgia state legislators liked the show even though they said it "contained an underlying philosophy inspired by Moscow. . . . Intermarriage produces half-breeds. In the South, we have pure blood lines and we intend to keep it that way." Touring companies had trouble finding Southern bookings.

The influential Boston critic Elliot Norton also suggested that the song be cut because of Boston's racist history—all the more reason, said Logan, to keep it in the show. But a few prominent New York critics also flinched at the song. Wolcott Gibbs of the *New Yorker* wrote that "something called 'You've Got to Be Carefully Taught,' a poem in praise of tolerance, I somehow found a little embarrassing." Distinguished theater critic John Mason Brown said he also was "somewhat distressed by the dragged-in didacticism of such a plea for tolerance as 'You've Got to Be Carefully Taught.'" Many reviewers and playgoers praised Hammerstein, but what likely bothered even sophisticated critics like Gibbs and Brown is that the number's unassailable sentiment is expressed a bit heavy-handedly—in a word, preachy.

South Pacific is based on two of the nineteen stories in Michener's book that won a Pulitzer Prize in 1948: "Our Heroine" (the Nellie Forbush–Emile de Becque romance) and "Fo' Dolla'" (about the Joe Cable–Liat love affair); both tales were cleaned up for the show. In the love story, Liat is all but sold to Lt. Cable by Bloody Mary, her hustler mother. ("'Pimping' is too strong a word," writes the show's historian, yet in the story and the show Bloody Mary labels Cable "a stingy bastard.") And in the original Michener tale, de Becque has eight daughters out of wedlock, including two dark girls whom Nellie refers to in the book as "nigger children." Rodgers and Hammerstein were suckers for stories set in Asian cultures—*South Pacific*, *The King and I*, and *Flower Drum Song*. Their only hit shows set in white America are *Oklahoma!* and *Carousel*, based on a play set in Hungary, *Liliom*; the team's other non-Asian musicals—*Allegro*, *Me and Juliet*, and *Pipe Dream*—all failed.

In *South Pacific*, gender stereotypes are vigorously on display—from the curvy nurses and Bloody Mary chirping her "Happy Talk" to the Luther Billis drag number "Honey Bun" and the sailors chanting **"There Is Nothin' Like a Dame."** It's an unexpectedly randy song from the romantic Hammerstein, but one of his best comic numbers, a showstopper Logan said he staged in twenty minutes.

It's a lusty list song, deftly unreeling the unique joys of dames by isolated if not quite sex-deprived GIs, who had their pick of nubile native prostitutes. But the lyrics never turn raunchy or even risqué: "There are no books like a dame. / And nothing looks like a dame . . . There are no drinks like a dame, and nothin' thinks like a dame." In the amusing bridge, the horny Seabees bellow, "We have nothin' to put on a clean white suit for. / What we need is what there ain't no substitute for." (Today there surely would be a "prostitute" rhyme, if it's not already implied in the line, where "tute" is heavily accented in "substi*tute*.") Hammerstein's introductory verse succinctly captures the sailors' frustrated sex lives: "We got sunlight on the sand, / We got moonlight on the sea, / We got volleyball and Ping-Pong / And a lot of dandy games! / What ain't we got? / We ain't got dames!"

My favorite stanza: "We feel restless. We feel blue. / We feel lonely and, in brief, / We feel ev'ry kind of feelin' / But the feelin' of relief. / We feel hungry as the wolf felt / When he met Red Riding Hood. / What don't we feel? / We don't feel good!" Their comic plea ends with a hearty two-fisted chorus: "There ain't a thing that's wrong with any man here / That can't be cured by putting him near / A girly, womanly, female, feminine dame!" Well-stated, guys. The song is now part of the culture, and not just American culture. When an English newspaper did a story on the difficulty of an actress ever becoming a Dame of the British Empire, the headline read, "There Is Nothing Like a Dame."

The show had no need of a choreographer. Logan staged the two semi-dance numbers himself—"Honey Bun" and "There Is Nothin' Like a Dame."

He put the latter in motion as a rowdy expression of wholesome all-American boyish, manly, male, masculine virility. (Trivia note: Thurl Ravenscroft, later famous as Tony the Tiger in Kellogg's commercials, and the singer of "You're a Mean One, Mr. Grinch," sang the song's memorable basso profundo vocal part.) In lieu of sissified choreography, the burly, swaggering Seabees stomp around the stage baring their tattooed biceps and hairy chests. No gays in this man's military.

Logan choreographed the number with the men pacing up and down in rows, like caged lions, in opposite directions, restless because they've been deprived of not only military action but also female action; the nurses are off-limits. He staged the entire number instinctively and saw no reason ever to change it; the cast instantly gave it a standing ovation. The song remains one of the wittiest and best remembered moments in a show chocked with hits, though Logan took more pride in other, more nuanced directorial touches nobody noticed—which, as he noted, is just as it should be.

If the most beloved song in Rodgers and Hammerstein's seven musicals is not **"Some Enchanted Evening,"** clearly it's the team's most signature ballad, a landmark love-at-first-sight song set to one of Rodgers's most melodic waltzes. The number is a hopeful expression of romantic bliss and fatalism—the notion that your "true love" may just be on the other side of the room and will "fly to your side" if the gods of enchantment should summon her. It's idyllic—we're talking true love here—but so simply and honestly stated: "Some enchanted evening / You may see a stranger, / You may see a stranger / Across a crowded room. / And somehow you know, / You know even then / That somewhere you'll see her / Again and again."

That's pretty much every single man's wish when he's looking for someone to love as he enters a crowded room—a universal fantasy whether you're a dude at a frat party or an aging French planter in the 1940s in the South Pacific; *she* might be there: "Someone may be laughing, / You may hear her laughing / Across a crowded room." Hammerstein tapped into the heart of unspoken romanticism, which he very much believed in, and he heads off any cynics in the room by asking, "Who can explain it? / Who can tell you why? / Fools give you reasons, / Wise men never try."

When Rodgers first played the song for Ezio Pinza, he told the singer, "This is going to be the hit song of the show," but Pinza was not so sure. In his memoirs he says he responded, "It's a very lovely song. One of the loveliest I know, but it can't compete in popular appeal with 'A Wonderful Guy.'" Pinza writes, "Rodgers seemed hurt by my remark, but he had his sweet revenge." A less grand but quietly compelling ballad, "This Nearly Was Mine," reveals de Becque's vulnerability.

Everyone knows "Some Enchanted Evening," and most are enchanted by it, but not everyone fell head over heels for the ballad. The respected musicologist/songwriter Alec Wilder was never a big fan of Rodgers and Hammerstein but worshipped the earlier work of Rodgers and Hart. Like others (myself included), Wilder felt the later team's work was overly solemn and that Rodgers had lost the freshness and irreverent twinkle he had with Hart.

Wilder says in *American Popular Song*, "While Rodgers continued to write great songs, and

In *South Pacific*, Mary Martin and Ezio Pinza are mutually enchanted in "Some Enchanted Evening."

even to top himself, generally speaking I find missing that spark and daring flair which existed in the songs he wrote with Hart." Wilder especially disliked "Some Enchanted Evening," which he called "pale and pompous and bland . . . I'm in church and it's the wrong hymnal!" He labeled it "didactic and sentimental." That's far more true of the team's prayerful "I'll Never Walk Alone" and "Climb Ev'ry Mountain" than of the lilting "Some Enchanted Evening."

To borrow Woody Allen's word, "seriosity" descended upon Broadway after *Oklahoma!*, *Carousel*, et al. Rodgers seemed to turn his back on his past with Hart, like a youthful fling he was now ashamed of. He rarely referred to their fruitful twenty-four-year collaboration that produced twenty-seven shows—not all brilliant, for sure, but many as innovative in their way as his later works with Hammerstein. But Rodgers now enjoyed a new exalted status that he embraced (a Pulitzer Prize will do that to a guy), although Josh Logan said he felt that Rodgers's "fun was gone." Logan said Rodgers's worldwide stature had turned him into "a monument," the George Washington of Broadway composers.

BACKSTAGE DISH

- *South Pacific* was a smash hit before it opened, with a half million dollars in advance ticket sales, then the biggest in Broadway history. It paid back a portion of investors' money by the first preview. The show was budgeted at $225,000, but it cost only $165,000 to open because the previews had gone so smoothly that money put aside for new sets, costumes, and orchestrations went untouched. James Michener said, "I went to bed an unknown and woke up to find Ezio Pinza famous."

- Ezio Pinza's contract included a clause that said he would not be required to sing more than fifteen minutes a night, total; the opera star, not used to singing every night, often lost his voice toward the end of each week. Mary Martin's contract stipulated that she not have to sing a duet with him; she feared her voice would pale next to his. (They do sing several bars together in a brief reprise of "Cockeyed Optimist" and also in counterpoint in the "Twin Soliloquies" duet.) Martin was envious that Pinza got the show's big solo, but she loved the score enough to let him keep the musical's major aria. Before the show opened, everyone thought Martin's jubilant "I'm in Love with a Wonderful Guy" would be the hit, not "Some Enchanted Evening." Audiences were disappointed that they never sang together, though they're heard in a duet in a finale reprise of "Some Enchanted Evening" on the cast album.

- Rodgers fretted at first that, because of the tropical setting, the *South Pacific* score would have to include guitars and ukuleles, both of which he hated, but Michener told him that the only instrument he had ever heard natives play in the islands was an empty gasoline barrel they pounded like a drum. Rodgers reassured the public that the show wouldn't be too exotic. As he told the *Los Angeles Times*, "There is no grass skirt business, no steel guitar or other such Hawaiian nonsense on these islands."

- Hammerstein's main concern was that he knew nothing of military life, but Josh Logan, a veteran, did and worked closely with Hammerstein on the libretto. Logan then wanted coauthor credit and part of the royalties, but R&H denied him a royalty payment, and Logan forever felt cheated (though he got a generous cut of the movie grosses in repayment). "Rodgers and Hammerstein" had by then become a corporate entity—a "brand" in current jargon—so Logan's name was displayed in smaller type despite his coauthorship of the script. The ads announced, "A Musical Play by

Rodgers and Hammerstein"; adding Logan's name would have cluttered up their trademark. Logan said Hammerstein told him, "Josh, Rodgers and Hammerstein cannot and *will* not share a copyright. It's part of the financial structure." Adding to the corporatization of R&H, *South Pacific* was one of the first musicals that peddled trinkets in the lobby—*South Pacific* neckties, lipstick, scarves, music boxes, dolls, and hair brushes and shampoo for the ladies to help wash men out of their hair. Mary Martin's pixie hairdo, made famous in the shower scene, led to a female fad for short hair.

+ Mary Martin's husband and manager, Richard Halliday, told Rodgers and Hammerstein that he had a great idea for the show's opening scene, writes John Lahr in his book *Joy Ride: Show People and Their Shows*: Martin would be revealed up a tree and, as she climbed down, her bloomers would catch on a branch—surefire laugh. When Rodgers and Hammerstein told Halliday it was a really terrible idea, Halliday stormed out, muttering, "All *you* guys care about is the *show!*"

+ One of the better tales of *South Pacific* is how rapidly Rodgers knocked out melodies for both "Bali Ha'i" and "Happy Talk." Known for the speed with which he could compose tunes—he was said to have done the entire score of *Oklahoma!* in six working days—Rodgers broke his own personal best with "Happy Talk," a sort of nursery rhyme, dashed off in about twenty minutes. And "Bali Ha'i" took him only half that long. He wrote the music in five minutes over coffee in Logan's apartment.

According to legend, Hammerstein sent the lyrics of "Bali Ha'i" to Rodgers by messenger and when he called a half hour later to see if they'd arrived, Rodgers told him they had and were now set to music. But Rodgers always took pains to explain that, whereas he could write a melody in ten minutes, it was really more like three months and ten minutes, the result of weeks of talking and thinking about a number—where it would go in the show, its dramatic purpose, how it should sound, and so on. "Bali Ha'i"'s first three notes also open the musical and set the show's idyllic island mood. Cole Porter was once at a dinner party where everyone was listening to "Some Enchanted Evening" on the radio, and a woman exclaimed, "Isn't that a wonderful song!" Porter agreed, then added, "If you can imagine it taking *two* men to write one song."

+ Rodgers biographer Meryle Secrest writes that it was an "open secret" that Pinza hotly pursued Martin, a rumor fueled by Pinza's torrid onstage kisses. Don Fellows, a sailor in the show, recalls hearing Martin telling Pinza in the wings, "Ezio, when you kiss, kiss me *nicely*," and Pinza's reply was, "When I kees, I kees!" Fellows said, "She'd be singing and he'd be whispering, 'Mary, I love you' into her ear. Pinza was like that with all the girls." In the wings, he kept stealing kisses from a nurse in the chorus, until she vowed, "If he kisses me one more night I'm going to bite his tongue. I'm tired of this." And she did. After a yowl, Pinza smiled and said, "Wonderful!" (Playwright Russel Crouse said, "Pinza has three balls and when he sings they all light up.")

✦ The first time Martin sang "I'm in Love with a Wonderful Guy," at Rodgers's apartment, she did the song's last twenty-six words in one breath, as written, and fell off the piano bench, exhausted. Rodgers bent over her and said, "That's exactly what I want. Never sing it any other way." She didn't—except for not falling on the floor every time. The lyrics include phrases made up by Hammerstein to sound like clichés that became part of the language—"corny as Kansas in August," "normal as blueberry pie"— which, one writer noted, finally became actual clichés.

✦ "I'm Gonna Wash That Man Right Outa My Hair" was intended to give Martin a big moment to balance Pinza's "Some Enchanted Evening," and her number stopped the show—indeed brought it to an unintended halt at first—but not for itself. It's a cheery enough number if not all that notable except for an original special effect—the onstage shower in which Martin scrubs her hair.

While showering at home one day, Martin is said to have come up with the idea to actually lather her hair onstage eight times a week while warbling "I'm Gonna Wash That Man Right Outa My Hair." "What a great idea!," Rodgers, Hammerstein, and Logan all exclaimed, instantly adding the bit to Martin's number as she sang it. But the song died in early previews and nobody could figure out why until a woman friend of Logan's told him it was such a great scene that women in the audience were all abuzz.

"Did you like the song?," he asked her. "Song?" she said. Logan reminded her, "She sang a song when she washed her hair." "Oh, well, that explains it," she replied. "I couldn't tell whether she was talking or singing. All I heard was the people around me saying how terribly clever it was"—which is why the song was dying: the shampoo shtick was distracting the audience from the actual song. As soon as Martin began soaping her hair, the audience started whispering, wondering what shampoo she was using. Would it damage her hair? Was she really washing her hair? Was it a wig? Logan found a shrewd way to get the audience's attention back on the song, not the soap. Martin first shampooed her hair and *then* sang the song, which fixed the problem. Result: instant showstopper (showerstopper?).

The number (or maybe the lather) got a huge hand every night, and before Martin left the musical she had washed her hair 861 times. Lesson:

audiences are easily distracted. Another example: Martin's joyous "I'm in Love with a Wonderful Guy" didn't get the expected reactions in previews until Logan realized she was singing to the other nurses. He cut the nurses and attention quickly swung back to Martin and the song.

+ Mary Martin was Rodgers and Hammerstein's vision of the ideal leading lady—a sweet, frisky gal next door, if maybe too goody-two-shoes for some tastes. They had offered her the role of Laurey in *Oklahoma!*, which she turned down in favor of a musical called *Dancing in the Streets*. Mary was a girl who could say no: she also turned down offers to play Eliza Doolittle in *My Fair Lady* and to star in *Mame*. Martha Wright took over the show when Martin left, but the role was a better springboard for Florence Henderson, Nellie in a 1967 revival at Lincoln Center. (Trivia note: In the London production, two of the Seabees were played by Larry Hagman [Martin's son] and Sean Connery.)

+ A song written for *South Pacific* and later discarded, called "Suddenly Lovely," was reborn as "Getting to Know You" for Rodgers and Hammerstein's next show, *The King and I*, and the tune for "Younger Than Springtime" was originally called "My Wife" and written for *Allegro* before it was cut.

+ The splashy Todd-AO movie version of South Pacific with Mitzi Gaynor and Rossano Brazzi was a box office hit but generally considered a charmless film and critical failure. The movie was sabotaged by color filters that changed every scene, no sizzle between Gaynor and Brazzi, and a reshuffled song order ("Bloody Mary" opens the movie). *Time* wrote that it was "almost impossible to make a bad movie out of it—but the moviemakers appear to have tried."

Doris Day turned down the Nellie Forbush screen role and Elizabeth Taylor got stage fright during her audition, but Rodgers nixed her anyway. When Gaynor was chosen, the film producer told Logan to sit on her to suppress what one writer called her "forced sunniness"; Gaynor does appear determined to outshine Martin's cockeyed optimism. Actors first offered the movie's male lead were Charles Boyer, Fernando Lamas, and Vittorio De Sica. Pinza died before filming began. If he had lived, Martin might have been cast, but she was deemed too old by 1958 to survive the harsh scrutiny of a wide-screen lens. Brazzi's songs were dubbed by opera star Giorgio Tozzi. The movie got the lavish "road show" treatment—reserved tickets, an overture, and entr'acte music. It didn't help. But at least Hollywood respected musicals then, and, as one writer notes, even if the screen versions weren't as good as the stage shows, "they kept theater connected to mainstream America."

+ In his memoir, Logan described Rodgers: "What is a Richard Rodgers? It's a brilliant, talented, highly intelligent, theatrically sound, super brain. . . . It's not given to smiling too much, and yet when it scowls it does not indicate anything unpleasant; it is simply making a judgment." Logan says in his memoirs that the general consensus on Broadway was that "the big one [Hammerstein] is a nice guy but the little one [Rodgers] is a son of a bitch." He writes that Rodgers "pretends to hate business, and yet my theory is that [he] is only really happy making contracts, haggling about royalties, salary or theater leases. I often believed [he] was a bit embarrassed about the ease of writing music, as though it were too easy, too soft a thing for a man to do," and that he "enjoyed being a hard-bitten businessman." About as astute a profile of Rodgers as anyone ever wrote.

+ Rodgers was always bedeviled by the fact that Broadway insiders felt that his music, however wonderful, needed skilled arrangers to make it successful—Hans Spialek when he worked with Lorenz Hart, Robert Russell Bennett after Rodgers joined Hammerstein. Bennett helped give Rodgers's melodies their lush sound—straightforward and unfussy, always tasteful. But arrangers always feel their work is underrated, that they're regarded as mere technicians rather than artists; none are known to the public. And composers are prone to grab credit for the success of a superbly orchestrated song. Rodgers was fond of the story of an arranger who claimed a composer was "nothing" without his arrangements. The composer whipped out a piece of blank sheet music, tossed it across the table to the arranger, and said, "Arrange me a hit."

CALL ME MADAM

◆ 1950 ◆

"(You're Not Sick) You're Just in Love"

After *Annie Get Your Gun*, *Call Me Madam* is Irving Berlin's most hit-packed stage musical and his final success, which he wrote at age sixty-one. He then lived another forty years without another hit song, let alone hit show. But he went out with a bang with the score's biggest showstopper, **"(You're Not Sick) You're Just in Love,"** one of Berlin's three best known countermelodies (he wrote six in all), along with "Play a Simple Melody" from a long-forgotten 1914 show and "An Old-Fashioned Wedding" from *Annie Get Your Gun.*

The jolly madam Sally Adams, played by Ethel Merman, was based on Perle Mesta, the flamboyant Washington hostess and newsmaking ambassador to Luxembourg (renamed "Lichtenberg" in the show) under Harry Truman. When he was asked to write the show, Berlin asked, "Who's Perle Mesta?" The 1950 musical is rarely revived, for some reason, considering how many irresistible Berlin songs it has, not even counting "(You're Not Sick) You're Just in Love."

The show, an affectionate political satire about America's postwar global influence, with a smart book by Howard Linsday and Russel Crouse (who later wrote the libretto for *The Sound of Music*), includes "Can You Use Any Money Today?," a nice jab at foreign aid and "dollar diplomacy" ("Two million. Four million. Six million. Eight million. Ten. / Take what you want, when it's gone you can come back again"). The score also features four more of Berlin's most melodic songs—"The Hostess with the Mostes' on the Ball," "The Best Thing for You (Would Be Me)," "It's a Lovely Day Today," and "They Like Ike," the basis for Dwight Eisenhower's winning campaign slogan when he decided to run in 1952; the song might even have given the reluctant candidate a little push into the 1952 race: "I like Ike, / I'll shout it over a mike . . . I like Ike / And Ike is easy to like"—not exactly Lorenz Hart, but it works in the show and inspired one of the most effective campaign phrases in political history.

The show's major crowd-pleaser, though, is the joyous second-act duet with Merman and the bespectacled, crew-cut actor Russell Nype, playing a nerdy lovesick aide to Merman, whom he seeks out for romantic advice. In the 1953 movie

Ethel Merman diagnoses lovesick Russell Nype in "(You're Not Sick) You're Just in Love" in *Call Me Madam.*

version, easily Merman's best film, she sings the number with a googly-eyed Donald O'Connor. The movie also features George Sanders as a starchy diplomat with his eye on Merman. The usually icy, sardonic Sanders turns out to have an unexpectedly warm, pleasing voice. Merman, for a change, is not bigger than life in the movie, but her legend preceded her. The show's *Playbill* included this note: "Neither the character of Mrs. Sally Adams, nor Miss Ethel Merman, resemble any person living or dead."

Berlin wrote the duet "(You're Not Sick) You're Just in Love" when the show was limping along out of town, hoping to replace two songs that had died earlier. Merman told Berlin, "I want a number with the kid," and he complied. Her relationship with her love interest, played by Paul Lukas, was less chummy. George Abbott, who directed the show, reports in his memoir: "Later on in the run she got angry at Lukas and wouldn't look at him. Night after night I would have to go backstage and give her notes telling her that she ought to look at the leading man during love scenes. She would agree blandly and look at him for a couple of performances, but when I returned the next week I'd find her standing there talking to the audience and leaving Lukas out on a limb all by himself."

When Berlin first played the countermelody for Nype he warned him not to tell Merman because she would hit the ceiling if she learned he hadn't sung it for her first. When Berlin presented it to her, she said, "We'll never get offstage," and she was nearly right. At the show's first out-of-town performance in Boston, the number got seven encores—long after musicals abandoned encores. In the number, Nype chirps, "I hear singing and there's no one there, / I smell blossoms and the trees are bare. / All day long I seem to walk on air, / I wonder why, I wonder why."

At that point Merman bursts in with her older woman's sage counsel: "You don't need analyzing, / It is not so surprising / That you feel very strange but nice. / Your heart goes pitter-patter, / I know just what's the matter / Because I've been there once or twice. / Put your head on my shoulder, / You need someone who's older, / A rubdown with a velvet glove / There is nothing you can take / To relieve that pleasant ache, / You're not sick, / You're just in love!" Whereupon they sing over each other as the jubilant number explodes and the audience goes wild with delight.

Countermelodies are rare but always hugely satisfying, just great fun to hear as two voices blend in pleasant opposition, crooning separate lyrics, usually resulting in a deserved showstopper. Philip Furia suggests in his Berlin biography that the songwriter might have been inspired by his own long-ago hit, "Play a Simple Melody," which had a 1950 revival just before *Call Me Madam* was written, when Bing Crosby and his son Gary recorded it, making "Play a Simple Melody" a hit all over again, and whose title (from the 1914 hit show *Watch Your Step*) became Berlin's lifelong hit-machine philosophy. *Call Me Madam* was Berlin's triumphal return to Broadway after he had deserted New York for Hollywood (returning for *Annie Get Your Gun*). His first love was Broadway, but, as much bookkeeper as pop prodigy, Berlin found films a more efficient way of getting his songs heard. He was a walking juke box who wrote about fifteen hundred published songs, plus another four hundred never published.

The idea for *Call Me Madam* (the phrase is found in Shakespeare, uttered by Mistress Quickly in *Henry IV, Part Two*) was hatched when co-librettist Howard Lindsay wrote to Russel Crouse from a resort in Colorado where he and Merman were both vacationing. "I have been studying her," he wrote Crouse, viewing Merman at poolside in a yellow swimsuit and bandana. "She seems so *American*," he told his partner, "raucously, good-naturedly, almost vulgarly American. I got to thinking how we could spot her in a foreign setting. And then I thought of Perle Mesta. How about making her Madam Ambassadress? She could be very funny as an American ambassador. . . . She could get the government into trouble and then get out of it by using sound American instinct and common sense. And she could turn out to be a hell of a good ambassador in the end and spread the democratic idea. The title could be 'Call Me Madame' or is that terrible?" It may sound like a fantasy out of a movie, too pat to be true, but Merman biographer Philip Furia quotes Lindsay verbatim that the show was born in just such an aha moment.

Call Me Madam, like other hit musicals of the era—*Bye Bye Birdie, Bells Are Ringing, Grease, Can-Can, On the Town, Milk and Honey, Finian's Rainbow*—was inspired not by a movie or book but by current events of the period: *Call Me Madam* made fun of foreign aid, *Bye Bye Birdie* mocked rock 'n' roll and Elvismania, *Bells Are Ringing* was about a new phenomenon called answering services, *Grease* focused on teen rebellion, *Silk Stockings* fastened on the cold war with Russia, and *Finian's Rainbow* took on Southern racial bigotry. Lyricists like Cole Porter, Comden and Green, Ira Gershwin, Adler and Ross, E. Y. Harburg, and others played off fads, newsmakers, and the mood of their time.

The songwriters created a world onstage that reflected and satirized the real world. Their songs, plots, and jokes came out of the news, freshly minted—shows about bootleggers, talking pictures, and the Florida land boom. In *As Thousands Cheer*, Irving Berlin and Moss Hart even used the daily newspaper as a theatrical device to write about everything from Herbert Hoover to lynchings. If Berlin, Porter, Gershwin, and Harburg were writing today, they would seize on cell phones, Bill Gates, Facebook, Donald Trump, the Kardashians, and climate change as sitting ducks for witty songs.

Merman loved the idea for *Call Me Madam* but first imagined it as a play, not a musical. She finally wanted a chance to rest her pipes and display her acting skills. (Her mother said, "Ethel can talk, too.") "I want a good solid dramatic role," she told Lindsay, but he insisted she sing the role, and Merman finally relented. "All right—a few songs if they could be worked in." (He worked in thirteen.) Berlin also saw it as a play and resisted writing songs for it. As he recalled, in a tone of hurt irritation, "I had to find a way of getting songs into a play that was strong enough to stand by itself without music, instead of a libretto full of song cues. They never seemed to worry about me or my work. They just sent me the text and said, 'Oh, send it off to Berlin. He'll take care of the music.'" Berlin was pretty good at that.

GUYS AND DOLLS

◆ 1950 ◆

"Adelaide's Lament"

The almost performer-proof soliloquy from *Guys and Dolls*, **"Adelaide's Lament,"** an all-time showstopper, is a richly layered character song that reveals with unexpected wit what's going on inside the head of the troubled female comic lead, a fretful, unwed showgirl. The role was originated on Broadway by Vivian Blaine, who, by a Hollywood miracle, was actually chosen to repeat her iconic performance on screen even though she wasn't a movie name, or really a name anywhere off Broadway.

In the number, Loesser has Adelaide searching for a medical link between herself as an unhappily semiengaged Hot Box doll and her sneezing jag, a self-diagnosis that hooks you from Adelaide's first line—"It says here [or "heah" as she pronounced it] / The av'rage unmarried female, / bas-i-call-y insecure ["in-se-cu-ah"] / Due to some long frustration may react / With psychosomatic symptoms, / Difficult to endure ["en-du-ah"], / Affecting the upper respiratory tract. / In other words, just from waiting around for that plain little band of gold / A person ["poi-son"] can develop a cold."

Part of the fun of the song is the juxtaposition of Adelaide's Brooklyn yammer as she tries to get her chorus doll's tongue around clinical terminology—"chronic organic syndromes, toxic or hyper-tense," "neurotic tendency." Loesser seamlessly mingles clinical jargon and showgirl slang. There's even a logical reason she might have a chronic cold, dressed half the time in skimpy showgirl attire.

The great character song fleshes out Adelaide's deep-seated worries about landing the elusive Nathan Detroit after a fourteen-year relationship—what is she doing wrong? It's simultaneously funny and heartfelt, a patter song on the surface that nonetheless makes us adore Adelaide and care about her plight. The number may not advance the plot, but it deepens it, or at least comically embroiders it. "Adelaide's Lament" takes us inside her head. She's not just a frowsy, dimwitted dame but a real, rounded, sensitive woman who reads books and is trying to psychoanalyze her physical and emotional condition. The song comes out of nowhere, and though we now know the words almost by heart, we still always care about Adelaide. Loesser's widow, singer Jo Sullivan, told me she has never seen the song performed any differently than Blaine first did it. "You can only do it in a certain way. They can't go crazy in some other way."

The song is an old-fashioned showstopper that engages us without a single excess or gimmick. No falling chandeliers, revved-up red cars, or flying actors required. The bells and whistles are built into Frank Loesser's ear-catching song, the engaging character, and a winning performance. Blaine's exacting delivery was funny but authentic. She said that when she was considered too sexy for the part of Salvation Army doll Sarah Brown, Loesser figured out how to fit her into the role of Miss Adelaide, though she seems born to play it. In the end, every bit of business, every sniffle and sneeze, was as good as copyrighted by Blaine when the show opened in 1950. Adelaide was the original Broadway baby.

The late lyricist Fred Ebb (*Cabaret, Chicago*), who knew a thing or two about comedy songs, said *Guys and Dolls* was the first musical he saw. Ebb analyzed the song for NPR's *Fresh Air* on the show's fiftieth anniversary: "Here's a girl who . . . says she has a cold 'cause somebody isn't going to marry her. That's a very rich comic notion. And she's got these hilarious punch lines, you know, like, 'If she's getting a kind of a name for herself and the name ain't

**Vivian Blaine, as Adelaide, lamenting her iffy relationship with
Sam Levene's Nathan Detroit in *Guys and Dolls*.**

his' and 'If she's tired of getting the fish-eye from the hotel clerk.' Every line
in it is worth something. It means something. It has impact. It has vitality. It
has humor and charm and appropriateness. And I don't know how you can
get much better than that." And Loesser keeps topping himself in succeeding

stanzas: "You can feed her all day with the vitamin A and the bromofizz, / But the medicine never gets anywhere near where the trouble is."

Loesser extended Adelaide's lament by allowing Nathan to answer her in "Sue Me," Sam Levene's only solo, which he was unable to start on the right note (*mi*) until Loesser devised a way to let Levene sort of sneak up on the song by way of a spoken phrase that segues into the tune's opening line: "Call a lawyer and . . . sue me, sue me, shoot bullets through me, I lo-o-ove you," which leads into their contrapuntal duet as Adelaide argues in exasperation, "Ya promise me this, ya promise me that . . ."

———

Faith Prince, who played Adelaide opposite Nathan Lane in the acclaimed long-run Broadway *Guys and Dolls* revival in 1992, needed to reinvent a landmark role in an iconic number originated by a famous performance and still put her stamp on it. "I just took it as if it was written for me," she told me. "There is no difference between a new work and a revival. When you look at the song itself, you have to look at it as *you*, not as a role, and say that whatever character you are is a dilemma. How would *you* say these words?"

Prince explains, "You have to begin to outline what the dilemma is, what the story is, and in this case I just took it at face value. Adelaide was a girl who had been in this relationship for fourteen years. She was frustrated and she was at a juncture. And I thought, if I were this girl in this situation, the stakes would be incredibly high. By doing that, you start to spin it in your own way as opposed to some caricatured generalization of what people think of that part. The song is laid out extremely well. There are real stakes and needs in it. You just try to carve it out as you." She worked to make Adelaide a real person, not just a lovable cartoon. "Comedy is about real tragedy," she said. "The more tragic it is and the more committed to it you are, the funnier it is."

Ken Bloom, the musicals historian, adds, "'Adelaide's Lament' originally had heart. Everybody now who sings 'Adelaide's Lament' makes it a caricature. It does not work as well as caricature. They are pushing the comedy and accent and all that, but originally it had a heart. It was a sad song. Even though you are laughing you are feeling bad for her."

Had Prince seen the movie with Vivian Blaine as Adelaide? "Probably growing up, but I didn't sit there and study it. Like when I did 'I'm the Greatest Star' in *Funny Girl* I didn't sit there and analyze Barbra Streisand. I'm not going to mimic her. It's like research. You look at the research and say, here are some interesting choices, but then you have to get into yourself and it has to come from yourself. That's what you do naturally." But don't directors often just want reproductions of a famous role or song? "Then I would not be working with that director," she declares.

Loesser's widow was involved in the Prince–Nathan Lane revival. Did Prince ever talk to her about the song? "A lot. She came in and saw things. But I never got any directions from her. She would come in and just oversee it. We did not discuss any specifics. I just remember her as being incredibly kind. Her thinking was to not make Adelaide a victim." Prince, Lane, and director Jerry Zaks discussed the relationship between Miss Adelaide and Nathan Detroit. "We all kept saying they love each other so much. That is what I meant about the positive. Because when you really love somebody you really want to make them happy. That was their reality in their world. Jerry always said, they love each other, but they just do not seem able to connect, and that's the dilemma." (You can compare Prince's version on YouTube with Vivian Blaine's, who so perfectly first nailed it.)

Prince said she had played Adelaide earlier in her career, in summer stock and in a regional production. "The first time I did it, I was maybe nineteen [but] I have always been an old soul. I just felt the truth of it. It was a not caricature for me even at nineteen. I felt, I know this woman, even though I didn't know about relationships like that. I knew how to innately relate to her dilemma and how to drive the high stakes in comedy. Musicals can hold more darkness and weight than is usually imagined. I just had that naturally."

She was taken aback by the show-stopping impact of the song when she performed it on Broadway: "I didn't know it was going to be as powerful as it was until the very first preview. She starts off reading the book and doesn't know what is going to be inside the book. She is researching, she is turning to the book for an answer." The concept of a showgirl reading a psychology book is just a funny premise to start with. "You don't think she is the brightest tool in the box. I played her as somebody like Judy Holiday." Prince continues, "When she gets into the book, she gets all stirred up. She gets sicker as the number goes on, and by the end she is so frustrated that she takes out her absolute frustration; it grows during the song. I think with any showstopper it is the way it is constructed, carved out. You have to travel some sort of arc that makes a huge statement, and the more you are able to articulate that the stronger it will be. It's all a story. It's not song and lyrics separately."

·············· BACKSTAGE DISH ··············

+ Producer Cy Feuer first had the idea for a musical based on Damon Runyon characters. He telephoned Frank Loesser, who later recalled, "He said the magic word 'Runyon,' and I said, 'Let's have a meeting,' and that was it." Loesser, then forty, was something of a Runyon character himself, with a gruff voice and street-smart manner. Feuer told him he wouldn't be free to produce the show for a year, but Loesser was so inspired by the idea of a musical based on Runyon's stories that he wrote the score without a script. The libretto was written around Loesser's songs by Abe Burrows, the perfect man for the job. Burrows, a "dese-dems-dose" guy, said Loesser "really worked from his gut. He was an incurable romantic. He knew he could write the big comedy songs, but what he wanted was to *reach* the audience, get into them." Loesser liked to say, "I'm in the romance business."

+ Adelaide was based on a character in a Runyon story named Cutie Singleton. Loesser renamed her and added Adelaide to the script for Blaine. Burrows borrowed characters like Nathan Detroit from various Runyan tales, partly for their vivid names: Harry the Horse, Nicely-Nicely Johnson, Liverlips Louie, Brandy Bottle Bates, Benny Southstreet, Big Jule. Loesser had a keen ear for urban slang, brand names, and streetwise banter. In the title song, he refers to Vitalis, Barbasol, "a breakfast-eating Brooks Brothers type," and "a Scarsdale Galahad." In "Take Back Your Mink," there's a reference to "Hollandarize" (a fur coat–cleaning process).

+ "Standing on the Corner," the big pop hit from Loesser's *The Most Happy Fella*, was originally written for *Guys and Dolls* but was cut, said Laurie Franks, a chorus girl from Loesser's show *Pleasures and Palaces*, who recalled him telling her that he decided to put it in *Most Happy Fella* when the show was in trouble out of town. Loesser, an ex-Hollywood songwriter, smelled a winner when he'd written one.

+ Sam Levene, still the definitive Nathan Detroit, began with the Yiddish theater and had played Runyonesque types on Broadway and in films but never had been in a musical before *Guys and Dolls*. He couldn't sing, and his voice didn't improve during the entire run of the show. At his audition, Loesser asked Levene to sing anything. Levene sang "Pony Boy" off-key. "Now let's do it the right way," smiled Loesser. "This *is* the right way," said Levene. "I can't do it any other way." Levene was so tone deaf that, during the ensemble title song, Loesser ordered Levene just to move his lips. Cy Feuer said Levene never sang his one song ("Sue Me") in tune the entire run, "but it was absolutely right for the character." If Nathan Detroit can't sing, why should Sam Levene?

+ Isabel Bigley (Sarah Brown), the original cast's last surviving lead character, recalled on NPR's *Weekend Edition* in 2000, "There had been musicals before, but they were always pretty boys and pretty girls." Loesser made a point of casting real-looking actors, like Stubby Kaye as Nicely-Nicely and the burly blue comic B. S. Pully as Big Jule, what he called "people with bumps." Bigley said, "In other musicals you knew when a song was coming up. In *Guys and Dolls* everything just blended. You went into a song and it came out of the script. It wasn't, 'We'll stop now and sing a song.'"

+ An oft-told backstage story involves the day Loesser smacked Bigley because she didn't perform part of a song ("I'll Know") as he wanted it—spoken at one point, not sung. "He started hollering and I giggled. I asked him, 'Why did you hire a singer if you don't want me to sing?'," she told Scott Simon on the fiftieth anniversary of the show. "And he hauled off and slapped me. I think he was as stunned as I was. I just continued on with the song like it had never happened. From that moment on, everyone was my pal because they thought it was so terrible. . . . You know, we all understood. There was tension; we were going to open in a couple of days and everyone was under tremendous pressure, working almost twenty-four hours a day." Frank never apologized, Bigley said, but Loesser's wife sent her flowers the next day, and coproducer Ernie Martin said Loesser apologized with a diamond bracelet. Neither Loesser nor Bigley ever mentioned it again. Martin added, "He's the only guy I ever saw punch a soprano in the nose."

+ Vivian Blaine was totally unknown to most filmgoers, so it's a tribute to her show-stopping stage performance that MGM reluctantly allowed her to duplicate the role on screen, which Frank Loesser made a deal-breaker. Producer Sam Goldwyn pushed for bankable Betty Grable, far too much the pinup bombshell to lament much of anything. Marilyn Monroe made a bid for the role; Monroe had a lot of Adelaide in her and might have brought it off. Goldwyn also wanted regal Grace Kelly to play the mousy Salvation Army doll Sarah Brown.

+ Frank Loesser went to the mat to cast Blaine as Adelaide on screen, but he buckled under studio pressure in the confused miscasting of Frank

Sinatra as Nathan Detroit and Marlon Brando as Sky Masterson, whose roles, many felt, should have been reversed. Despite his mob friends, Sinatra failed to deliver as believable a portrayal of a two-bit hustler onstage as had Sam Levene, who absolutely captured Nathan's ragtag character. Sinatra does a decent enough job but was too polished, unfunny, and cocky, too Sinatra—America's greatest male pop singer in a role created by Levene, one of its greatest nonsingers. It was like casting Sinatra as Broadway Danny Rose. Nathan is clearly a Jewish nudnik (in "Sue Me," he asks, "What can you do me?" and "It's true—so, nu?"), not a dapper Italian swinger.

✦ Loesser's daughter Susan says her father hated how Sinatra turned the rumpled Nathan into more of a smoothie, like Sinatra. Levene's husky untrained voice added to the song's charm, not to mention its believability. Finally, Loesser asked Sinatra if he might give him a few thoughts on the song. "If you want to see me," said Sinatra, "you can come to my dressing room." Loesser complied, but Sinatra's dressing room was packed with his pals; a radio was playing loudly. "How the hell can we rehearse in this atmosphere?" Loesser asked. Sinatra: "We'll do it my way or you can fuck off." End of rehearsal. Susan Loesser writes, "In the end, Sinatra sang the song his way and my father refused to see the movie." Adding Hollywood insult to injury, the movie dropped five great Loesser songs from the Broadway show: "A Bushel and a Peck" (a pop hit), "My Time of Day," "I've Never Been in Love Before," "More I Cannot Wish You," and "Marry the Man Today." The film added three new Loesser (much lesser) songs, only one of which, "Adelaide" (for Sinatra), had the flavor of the Broadway score ("But Adelaide, Adelaide, ever-lovin' Adelaide, is takin' a chance on me—talk about your long shots, taking a chance on me!").

• •

THE KING AND I

✦ 1951 ✦

"Shall We Dance?"

Unlike all of Rodgers and Hammerstein's shows except the virginal *Sound of Music*, *The King and I* is a virtually sexless musical, at least between the title characters. It is mainly remembered for its peppy tunes ("Getting to Know You," "I Whistle a Happy Tune") and tender ballads ("I Have Dreamed," "We Kiss in a Shadow") that accompany the romantic subplot: the troubled affair between Tuptim and her lover, Lun Tha, that allowed Richard Rodgers to spin out dreamy waltzes.

So love is very much in the air at the palace, but not sex, certainly not in the air that surrounds the adversarial principals. Anna Leonowens's wise, womanly counsel to the couple, "Hello, Young Lovers," is a longing reverie about lost love (her dead husband, Tom) and fading youth (her own). The show's leads—Anna and the King—never acknowledge their begrudging affection for each other (much like Henry Higgins and Eliza Doolittle) until deep in the second act, near the end of the show, when they suddenly find themselves, yes, dancing, of all things—if not quite in each other's arms, at stiff arm's length, much as they've related to each other throughout the show.

Suddenly, seemingly out of nowhere, with little motivation, the orchestra has struck up a polka (not exactly your classic Asian tempo or usual romantic music) so that Anna can teach the King of Siam how Westerners dance, part of her ongoing campaign to civilize him—or at least Anglicize him.

It's also Oscar Hammerstein's subtle way of suggesting a sexual connection that neither partner is aware of but that we in the audience have suspected—and are itching to see heat up. Anna is a warm single woman, alone, and the King is a royal stud (up to his stiff neck in wives)—so why wouldn't they desire each other? What's one more conquest to this virile emperor?—it is indeed good to be the king. There is no onstage romance, and yet there is—it hovers over the show until it finally, satisfyingly, detonates in **"Shall We Dance?,"** the show's most joyous, sunniest, spiciest, show-stopping moment. William Zinsser, in his book on great pop songs, goes so far as to call it "the most electrifying moment in all of Rodgers and Hammerstein musicals." Certainly near the top. Who, other than Lawrence Welk, would guess that a bounding polka could engender such sensuous feeling? But it's more than just a dance; it's a number that pushes the plot, and the lead characters, forward—right into each other's arms, before they quite realize it. A polka is totally unexpected coming from Richard Rodgers, the Broadway waltz king. But as musical historian Thomas S. Hischak notes, "The unconventional pair needed an unconventional way to have their big number."

This surprising song and dance gently links the couple—the only moment in the show when the leads actually touch and communicate as man and woman. It subtly hints, lyrically, at what is lurking in their hearts, a vague buried feeling that they could never speak—mainly because they're not aware of their feelings, but we are. Fred Astaire famously courted Ginger Rogers in dance, where it's expected, but in the royal palace a rousing song and dance comes out of the blue. It's the only real dance in the show unless you count "March of the Siamese Children" and the whimsical but long-winded Jerome Robbins comic ballet, "The Small House of Uncle Thomas."

Maybe we're reading too much feeling into this mismatched pair and into the number, but I don't think so. It's there for a major theatrical reason—to let the King and Anna finally connect, however indirectly and accidentally—because, of course, the King is about to die in the next few minutes. That makes their dance even more moving today, because, unlike audiences in 1951, we've likely seen the show or film and are aware he's doomed. We want their relationship to be, if not consummated, hinted at obliquely, and "Shall We Dance?" is just that musical aphrodisiac.

Ostensibly, "Shall We Dance?" is just a song about dancing, but like so many great songs about dancing ("Dancing on the Ceiling," "I Won't Dance," "Cheek to Cheek," "Change Partners," "Dancing in the Dark"), "Shall We Dance?" is all about coupling. It's suggested in the lyrics and by the physicality of the leads, finally in sync despite their harsh exchanges and criticisms of each other's ways and worlds. That's what makes the number so irresistible and it's what stops the show, striking the erotic spark that we've been patiently longing to see all night between, in the original production, Gertrude Lawrence and (then and forevermore) Yul Brynner. It warms him up for us.

Ted Chapin, head of the Rodgers and Hammerstein Organization, comments: "It's a polka, which is not a sexy dance, but one of the sexiest moments in musical theater is when the king puts his hand on her waist. The more we see going on between them before we realize where it is heading, the better. In Rodgers and Hammerstein there is some sexual underpinning to every one of their shows." Stephen Sondheim says that when he met Rodgers, he told him he was impressed that the second section of "Shall We Dance?" "was a melodic inversion of the first section." Rodgers gave him a blank look. Sondheim said he might have been speaking Eskimo to Rodgers, who just wrote intuitively and didn't intellectually deconstruct songs as Sondheim does.

Dancing is a tried and true theatrical metaphor, a kind of vertical foreplay, often used in shows (and movies) to suggest an unacknowledged longing. "I Could Have Danced All Night" from *My Fair Lady* ends in a similar covert, proper musical climax, as Eliza whirls through the room before collapsing in a big easy chair, exhausted, in a kind of postcoital pant. There's even a

In *The King and I*, Yul Brynner and Gertrude Lawrence
kick up their heels in "Shall We Dance?"

similarity between Anna and the King and the strained relationship between Eliza and Higgins—two adversarial pairs who find themselves drawn to each other against their will, one of comedy's most reliable ploys. It's a fond, familiar, and too often lame form of theatrical forbidden love—squabbling men and women who wind up in bed (*When Harry Met Sally*, et al.). They shouldn't be eager for each other, and don't plan to be, but they are, and everyone else knows it. What could be sexier?

"Shall We Dance?" builds until it erupts into a climactic moment, bringing Anna and the King together at last, telling the eager audience that— aha!—something *is* going on here after all, or *could* go on here. The King, alas, dies before anything can be consummated, before there can even be a chaste embrace, so their exuberant polka is the only embrace they'll ever have, but it's enough for us—a teasing, playful, almost rapturous song and dance that earns its place onstage.

It stops the show in its tracks because, like most showstoppers, it's an emotional payoff that the show has been hinting at all along. Rodgers's infectious melody has our hearts whirling, but why to a polka? For one thing, a polka has more energy than a proper waltz—more punch, more athleticism, more drive, more fire. A tango would have been too obviously torrid. "Shall We Dance?" feels sedate, almost like a souped-up minuet, because of Anna's hoop skirts and refined British manner—a kind of a warp-speed waltz masquerading as a polka.

To set up the moment, Anna explains to the King, "In my country the customs are very different. It's interesting to be a young girl at a dance."

Anna begins by dancing alone, explaining to the King how Westerners relate through dance ("Western people funny," to quote an earlier song, during which she reveals her own womanliness), in effect displaying herself for him, a sly, teasing, but polite invitation that seems quaint today. A governess would never ask her boss, his royal highness, to dance. That would go against her upbringing and feminine grain, not to mention breaking every Siamese rule of behavior. A cat may look at a queen, but he best not ask her to dance. So she sings, "We've just been introduced, / I do not know you well, / But when the music started / Something drew me to your side."

As Anna begins gently spinning about the palace, the King grows interested, maybe even aroused—he has never thought of Mrs. Anna in quite this way; unlike his chosen wives, she seems unattainable to his highness. We have seen her demure, stern, even angry ("Shall I Tell You What I Think of You?"), a clear indication that she cares about him, but we've not seen Anna engaged in pure physicality. In "Shall We Dance?" she is in effect performing for the King, a quasi-come-on, even a turn-on. Unaware that he is being seduced, however innocently, the ever-curious King is intrigued by one more weird Western practice—one more "puzzlement." The King gradually gets into it, almost against his will.

As the tempo picks up, Anna senses his interest and proceeds to teach him the polka (yet another classic courtship device). Midway through the song, after seeing her with new eyes as she sings and picks up her skirt, he decides to attempt this odd Western dance and, in charmingly clunky footwork, counts out the steps, "*one*, two, three and . . . *one*, two, three, and . . . ," then stops dancing to slyly slip his arm about her. Intrigued, he tries to lead rather than follow (emperors don't follow), at first stomping out the beat with his royal macho foot on the *bum-bum-bum*s, then gradually extending his hands and clasping Anna's when they begin to dance as a couple and spin about the palace. At this point the lyric takes over and tells us that what's really going on here goes well beyond their businesslike relationship so far. The musical questions Anna asks are full of "shall"s the audience silently answers, that really answer themselves.

Hammerstein's lyric is posed as a series of queries about the nature and purpose of dancing, but really it's a soliloquy that hints—as most social dancing does—at something more intimate this all may lead to, as the lyrics indicate: love, sex, the whole damn thing. It is wonderfully romantic, and sensuous, because it's phrased in such an innocent inquisition, chastely but rich in subtext—a little like the what-if themes in "If I Loved You" and "Make Believe" ("Couldn't you? Couldn't I? Couldn't we?"). As the introductory verse observes, prior to the release, "So many men and girls / Are in each other's arms / It made me think / We might be / Sim-i-lar-ly occupied." Such a deliciously understated, almost comic, phrase—"similarly occupied."

Against Rodgers's whirling melody, Hammerstein counters with a polite lyric that concludes with Anna's promising phrase, "Shall we then say 'good-night' / And mean 'goodbye'? Or perchance, / When the last little star has left the sky, / Shall we still be together / With our arms around each other, / And shall you be my new romance?" All of those repeated, ever-so-coy "shall"s cloak the daring nature of her proposal, before she plunges ahead and comes right out with it at the song's end: "On the clear understanding / That this kind of thing can happen, / Shall we dance? / Shall we dance? / Shall we dance?" We shall indeed. The presumably still respectable Anna is making a thinly veiled proposition—hey, your highness, let's see if "this kind of thing can happen" (Edwardian-speak for "Shall we perhaps consider getting it on?"). The idea of dancing with such a mighty, tyrannical king also seems to liberate, even excite the dignified Mrs. Anna.

The audience has been awaiting the moment all night, and here it is, disguised by Anna's discreet language that says so much without saying it. The push me–pull you power of Hammerstein's lyric is how it suggests a longing, a desire for something romantic to happen between Anna and the King in a plot and a place that makes it highly unlikely. So—again as in the last scene of *My Fair Lady*—the audience senses a romantic/sexual attraction that is never stated, only delicately suggested. It makes for an intense song and scene, setting off the charge for a blockbuster moment when the couple swirls about the palace, finally in each other's arms as Rodgers's infectious music propels these would-be lovers and this ecstatic number into Broadway posterity.

Hammerstein's first idea was a duet in which Anna and the King compare notes on male-female relationships as they dance. In his original notes, Hammerstein writes, "Anna tries to explain the Western idea of the love of one man for one woman. It will introduce a new song which will be Anna's attempt to describe a romantic love totally foreign to the King's idea of relations between man and woman. In his part of the song his logical arguments against sentimental monogamy must be difficult for Anna to answer. She can only fall back on the fact that in the Western world, this thing which seems so foolish and impossible to him is happening every hour of the day every day, and a man and a girl are falling in love, believing that they are the only people in the world for each other. At the end of the song, in which he does not admit that he is convinced to any degree, it is apparent that he has found her very attractive and somehow can feel this illogical impulse himself, however vaguely."

• • • • • • • • • • • • • • BACKSTAGE DISH • • • • • • • • • • • • • • •

+ Sandy Kennedy, who played Anna's son in the original production, reports that Gertrude Lawrence and Brynner got along "very, very well. During the overture every night, he would come backstage and give her hugs that made you think he had a lot more on his mind. But that was the kind of guy he was." When Brynner hugged Lawrence, recalls Kennedy, she would whisper, "Yul, the boy's here," and he would say, "Well, the boy's got to see it sometime." Kennedy comments, "They were playing around, but . . . whether there was any honest-to-God fire between them I honestly don't know. I was too young to care." Of Lawrence, he remembers, "To me, onstage, I now know, as an adult, how supportive she was of me." In their opening song, "I Whistle a Happy Tune," he felt, "We were really equal in that scene, which is why the scene worked. She made me feel like a real person, not like a little child in the presence of an adult who was a star. . . . She wasn't brassy or clever or cute. She was a very mature, solid, lovely woman."

+ When the show opened a run in Indianapolis with Constance Towers as Anna, Brynner had such severe laryngitis that his son Rock, whose voice had a similar timbre, read the lines from the orchestra pit as Brynner acted the part onstage, posing and strutting. Towers recalled, "He had such incredible presence that it didn't matter whether he could speak or not. The audience just wanted to see him." She added, "He created an atmosphere where we weren't competing and he wasn't threatened by me." Breaking a cardinal theatrical rule, Brynner would constantly give Towers performance notes, but she didn't object. He became the onstage director, attending to details of every production.

✦ Another Mrs. Anna, Patricia Marand, said, "He really thought he was the King, offstage and on, and once you understood that, your life was a little bit easier." He always insisted his dressing room be repainted brown, but still another Anna, Mary Beth Peil, recalled, "This man was spending ten months of the year on the road! The theater was virtually his home, and the only way he could create any kind of stable ground was if he painted the walls of those drecky dressing rooms a warm chocolate brown color he found soothing." When *Variety* printed a list of his demands, he just laughed. Brynner wanted everything in the dressing room the same color—brown walls, brown ceiling, brown carpet, two brown sofas, two brown chairs, brown telephone. Carol Channing joked that after he put on his brown makeup you couldn't find him in his own dressing room. Peil had heard rumors that his leading ladies were never to look him in the eye onstage, but it didn't apply to her. "Yet a lot of people were afraid of him."

Actor Russ Thacker, on tour with him in the show, said, "There were a lot of bad stories about his temperament, but I saw none of that. When I first met him, I was sort of crunched down, trying to make myself shorter. When he asked me why I was standing all scrunched up, and I told him it was because he was so short, he really loved that." Thacker recalls that Brynner would invite him to visit while he got made up. "He loved to have people watch him make up. It was like a Kabuki sort of thing, a whole ritual with him." He once gave Thacker $1,000 when he was not working and said, "Just keep it. Spend it." Thacker says Brynner did a lot of charity work he didn't want publicized because he felt it might ruin his imperial image.

✦ The movie version, with Brynner and Deborah Kerr, filmed but never used three numbers from the stage show—"I Have Dreamed" and "My Lord and Master," for failing to advance the plot, and the sharp-tongued "Shall I Tell You What I Think of You?," where Anna tells off the spoiled emperor.

✦ Patricia Morison, who made a splash as the original and highly kissable Kate in *Kiss Me, Kate*, followed up that milestone production by playing Anna for two years opposite Brynner. Morison was the last Anna in the original Broadway run and toured in the show with him for a year. Brynner treated his leading ladies, she quickly discovered, like one of his wives in *The King and I*, expecting to make a conquest of each of them, one by one.

Morison, ninety-eight when we spoke, recalls, "Before I went into *The King and I*, I heard that they asked him, 'What would you think of having Patricia Morison in it?' He said, 'I don't know, I haven't bedded her yet.' In my mind, that was not going to happen. He finally showed up on the last day of my rehearsal, and he said, 'Miss Morison would you stop by my dressing room on your way out? We have to know each other before we start working together on Monday.' I knocked on the door, and he was sitting in front of the mirror completely nude. I said, 'You wish to see me, Mr. Brynner?'" He fed her some line about a need to stay in touch with his body before each performance, but Morison was not interested in staying in touch. "I had made up my mind I was not going to go out with him or anything."

Publicist Josh Ellis's response to Morison's bedtime story: "I can see him telling her that as a total joke. That was his sense of humor. It doesn't surprise me. And if you took it seriously when he was intending it as a joke, he would enjoy it all the more." The stars' cat-and-mouse relationship very much mirrored what was happening onstage. The pair of self-possessed actors had authentic onstage electricity, says Morison. "The two of us had such great rapport, it came across. The great Gertrude Lawrence played the original Anna, and she was lovely. But everybody said we were the most exciting combination."

Brynner didn't give up easily and kept trying to seduce Morison, to no avail, she says. "And then we became very good professional friends. No matter the time and performance, the minute he hit the stage, no matter what condition he was in—if he had been out all night sometimes, or water-skiing all day—he had this tremendous energy and it affected the entire cast." Josh Ellis, who became a friend of Brynner's, comments, "His magnetism was the same whether he was doing the show in a 2,000-seat theater or having a meal with you."

Morison says, "Yul was a naughty boy, and all the ladies in the show crowded around his dressing room door all the time. He was busy in that respect. All the girls were happy. Every time we hit the stage together that kind of spark was there. It was exciting. He had a lot of charisma." One of his assistants, Charlotte Paley, said, "There's an awful lot of animal in this man. He walks like a panther. He can say hello in the most romantic way. It knocks you out." Much of Brynner's appeal was his mysterious, supposedly exotic past: Mongolian? Siberian? Swiss? Was his mother a Romanian gypsy? Nobody ever knew for sure where he came from—he may have grown up in Wichita, Kansas—but he was born (so he said) Yuliy Borisovich Briner.

• •

WONDERFUL TOWN

✦ 1953 ✦

"Ohio"

One reason that **"Ohio,"** a wistful comic duet from *Wonderful Town* sung by two sisters who come to New York from the Midwest, is so tender is that it's one of only two quiet moments in an otherwise jokey score. The Bernstein–Comden and Green classic is one of those musicals that exists a bit better in memory than in viewing—a succession of comic songs, slapped together in six weeks, most of which have a slightly contrived sound. They're still fun, but they don't pull you into the plot like "Ohio" does. It's the song that grabs you and tells you, *You're gonna love this show.*

"Ohio" wasn't a hit. It is very much a theater song whose appeal is linked to character and plot, but it may be the most fondly recalled number in the show. "Ohio" is a great musical theater song—a heart-tugging moment in its quiet way, an antishowstopper in a show overloaded with flashy numbers that dazzle but don't grab us, as "Ohio" does without breaking a sweat. The only problem with *Wonderful Town* is that it needs a couple more "Ohio"s—songs that explain the characters' plight.

"Ohio" is decidedly different. It doesn't want to knock you out like "Conga!," "One Hundred Easy Ways," and "What a Waste," clever revue-style numbers that appeal to the head, not the heart. "Ohio" dares to look inward ("Why oh why, oh why-o / Why did we ever leave Ohio?"), a ballad that's not even a love song, just a plaintive wish by the sisters to go home after a few weeks in scary, crazy-making New York City.

The sisters, sexy Eileen and smarty-pants Ruth, played by Edie (billed then as Edith) Adams and Rosalind Russell, who have come to New York to pursue acting and writing careers, sit on their street-level bed and—after a series of explosions from subway construction below their cheap ground-level Greenwich Village apartment—pour out their worried homesick hearts, wondering if maybe they should have stayed "back home in O-H-I-O." Suddenly we see them stripped of their big-city Manhattan ambition, fake bravado, and would-be sophis-

Edie Adams and Rosalind Russell console each other as they pine for "Ohio" in *Wonderful Town*.

tication as they come face-to-face with their real midwestern selves: "Why did I wander / To find what lies yonder / When life was so cozy at home? / Wond'ring while I wander / Why did I fly? / Why did I roam? / Oh, why oh, why oh / Did I leave Ohio? / Maybe I'd better go / O-h-i-o / Maybe I'd better go home."

It's a deceptively simple song—the least gimmicky number in the show—but it never fails to please because it creates a true nostalgic moment that anyone has felt who ever left home and journeyed to Manhattan, only to have grave second thoughts after months of getting nowhere, being ignored, and trying to cope with a noisy indifferent city.

What adds to the song's strength is that, between the longing sentiments, Ruth and Eileen argue with their own nostalgia, recalling the reality of life in Ohio in an unrhymed narrative duet: "Now, listen, Eileen, Ohio was stifling. We just couldn't wait to get out of the place, with mom saying, 'Ruth, what no date for this evening?'" Eileen: "And pop with, 'Eileen, do be home, dear, by ten.'" Together: "Ugh!" Ruth: "The gossipy neighbors, and everyone yapping who's going with whom." Eileen: "And dating those drips that I've known since I'm four."

The other songs are spirited and amusing as you're watching them, but they don't get to you as "Ohio" does, don't make you take the sisters to heart, or take them seriously. After that endearing little duet, we're drawn to Ruth and Eileen and on their side, rooting for them to stick it out. They're afraid they've made a horrible mistake and want to flee to safe familiar ground back in Columbus. Bernstein's gently nostalgic tune matches Betty Comden and Adolph Green's homey lyric.

Bernstein's mooning melody is a lazy lullaby reminiscent of Irving Berlin's "Moonshine Lullaby" in *Annie Get Your Gun*. Together with Comden and Green's heartfelt lyrics, it creates a dramatic moment, a needed lull in the otherwise '50s jazzy Bernstein score ("Wrong Note Rag," "Christopher Street"). The fact that it's a duet doubles its appeal. You want to hug the sisters and tell them everything is gonna be OK. We easily identify with their worried mood.

"Ohio" is the song I hear whenever I think of *Wonderful Town*, a wonderful tune that doesn't stop the show so much as pull us into it. It's the show's second song, but from then on you're involved and care what happens to the sisters. You want them to succeed; you *don't* want them to go back to Ohio, defeated. After "Ohio," there is something at stake in the show, much of whose success, I suspect, stems from this one little tossed-off duet.

———

Wonderful Town put Edie Adams on Broadway, though she was already known to TV viewers as a sexy foil to her husband Ernie Kovacs on his surreal comedy shows.

"Ohio" was composed conversationally by Leonard Bernstein to take advantage of star Rosalind Russell's thin, narrow singing voice, so shaky that Russell almost turned down the role. She had never been in a musical and knew nothing about singing, as she admits in her post–*Auntie Mame* memoir, *Life Is a Banquet*. While Bernstein, Comden, and Green sat around discussing songs, she writes, "I listened, bug-eyed." Bernstein asked her to sing for him "as soon as the others leave." When everyone began leaving, she tore down four flights of stairs to escape Bernstein, thinking, *I cannot let him hear this voice.* Finally, after a week, he trapped her and said, "Roz, I have to hear your range." She didn't realize she had a range, she recalls, other than the one in her kitchen.

Bernstein sat down at the piano and began to sing, "Why, oh why, oh why-o / Why did I ever leave Ohio?" "I'm so nervous," she told him, but tried to imitate him. He was satisfied. "Lovely. Now we'll just change the key." She told him she'd learn it by tomorrow, but Bernstein told her, "Oh, you don't sing the melody. You sing the harmony." She had no idea what he was talking about. "The *harmony*? I'll never learn the melody, much less the harmony. The harmony is what you make up as you go along, isn't it?"

That night, the musically clueless Russell consulted a friend, director Josh Logan, who advised her, "If you can't sing, whisper. Listen to Walter Huston sing 'September Song.' He whispers it." Logan then realized that wouldn't work for her and told Russell to concentrate on the words. "People won't pay so much attention to the music if there are lots of words." She learned to harmonize the song well enough to get through it, but Adams suggested Russell see a vocal coach to help get rid of her raspy voice on the low notes—"a lighthouse calling to its young," Adams called it, imitating Russell's deep sardonic voice.

"Whenever we would start to sing 'Ohio,' she couldn't find the first note," Adams told me in her home. So at every performance, when they began their duet, Adams would softly hum the first note of "why," making like a pitch pipe to let Russell know where to begin the song. When Adams had a cold, Russell was afraid her costar might miss a performance and, in a panic, sent over her driver with cough medicine. Adams, on the other hand, was a Juilliard-trained coloratura, which got Bernstein's respect ("He thought I could do anything"); he even wanted to cast her in *Candide*, his next show.

Russell was totally dependent on Adams to give her that crucial opening note, her first note in the show. Adams: "Here she was, a big star from Hollywood, and I was in my first show." The challenge was to keep her on key, but Russell managed to stay in sync throughout the run, thanks to Adams. Even during songs that didn't involve Adams, Russell wanted her costar around during rehearsals of other songs, to alert her when she began swerving off-key. "Roz couldn't have been sweeter to me," recalled Adams, "but I was more impressed by the authors"—Bernstein, Comden, and Green, who had been brought in only five weeks before rehearsals to replace Leroy Anderson and Arnold Horwitt. It was a chaotic month—much shouting, tension, and uncertainty—but somehow Comden and Green wrote a score in a pressure-filled few weeks, which may account for the show's slapdash revue feeling. Jerome Robbins was also brought in to give choreographer Donald Saddler an uncredited hand.

George Abbott, who directed the show, recalled in his memoir, "There was more hysterical debate, more acrimony, more tension and more screaming connected with this play than with any other show I was ever involved with." He'd been involved in a few. Not even the rave reviews patched things up. Abbott writes, "Sometimes a success will make all problems disappear, all differences evaporate, but in this case the antagonism between the writers of the book and all the rest of us continued. They were in the enemy camp and they never fraternized with us."

Even though Adams was a recent Juilliard graduate, or perhaps because of it, she was a little full of herself at twenty-one. Indeed, when she had earlier auditioned for Richard Rodgers for the road company of *Carousel*, she turned him down when he offered her a chance to understudy the female lead. "I didn't want to be an understudy. I was very snippy."

When she tried out for Eileen, and was given a curt "Thank you," she went home "furious" at being so quickly dismissed. "I was on TV every day [with Kovacs]. I felt I had more musical knowledge than a lot of these Broadway people!" But after she got home, the phone rang, and stage manager Hal Prince said, "Where were you? You got the part." She had no hint that she had even made callbacks.

When the TV version was cast, suddenly Russell didn't want Adams in the cast, despite all she had done to help the star vocally during the Broadway run—most likely because of Adams's youthful glow, voice, and shape (famous from her sultry Muriel Cigars commercial: "Come up and *smoke* me sometime"). After not being cast in the TV version, Adams didn't speak to Russell for ten years. She was replaced by an unknown, Jacquelyn McKeever—"who was never heard from again," said Adams, still seething a little. "It was very hurtful."

Adams's theory is that Russell worried the young singer, who came out of TV, might upstage her on camera and make her look old. "I'm a team player. I wouldn't do that, but she wouldn't hear of it. There was just something about her. She didn't know the role for TV, she knew it for theater, and it scared her. I knew TV better than she did. I could've *helped* her performance. I knew how TV worked. She was doing a [shouts] FULL-OUT BROADWAY PERFORMANCE on a tiny TV screen."

After Adams got raves in *Wonderful Town*, she said, Bernstein begged her to star in *Candide*, but she had also been offered the role of Daisy Mae in *Li'l Abner*. Undecided, she again consulted George Abbott, the Broadway sage. The pragmatic, ever-commercial Abbott advised her to take *Li'l Abner* over *Candide*, advising her, "*Candide* will have a short run on Broadway and then go to a few colleges and small opera companies." As Daisy Mae, he said, "You'll be in a short skirt, you've got good legs, you're very attractive. You need a sexy role." She took it—"I needed the money" ($1,000 a week)—and, indeed, *Li'l Abner* ran 693 performances to *Candide*'s seventy-three. Someone named Barbara Cook got the Cunegonde part in *Candide*. Cook did pretty well, too.

DAMN YANKEES

◆ 1955 ◆

"Whatever Lola Wants," "Heart"

The va-va-voom number that Gwen Verdon vamped to stardom, **"Whatever Lola Wants,"** is one of several take-home songs in *Damn Yankees*, in which an aging and anguished Washington Senators fan, Joe Boyd, sells his soul to the devil in order to be transformed into a young slugger named Joe Hardy to help his losing Senators whip the indomitable and damnable New York Yankees. *Playbill* writer Harry Haun once described the show as "Who's on Faust?"

As Lola, the devil's plaything employed to entice the hero from his happy home (Boyd's wife's friend was Jean Stapleton), the redheaded Verdon purposely overdid her sexpot seductress, making Lola not just flaming but funny, a mocking temptress. "Whatever Lola Wants" is Lola's comic declaration of seduction, in which she announces that anything Lola desires, Lola never fails to achieve—total female domination. A YouTube clip from the movie reveals Verdon in full come-hither regalia, peeling off a black mesh body stocking and flouncing about the locker room before a stunned, mute, immobile Tab Hunter.

 By the time the show opened in 1955, she was highly experienced at stopping shows after her second Broadway musical, *Can-Can*, in which, cast as the snake in a Garden of Eden ballet, she snaked her wicked way into audience's hearts. John Chapman fell hard, writing in the *New York Daily News*, "Miss Verdon is entirely, absolutely, utterly and simply bewitching."

Damn Yankees is the only musical about baseball ever to become a hit, yet it's rarely revived. Two others, *Diamonds* and *The First* (about Jackie Robinson), never got to first base, but *Damn Yankees*—score by composers and lyricists Richard Adler and Jerry Ross (each wrote music and lyrics)—hit a grand slam with four hit songs. The score captures the essence of the game, as did the Douglass Wallop novel it's based on, *The Year the Yankees Lost the Pennant*, with a savvy inside-baseball sensibility. Two numbers made the Hit Parade—"Heart" and "Whatever Lola Wants," plus a semistandard ("Two Lost Souls"), a rousing two-bagger ("Shoeless Joe from Hannibal, Mo."), and a Bob Fosse custom-built Verdon tour de force, "Who's Got the Pain?," a mambo out of left field about the agonies of dancing. Without Verdon it's unlikely the show would have run nearly as long as it did.

"Lola" isn't that punchy a number out of context, but Verdon turned the little twelve-line song into a showstopper with her slinky trademark style, in a see-through leotard, choreographed by future husband Bob Fosse. It's typical Fosse, all hips, dips, and fingertips. Director Greg MacKellan notes, "It's interesting that the song became such a big hit because it's so specific to that show."

Verdon had a much more clever, interesting, and amusing number about herself in the show, "A Little Brains—A Little Talent," in which Lola admits she may not be too bright but that her major power

In *Damn Yankees*, Gwen Verdon's mesh-covered devilitrix reveals her MO in "Whatever Lola Wants."

lies south of her brain. "Lola" is really a one-note hoochy-koochy star turn meant to inveigle the square hero, and the audience, but "A Little Brains—A Little Talent" has witty meat on its bones that makes Lola not just sexy but cute—and literate. Verdon sang it in a baby-talk voice that made it even sexier. This is exactly the sort of bright number that separates show tunes from pop songs. In the song, Lola confesses she may not be too bright but her major power lies south of her brain.

"Heart" of course is the heart of the *Damn Yankees* order—a cheery 11 o'clock number sung by the hapless, hearty, and close-harmonizing Washington Senators, who couldn't play ball terribly well but led the league in singing and dancing. Eddie Fisher turned it into a huge hit even outside the ballpark. The number is just an all-out gleeful shout of resolve (most people can still quote the lyrics). It's not a great lyric—about how you need to defeat losing odds, pick yourself up off the floor, smile, have hope, and just wait till next year—but the melody sells it and the singers look and sound like rough-hewn ballplayers.

My vote for the show's most valuable player (next-to-last baseball metaphor) goes to Ray Walston, as Satan in a business suit in both the original show and movie, singing "Those Were the Good Old Days," a soft-shoe tribute to the bloodiest events in human history. Walston performs it as Lola's boss, a devil-may-care charmer named Applegate. Decked out in red tails, red socks, and cane, Walston sang Adler's lyrics in a pure devilish deadpan, telling us how much he longs for the golden days of the rack, the plague, scalping, and the guillotine. Jerry Lewis later played Applegate on Broadway and on tour and did a credible job despite hamming it up with Lewis shtick.

Generally it's just a gleeful show that deserves to be more revived, as Bebe Neuwirth pointed out when she played Lola in a 1994 Broadway revival: "*Damn Yankees* does something to an audience I've never seen before," she told *Playbill*. "*A Chorus Line* you could feel them moved by, *Sweet Charity* you could feel them delighted by—but I've never seen or felt an audience get as purely happy as they do with this show. You sense them falling in love with the ballplayers, then getting happy—and staying happy—through the whole show." *Damn Yankees* isn't a top-tier musical, but it's near the top of the next tier, the sort of workmanlike musical that sustained Broadway for decades, without any need to overwhelm everyone. As John Chapman wrote, "The show makes no claims to art but it is a fine amount of fun"—that is, solid enough for playoff contention if not quite a World Series trophy.

MY FAIR LADY

◆ 1956 ◆

"The Rain in Spain," "Get Me to the Church on Time"

In a musical wallowing in showstoppers, **"The Rain in Spain"** is by no means the greatest or cleverest song in *My Fair Lady*. Yet it causes the biggest onstage ruckus, the purest glee, when it arrives in the show—maybe because it comes out of nowhere and reveals that Henry Higgins and his prize pupil have finally triumphed: ex-guttersnipe Eliza Doolittle at last is able to speak proper English; her makeover is complete; Higgins has won his little bet; and Eliza is at last a fair lady.

Nearly all of the other songs in the score are pretty much of a piece—brilliant and British, like "Why Can't a Woman (Be More Like a Man)?" It's startling to read that *Variety*, supposedly the hardest-nosed of showbiz journals, wrote in its review, "Despite the gaiety and infectiousness of the Lerner and

Loewe score, there isn't a real audience-stampeding song in the show." Only four or five.

"The Rain in Spain" overcomes the show's general decorum and allows the pompous linguistics teacher to explode with delirium for the first and only time in the show. Higgins has finally produced an intelligible Englishwoman from "a squashed cabbage leaf" of a Cockney flower girl, coming closer to winning his bet with Colonel Pickering that he can pass Eliza off in society as an authentic lady—the wager that sets the plot in motion.

When Eliza finally sheds her squalling accent and learns to enunciate correctly after weeks of laborious tutoring, the cynical elocution scholar and his Watson-like associate, Pickering, go slightly berserk and celebrate the moment with a tango in the professor's study. In the original Shaw play, *Pygmalion*, there is only a brief instruction scene, but we never see the technique by which Higgins actually transforms Eliza—*how* he teaches her to speak well. We're asked to take it all on faith.

Librettist and lyricist Alan Jay Lerner expanded the scene into what becomes the most dramatically joyous musical moment in the show, and effectively stops it. Lerner neatly tops Shaw. The famous catchy "rain in Spain" phrase isn't actually from Shaw, or even from Lerner, but from the screenplay of the 1938 film with Leslie Howard and Wendy Hiller. The film's producer, Gabriel Pascal, according to his wife's biography, introduced the phonetic exercises in "The Rain in Spain" into *Pygmalion* and in fact made up the line "The rain in Spain stays mainly in the plain" that Shaw wrote into the film script. (Meteorological note: a Wikipedia climate authority maintains that

the rain in Spain does *not* fall in the plain at all but, rather, falls mainly in the Northern Mountains.)

Up until that point in the story, it has begun to seem that Higgins will be defeated, but through Eliza's perseverance, goaded by her bombastic mentor's ridicule, the girl has broken through her social level to show (as Shaw insists) that anybody can

In *My Fair Lady*, **Rex Harrison and Robert Coote do a meteorological tango to "The Rain in Spain" as said fair lady, Julie Andrews, urges them on.**

become an instant aristocrat with a few diction lessons. It's a great victory for Eliza, for Higgins, for English, and for democracy. She and Shaw shatter British society's class ceiling.

Higgins tries to badger Eliza into speaking correctly, even forcing her to blow out a candle to learn how to enunciate her *H*'s (the Spanish rain that falls equally in "Hartford, Hereford and Hampshire, [where] hurricanes hardly ever happen"). In the background, like a Greek chorus, with clocklike ticking sounds played on a xylophone, the servants chant, "Poor Professor Higgins! / Night and day / He slaves away . . . up and down until he's numb . . . on he plods / Against all odds," as blackouts indicate time passing with seemingly no progress at all. Eliza finally pleads with Higgins to stop—"I can't [go on]. I'm so tired! I'm so tired."

The hardheaded Higgins relents and tries a whole new tack—empathy, handing Eliza an ice pack for her pounding brain and giving her a gentle pep talk: "Eliza, I know you're tired. I know your head aches. I know your nerves are raw as meat in a butcher's window. But think what you're trying to accomplish. Think what you're dealing with. The majesty and grandeur of the English language. It's the greatest possession we have. The noblest sentiments that ever flowed in the hearts of men are contained in its extraordinary, imaginative and musical mixtures of sounds. That's what you've set yourself to conquer, Eliza. And conquer it you will. Now, try it again."

So she gives it one last sporting try and finally gets it right. "What was that?" he asks her, and she repeats the line properly and deliberately—"The rain in Spain stays mainly in the plain." Then he tests her again: "And where's that soggy plain?" "In Spain, in Spain." Higgins then bursts into Frederick Loewe's unlikely tango (a habanera, actually), a celebratory dance that finds the bookish, buttoned-up Higgins and Pickering, a pair of stuffy old phonetics experts, miming a bullfight as they dance their pointy heads off in the library, deliriously drunk with victory. The applause after the first preview performance, said Lerner, "exploded like nuclear fission." Director Moss Hart's assistant Biff Liff recalled, "They finished the song and the audience went wild. There were Robert Coote [as Pickering] and Rex Harrison, experienced professionals, and they didn't quite know what to do." Liff says Julie Andrews (who played Eliza in the original production) grabbed their hands and made them take a bow to stop the applause. "So it was Julie who then became the really big professional."

The little ditty was written in about ten minutes ("It happened so spontaneously and easily we were suspicious of it," notes Lerner in his memoir) and is totally out of character, both in the score and for Higgins and Pickering, playing a bull and a matador. It's a zany musical surprise that delights the audience, a pure theatrical moment by Lerner that turns *Pygmalion* from a witty play with music into a full-blooded musical. The song not only stops the show but is also the number on which the plot smartly turns. One theater historian calls it the song "that defined *My Fair Lady*'s individual brilliance." The *New Yorker*'s tough critic Wolcott Gibbs pronounced the scene "the most brilliantly successful" scene he had ever witnessed in a musical. "It has practically everything—charm, style, wit, gaiety—and I will cherish it as long as I live."

A tango could not be more out of place in a setting of such utter sobriety, Higgins's dark study, with its elocution charts and vocal diagrams (like the "Moses Supposes" set in *Singin' in the Rain*), but the number works precisely because of that, much as "Marian the Librarian" delights us in *The Music Man* because it occurs in a small-town library, amid NO TALKING signs and a stern hush-hush atmosphere. A tango breaking out in *My Fair Lady* is as likely as a hoedown in *The Phantom of the Opera*.

It couldn't be a simpler lyric—a child's rhyme, really—that Lerner created without leaning on Shaw. Many of Lerner's lines and lyrics in the show are either lifted or directly influenced by words or phrases from *Pygmalion*, but the elocution fandango was all Lerner and Loewe, a number that reveals Higgins in a rare unguarded moment of exuberance. It's quickly followed by "I Could Have Danced All Night," Eliza's own giddy reaction to her linguistic glory that she has been rudely excluded from in Higgins and Pickering's private "Rain in Spain" celebration. "You did it!" they later exclaim in song as Eliza seethes, knowing that *she* is the one who did it.

Director Greg MacKellan notes that "The Rain in Spain" "will never work as well as it worked in the first few months of the show's run, when it was still a surprise." "The song makes a plot point and there was suspense in it," he notes. "The way they built the tension—she's just not getting it—'the rine in Spine.' There was such tension if you didn't know the plot: is she ever really going to get this? It became this delightful moment when they're dancing around singing this silly song. But that no longer exists for an audience today." Yet for young *My Fair Lady* first-timers, the moment still casts an ageless spell.

The show-stopping song also gave rise to the show's most quoted line, "By George, she's got it!" It's hardly a brilliant epigram in a script brimming over with witty lines, but the phrase has ever since been quoted in every possible circumstance by people who may not even know where it originated—the ultimate expression of triumph for a sudden eureka! moment. Of course, we know all along that Eliza *will* get it—not just because we've seen the show or film but because we've seen Cinderella and Snow White and hundreds of similar makeover jobs in plays and movies. Even so, we share Higgins's merry triumphal moment, his astonishing achievement.

When all is said and sung, *My Fair Lady* is the classic tale of a bedraggled nobody who cleans up real nice and becomes—lo!—a somebody. In this case, of course, she gets a linguistic as well as a literal scrubbing. When Eliza finally sheds her dingy Cockney rags to don Higgins's aristocratic verbal finery, we bask in Eliza's transformation, in the tattered but dogged girl's hard-won victory over not just the English language but also Shavian male chauvinism and class snobbery. By George, she has got it, and, from that moment on, the show has got *us* for good.

"Get Me to the Church on Time" sounds like an authentic old-fashioned English music hall favorite, as does "With a Little Bit of Luck," two of the show's sunniest moments. It's a classic blow-'em-out-of-their-seats 11 o'clock number, bracingly sung in the original (and on screen) by Stanley Holloway. You can't imagine anyone but Holloway, as Eliza's scruffy, aptly named father Alfred Doolittle, performing it. After Holloway's career of playing similar rowdy roles, "Get Me to the Church on Time" became his ultimate glory.

It's the song people tend to leave the show humming: "I'm getting married in the morning, / Ding dong, the bells are gonna chime, / Pull out the stopper, we'll have a whopper! / But get me to the church on time . . . Kick up a rumpus, But don't lose the compass, / And get me to the church, get me to the church, / For Gawd's sake, get me to the church on time!" It's an irrepressible song that gives the show a second-act lift and proves that even a rebel who has avoided marriage can be happily corrupted overnight by a change in his social status.

Other songs in the score are cleverer and more crucial to the plot, but none is more exhilarating and just plain singable than this showstopper. The lyric doesn't say anything of interest (the title says it all), and the song might easily be dispensed with unnoticed, but the show *needs* a number like this, as well as Holloway's other jolly declaration, "With a Little Bit of Luck." The musical's one-two punch elevates the audience's spirit and gives them two big fat giddy songs that are nothing but pure pleasure, especially performed by a powerhouse charmer like Stanley Holloway.

·············· BACKSTAGE DISH ··············

+ A musical based on *Pygmalion* had flummoxed Rodgers and Hammerstein, who after a year couldn't figure out how to make it work as a show, a play with music, a whatever. "It can't be done," Hammerstein proclaimed. Cole Porter, Howard Dietz and Arthur Schwartz, and E. Y. Harburg all said no to musicalizing the play, feeling Shaw's classic was too perfect to tamper with; none of the songwriters felt it was quite their cup of Earl Grey. Mary Martin, when she first heard songs from the score, was unimpressed and turned down the show, saying, "Those dear boys have lost their talent." In fairness to her, three of the five songs Martin and her husband, Richard Halliday, listened to were eventually dropped out of town, but it's hard to imagine Mary Martin as a Cockney flower girl; she was probably smart to say no, if for the wrong reasons; she also turned down, less wisely, *Annie Get Your Gun* and *Mame*. Lerner relates in his memoir that Martin's husband told him, "Alan, 'Just You Wait' is simply *stolen* from 'I Hate Men' in *Kiss Me, Kate*, and 'The Ascot Gavotte' is *simply* not funny. It's *just* not *funny* at all." His last heartfelt words to Lerner: "I'm so sorry. *Really*, Alan. We're so *sorry*." He was the last one who was.

+ Lerner conquered *Pygmalion* largely by leaving it alone, lifting much of its dialogue and reupholstering the play with unforgettable songs. He and Loewe weren't cowed by the idea of revising a masterpiece and yet, through the songs, made it very much their own work, even as it adheres tightly to Shaw's play. Most importantly, *My Fair Lady* captured, and is infused with, the master's Shavian spirit. Lerner and Loewe didn't try to conquer Shaw; they considered him a third collaborator. As Ethan Mordden puts it, "Lerner didn't make *Pygmalion* into a musical. He made a musical into *Pygmalion*."

+ *My Fair Lady* was mired in rehearsal trauma, from Rex Harrison's preopening night panic that he was going to embarrass himself singing when he had never sung onstage before, and threatened not to go on, to Julie Andrews's inability in early rehearsals to portray a Cockney flower girl. In photos of Andrews in the show, she still looks far too refined for the early Eliza, as did Audrey Hepburn in the movie version. Discreet smudges of soot prettily applied to their downy cheeks failed to turn them from proper fragile young things into convincing Covent Garden street venders, like the much more convincing Wendy Hiller in the movie of *Pygmalion*. Barely rumpled, both Andrews and Hepburn looked like extremely fair ladies even in the gutter. Jack Warner wanted Cary Grant to play Higgins in the movie, but Lerner nixed it, citing Grant's own Cockney accent, and Grant wisely turned down the offer, telling Warner that only a fool would try to follow Rex Harrison.

+ After mulling over titles for months, Lerner and Loewe halfheartedly decided to call their show *My Fair Lady*—"the least objectionable name," explained Lerner. The more objectionable titles that were rejected: "Lady Liza," "London Pride," "Promenade," "Come to the Ball," and "Fanfaron," which was Lerner's favorite; it means braggart or fanfare.

+ When Julie Andrews, fresh from rave reviews in *The Boy Friend*, playing perky Polly Browne in Sandy Wilson's sharp, bouncy parody of 1920s musicals, auditioned for *My Fair Lady*, she was told, in a burst of enthusiasm, "That was absolutely adequate." Andrews was less than adequate once rehearsals began. After three weeks, Harrison stomped out of rehearsal, shouting, "If that bitch is here on Monday, I'm quitting the show." It was the first of his many empty threats to leave the show. At one point, director Moss Hart turned to his wife, Kitty Carlisle, in a taxi and asked, "Is she as bad as I think she is?" "Worse," said Carlisle. He told her, "If I was [legendary tough director] David Belasco, I should take her away and paste the part on her." "Why don't you?" his wife suggested.

Their "weekend of terror," as Hart and Andrews later called it, occurred at the New Amsterdam Theatre at 2:00 PM on a Saturday afternoon, where Hart told her, "Julie, this is stolen time, time I can't really afford. So you mustn't take offense because there aren't any second chances in theater. There isn't time to sit down and do the whole Actors Studio bit. We have to start from the first line and go over the play, line by line." That weekend, Hart did indeed paste the part on her. Hart became her Henry Higgins, molding Andrews into Eliza, Pygmalion-like. "If Julie wavered at all," said Biff Liff, Hart's assistant, "he brought her back sharply. He certainly wasn't cruel, but there was no time for politeness." Hart told her, "You're playing this like a Girl Guide [British Girl Scout]. You're not thinking. You're just oozing out the scene. You're gabbling." By Sunday night, by Moss, she had it. Miles Kreuger, another of Lerner's assistants, recalls, "All I can tell you is that Julie Andrews had it all, way down deep somewhere, because it was like lifting the veils."

+ At the first out-of-town preview in New Haven, Harrison came down with acute cold feet after performing his songs for the first time with an orchestra, which terrified him. Lerner's wife at the time, actress Nancy Olson, recalled that Harrison "just went to pieces" and locked himself in his dressing room, refusing to do the show that night, feeling he needed more rehearsal with the orchestra. "I am not ready to do it!" he bellowed. At 6:00 PM, with people lined up in the snow outside the theater, Harrison's agent was summoned and yelled to him through the dressing room door, "Come out! You've got to do this! If you don't you'll never work again." He came out and went on.

+ During the Andrews solo "Without You," Harrison was directed to stand in place and just listen, but he informed Hart, "I am not going to simply stand onstage and make a cunt of myself while this girl sings at me." Lerner devised a line for him to respond to her—"You did it!" (echoing his earlier song), shifting the focus and placating the jittery star. Harrison confessed in his autobiography that he had been "a first-class prick" in his rehearsal shenanigans, blaming his behavior on a fear of singing. But Harrison's musical speaking voice made his lines sound almost like singing. He convinced Lerner and Loewe he could sing well enough when he sang "Molly Malone" for them. Loewe stopped him after one verse and said, "Fine. That's all you need."

Lerner wrote that Harrison sang in a tenor timbre that would carry over an orchestra and that he had a "faultless" sense of rhythm. The lyricist realized that the secret was to write lines for Harrison that could be equally sung or spoken, such as, "Let a woman in your life and your sabbatical is through." A song like "I'm an Ordinary Man" is more recited than sung, and Harrison's natural whine, and his rising and falling delivery, gave his songs a melodic lilt.

+ Instead of humiliating himself, Harrison's singspiel style of talk-singing blazed a trail for other untrained leading men singers (Richard Burton in *Camelot*, Robert Preston in *The Music Man*, Sydney Chaplin in *Funny Girl*), though a couple of other nonsingers preceded him—Sam Levene's raspy out-of-tune Nathan Detroit croaking out "Sue Me" in *Guys and Dolls* and Yul Brynner's profound recitation of self-doubt, "A Puzzlement," in *The King and I*. Harrison, Levene, and Brynner all proved that a dynamic, charming, persuasive stage presence can make up for a great singing voice. Had the studio not insisted on Marni Nixon dubbing Audrey Hepburn's songs in the film version, Hepburn could have brought it off with her small but endearingly honest if imperfect voice. It's a little odd hearing the slender fawnlike Hepburn belting songs in the film—and later on the much-awaited cast album that every home owned; the bestselling cast album, like the show's very theme, seemed to cut across social classes.

+ Harrison turned down the show initially after hearing two of the songs, one of which was "Why Can't the English?," which he later made into one of the show's high spots. He sniped, "I hate it. It makes me sound like an inferior Noël Coward." But Harrison's own waspish, fussbudget temperament was totally Higgins and helped Lerner mold the character and actor into a seamless blend. He said, "I had the feeling that in finding a style for Rex I was also finding a style for myself."

+ Despite his prickly nature, on one occasion Harrison proved himself a trouper. During a performance, chandeliers that were supposed to rise out of sight were mistakenly lowered. As a stagehand reversed the chandeliers' course, one of them snatched Harrison's toupee and it rose skyward attached to a chandelier. Biff Liff was again summoned to the theater and burst into Harrison's room to calm him down, promising that the stagehand would be fired. Harrison told Liff, "Biff, old boy, wait, it's not that serious." Lerner, in an aside foreshadowing The Phantom of the Opera, observed, "Nothing impresses an audience more or produces a more dependable, spontaneous burst of applause than to see a chandelier appearing from on high. Two chandeliers—ecstasy. Three are a collective orgasm."

+ Harrison always stuffed a copy of Pygmalion in his hip pocket and felt more secure uttering lines by Shaw than by Lerner. After a speech Harrison particularly liked, he told Lerner, "That's a damn fine speech. Where in Shaw did you find it?" Lerner boasted that he had written it himself. "From then on," Lerner writes, "he lost respect for the line and seldom got it right." After that, Lerner always reassured the actor that any passage he liked had come from Shaw's letters or essays. Harrison told the London Times before the show opened that there were only six lines in the play Shaw hadn't written.

+ Harrison, every inch as much the womanizer as Alan Jay Lerner (about a dozen marriages between them), once told Lerner when they were comparing their mutual female problems, "Alan, wouldn't it be marvelous if we were both homosexual!," which directly or indirectly led to Lerner's wry song, "A Hymn to Him," in which Higgins wonders, "Why can't a woman be more like a man?"

+ Lerner said "I Could Have Danced All Night" "was far and away the most popular song Fritz and I have ever written," but he went to his grave hating one line in it—"Why all at once my heart took flight." He writes, "I have a special loathing for lyrics in which the heart is metamorphosized and skips or leaps or jumps or 'takes flight.' I promised Fritz I would change it as soon as I could. I was never able to."

✦ At the end of the play *Pygmalion*, Higgins asks Eliza to do some errands for him, but she appears to ignore him, dons her coat, and walks out of the house, leaving us to wonder if, like Nora in *A Doll's House*, she is gone for good. Shaw felt she had her independence so she didn't need Higgins. Shaw wants us to wonder if Eliza will be back but strongly resisted tying up Henry and Eliza's relationship into a pretty romantic pink bow, which is how *My Fair Lady* concludes. Lerner's script tries to have it both ways, with Higgins slouched contentedly in his chair listening to a recording of Eliza's voice (overlaid with her live voice offstage), as he asks peevishly but with husbandly intimacy and a smug, satisfied smile, "Eliza? Where the devil are my slippers?"

Lerner reveals that Mrs. Patrick Campbell, for whom Shaw wrote the play, refused to perform the last scene as written and on its London opening night, "much to Shaw's horror, added her own last line." As Liza is saying farewell, Higgins tells her to stop off and buy him some Stilton cheese and a pair of gloves. In the script, she ignores him and walks out while Higgins breaks into "enigmatic gales of laughter" as the play ends. But on opening night, Mrs. Campbell came back onstage and said, "What size?" Lerner writes, "The curtain fell, along with Shaw's jaw."

✦ Most audiences assume, because they crave happy endings, that Henry and Eliza are romantically drawn together and will eventually marry. Shaw disdained such easy traditional endings, writing about the "lazy dependence on the ready-mades and reach-me-downs of the rag shop in which Romance keeps its stock of 'Happy Endings' to misfit all stories." Shaw called *Pygmalion* a romance, but "love" is never mentioned. When the play was first performed in 1914, with Sir Herbert Beerbohm Tree as Higgins, Shaw was aghast at how it had been sentimentalized and let Tree know about it.

Tree, a major star of the day who also directed the play's debut, replied, "My ending makes money. You ought to be grateful." Shaw snapped, "Your ending is damnable: You ought to be shot." Shaw wrote his wife, "For the last two acts I writhed in hell." Shaw scholar Shmuel Ross wrote in 2010, "Critics have insisted that Tree got it right, and romance was in the air." Shaw much preferred keeping the ending intriguingly unresolved, but he liked the film version (it made him a star and pots of money) and didn't voice loud objections to a happy ending, but he may have finally just given up. The musical concludes as the movie does, *suggesting* domestic bliss without saying so. Ross writes, "Many of the changes made for the film were incorporated into the play itself in its 1941 'definitive text.'"

In the 1938 movie *Pygmalion*, the two characters clearly have strong feelings about, and *for*, one another. Yet the question of whether Eliza will live with Higgins after he wins his bet is left tantalizingly open, with many unanswered questions, such as does she want to stay, and does he want her to stay? She loathes him because he's self-centered and doesn't respect her ("I shall always be a flower girl to Professor Higgins!"), but she's drawn to him against her will; likewise, she rankles Higgins, but he is drawn to her despite his fiercely independent streak. "I can do without you, don't think I can't!," she protests, maybe a bit too intensely, and he replies, "You haven't asked if I could do without you." So it's a delicious tangle of emotions, not just between the couple but within each of their hearts. "I have grown accustomed to your voice and appearance. I like them, rather, he tells her," is as far as he goes in the play and film. And she says, "I want a little kindness—I'm not dirt under your feet. If I can't have kindness, I'll have independence!" Thus the seeds of both of their final songs, "Without You" and "I've Grown Acccustomed to Her Face," are taken directly from Shaw's dialogue and made their way into the Pascal film and then the musical.

Higgins doesn't want her to leave but won't ask her to stay. She mocks his arrogance, and he both loves and hates her newfound freedom. She hates his hauteur. In the end, his slippers become a symbol of domesticity, so when Higgins asks Eliza to fetch them (like a dog, as she sees it), her answer is crucial. But in the film and in the musical, there is *no* answer. Shaw loved leaving their future up in the air in the play, but in the movie, despite all, Eliza returns—and the audience, if not the author, goes home happy.

Keith Garebian also points out in his study of *My Fair Lady* that "the word 'love' is never uttered by any of the principal characters [but Eliza does mention love in "Show Me"]—not even the love-struck Freddy Eyns-ford-Hill, who has the only explicit love song," which Garebian contends is "arguably out of place in the work"—Broadway sugarcoating literature. "On the Street Where You Live" sounds like a big reach for the pop charts: "And oh! the towering feeling! / Just to know somehow you are near! / The overpowering feeling / That any second you may suddenly appear!" It's hard to find much of Shaw there; GBS didn't know from towering feelings of adoration. The ballad seems to have wandered in from another musical next door.

Reality, however, reared its ugly capitalist head, and Shaw decided—or simply knuckled under to producers who disliked his cold, uncertain, unromantic ending—to write an epilogue explaining that Eliza winds up marrying Freddy, the mooning wannabe spouse (better he than Higgins, Shaw felt), but she keeps in touch with Higgins. Shaw wrote, "Galatea [the statue created by Pygmalion who comes to life] never quite does like Pygmalion; his relationship to her is too godlike to be altogether agreeable." If there's a weakness in *My Fair Lady*, it's that the stubborn, haughty, and cranky Higgins caves in too easily to Eliza without a strong, honest motivation, and suddenly he warbles the tender ballad that is meant to reveal his love for her, "I've Grown Accustomed to Her Face." The real, thornier, more Shavian question is, has she grown accustomed to his?

• •

WEST SIDE STORY
◆ 1957 ◆
"America," "Gee, Officer Krupke"

You would hardly expect to find two such explosive comic songs as "America" and "Gee, Officer Krupke" in a tragic musical like *West Side Story*, the 1957 milestone whose two biggest showstoppers might almost have come from any traditional mid-'50s musical. Both numbers are rambunctious rebukes to idyllic life in America and to the country's vaunted social justice system, wryly translated from national clichés into the street reality of Manhattan's Upper West Side (where Lincoln Center is now). The pre–urban renewal neighborhood of tenements, poverty, and ethnic gangs is where the show plays out against a menacing backdrop of rusting fire escapes and deserted playgrounds surrounded by wire fences—as much to keep the unwanted kids confined as to keep intruders out.

In the first draft of **"America,"** Stephen Sondheim wrote the song as a bantering debate between Anita (Chita Rivera in the original cast, Rita Moreno in the movie) and Maria's brother, Bernardo, that explored their relationship with their new country—and with each other. Besides the fun of listening to the taunting byplay, the original lyric made it clear that Puerto Ricans were hardly of one mind about their adopted land: "I like the island Manhattan," sings Anita, adding a lovely mixed-up Americanism, "Smoke on your pipe / And put that in!" The girls chirp, "I like to be in America / Okay by me in America / Everything free in America," answered by Bernardo's sardonic "For a small fee in America." She boasts, "I'll have my own washing machine," answered by, "What will you have, though, to keep clean?" Back and forth it goes. Bernardo: "Free to be anything you choose." Anita: "Free to wait tables and shine shoes." And the capper: "Life is all right in America," "If you're all white in America." But Jerome Robbins wanted to create an all-female number in counterpoint to all the men's numbers, so Anita faces off with acerbic retorts to her girlfriend Rosalia's rosy view of America, rebutting her friend's platitudes about Puerto Rico, efficiently batting every banality back in her face.

When Sondheim wrote the lyrics he said he had never actually met a Puerto Rican, yet he managed in "America" to mock favorite immigrant myths of our national life. When the movie was made four years later, the original lyric battle between Anita and Bernardo was restored to dazzling effect. Whether in the original Anita-Bernardo lyric that spoke of immigrant hardship, or in the all-female Broadway lyric that ridiculed romantic ideas toward one's homeland, the song reveals immigrants adjusting to a new country. Even the title, "America," subtly plays off the hallowed anthem rich in patriotic images about amber waves of grain and purple mountains' majesties. There are few spacious skies, amber waves of grain, or majestic purple mountains on the Upper West Side.

"America" was first staged by associate choreographer Peter Gennaro, but it didn't work in rehearsal until Robbins reshaped the dance with more vitality and ingenuity. Gennaro had a silent hand in many of the show's dances, but Robbins was protecting himself legally, surmises Sondheim, and insisted Gennaro sign a contract with the line, "You hereby assign to me any and all rights in, and to any and all choreographic material created or suggested by you in connection with, the play." At the Tony awards, Robbins failed even to acknowledge Gennaro's contribution to the show in his acceptance speech.

The tune itself was a Bernstein leftover from an unproduced ballet, "Conch Town," inspired by the composer's vacation in Key West, where he discovered

Chita Rivera dances her way across "America" in *West Side Story*.

a Latin folk music called *huapango* that eventually became the basis for the music in "America."

The clever, cutting lyrics in "America" compete with the rowdy choreography that covers up some of Sondheim's best rhymes and lines. Audiences are so captivated by the flashy footwork and flying skirts that lyrics get lost; but because the music needs to be noisy and the dancing exuberant, there seems no way to avoid burying some of the jokes. "Gee, Officer Krupke" includes shouted comic lines that are easier to catch than the packed lyrics of "America." Whereas Sondheim doesn't miss any opportunities to take pointed digs at American life seen through the jaundiced eyes of Puerto Ricans, the cracks aren't mean, hostile, anti-American, or anti–Puerto Rican, just amusing and on the money, wryly countering the popular image of the island. But as Sondheim readily admits in Meryle Secrest's biography, the song is too stuffed with words. "'America' has 27 words to the square inch," he told her, "and the audience becomes confused. I have this wonderful quatrain, 'I like to be in America / OK by me in America / Everything free in America / For a small fee in America.' The little 'for a small fee' was my zinger—except that the 'for' is accented and 'small fee' is impossible to say that fast, so it went 'for a smafee in America.' Nobody knew what it meant."

Many of Sondheim's catchiest lyrics in his shows are equally hard to catch, frustrating audiences that dote on his incisive wordplay. Sondheim, as always his toughest critic, says the lyrics to "Something's Coming" and "Jet Song" "are too self-conscious and pretty embarrassing," but that's him speaking in 2003 (on NPR's *Fresh Air*), with a different, higher standard than in 1956, when they didn't seem at all self-conscious or embarrassing. He has long blasted his lyrics to "I Feel Pretty" as being too sophisticated ("It's alarming how charming I feel") for a Puerto Rican shopgirl. (Sondheim says that only four of his songs turned out as he wanted them to, all but one from commercial failures: "Bounce" from the ill-fated *Bounce*, "Someone in a Tree" from *Pacific Overtures*, "Opening Doors" from *Merrily We Roll Along*, and "The Miller's Son" from *A Little Night Music*.)

Karen Ziemba, who was in *Jerome Robbins' Broadway*, describes some of Robbins's choreographic artistry in the show: "He had the ability to have a dancer just be walking down the street like a pedestrian and then go into dance as if it was the most natural thing for anybody to do. He knew how to create choreography so it did not seem as if we are going into a dance. The dance was always out of some emotional or comical thing going on with the character. He made it look as if it were coming out of a person's own mind and body. That's where he was extraordinary. He made you feel as an onlooker that you could do the dance, like it wasn't difficult, like anybody could do it."

———

"Gee, Officer Krupke" is Sondheim at his most accessible and witty and Robbins's staging at his most flamboyantly original. It's an old-fashioned patter list song—Sondheim in a number studded with gags that pop up out of nowhere amid the show's bloody killing fields. The song is a welcome and totally unexpected comic relief in mid–act 2 from the cataclysmic *West Side Story* drama, inspired by *Romeo and Juliet*. Shakespeare would have been impressed at the unlikely juxtaposition of mayhem and humor.

The number originally was written as a first-act song, but Robbins, over Sondheim's strenuous objections that it would interrupt the gruesome events of act 2, moved it deep into the second act, where it became an unlikely show-stopper, sandwiched between two brutal deaths; you could say Robbins got away with directorial murder. Sondheim eventually and reluctantly agreed that the song somehow works better in act 2 than in act 1, providing a needed comic breather. As Sondheim explains in his book *Finishing the Hat*, "I had severe doubts about it: it was hard for me to believe that a gang on the run from being accessories to a double murder would stop on the street to indulge in a sustained comic sneer. My collaborators disagreed, on the traditional theatrical grounds that, as the drunken porter in *Macbeth* exemplifies, comedy in the midst of melodrama makes the comedy more comic and the melodrama more melodramatic. I grumpily acceded." Placed early in the film version, it didn't work as well because there is as yet no tension that needs relieving. Martin Charnin, who played one of the original Jets, says, "Jerry was right. The show needed it more there. To do it early in the first act you don't really know the kids well enough to justify them acting like that. It's a release from the horror that occurred previously."

The gang of "juvenile delinquents" depicted in the number are not easy stereotypes but self-aware guys hip enough to satirize their own dreary plight and the inept social agencies that try to understand them—to wit: "My father is a bastard, / My ma's an S.O.B. / My grandpa's always plastered, / My grandma pushes tea. / My sister wears a mustache, / My brother wears a dress. / Goodness gracious, that's why I'm a mess!" (That prissy "goodness gracious" makes the line.)

Sondheim says, "That's not exceptionally funny on its own [wrong!], but it brought down the house every night, because the form helps make it funny. . . . It uses a favorite technique of mine, parallel lines where you just make a list." He told a biographer, "It is always better to be funny rather than clever, and much harder to do. There are very few times when you laugh out loud in the theater at a lyric joke. One laugh per score is a lot for me."

He notes that the song was also funny because "it depended not on cleverness but on the kids' attitudes, and that's what humor is all about: character, not cleverness." Sondheim wrote eight other equally cutting stanzas that didn't make the final cut. He comments, "Most people who write lyrics don't understand why rhyme is used. They just rhyme at the ends of lines to neaten it out, like tying up a package, without giving proper thought to the fact that a rhyme gives point to a word. If you don't want that word pointed up, don't rhyme it. . . . Rhyme will often get in the way of sense."

In the case of "Gee, Officer Krupke" the rhymes never get in the way, not even with Robbins's comic vaudeville choreography, in which the nimble Jets assume a variety of acrobatic positions, imitating judges, social workers, shrinks, and cops. The lines are delivered in rapid-fire bursts, but every syllable is audible: "Dear kindly Sergeant Krupke, / You gotta understand, / It's just our bringin' upke that gets us out of hand. / Our mothers all are junkies, / Our fathers all are drunks. / Golly Moses, natcherly we're punks!" It's a long number, but each joke pays off, largely because the Jets strike a savvy comic attitude that ridicules social worker banalities.

Between all the do-gooder cant, Sondheim has other gang members respond in mock earnestness, followed by a clueless judge on the bench (two kneeling Jets): "Hear ye, hear ye . . . this child is depraved on account / He ain't had a normal home," as the defendant gleefully cries, "Hey, I'm depraved / On account I'm deprived!" And so it smartly goes, as the delinquent is passed along to a series of case workers, which tells a story of inept juvenile justice beyond comic performances. There is no better example of a showstopper. Everything clicks: the idea, the acting, the attitude, the catchy tune (which Bernstein had first used for a song in *Candide* called "Where Does It Get You in the End?"), and, to be sure, the ingenious Sondheim lyrics. Robbins choreographed the number in three hours, says Sondheim, "one of the most brilliantly inventive [stagings] in one number I've ever seen."

The last line of the song has its own story, which Sondheim relishes telling—how he was looking forward with great glee to breaking songwriting ground by including a then-verboten word on a Broadway stage in the song's tag line: "Gee, Officer Krupke, fuck you!" Before that, Sondheim says, the foulest expletive ever heard on Broadway was Big Daddy's "Bullshit!" in *Cat on a Hot Tin Roof.*

The problem was, if the F-word was included on the Columbia Records cast album, it would be illegal to ship it across state lines because of obscenity laws, which sounds like 1857, not 1957. "I was in despair," Sondheim recalls, "until Lenny [Bernstein] came up with 'Krup you!,' which may be the best lyric line in the show, and which actually was an improvement, since it fitted the kidlike nature of the Jets better than the harsher and more realistic expletive." Columbia also had Sondheim replace "shmuck" (Yiddish for "penis" or "reprehensible person") with "schmo" (also Yiddish, for "dummy"), which in the movie was changed yet again to "slob."

BACKSTAGE DISH

+ Stephen Sondheim, in retrospect, is not that great a fan of *West Side Story*. "What the critics didn't realize—and they rarely realize anything," he told his biographer Meryle Secrest, "is that the show isn't very good. By which I mean, in terms of individual ingredients, it has a lot of very severe flaws: overwriting, purpleness in the writing and in the songs, and because the characters are necessarily one-dimensional they're not people. What lasts in the theater is character, and there are no characters in 'West Side Story,' nor can there be. It's the shortest book on record, with the possible exception of 'Follies,' in terms of how much gets accomplished and with how little dialogue." He said librettist Arthur Laurents "wrote one-dimensional characters for a melodrama."

+ Even though *West Side Story* has become an iconic musical, it mostly got respectful but not "money" notices. (The dancing got most of the raves, not the songs, and in a few reviews, amazingly, including the *New York Times*, Sondheim's lyrics were not even mentioned.) A few critics recognized it was a masterpiece, but it was not a mass audience favorite. Prince says, "The reviews were good but begrudging." "Everyone thinks it was an enormous hit, but it wasn't," Sondheim told author Craig Zadan. "The show, specifically, was not one that people wanted to see. It was a big hit with theater people but not with audiences," who considered it too much of a downer; it may be the first musical in which major characters are murdered onstage. (Billy Bigelow stabs himself to death in *Carousel* rather than face prison, and Lt. Cable in *South Pacific* is shot down by Japanese gunners offstage.)

+ Sondheim may have been ignored by Brooks Atkinson, but he did not go unnoticed by the paper's medical writer, Dr. Howard Rusk, who took exception to a line in "America" that calls Puerto Rico "an island of tropic diseases." Puerto Ricans who objected were supported by Rusk, who argued, "Today, Puerto Rico has no significant disease problems related to its tropical climate . . . last month showed no cases of cholera, dengue, filarisis, typhus or yellow fever this year and only one new case of Hansen's disease [leprosy]. . . . 'West Side Story' is a dramatic and effective production and Puerto Rico is a healthy island." Sondheim's aesthetic defense: "I'm sure his outrage was justified, but I wasn't about to sacrifice the line that sets the tone for the whole lyric."

♦ The movie version, directed by Robert Wise (not Robbins, whom the film's producer fired before filming began because he was regarded as too difficult and demanded extensive, expensive rehearsal time), made the stage show a belated hit and has kept it in revival for sixty years. The screen score got plenty of airplay, which made the songs suddenly famous and "hummable"—the old knock against Sondheim's tunes. He told Zadan, "When people say [a song] is not hummable, it makes my blood boil. It's really a question of how many times you hear it. People have lazy ears."

In the four years between the Broadway show and the movie, two songs from the show became single hits, notes Sondheim, because the film company spent hundreds of thousands of dollars promoting the picture, and, bingo, the songs suddenly became hummable. "Hummable really means familiar," says Sondheim. Theater audiences, he says, are distracted by costumes, scenery, lighting, choreography, and performers. Songs reprised in a show have a better chance of being remembered, and becoming hits. When collaborating on *Do I Hear a Waltz?* with Richard Rodgers, a great believer in reprises, Rodgers wanted a ballad reprised called "Take the Moment." Rodgers said, "I want them to hear the tune again." Sondheim: "For me, that isn't reason enough."

"Lyrics have to be underwritten," Sondheim explains. "They have to be very simple in essence. That doesn't mean you can't write convoluted lyrics, but you have to stretch it out enough so that the listener has a fair chance to get it. Many lyrics suffer from being much too packed"—his own very much included. Songwriter Lauren Mayer wrote a superb parody of Sondheim, "Another Hundred Lyrics," which begins (to the tune of "Another Hundred People" in *Company*): "Another hundred lyrics just flew out of my brain / As I stand here on stage / With another hundred lyrics that I'll never recall / And on every damn page / There's another hundred lyrics that'll drive me insane / Right in front of you all, 'cause the words are a pain / Not to mention the sprawl of the melody. . . . But we're all singing Sondheim—some songs are sweet, some are strange /

But we're all singing Sondheim, there's not one damn tune in my range / And every song is too damn long."

+ Bernstein wrote lyrics to some of the show's ballads, but just which ones remains a well-kept secret. In his memoirs Laurents says "most of the florid lyrics were written by Lenny." The composer generously let Sondheim take sole credit for the lyrics, crucial to the young songwriter at that point in his career. Laurents called Bernstein's gesture "the most magnanimous act I ever heard of in the theater." Ethan Mordden, in his book *On Sondheim*, says Bernstein even offered to give up his royalty percentage for the lyrics "but a grateful Sondheim thought that might be too much to want."

+ Whereas many numbers in *West Side Story* still move audiences—"Somewhere," "Something's Coming," "Maria"—the show itself has not aged so well, and efforts to update it don't really work. The show is very much a product of its time. When it was revived in 2009 by Arthur Laurents, in his nineties, he decided parts of songs should be sung in Spanish, which was innovative but self-conscious. A central problem with the show today is that the Jets and the Sharks seem almost innocent by today's violent gang standards. Even in 1957 the Jets and the Sharks never looked much like street toughs, though Robbins purposely cast rugged-looking males for the chorus, not slender ballet dancers. An editor who saw the original show in New York, who had covered gang wars in Berkeley, said the onstage gangs were far too likable, but then it is a musical, not a documentary, though the show's torn-from-the headlines premise gave it much of its primal power.

One of those original Jets, Big Deal, was played by Martin Charnin, who was not a great dancer, but Robbins liked his nondancer look and cast him in the chorus. (Charnin soon left performing and became a director and lyricist, most famously for *Annie*.) Charnin did the role for a thousand performances, replacing an actor who broke his wrist. (He notes that Robbins's staging of "Krupke" drew on many of the cast's ideas.)

Charnin reflects on working amid four major talents—and egos: "They were all mind-bogglingly smart, opinionated, and dedicated. They never collaborated again after this show. Jerry and Arthur and Steve worked together but never with Lenny in the mix. Steve always wanted to leave the quartet to write his own music." Of the difficult Robbins, Charnin says, "Jerry was a perfectionist. He was not the most communicative at expressing his thoughts. He could express his body thoughts to dancers more than he could to actors. He could express negative thoughts, even cruel things, but in the final analysis Jerry was a genius."

Of another genius, Bernstein, he says: "Lenny was very involved, and then he was gone. He had one foot in musical theater and the other in his work, writing music and TV series, etc. I think everybody in the company was much more in awe of Lenny than anybody else in the group." Laurents and Robbins were a volatile blend, tarantulas in a bottle. "He and Jerry were at loggerheads a lot of the time," recalls Charnin. "There were times when Jerry would go away to Spoleto [Italy] or somewhere and Arthur would come in and redirect what Jerry had done. Next thing, Jerry would come back and change it all back. That was sort of the routine."

As for Sondheim's presence, Charnin recalls, "He made his voice heard, but I think he was intimidated by the experience of the others. They all acquiesced to each other's ideas. It was one of those shows where everything went in the direction of making it better, to make the show work. Everyone seemed to sense *West Side Story* was unique. We knew it when we were out there doing it, no question about it. It was not after the fact. They knew how sensational a piece of theater it was—we all knew."

• •

Of the four lead performers in *West Side Story*, only Chita Rivera went on to have a major career on Broadway. Carol Lawrence pretty much faded away after playing Maria, and Larry Kert had only one more Broadway leading role, in *Company*, replacing Dean Jones. Tony Mordente, in the fourth lead role as Bernardo, is forgotten. None, of course, were cast in the movie version.

Rivera got the role of Anita when she went to an audition with a friend from the American School of Ballet, but her agent later told her to audition herself, and, after five callbacks, she got the part. Rivera remembered it all vividly when we talked by phone.

"America" stopped the show every night, but how did you make yourself heard above the excited, raucous orchestrations?
I have given credit to that show for giving me very strong lungs and excellent diction. You had to dance and sing at the same time. The rhythms were very intricate and there were a lot of lyrics and fast steps. It's training. You have to do it over and over again. You can't be lazy. It's good for you because it changes your mouth and your tongue and then you have to act it out. And then you have to make it look simple. You have to make it all look easy.

"America" was a little controversial because of the "tropic diseases" line. Did it bother you?
I was amazed people didn't get it. I was shocked; it was meant to be tongue in cheek. One minute you have a lovely island of tropical breezes and then you have a clever lyricist who puts in tropical diseases.

Sondheim was writing more about the image of Puerto Rico than the reality.
Absolutely. It was just a line. The small-minded people just didn't get it.

***West Side Story* was the first Broadway show to depict Puerto Rican culture, and you were the first Puerto Rican to star in a major Broadway show. Did all that weigh heavily on you?**
Not at all. I was just a dancer who wanted a job. When I auditioned I realized this was material I really loved. I did not know Jerome Robbins was a genius; I didn't know Leonard Bernstein was a genius. He was sweet and kind and fun and easy, maybe one of the easiest people in the world to be around. You just work and you grow with it. And the aftermath, when the pieces are put together, you go, wow! We didn't realize it was going to be as exciting to anybody else until we had our first run-through. That was when we started bumping into each other, after "America" stopped the show dead.

You once said you realized *West Side Story* was not just another show when you came out of the theater during previews and found real gang members hanging around outside.
They wanted to check the guys out. They were saying, *Let's see these guys who are portraying us.*

Might they actually have been checking you out?
My goodness, I never thought of that.

There was a rumor at the time that you weren't cast in the movie version because you were "too old" by then, when in fact Rita Moreno was two years older than you.
Who said I was too old? It's the first time I have ever heard that. People lie. What happened was, I was in the show and my agent asked if they could postpone the movie, which made me laugh. Can you imagine the audacity to ask a film company to postpone the film for me? I would never have dreamt of leaving a company I had given my word to. I was not going to get out of the

show and they could not postpone the movie. They actually apologized and said we can't do that.

Lin-Manuel Miranda, the author, director, and star of *Hamilton* and *In the Heights*, said that *West Side Story* "was Puerto Ricans' greatest blessing and greatest curse," meaning the show featured Latinos but also furthered Latino stereotypes.
I don't understand why it would be a curse. Unfortunately, stereotyping is still happening. What we did was to open it up and make everybody aware of it. Where it went from there was up to the world. How could it possibly have been a curse? I loved *In the Heights*. *West Side Story* made it easier for him to write that.

Jerome Robbins was known as a tyrannical taskmaster. Larry Kert said, "Jerry Robbins is an incredible man I'd work for in a minute, but he is a painful man—a perfectionist who sees himself in every role. If you don't give him exactly what he's pictured, he destroys you. People thought we were puppets on strings, and in some ways we were." And the dancer Helen Gallagher said, "He would strip you naked, pull the flesh right off your bones, and then rebuild you. He wasn't fun to be around." Did he ever pull the flesh off your bones?
Never ever with me. I believe you have to have a bit of both genius and tyrant to make us do what we did. It's not natural for a boy to be flipping in the air or running up walls. He made us do it. You have to have a taskmaster. He and I had a very special relationship. I used to make him laugh.

Robbins's sharp criticisms of dancers could make them cry.
Not with me. Some people had to be pushed harder, so he pushed. They should be thankful to this very day because they all came out brilliantly. Their careers have gone to wonderful places. It's tough, but I like tough. It's hard work. The theater is hard work and you have to take it.

What do you recall of Robbins's staging of "America"?
First of all, there were both girls and boys. I thought it was genius to include girls, too. It was a huge statement in a male-dominated show. We came in and Peter Gennaro had choreographed something terrific and then we were excused, and when we came back to rehearsal the boys were gone! It became a completely different idea.

Martin Charnin says "America" was Peter Gennaro's number.

Peter was responsible for many of the things the Sharks did, much more so than what the Jets did. Peter took care of the women and the Sharks.

Gennaro also staged the memorable mambo at the gym, but his name is lost in the show's legend. "There were these four gigantic egos," Martin Charnin said. "There was not a lot of room for a fifth ego." Which of the four egos do you most recall?

Lenny—oh my god, what a ray of sunshine! What a passionate and energized human being. It was like osmosis that we just sucked up. He made us believe that we could do things we never thought we could do. And he made us do it. We knew there was genius present. It was Jerry and Lenny's voices we heard.

Your other big number, "A Boy Like That," was not a showstopper and wasn't meant to get a hand. It was just the opposite, but a dynamic theatrical moment.

I learned that a big hand sometimes can ruin the moment. We discovered that. "A Boy Like That" started out with the audience wanting to applaud at the end, but it was up to us to keep it going, and when we never got a hand it was really a wonderful feeling. We knew then that we had made it work.

THE MUSIC MAN

◆ 1957 ◆

"Ya Got Trouble," "Seventy-Six Trombones"

The Music Man is as close to a perfect musical as exists—the story; the characters; the early twentieth-century sentiments, attitudes, and language; and, to be sure, the great songs. Everything about it sounds right, feels right, smells right. It's as authentic in its style as *Guys and Dolls* is to Times Square, *Oklahoma!* is to 1906 Oklahoma, and *Fiddler on the Roof* is to Russian shtetl life.

The Music Man is worth cheering as a show that came out of its writer Meredith Willson's gut, unlike most musicals of recent decades, corporate deals willed into being—movie adaptations, piggyback versions of tired icons, re-creations of old hit shows. Broadway today mostly seems to be living off the pop culture of the past rather than producing original musicals like this and many of the vintage shows in these pages.

The defining moment of Willson's 1957 masterwork, the mesmerizing **"Ya Got Trouble,"** is a textbook example of Musicals Appreciation 1A. There is even a kind of textbook, a guide for community theater directors and actors, called *Deconstructing Harold Hill* that examines the show in detail. But if ever a musical seemed *not* to have been constructed, that simply grew organically onstage, *The Music Man* is that show, so purely does it seem a product of rich Iowa topsoil. It's a fully realized musical that emerged from Willson's fertile memories of his Mason City, Iowa, boyhood. "I didn't have to make up anything for *The Music Man*," said Willson. "All I had to do was remember."

It wasn't quite that simple. He said in 1980, at the age of seventy-eight, "I had never tried to write a musical comedy, and it didn't come easy. I think I must have done thirty or forty rewrites before I got it right." To get it right he needed help from playwright Franklin Lacey (still credited as a co-librettist), who helped Willson structure the story, which stumbled through several versions. One of Lacey's most crucial contributions was changing the little boy in the show from a spastic child into just a kid with a bad lisp.

Here is a musical that not only doesn't date but that gets richer every time you see it, when performed with care and affection. It remains one of the most inventive musicals ever written, and you marvel anew at its brilliance with every song cue. Even so, Brooks Atkinson neglected to name a single title from the score in his *New York Times* review, calling it a mix of Mark Twain and Vachel Lindsay (the so-called prairie troubadour).

In the show, Willson captured forever the flavors of another time in a musical without a single mediocre tune, but it relies almost completely on a vital, captivating leading man. Whether it was the original "Professor" Harold Hill, Robert Preston, onstage at the Majestic Theatre on Broadway in 1957, or Dick Van Dyke in a later touring company, or Craig Bierko in the 2000 Broadway revival (or even attorney Richard King in a long-ago 1970s community theater version I covered at Woodminster Amphitheater in Oakland), the controlled coiled energy required to perform the number remains the same. The dynamic role demands extraordinary performing prowess, precision timing, and a sly, ingratiating satirical persona to bring it all off with charm, style, and easy authority. Preston also infused the character with magnetic energy and wit, built into every one of his lines, such as, from "Trouble," "are certain wor-r-rds creeping into his conversation?"

Robert Preston warning citizens of River City of the dire "Trouble" that awaits them.

Preston's original galvanizing performance made him a legend and transformed him overnight from a solid B-movie character actor into an A-Broadway leading man. He had played in a few 1950s Broadway comedies but had never been in a musical. I watched him from a standing-room-only stall in 1958, in one of the half-dozen greatest displays of sheer theatrical sizzle I've witnessed. Preston starred in other musicals after that (*Ben Franklin in Paris, I Do! I Do!, Mack and Mabel*), but none approached the ornate style and spellbinding oratory he brought to a part he was clearly born to play. Even so, at least eight established stars supposedly turned down the role before they thought of Preston—Ray Bolger, Andy Griffith, Phil Harris, Art Carney, Dan Dailey, Danny Kaye, Gene Kelly, Jason Robards, and Bert Parks.

Preston was one of the last virile leading men in Broadway musicals of that era—an actor whose swaggering vitality and charisma is as indelibly stamped on the character as Rex Harrison's is on Henry Higgins, Richard Kiley's on Don Quixote, or Yul Brynner's on the King of Siam. Barbara Cook, who played opposite him in the show, said of Preston in a 2011 TV interview, "He had enormous sexual power onstage. The show doesn't make sense without that. Everybody in the show is in love with Harold Hill. You'd go anywhere with him."

Sixty-five years later you can still revel in his performance by watching the unusually faithful 1962 movie version, with all his precise theatrical gestures. Preston, in his flashy con man's white suit, tippy-toes through "Ya Got Trouble," making his flim-flam man's case suavely and persuasively. He's like a slick attorney working a dubious jury, carefully trying not to alienate the skeptical River City parents he needs to inveigle, fearful of coming on too strong while presenting evidence that trouble is brewing amid River City's youth. He coaxes and cajoles in a modulated, reasonable voice, sounding simultaneously urgent but understanding, a rascally but far more lovable Elmer Gantry.

Preston, as they used to say in movie ads, *is* Harold Hill, from his silver-tongued spiel to his snazzy shoe tops. Other stars who played the role after him (Forrest Tucker, Van Dyke, Bierko, even John Davidson, and Eddie Albert, who followed him on Broadway) might turn in winning versions, but they were just that—versions of the maestro. Much of the personality we now consider inherent in the character of Harold Hill is borrowed, if not channeled, from Preston.

In the 2001 revival, Bierko was no Preston—they're all out of those—but he gave an invigorating performance (staged by Susan Stroman) that recalled Preston yet fell short of mimicking him. But by now it's impossible to say where Preston's Hill leaves off and everybody else's begins. When I once raved about Bierko's performance to Barbara Cook, Preston's original Marian the Librarian, and said he didn't seem to be copying Preston, she scoffed, "I wouldn't be quite so sure about that!" Stroman thinks "the shadow of Mr. Preston" may have scared off later pretenders, and Bierko himself concedes, "He kind of haunts this performance." Harold Hill is a role that inspires most performers, as highly charged a male musical lead as Dolly or Gypsy is to female performers. A limp 2003 TV version starred a wildly miscast Hill— the aging boy next door Matthew Broderick—with Kristin Chenoweth as Marian.

Rebecca Luker, who played Marian opposite Bierko, recalls, "He just made it easy. He even sounded a little like Robert Preston, which, good or bad, I found comforting. But his physicality wasn't like Preston, who sort of did the part like a panther. If I was a man that would be the first role I'd want to do." Luker captures the show's essence: "Every word and note that Meredith Willson wrote is a little gem. Not one boring moment. It has a unique quality—nobody had ever written anything quite like it, like the opening number on the train. He broke all sorts of barriers. It's laugh-out-loud funny, and it makes you cry, and it's sweet. The perfect American musical."

In "Trouble," Preston set the tone, the template, for thousands of Harold Hills to come, but the song's meter is so indelibly encoded in us that it's impossible to imagine any actor doing the role any other way. Every Hill owes its spunk and sparkle to Robert Preston, a wired, wily performer who let loose bolts of theatrical electricity. But Preston told me long ago it wasn't so tough: "Once you fall into the cadence of the number, the rest is easy."

Preston's Hill whispers, he whimpers, he warns—shaking first a finger and then a fist, using lithe body language to transfix the crowd with worried eyes and waggling fingers as he talk-sings the words in insinuating inflections. He draws out a phrase or lingers over a word to give it its full mock-menacing meaning, warning parents what signs to look for in their sons ("Does he re-buckle his knickerbockers below-w-w the knee? Is there a tell-tale scent of Sen-Sen on his breath?"). Every line has a built-in wink, as if letting us in on the con. And like so many songs in the show, the number segues naturally out of the dialogue, far more seamlessly than in most scores, as the last line of a speech becomes the first line of a lyric, like the verse to "The Sadder but Wiser Girl" that starts out spoken—"No wide-eyed, eager, / Wholesome innocent Sunday school teacher for me. / That kinda girl spins webs no spider ever— Listen boy . . . ," then slip into the spritely tune.

Few musicals are packed with as many satisfying moments. The melodies drift in and out easily, inevitably, through this midwestern fable, the romance flowers naturally, and each song—detailed in a close look at "Rock Island" in Part I of this book—grows out of the sounds of small-town America. As Philip Furia observes in *America's Songs*, "What is distinctive about the musical is Willson's reliance on unusual rhythms to take the place of rhyming, as in 'Rock Island,' 'Iowa Stubborn' and 'Ya Got Trouble.'"

Much of the fun of the lyrics in "Ya Got Trouble" is built into the rise and fall in a breathless gospel tempo, as Hill, a two-bit Billy Sunday, mounts a secular sermon. The stem-winding number starts unremarkably, with Hill gathering his congregation of concerned parents about him as he takes to an imaginary pulpit to spell out the certain "depredation" sure to befall their children if the parents fail to buy band uniforms from him to save their innocent boys and girls.

He appeals to their filial duty, their moral values, their community spirit, their cultural obligation, their patriotic zeal. It's a fiery sermon that pushes every parental button: "Now I know all you folks are the right kind of parents. / I'm gonna be perfectly frank. / Would ya like to know what kinda conversation goes / On while they're loafin' around that hall? / They're tryin' out Bevo, tryin' out Cubebs, / Tryin' out Tai-i-lor Mades like cigarette fiends!" Slowly, inevitably, the good folks of River City are suckered into Hill's fire-and-brimstone message of Satan about to take up residence in a new pool hall, lurking behind an eight ball. The citizens congratulate themselves for finally seeing Hill's point and then agree with him that a pool room will indeed corrupt their vulnerable River City youth unless they fund a righteous solution—a boys' band. What a *swell* idea!

Hill raises the specter of juvenile sloth: "And all week long your River City / Youth'll be fritterin' away, / I say, your young men'll be fritterin' / Fritterin' away their noontime, suppertime, choretime, too! / Get the ball in the pocket, / Never mind gettin' dandelions pulled / Or the screen door patched or the beefsteak pounded. / Never mind pumpin' any water / 'Till your Parents are caught with the cistern empty / On a Saturday night." Willson sketches small-town life in such exacting detail, with words like "fritterin'," "choretime," "screen door," "beefsteak," and "cistern."

By the time the song ends, Hill has convinced the parents that there is no other solution for the peril of a pool table downtown. Carefully enunciating every cautionary word, he says, "Well, either you're closing your eyes / To a situation you do not wish to acknowledge / or you are not aware of the caliber of disaster indicated / By the presence of a po-o-ol table in your community." He subtly slips in scary hyperbole like "the caliber of disaster."

What a beautifully logical yet cunning sentence it is, worthy of history's most evil demagogues, encapsulating in a phrase the cant and cautionary appeal of every fraud who ever hawked his wares—from rabid tyrants, televangelists, pseudopsychics, and Vegematic spielers to tin-horn politicians, born-again ministers, and major despots. Not finding a problem and fixing it but, rather, alerting you to a crisis you were not aware of that only *he* can cure—in this case, by the simple purchase of a uniform or a trombone. He lays it on the line—it's up to them. Harold Hill is a jolly Jim Jones hawking salvation.

Beyond the enjoyment of the song itself, and to be sure the buoyant performance it inspired, the number makes a major plot point. "Ya Got Trouble" is not just an irresistible showstopper but also neatly nudges the story along. In fact, it does many things: it makes gentle fun of the townsfolk's unreasoning fears and worst suspicions; it solidifies Hill's hold on the community by convincing it of the need to band together to ward off wayward youth soon to undermine the town's decency; it even impresses the skeptical, comely librarian he has his eye on.

The song is a Sears-Roebuck catalog of period lore, of midwestern Americana in 1912, jammed with references to *Capt. Billy's Whiz Bang*, Sen-Sen, and phrases like "So's your old man!" and "Swell!" The number is full of information, about the difference between a gentleman's game of billiards and a hustler's game of pool (with inside references to "a three-rail billiard shot" and "a balk-line game"); about fashion ("the next thing you know your son is playin' for money in a pinch-back suit"); about "wholesome trottin' races" versus low-class horse races ("where they set right down on a horse!"); about "shameless music" like ragtime and mentions of "libertine men," "scarlet women," and "some big out-a-town Jasper."

Willson's rabble-rousing snake-oil salesman precisely captures the lingo of Iowans—"Well, ya got trouble, my friend, right here, I say trouble right here in River City" (note that extra "I say")—begins the chant, then veers into the spiel of a hustler zeroing in on that very trouble. He twists words to get across his pitch, as the line famously continues, "trouble with a capital 'T' and that rhymes with 'P' and that stands for pool!" Hill fastens on a pool room about to be built in town, sure to turn River City kids into overnight delinquents, but he guarantees a boys' band will "keep the young ones moral after school"—every parent's fervent wish.

Yes, of course!, nod the once wary but suddenly transfixed and appalled townspeople, catching his drift, as a fervent chant goes up from the crowd, as at a revival meeting ("Trouble, trouble, trouble . . ."). Musical director Arthur Masella noted, "It has a pulse that starts" with the first note of the opening train number. "Not only is the show built around that pulse, so is the character of Harold Hill."

Susan Stroman, who staged the robust *Music Man* revival in 2000, the first Broadway revival since the 1957 original, approached the entire show "almost as a journey of movement." When Harold Hill first comes to the town, "everyone is very stiff—the way they treat strangers, with a very stiff way about them"—as in the show's second song, "Iowa Stubborn." Then, explains Stroman, as the show unfolds, the whole town starts to move easier and everyone gets friendlier with one another. She calls it "a movement journey." Hill's body language gradually loosens up the townspeople, bursting open in later numbers, "infusing the entire town with music," just as he has promised.

"Ya Got Trouble" is not just a terrific song, it's a minidocumentary of its time, like most of the score. In "Marian the Librarian," Hill threatens to disturb the library's quiet by dropping a bag of marbles on the floor, but he doesn't stop there—he details "six steelies, eight aggies, a dozen peewees and one big glassie with an American flag in the middle." As Ethan Mordden notes, "A goodly portion of the show's content had been retired to the American memory bank by the 1950s."

Even if you didn't grow up in Mason City, Iowa, like Meredith Willson, "Ya Got Trouble" and its nostalgic allusions set you down firmly there. It's clear Willson knows every square foot of the territory. But Willson left home fast, a musical prodigy who played piccolo in John Philip Sousa's band at nineteen, then with Toscanini, and scored Chaplin's *The Great Dictator*. He became a radio band leader and comic foil opposite Tallulah Bankhead on *The Big Show*, when he first thought of the musical.

Despite Willson's romantic recollection of his Iowa boyhood, the score never sounds corny. Songs and dialogue revel in the period and its people, but Willson was adamant that the show never mock River City. He told directors the show "was intended to be a valentine, not a caricature" (despite a quick visual parody of Grant Wood's *American Gothic*). Willson's widow said in 2000, "A lot of Meredith is in 'The Music Man'—not the con man part but the sincerity." Willson took painstaking care that subsequent productions treat the material with total sincerity. He wrote a note to the director of a Beijing production: "Please do not let the actors . . . mug or reach for comedy effect. The Delsarte ladies also should be natural and sincere, never raucous, shrewish, or comic per se. The humor of this piece depends upon its technical faithfulness to the real small-town Iowans of 1912 who certainly did not think they were funny at all."

"Seventy-Six Trombones" is the big fat obvious *Music Man* showstopper, the best-known song from the show. In his encyclopedia of American musical theater songs, Thomas S. Hishack calls it "the most famous march to come from the Broadway stage since the operettas of the 1920s." It's lively if not as interesting or as surprising as "Rock Island" or "Trouble," but it's a colossal march that, were there any doubters in the audience, pushes the show well

Robert Preston's Harold Hill in *The Music Man* ready to lead "Seventy-Six Trombones" and all of River City in the parade of parades.

over the top near the end of act 2 and brings the musical to its inevitable and joyous climactic conclusion.

The number has a major distinguishing factor that gives it a unique niche in musicals: Willson slowed down his brassy foot-tapping march to create an earlier tender ballad, "Goodnight, My Someone," sung by Marian to a lover yet to arrive. Even many who have seen the show a few times are unaware that "Seventy-Six Trombones" is the same tune as "Goodnight, My Someone." I don't know any other musical that does that as triumphantly—uses the same melody twice in the same show in opposite tempos, though it's common in opera; it's such a splendid original idea that nobody seems even to have dared try to duplicate it.

Not content with that invention, Willson later weaves both songs into a counterharmony, a duet with Harold and Marian singing the two songs to each other after they've fallen in love, uniting them musically. He then adds a further romantic touch: in a reprise duet at the show's end, they switch and sing each other's song: the newly reformed Hill croons "Goodnight, My Someone" while a reinvigorated Marian sings "Seventy-Six Trombones." It's an exchange of musical gold rings.

"Seventy-Six Trombones" is Willson's salute to Sousa, whom he played under from 1921 to 1923, his first major gig. In the number, Willson refers to all the great band leaders besides Sousa—Gilmore, Pat Conway, Libertini, the Great Creatore, W. C. Handy—whom Hill claims once, in his youth, "all came to town on the very same day!," which explains why there are seventy-six trombones and not merely thirty-seven, plus those 110 cornets right behind. It's a rousing march but, more than that, it's a fond tribute to the instruments themselves: "There were copper-bottomed tympani in horse platoons / Thundering, thundering all along the way. / Double bell euphoniums and big bassoons, / Each bassoon having its big fat say!" Clearly this is a song written by a guy who did time in a marching band: "Clarinets of ev'ry size / And trumpeters who'd improvise / A full octave higher than the score!"

Hill uses the song as a sales tool, conjuring a vision of a great marching band and, like all ace scammers, believes his own con. "I always *think* there's a band," he confesses to Marian, which makes him seem less a weasely money-grubbing charlatan than a self-deluded wannabe band leader, a fond poetic sentiment that wins Marian's suspicious heart. What starts off as a fraud winds up as a symbol of faith, redemption of a kind, when the band actually materializes, the boys magically learn how to play, and, in the show's finale, they parade onstage playing a wobbly version of "Seventy-Six Trombones" in their sharp gold-braided red uniforms; the proud parents naturally think the kids are fabulous. The moment turns Hill from a scoundrel into a rainmaking faith healer. The audience is so caught up in the number that it claps along in unison, making the song not just a traditional showstopper but a sneaky applause stoker. Meredith Willson was himself a canny music man.

"Seventy-Six Trombones" bookends the show with the same punch that opens it with "Rock Island," as the cast parades behind high-stepping Harold Hill, twirling a baton and grinning broadly. The prank Hill planned to play on the town has turned on him and converted him from a slippery con artist and philanderer to a River City hero and fervent lover of the town librarian.

Susan Stroman treated the curtain call as a final opportunity to stop the show before it officially ended: "The curtain call was the most fun and what I'm most proud of in that revival." She asked the producer if she could give trombone lessons to the entire company. She told him, "If it works, we will all play the trombone, and if it doesn't work we will just come out and take a bow. So every day at 4 o'clock they'd all go into trombone lessons. I'd walk down the hall and it really sounded terrible. I thought this is never going to work. Then I became one of those mothers saying, 'Oh my god, that's my kid!' And finally they really *could* play, and at the curtain call every single cast member comes out in a marching band and they're all playing the trombone—all of them!"

Hill preaches that, if you just believe in a boys' band it will somehow materialize, what he calls his "think method"—sheer hokum, yes, but a fairy-tail ending you don't want to examine too closely. This is musical comedy, after all, not Eugene O'Neill, although Willson's pipe dreams are not that far away from O'Neill's Hickey. Harold Hill and Hickey are theatrical cousins. This isn't *The Iceman Cometh*, it's *The Music Man Cometh*.

•••••••••••••• BACKSTAGE DISH ••••••••••••••

+ On NBC Radio's *The Big Show*, as its conductor, composer, and comic stooge, one of Willson's shticks was talking about "that obscure little hamlet of yours," as hostess Tallulah Bankhead derisively called Mason City. He and his Iowa stories were so linked on the radio show that *The Music Man* was a natural outgrowth of his on-air rube character.

+ For the movie version, Jack Warner wanted either Frank Sinatra or Cary Grant (who else?) to play Harold Hill; either would have been a disaster. Willson insisted on Preston, and, with Morton DaCosta again directing and Onna White back as choreographer, the movie is one of the few reliable filmed versions of a Broadway musical; even Brooklyn stand-up comic Buddy Hackett as Hill's buddy Marcellus didn't wreck it. All the songs in the show were kept except "My White Knight," which was dropped in favor of a generic love song for Marian, "Being in Love." Songs added to movie versions of stage shows rarely measure up to the original score, always tacked on to give a film star another big number.

+ Prolific and usually shrewd *Guys and Dolls* producers Cy Feuer and Ernest Martin passed on *The Music Man*, but *Guys and Dolls* songwriter Frank Loesser encouraged Willson and kept prodding him to finish the show. Six years and thirty rewrites later, it finally opened, produced by Kermit Bloomgarden. Loesser remained with the show as associate producer, publisher, and licensor—giving rise to a rumor that Loesser wrote "My White Knight," supposedly left out of the movie for that reason. It's unlikely Willson would have allowed a song by an outsider infiltrate his intensely personal Broadway show, plus Willson hardly needed help with a score that overflows with inventive songs. "Till There Was You" was first recorded by Eileen Wilson in 1950, under the title "Till I Met You," then sung on the air in 1951 by Fran Warren on Willson's *The Big Show*.

+ Protective of his meal ticket to posterity, Willson was not flattered when song satirist Allan Sherman asked him if he could record a parody titled "Seventy-Six Sol Cohens." According to Mark Cohen's biography of Sherman, Willson turned Sherman down cold—allegedly throwing him out of the house, shouting, "Get out of here—you're crazy!" The humorless Richard Rodgers also told Sherman to get lost when he requested permission to record "There Is Nothing Like a Lox." Both songs are now happily available on a CD of lost Sherman parodies of Broadway classics.

+ *The Music Man* opened the same season as *West Side Story*, only weeks apart, and narrowly beat out *West Side Story* for a best musical Tony by one vote. They were two totally different but equally inventive shows—one a comforting, rose-colored view of America's small-town past, the other a dark, starkly realistic look at the country's troubled urban present. *West Side Story* was more blatantly innovative, because of its topical subject matter and hip portrayal of New York street gangs, but whereas *West Side Story* impressed Tony voters, *The Music Man* simply charmed them.

GYPSY

✦ 1959 ✦

"Everything's Coming Up Roses," "Ya Gotta Get a Gimmick," "Rose's Turn"

Gypsy was a game changer for musicals when it arrived in 1959, at the close of an era dominated by Rodgers and Hammerstein, whose idealistic shows glorify romance (*Oklahoma!*, *South Pacific*) and redemption (*Carousel*, *The King and I*). In R&H land, good invariably triumphs over evil. *Gypsy* put the lie to all that, with a new, darker, cynical, more wrenching rewrite of the American showbiz dream.

Critic Frank Rich calls *Gypsy* "one of the most enduring creations of the American theater, regardless of the star" and compares it not just to other great musicals but to dramatic classics like *Death of a Salesman*, *The Glass Menagerie*, and *Long Day's Journey into Night*—all, he writes, "blood-letting plays about paired siblings, problematic mothers and vanished (or vanishing) fathers." Pretty heavy company.

The show's lyricist, Stephen Sondheim, believes that "it holds up the way *Citizen Kane* holds up. Every scene is juicy. The characters are vivid. The songs are sharp and entertaining. You can't get bored in *Citizen Kane* and you can't get bored in *Gypsy*." Critic Kenneth Tynan said, "The evening tapers off from perfection in its first half to mere brilliance in its second." Like only a handful of musicals—*Annie Get Your Gun*, *South Pacific*, *Follies*, *Babes in Arms*, *Cabaret*, *Show Boat*, *Funny Girl*, *Chicago*—*Gypsy* is so packed with great songs that it's a little unfair to limit the choice of showstoppers. With Ethel Merman, almost every song she belted threatened to bring the show to a screeching stop.

The musical was devised with Ethel Merman in mind, so if it was almost a one-woman show it was sort of meant to be, and in any case she easily turned it into one—but without upstaging the character or distorting the story. "On Merman's Broadway," Ethan Mordden writes, "the star *was* the character." The character she plays—the brash, tough, conniving, never-say-die trouper who blasts her way through anything and anyone in her path to make it in show business for her and her two daughters—played into Merman's stage (and real-life) persona. It was, as everyone said, a custom-built part, unlike another major role she squeezed into that didn't fit her—Annie Oakley.

Only the Perle Mesta character in *Call Me Madam* suited Merman's crass, outsize persona as snugly as Momma Rose. (Note: she is never called that in the show, and purists rail against the phrase, but it's who she is—there's even a song in the score called "If Momma Was Married" and a line in "Rose's Turn" that goes, "Momma's talkin' loud / Momma's doin' fine.") Ethan Mordden notes, "She had played a fake Merman all of her life; now she would play someone real." The real Rose, as depicted in photos, looks less fearsome than the stage mother in the musical—prettier, more winsome, smaller, almost fragile looking (and lesbian), far less bombastic than the loud, swaggering, fearsome ball-buster in Merman's legendary version. In her memoir, the actual Gypsy paints her mother as a woman of some charm.

Sondheim adds, "She's a very American character, a gallant figure and a life force." Well, maybe not so gallant: the real Rose tried to shoot the boy who stole Dainty June from the act (named "Tulsa" in the show), but the safety catch was on. Rose later allegedly shot and killed a young woman in Upstate New York. She ran a lesbian boardinghouse and reportedly pushed a woman out a window. In any case, Rose was not a lady to be messed with. Her other daughter, actress June Havoc, described her as "a mentally disturbed person who looks healthy, and who was so utterly adorable that you couldn't possibly think anything was wrong. She was a beautiful little ornament that was damaged."

In its bones, *Gypsy* is just another backstage musical, Broadway's favorite subject (applauding its own guts and glory), but with a big difference. It details the ups but mainly downs of showbiz—the repeated rejections, dingy theaters, shady producers, and hand-to-mouth existence. *Gypsy* is about the tawdry, pathetic underbelly of show business embodied by Momma Rose's saga, with none of the glamour except in a final scene where we see the fully grown, now famous, Gypsy Rose Lee. But Gypsy (and her success) is not the focus of the musical, just a footnote to the real story of Rose's rise to the bottom.

Arthur Laurents didn't want to write a show about Gypsy Rose Lee when first handed her memoir to adapt—until he realized that the central character wasn't Gypsy but her mother. "And once he made that decision," recalls Sondheim, "which seems an obvious choice now but not when you're sitting down with a book written from a daughter's point of view, everything fell into place." The show was finished in four months, record time for a contemporary musical, which can take five to ten years to get themselves born.

In *Gypsy*, not just Merman but everyone involved was working at the top of their talent: Arthur Laurents, who wrote the libretto and saw that the true heroine was not the stripper but her hard-driving mother Rose; Jule Styne, who some felt was too much a Hollywood guy to handle a full-blooded dramatic Broadway musical, even though he had composed scores for *Gentlemen Prefer Blondes* and *High Button Shoes* (before *Gypsy*, Styne had mainly been a writer, often with Sammy Cahn, of movie songs and pop hits for Frank Sinatra); and finally Sondheim, whom Merman had rejected to write the music in favor of Styne ("Steve's a clever boy, but he can't write for me. He doesn't know who I am"), yet whose lyrics gave the show—and the character—its flavor, richness, charm, wit, and soul. This was the second of three shows for which Sondheim was credited as lyricist alone, but Styne's zesty tunes gave the lyrics a vitality that make them among his most invigorating, inviting, and lasting. Even so, Elliot Norton, the esteemed Boston critic, failed even to mention Sondheim's lyrics in his review, giving Styne sole credit for an "agreeable score."

Styne's greatest asset was that he knew how to write for Merman's voice. Her biographer Brian Kellow observes, "He thought of her voice as a trumpet, and he wrote for it as he would an instrument. What he came up with was an exhilarating score that felt as if it had been shot from a cannon. It played to all of Ethel's strengths. With the exception of 'Small World' . . . all her numbers have a pulsating, relentless drive . . . that required them to be hurled at the audience. Ethel wept when she first heard the songs." Sondheim once said, "When you write for a musical comedy star, you write for not just the character but the character played by that personality. This is a lesson that stood me in very good stead ever since."

Styne was seen as the hard-boiled Hollywood hand, Sondheim as the esoteric genius. Sondheim (at his mentor Oscar Hammerstein's urging) reluctantly took the job writing just lyrics, but Hammerstein told him it would be good experience writing for a seasoned star. Actress Benay Venuta, Merman's chum, said, "Ethel didn't get along with Stephen Sondheim. And to the very end of her life, she couldn't understand why he was such a great success." It was a shotgun marriage that worked out.

"Everything's Coming Up Roses," an exuberant declaration, was Sondheim's ingenious coining of a phrase that many assume is an old saying when, in fact, it never existed until Ethel Merman sang it in *Gypsy*. The phrase harkens back to "come up smelling like roses," but Sondheim neatly recast the expression.

Sondheim was searching for a phrase that would express Momma Rose's jubilant moment, found none he liked, so he invented his own, now part of the language. Beyond that, it's also a pun on the name of the character who sings it, yet it doesn't sound forced. But when Jerome Robbins first heard the song sung by Sondheim, he didn't get it. "But that's her name," Robbins protested. "Everything's coming up Rose's *what*?" (It's actually a triple pun, referring to roses, Momma Rose, and the future Gypsy Rose Lee.)

"Everything's Coming Up Roses" is reminiscent of other numbers from shows that sound like they're borrowed from an earlier era—"Lida Rose" in *The Music Man*, "The Best of Times" in *La Cage aux Folles*, "Tomorrow Belongs to Me" in *Cabaret*, "Edelweiss" in *The Sound of Music*—but are in fact the creations of songwriters who devise a song so right for a nostalgic moment in a show that audiences assume it's actually from the past.

The tune for "Everything's Coming Up Roses" was cut from *High Button Shoes* with lyrics by Sammy Cahn and titled "Betwixt and Between." That show's choreographer, Jerome Robbins, had liked the song and suggested recycling it to Styne. The rewritten number grabs you with its showbiz tang "Curtain up! Light the lights! / You got nothin' to hit but the heights!" It feels so organic to Merman/Rose that the lyrics might almost have been written *by* her, a statement of unbridled can-do spirit, not unlike Styne and Bob Merrill's "Don't Rain on My Parade."

Ethel Merman announces her big plans for the big time in *Gypsy*.

The song reveals Rose's insistence that, even as her world has begun to fall apart and her dream is crumbling after her more gifted daughter June elopes with a chorus boy, all will still be just dandy. Fantasy is what holds her world together, like any self-deluded dreamer with unrealistic expectations. So while the number is a battle cry of belief, it's also sad. "It's a little scary," adds director Greg MacKellan. "Herbie and Louise tell what they're planning to do now that June has left, while Rose in her head is preparing one more assault [on the big time]. When she shouts, 'You'll be swell! You'll be great!,' it's meant to be a picker-upper, but they're appalled Rose is not going to give up. If there's no June to make into a star—well, there's still Louise."

Rose has nothing much to cling to except her stubborn faith that everything will turn out well. She'll figure out something: "I had a dream, / A dream about you, baby!," she tells the shy, neglected, suddenly embraced Louise. With a bravado shout, Rose shares her optimistic dream: "You'll be swell! You'll be great! / Gonna have the whole world on a plate! / Starting here, starting now, / Honey, everything's coming up roses! / Clear the decks! Clear the tracks! / You've got nothing to do but relax!" All of which of course terrifies Louise, who has never had any hope of a showbiz future, let alone dreams of glory. No roses for her.

Momma Rose is intrepid, vowing to push Louise into the spotlight: "You'll be swell! / You'll be great! / I can tell. Just you wait! / That lucky star I talk about is due! / Honey, everything's coming up roses for me and for you!" For timid, lackluster Louise, it's less a promise than a threat. Sondheim said of the number, "I wrote a song of the type that Merman had sung all her life, like 'Blow, Gabriel, Blow,' which only requires a trumpet-voiced affirmation." But she gave much more to it. "Her intensity came as a surprise," he said. "Ethel was not one for analysis of character. I just knew she could do double takes." Sondheim's power surge number chillingly convinces you, despite her obvious delusion and desperation, that "lucky star" Rose crows about will come true by the end of the evening, if this stage mother from hell has anything to say about it. The song was perfectly placed in Merman's sweet spot, and she blasted it into posterity. It's impossible to listen to the song, or just the tune, and not hear Merman's voice. And in the end, by the way, Momma was right.

Gypsy was not Jerome Robbins's kind of show, with no dancing of any consequence, but he tried to put his stamp on the musical by envisioning it as a "panorama of vaudeville," a fond recollection of a dead entertainment era. He even auditioned acrobats, jugglers, animal acts, and burlesque comics—a vision that librettist Arthur Laurents declined in favor of Momma Rose's grim showbiz survival saga. The closest the show came to a panorama of vaudeville was its most flagrant showstopper, **"Ya Gotta Get a Gimmick,"** the burlesque parody performed by three strippers, the virginal Louise's shocked introduction to the sleazy world of striptease that she later conquered.

The first version was a raunchy twenty-minute miniburlesque show Robbins devised, with an aging comic playing a little girl dressed as Shirley Temple opposite a lecherous Santa Claus. That was quickly cut and replaced by dancers playing three strippers who strut their specialty numbers—Tessie Tura (Maria Karnilova in the original), Electra with the blinking pasties (Chotzi Foley), and Faith Dane as Miss Mazeppa ("Once I was a schlepper, now I'm Miss Mazeppa"), who ends the song with her show-stopping routine, bending over and blowing a horn between her legs, unfailingly bringing down the house. Dane was hired before there was a song for her, but she knocked everyone out with her audition, bumping and grinding to "The Call to the Post," the racetrack fanfare before each race (that leads off "Fugue for Tinhorns" in *Guys and Dolls*). Just the sort of gimmick that inspired "Ya Gotta Get a Gimmick." But Gypsy Rose Lee wound up with the best gimmick of all—a striptease that was all tease and little strip.

That was a big moment in *Gypsy*, so much so that Dane sued the show when it went on the road without her, using the bit that Dane claimed was her property, even if the music was Styne's and the lyrics Sondheim's ("If you wanna bump it, / Bump it with a trumpet"). Sandra Church, who played Gypsy, told me, "She said, 'You can't do that. It's mine.' She said it was her number. I don't think she won anything, but she did go to court. She went against [coproducer] David Merrick. She said she had brought [the number] to them and they had no right to it." Dane was in the movie but never did the show again despite repeatedly auditioning for it. She ended up as a wannabe politician and ran for mayor of Washington nine times, most recently—at age ninety—in 2014, when she again auditioned for the role she created, was yet again rejected, and filed an age discrimination suit.

In the show, Rose can't even bask in Gypsy Rose Lee's fame that she fanned into flame because she realizes it's really all been for her, not her daughters, revealed in the long dramatic finale, **"Rose's Turn,"** when Momma Rose finally sees her life as a push for her own thwarted recognition. In less talented hands, the scene might have come off as a musical version of *Stella Dallas*, but Laurents's harsh, unblinking book and Sondheim's unsentimental lyrics keep it from turning maudlin. "Rose's Turn" is a complex song cycle, divided into roughly four sections, each part referring back to earlier songs, a jagged patchwork that fits together seamlessly and ends with a discordant vamp that leads into Rose's manic collapse.

What starts out as a mock performance becomes, by the finish, a cry for help, or at least attention. Using snatches of earlier songs with a bitter twist, "Rose's Turn" is an intense ten-minute solo that starts with Rose announcing her own entrance—"Here she is, boys! Here she is, world! Here's Rose!" She resumes speaking: "Play it, boys," then segues into "You either got it, or you ain't—and boys, I got it! You like it?" The orchestra shouts, "Yeah!" The number sounds like a strip parody, as if to ridicule Gypsy or go her one better. As British critic Robert Cushman put it in a 1973 review of the revival with Angela Lansbury, "In a musical ostensibly about stripping, we watch the baring of a soul." He called it "the most tumultuous reception I have ever heard greet a single number." Merman had trouble with the number's climactic moment, when Rose falters in a near breakdown, because, in one critic's words, "Rose wasn't a falterer."

Angela Lansbury, who did an equally lauded version in London, said in 1970, "What makes Rose palatable is that she's a mass of good intentions that go wrong . . . then I think you forgive her. And she's very vulnerable. . . . You also hate her a lot, but hopefully you can smile at her too. She's a tragic figure, but I hope she's funny as well, realizing that this woman is a total failure." Tyne Daly, in a major revival in 1989, commented, "She wants something that she doesn't have, but it's not fame, or to be a great performer. Her yearnings are for something so unspecific that it breaks your heart."

Rose resumes singing, with a clever echo of her first song in the show, "Some People": "Well, I got it! Some people got it / And make it pay, / Some people can't even / Give it away. / This people's got it / And this people's spreadin' it around. / You either have it / Or you've had it." She then introduces herself, Gypsy style, "Hello, everybody! My name's Rose. What's yours? [*bumps*] How d'ya like them egg rolls, Mr. Goldstone?"

The number is an anthology of her fractured life story, a quick reprise of the show itself, and concludes with Momma Rose crumbling as she realizes why she sacrificed her life for her daughter's careers ("This time for me! For me! / For me! / For me! / FOR ME!"). For me, it's always seemed a too-pat cathartic moment, a dramatic device repeated in the crack-up number at the end of *Follies* in which the successful but miserable Benjamin Stone, in a lavish number called "Live, Laugh, Love," confronts his empty life and dismal marriage, as he crumbles onstage.

After Sondheim first sang "Rose's Turn" to Merman and others, Styne says in his biography that both the conductor Milton Rosenstock and the star were weeping. Merman exclaimed, "It's a goddamn aria!" To friends, she less politely called it "a motherfucker to sing." Merman realized Rose was the role of her lifetime, likely her last, and was willing to submit to Robbins's stern direction. She had never really been challenged in earlier shows, where she was just a big voice on legs—you could hear every syllable but that was it, not much dramatic interpretation. Laurents said later, "I'm very grateful to Ethel Merman because I don't think we would have done the show without her, even though she was on the skids at that time. She had had a few flops. She did us a great service and for that time she was terrific, but it was never what I thought the performance should be."

Robbins's early plan was to close the show with a nightmare ballet, but two weeks into rehearsal he suddenly notified Sondheim and Styne he didn't have time to stage the number. He agreed to meet Sondheim onstage one night, and Robbins said, "Let's try ad libbing something," which became a montage of the musical climaxing in Rose's dark turn. It was like a scene out of a '40s musical, noted Sondheim ("where the Gershwin kind of character is in his penthouse overlooking the city and writes his Manhattan symphony and it comes out all at once"), both men improvising late at night under just a work light. "I started to play the piano and he started to move, and he said, 'Play it in strip rhythm.' We worked for about an hour and a half. It was now 12:30 a.m. I was so excited. . . . Jerry and I improvised 'Rose's Turn.' I wrote the lyrics, utilizing all the songs Jule had written. I couldn't wait to get home and sketch the whole thing out. I wrote it all down and brought it to Jule the next morning." Styne approved it.

Laurents had asked Merman at the start of rehearsal, "How far are you willing to go?" and she replied, "I'll do anything you want me to," and she did. Laurents didn't just give her line readings but also lyric readings on "Rose's Turn"— "softer," "slower," "starting flat then building." Sondheim had grave misgivings that Merman wasn't enough of an actress to pull off such a dramatic moment— he once called her "a talking dog." Merman did as she was told because "she wanted a showstopper," writes Keith Garebian. "She wanted a blazing ending." Merman had trouble shifting gears, Laurents writes, when the number goes to the climactic breakdown when she stumbles on the word "Momma."

Sondheim later commented, "I thought in the first act, which required her comic skills, she was nonpareil. In the second, where it required dramatic skills . . . there was something less fulfilled." He told Brian Kellow, "Brains

rousing hand so interrupted the final scene that the audience "listened to the last scene less than it had before, because the prolonged bows cued a curtain that didn't come down but should have."

Veteran Broadway publicist Josh Ellis recalls a dinner with Merman where he asked her about creating "Rose's Turn." "She just glared at me. So I ask her again. This time she says, 'Jule Styne is sitting at a piano, Jerry Robbins was standing on a platform. Jule played and Jerry did the whole number for me. Jerry said, "Now Ethel, you do it." So I went up on the platform and did it the way Jerry did it. When I was done, Jerry said, "That's fine Ethel."' Then Merman paused and said, 'OK, who wants dessert? I want cherries jubilee.' That was her whole story. She did not analyze it. She only cared about getting it technically right. She had so much talent she didn't need to analyze it. She just did it, and it worked."

•••••••••••••• BACKSTAGE DISH ••••••••••••••

+ The list is long of people who turned down an offer to write the *Gypsy* score—or were turned down. Cole Porter was too ill; Irving Berlin didn't like the story. Styne said, "All sorts of composers were auditioning for it, I heard. I felt left out. I said to myself, 'Why are they auditioning composers when Steve Sondheim is there?'" Merrick finally told him Sondheim was reluctant to collaborate with him—or anyone; he wanted to do both lyrics and music. "He collaborated on *West Side Story* with Lenny Bernstein. Why can't he collaborate with me?" Styne asked Merrick, who replied, "Steve's very sensitive." "So am I," said Styne. Critic Martin Gottfried wrote that it shouldn't have been surprising that Styne could write for Merman. "He had been writing one Frank Sinatra hit after another and had already tailored 'Diamonds Are a Girl's Best Friend' to Carol Channing."

When Merman demanded Styne do the music, Sondheim relented and, despite early doubts, was persuaded by Styne's "enthusiasm with which he attacked the keyboard, and by his nervous good humor." Styne was apprehensive on meeting Sondheim: "I thought he might hit me over the head, knowing that he wanted to do the whole show. He was young, ambitious, and a huge talent. But he was also very gentle and we got along fine."

The Styne-Sondheim collaboration was a seamless merging of eras and sensibilities, which doesn't always work out (like the later disastrous teaming of Sondheim and Richard Rodgers). Styne was a great journeyman composer, an enthusiast who bubbled over with melodies and optimism; Sondheim was a much quieter, painstaking, more skeptical soul who seemed to bleed every note and word. Arthur Laurents didn't have much faith they would click. "Jule wrote big fat pop hits, great tunes, but *Gypsy* was not going to be a razzamatazz Ethel Merman show; it was going to be a tough musical with a dramatic range. Jule Styne music? I doubted it." Sondheim was a dawdler and procrastinator, whereas Styne was so prodigious that, like Cole Porter, he would rather write a new tune than revise one that didn't work. Like most songwriters, Styne was eager to reuse tunes cut from other shows, a practice that appalls Sondheim, who feels each song should be inspired by its unique moment in a show. He was unhappy to learn that Styne had dipped into his trunk for used tunes.

+ Styne threatened to quit the show if Robbins cut the tender "Little Lamb," another of Styne's trunk tunes (originally called "Untamed"). Sandra Church, as Gypsy, also threatened to leave the show if they cut the song, one of her only two solos. "Jule was adamant—he felt it was a very important song for her character," she says. Styne, never a guy to mess with, told the director, "Mr. Robbins, I have notified my lawyers in New York that I'm withdrawing the entire score unless 'Little Lamb' is put back in tonight." Louise got back her little lamb.

+ The pivotal phrase in the score, "Let Me Entertain You," begins the show as a kiddie vaudeville turn, "Let *Us* Entertain You," sung by Louise and June. It came to Sondheim while searching for a way to bookend the story with the same number. Robbins suggested, "Just say what [the show's] about." Sondheim: "Like what?" Robbins: "I don't know. Something along the lines of, 'Let us entertain you'?" Sondheim, annoyed, thought, "How like a nonwriter—blunt and flavorless," but jotted it down anyway, later realizing, "I saw that Jerry's phrase could, with a simple pronoun change, serve as a refrain for both Baby June's bright-eyed vaudeville solo and grown-up Louise's sultry burlesque come-on."

+ Laurents wanted to cut the charming "You'll Never Get Away from Me," which both Styne and Sondheim thought would be a hit. Laurents finally gave in. The melody was yet another Styne trunk song he had smuggled past Sondheim, originally called "I'm in Pursuit of Happiness" from the TV musical *Ruggles of Red Gap*, which began life even five years earlier as a tune cut from *The Girl in Pink Tights* with Marilyn Monroe. Styne defended song recycling by pointing out that even George Gershwin did it with "The Man I Love": "The song was in five other shows before it found the right home." Styne had infinite confidence in his tunes. He would demonstrate songs after setting down the lead sheet and grandly announcing, "May I say: another classic!" Styne usually got his way, like the time he felt the orchestra was too low in the pit to be fully heard and asked Robbins to raise it a little. Robbins ignored him until, finally, Styne went up onstage and told him, "You've got to do this right now, and if you don't I'm going to throw you into the pit and they won't hear you either." Styne won that one, too.

✦ Gypsy Rose Lee was overjoyed to have a musical about her life and laid down only one rule—the show had to be called *Gypsy*. Her envious sister June Havoc was a tougher sell but finally came around after Laurents changed her name in the script to Claire to avoid a lawsuit. Havoc, on second thought, insisted he change it back to June and signed off on the show. Gypsy answered June's objection to the embellished stage version of their lives by subtitling it *A Musical Fable*: "It's my monument. . . . It doesn't have to be factual, it only has to be big, exciting, and—a smash!" June protested, "You were never a pathetic Cinderella," and Gypsy rebutted, "They can't make a musical out of that, June. I don't care what they say about me as long as my name is up there."

✦ In his book *The Making of Gypsy*, Keith Garebian quotes a deathbed speech by the real Rose, true to the spiteful spirit of the re-created stage version that seems almost tepid by comparison. Rose vowed, with a bitter theatrical flourish no mere librettist could top, "This isn't the end. Wherever you go, as long as either of you lives, I'll be right there—and I swear before God you're always going to know it! . . . You'll know I'm there. I'll see to that. So go on, Louise, tell all your classy friends how funny I was, how much smarter you were than me. When you get your own private kick in the ass, just remember: it's a present from me to you. A present from your funny, un-bright mother."

✦ Cole Porter, who had been too ill to write *Gypsy*, wanted to hear some of the numbers, so his pal Merman arranged for her, Sondheim, Styne, and writer Anita Loos to have dinner at his apartment in the Waldorf Towers. Sondheim recalls a moving moment during the evening: "By then [the crippled Porter] was being carried around by his strong servant, piggyback. My memory is that when we sang 'Together,' the song from *Gypsy* has a quadruple rhyme: 'Wherever I go I know he goes. / Wherever I go I know she goes. / No fits, no feuds and no egos, / Amigos'—and when

I said 'amigos' I heard him go 'Ah!' right in the corner of the room. It's a very Cole Porter line, because he would use these foreign languages for rhyme, for effect, and he didn't see it coming." For Sondheim, Porter's delighted gasp was the highest possible accolade.

✦ One of musicals freaks' most fevered debates is over who was the best, most definitive Momma Rose—Merman, Tyne Daly in the rave 1989 revival, Angela Lansbury in London, Bette Midler in a TV version, Bernadette Peters in the New York revival in 2003, or Patti LuPone on Broadway in 2008, who had lost out to Peters five years before. LuPone surpassed all former Roses for sheer ferocity; critic Michael Feingold wrote, "She pushes both of the huge act-ending numbers to the point of mania; I wondered why Herbie and Louise hadn't called the men in white coats to take her away."

Tyne Daly usually gets the most votes for best-acted version, with Lansbury a close second, but Peters's version most divides avid *Gypsyphiles*. Sondheim said that Linda Lavin, in the 1990 Broadway revival, came closest to capturing the charm of the original Rose. Ben Brantley wrote in his *New York Times* review that, instead of playing her usual "delectable waif," Peters's Momma Rose revealed "damning glints of self-awareness." The dynamic cutie pie with the top-heavy hourglass figure finally brought sex appeal to the role of Rose, usually played as a sexless battle-ax, in the 2003 London revival directed by Sam Mendes, who explained, "Rose was a sexual animal. She used her sexuality to get her girls ahead, whereas everybody's always played her as a truck driver."

In any case, Momma Rose has become the King Lear (or maybe Lady Macbeth) of musical roles, which seasoned performers feel they must do to prove their musicals chops. Lansbury turned down the role in London for years, saying, "I can't beat Merman at the singing game, and she can't beat me at the acting game, so no contest," to which Merman responded, just a tad cattily, "I have no hard feelings—why should I? . . . I am just glad I created the role so others can enjoy it."

✦ One of those others was Rosalind Russell, who starred in the movie version of *Gypsy* after producer Mervyn LeRoy had promised Merman the film but was talked out of it by Russell's wheeler-dealer husband Freddie Brisson, known in showbiz as "the Lizard of Roz." Merman felt she'd been double-crossed. Jack Klugman told Sondheim biographer Caryl Flinn that LeRoy "regally screwed Ethel. He was constantly with her and told her he wouldn't do the picture without her." In 1962, Russell admitted that her songs were dubbed by Lisa Kirk (except for "Mr. Goldstone"), but in her 1977 autobiography she changed her tune, saying she nixed the dubbing after hearing it and convinced Warner Bros. to let her sing on screen. "People will say I didn't, but that's Roz and nobody else on the soundtrack." The movie—a faithful if uninspired reincarnation drained of its human juices—was blasted by critics who had seen Merman and refused to accept anyone else as Rose. A Toronto critic called the film a "debacle," writing, "Merman had stopped the show and rightly so. The chief fault must rest on Miss Russell, who can only pick up the crumbs her limited talents in this area allow her."

Merman was flattered her name was always mentioned in reviews of the movie, but Klea Blackhurst says, "She was devastated by not getting the movie. I think it did her in. She was told over and over it was hers. There's not a person I know that doesn't wish she was captured on film." Bosley Crowther in the *New York Times* wrote, "That tornado of a stage mother that Ethel Merman portrayed on Broadway comes out little more than a big wind in the portrayal that Rosalind Russell gives her. . . . She misses the Merman magic." Pauline Kael called the movie "heavy and coarse" and "extremely unpleasant."

✦ Though it's now considered a benchmark musical, *Gypsy* was a tough sell when it opened, despite the rave notices. "It was an unpleasant show by the standards of 1950s musicals, where everyone ends up happy," notes Sondheim. "In *Gypsy* one daughter is lost and the other is lost in another way." Albeit nominated for ten Tonys in 1960, neither the show nor its great star, nor anyone, won any. Both the show and Merman were soundly beaten by both *The Sound of Music* and *Fiorello!* (in a tie). The *New York Times's* Brooks Atkinson liked the star and her show ("a thoroughly professional musical," whatever that meant) but was underwhelmed by the score. "The music is fresh and lively in the musical-comedy tradition," he all but yawned. "Jule Styne has written dramatic songs, as well as Tin Pan Alley tunes."

• •

Apart from Stephen Sondheim, the major surviving member of the *Gypsy* team is Sandra Church, who originated the role of Gypsy in the show at twenty-two. Now close to eighty, Church lives in San Francisco, a longtime showbiz refugee whose first—and only—Broadway show was *Gypsy*, also her first and last musical. It cured her for life.

Church's role was central to the show, yet she made only a small but charming impression in it, playing the adolescent Rose Louise Hovick who blossoms prettily into the classic, and classy, stripper Gypsy Rose Lee. Gypsy became famous for what she *didn't* take off, when in fact she revealed more than legend suggests—just dropping a shoulder strap or peeling a glove. According to sister June Havoc, Gypsy sang "Minnie the Moocher" naked. "She was out there like all the others," said Havoc. "I couldn't stand it." Gypsy's defense after a Minsky's raid: "I wasn't naked. I was completely covered by a blue spotlight." In her memoir, Lee boasts, "I could be a star without any talent at all!"

When working on the script, Laurents asked Lee if there was any nudity in her act, and she told him, "I wouldn't know," ever the coy girl. In *Vanity Fair*, Laura Jacobs contended, "Her strip was still pretty strippy, still showing a lot of skin, ending up in net panties. She removed her clothes by plucking out the dress-making pins that held them together, dropping the pins into a tuba—*plink, plink, plink.*" It got laughs. "That's where she triumphed," said Havoc. "Somebody who would be unavailable, tall, and who would use her femininity and allure to get laughs as well as for sex, without doing dirty things. And that was genius. She's the only one that climbed out of the slime." In her memoir, Gypsy famously wrote, "You make 'em beg for more—and then don't give it to them!" Laura Jacobs refutes that, contending, "You couldn't just drop a shoulder strap or remove a glove, as Gypsy does in both the memoir and the musical. The men would hoot you off the stage."

Jacobs reports that the most Lee might expose was a nipple, before quickly covering it with a black lace bow. The song "Zip," from *Pal Joey*, performed by one Gladys Bumps, is a tribute to Gypsy's act, in which Gladys reveals her thoughts while removing items, much like one of Gypsy's lines in her act: "When I raise my skirts with slyness and dexterity / I'm mentally computing just how much I'll give to charity." At the end, down to a black lace G-string, Gypsy would duck behind a curtain after saying, demurely, "Oh, boys, I can't take *that* off. I'll catch cold!" Filmmaker D. A. Pennebaker recalled, "It was like your mom coming out. That's what made it work."

In the show, Gypsy is presented teasingly but not really comically. Church had two solos in the show and a duet, "If Momma Was Married," with June. In her big number, she segues from teenage tomboy to sophisticated strip star singing the come-hither "Let Me Entertain You." It's a crafty theatrical moment but less sensual than intended. Church was too prim to display the song's intended sexual flavors, and in fact she refused to wear pasties and a G-string, but Brooks Atkinson was charmed: "Sandra Church gives a lovely performance." Lovely if not terribly sexy.

Although Church got nominated for a supporting actress Tony, *Gypsy* was an unpleasant experience for her. "It sent me into analysis. My first analyst said, 'You are sort of playing your own life every night.' I had a stage mother and here was Ethel Merman, also a stage mother, who was not nice frankly. She was pretty terrifying. I was really scared most of the time. I scare easily. The show was very disturbing."

Before auditioning, Church, who was only interested in acting, took a few singing lessons and beat out Suzanne Pleshette for the part. Church was considered the better singer. Pleshette was dating producer Norman Twain, later Church's first husband. "She [Pleshette] auditioned for Gypsy, and when she didn't get it he told me she smashed a mirror. She was furious." Church nearly didn't get the role either, because she looked too naïve to evolve into the erotic Gypsy; after five auditions she was finally hired.

Both Laurents and Robbins were petty tyrants, Church verifies. Robbins, she recalls, "was just awful to Lane Bradbury, who played Dainty June." In rehearsals, Bradbury kept forgetting her batons for a number, so opening night Robbins hid her batons. "She was doing her splits in tears. She was doing this number with her hands, without the batons. He was so mean." Bradbury said, "He has a warm open smile, and then he sticks the knife in." "He didn't do that to me," recalls Church. "What he did do, he just refused to deal with the strip." Church's striptease scene never played convincingly, because it was never decided how much of a strip Church should do. "In Philadelphia, they were always cutting this and cutting that, and then the audience would get mad because I didn't strip in the number. They just couldn't get the strip right, adding more and then less." Laurents once had Ethel onstage during the strip, paralyzing Church. "They decided that didn't work."

Church wasn't a dancer so Robbins left staging the strip number to Laurents, whose bawdy striptease direction she didn't like. On her last night in the show she did it her own way, more demurely. Laurents writes in his memoir that Church was too tentative, even timid, to portray the grown-up Gypsy Rose Lee. "Sandra shrank. Her Method training was of no help. Jerry lost patience and asked me to rehearse Sandra's scenes in the ladies lounge. Jerry had turned against Sandra. Her terror blocked her and in turn, when they got to the strip, blocked him from inventing. He had to work it out on her, but a trembling body, however shapely, was less than inspirational. Gyspy Rose Lee hadn't had a good body but she was smart enough not to expose it. She seduced the audience with her wit; her gimmick had been fresh and original: talking."

Ethel Merman was an equally traumatic experience for Church. "She was terrible. She wouldn't speak to me for six months." Merman had heard that

Church made a crack about her going on too long at an Actor's Fund benefit, when in fact Church was criticizing someone else. "During the show, when we were in the wings, I said, 'Ethel I want to explain,' and she turned away. It went on like that for six months." She blames the misunderstanding on Laurents and a "bitchy" stage manager who caused a rift between her and Merman. "So I go in that night and go downstairs to Ethel's dressing room. Her dresser just pushes me out and says, 'No, you can't come in.'"

Church continues, "Finally, at Christmastime Ethel sends her dresser up with a little Christmas present for me. I go dashing down and rushing into her room and threw my arms around her and said, 'Ethel, I just love this present!' Then it was like nothing had ever happened. We never mentioned it. Everybody said she was tough. Jack Klugman got on with her. He was a man. I was a real threat, and I was with Jule Styne [in a brief affair] and that bothered Ethel. Working with somebody who is that jealous is very difficult." Biographer Brian Kellow reports that Laurents caught Merman peeking through a keyhole into Styne's room to see if he was in bed with Church. Once, at the Variety Club, he quotes Laurents as saying that after a few drinks Merman supposedly asked everyone at her table, "So! Is Jule fucking Sandra? Is he?"

Merman, Church says, was wary of everyone, especially of an actor doing anything behind her—a movement, a look, a gesture that might distract from her performance. "She would tell an actor, 'You're doing something.' She knew! She couldn't see it, but the audience's eyes were wandering. She could tell by the audience. And she would say, 'Whatever you are doing, don't do it.'" In *Annie Get Your Gun* a stage manager asked Jerry Orbach what he was doing while Merman was singing. He said, "I'm just reacting to what she sings." Her reaction: "I'm not reacting when he sings, so he should not be reacting to what I sing."

Edie Adams said Merman was "paranoid about being upstaged by a younger female performer. Even if the girl was not doing anything to call attention to herself, just her younger, prettier presence would freak out Merman." Russell Nype, her costar in *Call Me Madam*, claimed, "She really was a very insecure woman." Church says, "After *Gypsy* they wanted me to do a musical with Phil Silvers. I said no, because I looked at Phil Silvers and thought he was another Ethel Merman type and I didn't want to do it."

Yet stories emerge of unexpected Merman kindnesses, once toward an understudy, Merle Louise, who went on for one of the girls in *Gypsy* and got a laugh on a line that hadn't got one before. "Hey, this kid gave the show a real kick in the ass," said Merman in the wings, and sent her a bouquet of roses.

The next day, Merman called David Merrick and commanded, "I want Merle in that part."

Merman wasn't known for mingling with lesser lights in the show. Her friend Benay Venuta said, "She liked being called 'Miss Merman' and she liked being respected. She was not chummy with the chorus. I had some friends in the *Annie Get Your Gun* company, and I said to Ethel, 'You've got to meet them.' And she said, 'But they're in the chorus.' And I said, 'Yes, but they're very nice people.' She really was in an ivory tower. I said to her once, 'Do you realize you never went through a period where you had to audition or be turned down? You just became a star.'" Georgia Engel told Klea Blackhurst that when Merman played the last Dolly in the original Broadway run of *Hello, Dolly!*, in which Engel was playing milliner Minnie Fay, Merman played all their scenes to her forehead, and after six months she moved down to her eyes. Engel said, "That was the proudest moment of my life."

Church and Styne's romance also left a sour aftertaste. "He brought me milk shakes. That's how it started. I was young, and he was actually living with Ruth Dubonnet [of the Dubonnet wine family] at that point." Did Styne coach her much on delivery? "Sure. A lot. More than Steve. He was more open. Steve was very shy and withdrawn then." As Church remembers Styne, "I must say, in retrospect, I don't think of him kindly. He was very volatile and really neurotic and he took it out on me. He was a compulsive gambler and he borrowed money from me. He hadn't paid off the gangsters. Here I am making $350 a week! It's just bizarre. He knew I had a couple of thousand dollars hidden in my apartment. He was looking around trying to find it. That's a craziness! It's just awful. So I don't remember him kindly."

Her recollections of Gypsy Rose Lee herself are a lot warmer. "She was wonderful to me. I loved her. I was taken over to her house. She went over her scrapbooks with me and gave me pictures, which I still have. She could not have been more helpful and kind. I went over to her house a couple of times and she would tell me stories." Lee liked Church's performance, she says, and gave her some stripper tips. "She told me about the gloves and stripping." Church paid a stripper, Tempest Storm, to teach her how to strip for the audition. (Broadway incest note: when Merman left the cast of *DuBarry Was a Lady* in 1940, who should take over the role but . . . Gypsy Rose Lee.)

Church stayed with the show eighteen months until her contract was up, and even leaving the show left a sour taste. "I could not have been happier to leave. I was not happy in the show. Jack Klugman was bitching and was tired, but he stayed on because they gave him a big raise. He was buying a house, and he said, 'I have to do this, Sandra.'" She had wanted out of the show earlier to accept movie offers "when I was really hot," but the producer refused. So when they changed theaters and knew the critics would be back, they wanted Church to leave so her understudy could assume the role and get reviewed, but she said no. "I told them, 'You would not let me out when I wanted it, so now I am not going.' That's when I decided to quit the theater." She enrolled at Columbia to study archaeology but got a degree in English and wound up in art history. "After I quit and got married, Hal Prince asked me to do a show, so sometimes I'm sorry I left because it would have been a different life."

BYE BYE BIRDIE

◆ 1960 ◆

"Put on a Happy Face"

Not all showstoppers have a blockbuster mentality. Some, like **"Put on a Happy Face"** from *Bye Bye Birdie*, can light up an audience with just a simple jump for joy. This is the feel-good song of all time (and later wound up as the theme song for TV's *The Hollywood Palace* for six years).

The little throwaway number, barely three minutes long, just a few lines with a modest dance in the middle, succeeds in stopping the show with no knockout staging, no witty lists, no thumping theatrics—nothing but an innocent, playful, totally captivating spirit. It's a number that does exactly what it says. It's impossible not to smile when you hear it.

Like many great "charm songs" that don't advance the story, it almost got tossed out in rehearsal when it was first staged in act 2 with Dick Van Dyke serenading *Ed Sullivan Show* stagehands. Director Gower Champion's astute wife, Marge, thought it would work much better if Van Dyke sang it to teenage girls in act 1 who were miserable because their rock idol Conrad Birdie was going into the army. The song wasn't clicking as staged, and Van Dyke didn't feel he was any good singing it. Not even Charles Strouse, who wrote the infectious tune, liked it; too corny, he said. "I knew the song had to go."

Marge Champion—Gower's partner in movie musicals (most memorably *Show Boat*, strutting through "Life Upon the Wicked Stage") and, after their marital split, his career confidante—had a major hand in "Put on a Happy Face." He often looked to his old partner for dance ideas.

Champion, a cheery ninety-four when we spoke by phone, said, "*Bye Bye Birdie* was the first show Gower both choreographed and directed." She recalls going into the basement of the Shubert Theatre in Philadelphia to rehearse Chita Rivera in "Spanish Rose," her big *Birdie* number, in which she slithers around under a table full of Shriners—a wild, giddy, extraneous number but, says Marge Champion, an "enormous" showstopper.

"Put on a Happy Face" was originally written for Rivera, but, recalls Champion, "Gower said, 'Chita doesn't need another showstopper and this young man does.'" The initial idea was for Rivera to sing the song to Van Dyke, to cheer *him* up. Susan Watson, the original teenager Kim MacAfee in the show, recalls, "Gower said it isn't working; it slows down the plot. We were well into rehearsals by then, but it was obvious it would work, just watching Dick move. He would do these silly walks and stuff like that. It was just so playful."

Charles Strouse's version: "Marge had this idea of doing a tap dance with the kids in the first act when Birdie is leaving so I decided to try it her way. I was secretly very embarrassed about that song. It was my first Broadway show and I thought, *Oh my god, this is one of the first songs in the show and it's a tap dance!* But it stopped the show every time." Marge insists Gower should get all the credit for it but admits she may have suggested the idea to him.

Van Dyke had a hard time early in rehearsals because he had no confidence he could do a big Broadway musical. Champion says, "I remember it well. He had not danced. He had an act [the Merry Mimes]. He was a mime. He always gives me credit for giving him some tips." More than anything she gave him confidence. "He gives me credit for saving his life in that show, but really Gower deserves all the credit. Gower said Dick is going to be a great star, but we have to give him the right material." Van Dyke is that rare no-sweat performer who makes everything look easy, most of all in the little light-footed number that pops up in the first act. He's also one of the world's most likable performers, radiating feel-good vibes in any role.

Bye Bye Birdie, with songs by Strouse and Lee Adams, was an unlikely hit that satirizes the emerging '50s teenage invasion, the rock phenomenon, and a new celebrity culture epitomized by Elvis Presley. It was really the first musical to chronicle the generation gap. Creating a show around Elvis being drafted into the army seemed a far-fetched idea, but Strouse and Adams, with Champion's bright dances, plus the cheery presences of Van Dyke, Chita

Rivera, Susan Watson, and Paul Lynde, made the show much more fun than anyone might have guessed.

Susan Watson told me she wasn't sold on *Bye Bye Birdie* after first reading the script. "I remember thinking, *This is so dumb!* The whole Elvis Presley thing—and I was never an Elvis fan that much. I was into classical music, studying to be in opera in Tulsa, Oklahoma. But these were fun upbeat songs. Then I realized it was a spoof on how people reacted to Elvis and the parents versus the children, and as the show grew I realized, *Hey, this is kinda funny.*"

The musical depicts the intersection of pop-crazed America and real people (Kim MacAfee's family in Sweet Apple, Ohio), reminiscent of radio star Sheridan Whiteside descending upon another family in Ohio in *The Man Who Came to Dinner.* The man who comes to dinner in *Bye Bye Birdie* is the world's most famous rock star, and Kim is chosen to kiss him farewell on *The Ed Sullivan Show*—another pillar of pop Americana, lovingly razzed in "Hymn for a Sunday Evening," sung by a reverential viewer (Paul Lynde).

Bye Bye Birdie is a great example of a musical that reflects the national zeitgeist, that captures something in the air, comments on it sharply, and turns it into something amusing and melodic—that is, a Broadway show. Rock 'n' roll was a sitting duck, as was the runaway teenage cult that was hijacking pop culture, with fierce turf wars between parents and adolescents. Strouse and Adams took the rock sound and turned it into musical comedy terms in songs like Birdie's "One Last Kiss"—maybe the world's first Elvis impersonation. The show was such a must-see hit (644 performances) that a misbegotten sequel in 1981 was not as inevitable as it must have seemed at the time. *Bring Back Birdie* lasted four performances; its moment, so keenly skewered two decades earlier, had long passed.

The show makes fun of teenagers, TV, and rock stars without taking a mocking, superior attitude. As the writer Mark Steyn noted, it was an unusual (for the time, 1960) "young show" when most musicals then were about grown-ups. Critic Kenneth Tynan compared its "affectionate freshness" to Rodgers and Hart's 1938 *Babes in Arms.* It made fun of "Kids," in Paul Lynde's anguished solo, but it genuinely liked the kids it was kidding, and the show simultaneously kids parents: "Why can't they be like we were? / Perfect in every way. / What's the matter with kids today? . . . Why can't they dance like we did? / What's wrong with Sammy Kaye? / What's the matter with kids today?" (Square '40s and '50s bandleader Sammy Kaye is a perfect archaic '50s reference.) As a result, the show remains a revival favorite in high schools even now, when Elvis is medieval history. "Put on a Happy Face" later was deftly used in commercials for makeup, Kool-Aid, and even a cold-sore remedy ("Cold sores are gonna clear up / Put on a happy face!").

What made the number work so well was the contrast of Van Dyke's sunny manner—even his body language radiates humor—and two glum little girls' hangdog expressions. Nobody could not be transformed when confronted by Dick Van Dyke telling you, "Gray skies are gonna clear up, / Put on a happy face . . . / Stick out that noble chin / Wipe off that full-of-doubt look / Slap on a happy grin!"

The lyrics could not be more basic, but Adams snuck in a brilliant interior rhyme in the next line: "Take off the gloomy mask of tragedy / It's not your style. / You'll look so good that you'll be gladja de- / Cided to smile!" Tony Bennett, in his hit recording, messed up the line and the rhyme, clumsily singing, "Take off that gloomy mask of tragedy / It's not your style. / You'll be so good that you'll be glad / You decided to smile!" This is the sort of thing that ages lyricists prematurely. (For a quick mood fix, YouTube has a black-and-white clip of Van Dyke singing the song, most likely on, yes, *The Ed Sullivan Show*).

"Put on a Happy Face" is a simple song of exuberance of the kind that only musicals can provide. Champion might have turned it into a rousing tap-dance extravaganza with a big chorus (as he first considered), but it's exactly right as staged—just Van Dyke and two teenage girls interacting. It stays human and unshowbizy, but it gets the job done. Indeed, it kills, even if it has nothing to do with the show's rock 'n' roll theme.

The show began as a musical about teenagers, originally called "Let's Go Steady," but Champion felt the story needed a timely twist, which turned out to be Elvis's headline departure into the army in 1958. So the title was changed to "The Day They Took Birdie Away" and then "Goodbye Birdie" before it landed as *Bye Bye Birdie*. That gave the show a news angle, just the hook it needed to grab audiences in 1960. (Conrad Birdie's name was a play on rock 'n' roller Conway Twitty; real name: Harold Jenkins.)

The movie version was a misguided mess, a truly dreadful adaptation of a Broadway musical. Not even Van Dyke could save it. Janet Leigh played the Chita Rivera role of Van Dyke's Hispanic girlfriend, Rosie, except she's not Hispanic in the film, so Rivera's big number "Spanish Rose" was cut. Leigh was sexy, but a Spanish spitfire she was not. Lynde was recast, but looked miscast, and Van Dyke's mother was embarrassingly portrayed by Maureen Stapleton as a nattering Jewish yenta with a Waspy son. Most glaringly, the adorable Susan Watson, musicals' all-time ingénue (Luisa in *The Fantasticks* and naïve Nanette in the 1971 revival of *No, No, Nanette*), was ousted by hip-swinging Ann-Margret, who turned sweetheart Kim into a teenage sex kitten, not quite the original idea.

Charles Strouse well remembers the creative battles staging the song because it was his first Broadway show. "Gower was a very tough guy. Big numbers were Gower's specialty. One of the biggest numbers he tried to stage was 'Put on a Happy Face.' Dick Van Dyke's particular talent was his very plastic face, and Gower had the spotlight guy keep changing colors on his face. It was very intricate. It was really wonderful and it didn't work. One of the big arguments that I had was about this song. I said, 'OK, let's do another number.' I am not shy about throwing out a song. But they insisted on keeping it in. Then Marge Champion had this idea that he cheers up two girls and they do a tap step."

Strouse was actually ashamed of the number at first. "I was just out of music school, a graduate of the Eastman School of Music. I had studied with Aaron Copland in Paris. I'd been schlepping around New York accompanying singers at piano bars. So this was my first show in New York, and I thought it would be an embarrassment if I wrote a tap-dance number. And yet it was theatrically so right. It turned out to be such a wonderful number for those little girls and for Dick."

It was Strouse who helped Van Dyke land the part. They had been friends before the show. "I was a pianist on a revue that he was in as a second banana and we'd go out for coffee. I would say, 'I have a Broadway show I think you would be very good for.' When we got the money, we wanted everybody in the world. Nobody had ever heard of Dick Van Dyke. We wanted Jack Lemmon, and he would have been wonderful, but we didn't know Jack Lemmon or even anybody who *knew* Jack Lemmon."

When Lemmon proved ungettable, they took a chance on Van Dyke. "His personality was stamped on the show," Strouse goes on. "He was able to bring that cartoony quality that [librettist] Mike Stewart wrote into it. It's not *Carousel*. These people, though they are real, are living in a world of screaming teenagers." He confirms that Van Dyke is as nice as his image but adds, "I later read in a *Playboy* interview where he said that all during *Birdie* he was fighting alcoholism. I never knew he was drunk when we did *Birdie*. I never saw it, and we were very close friends. He never said he was an alcoholic."

————

Dick Van Dyke, to everyone's astonishment (mainly his own), is now ninety, yet a still boyish-sounding eighty-eight when we spoke by phone.

The very idea of a ninety-year-old Dick Van Dyke is absurd, clearly a crime against nature. You can imagine him mimicking a ninety-year-old geezer but never actually being one. He sounded as chipper as you would expect, with that same chuckly voice heard each week on his landmark sitcom. Van Dyke remains the ultimate Mr. Nice Guy.

In your autobiography, *My Lucky Life In and Out of Show Business*, you claim "Put on a Happy Face" changed your life.
Well, it did. We were already in Philadelphia at the Shubert Theatre doing previews, and they thought I needed another song in the first act. I had practically nothing to do in the first act. Charles Strouse wrote the song overnight. He came in, played it, and I loved it.

How important was that number to the show's success? It's a bouncy song but not germane to the story and easily could be taken out, which often happens with even great songs that are holding up the plot or are extraneous.
It's one of these songs that people remember. Maybe it's just the subject matter. It was my high point, and I think I won a Tony because of that number.

You had four songs, including the swingy "Rosie" and "Baby, Talk to Me."
I thought "Baby, Talk to Me" would be the hit song. It's a beautiful song. Frank Sinatra recorded it.

It was really "Put on a Happy Face" that kept you from leaving the show the first few weeks?
I had never done a Broadway show, and opening night I was a physical wreck. Opening night [out of town] I actually thought maybe I ought to leave town. Oh my god, I was scared. In one really good review the show got, it said at the end, "Mr. Van Dyke was adequate" or something like that. But then as I got used to it, and when I began to enjoy myself, the performance got a lot better.

The New York critics were not ecstatic.
I usually get better reviews from the public than I get from the critics.

Gower Champion was confident he could turn you into a dancer.
Gower was so good because he knew I was not a dancer by profession and was able to take what I *could* do well and showcase it. I think I got the job partly because we were about the same size and build. I think he saw himself in the role.

You say in your memoir that the producer didn't think, before that number, you were cutting it. Why?

Well, I probably was still trying to fit in, and thank god I didn't hear that story until many years later. Marge Champion told me that they were going to fire me and replace me in Philadelphia, and she said that Gower came to my defense and said I would be all right. I think I just hadn't really gotten into it yet. I was still tentative and nervous and really didn't open up and do the performance.

That number lifted the show and propelled it forward.

Yes, the show had been a little slow before that song. "Put on a Happy Face" just pops up at that moment. It got the pace going and the rest of that act went really well.

Did you immediately like the song when Strouse played it?

Absolutely! I loved it! It was so up. I just loved everything about it. I added a few little fillips to the dance number. I started to have a lot more fun with it, clowned around a little bit, my sense of humor finally came back, and it became much more of a performance. If I'm not enjoying something, I'm pretty bad.

What did you think of the movie version of *Bye Bye Birdie*?

I was very, very disappointed. They Hollywoodized it. It became more of a vehicle for Ann-Margret. It was rather smaller than on Broadway. They used it to build her up. Some of the very best songs fell out, and they ruined a couple of songs.

It's disappointing, in light of your huge success in *Bye Bye Birdie*, that you didn't go on to appear in more musicals on Broadway.

Mainly I had a family and I was looking for something a little more constant than going from show to show. I had a number of people who said I should stay in New York, that I wasn't meant for television, but then I read Carl Reiner's script for the TV series.

Who said you weren't right for TV?

Chita and the producer and most of the people in the cast and people who saw the show. They all said, you really should stay [on Broadway], and for my own welfare I would have.

HELLO, DOLLY!

◆ 1964 ◆

"Hello, Dolly!"

The first time he heard it, Gower Champion said, "If I can't make a show-stopper out of **'Hello, Dolly!'** then I better get out of show business." He staged the number the first day of rehearsals but refined it over the next two weeks. "It has never changed since that afternoon," recalls its creator Jerry Herman. "On the first day, Gower said, 'Let's get this over with.'"

The all-time show-stoppingest showstopper, "Hello, Dolly!" is more than just a famous rousing number. It's synonymous with your basic through-the-roof blockbuster, one that defines the very word *showstopper* and defies you not to embrace it—a huge hug of a song. In memory it's a kitschy production number that wears its love-me sentiment so brazenly on its sleeve that the song has become a cliché, even a bit too blatantly over the top. Until you see it again in all its splashy glory and are knocked out anew.

Like many a show tune that seemingly has worn out its welcome by over-exposure and ragged imitations in undernourished revivals, "Hello, Dolly!" reestablishes itself as a classic when it comes straight at you, all jubilant banners flying, five decades after it was conceived. In musical theater's current mood, for a show tune to be quite so unabashedly joyous is not just suspect on Broadway but almost subversive.

In a *New York Times* story announcing that Bette Midler had signed to star in a spring 2017 revival of the show, Midler called the musical "a very American thing, with a joyous quality, a kind of can-do quality, and an incredible sweetness, and in these dire times, when the whole world seems to be on fire, it seems like something people would love to see."

Hello, Dolly! was the musical that not only established Jerry Herman's credentials on Broadway in 1964, after his modest first hit *Milk and Honey* three years earlier. It also stamped his heart-pumping, toe-tapping, show-stopping style all over the musical theater of that era; and it made him a marked man for proponents of new pointed, complex, dark, cynical Stephen Sondheim musicals.

For Herman, the show was the culmination of a career that had barely begun, a show he would never top but nearly equaled with *Mame* and *La*

Cage aux Folles. The musical became the gold standard for smasheroo musical comedies—so much so that Mike Nichols once said, after being asked how he had liked *Hello, Dolly!*, "It's very good, but it's no *Hello, Dolly!*"

The show's title song was an instantly embraceable, smiley-face, take-home tune, but it was as much Louis Armstrong's unlikely hit record as Herman's song that nailed it for all time—along with Gower Champion's razzle-dazzle choreography and Carol Channing's career-clinching presentation. By the time Channing had finished her milestone song, the night of January 16, 1964, three careers sped into orbit (four, if you count producer David Merrick): hers, Herman's, and Champion's.

With *Hello, Dolly!*, Herman became the overnight master of the Broadway showstopper. His later musicals—*Mame, Mack and Mabel, La Cage aux Folles*, even parts of the failed *Dear World*—would reconfigure the happy all-stops-out spirit he first displayed in this ultimate showstopper, which says very little beyond "You're looking swell, Dolly, / We can tell, Dolly / You're still glowin', / You're still crowin', / You're still goin' strong." Harold Prince says he turned down the chance to direct *Hello, Dolly!* after hearing the song. "When I was asked to direct it, they played me the title song, and I said, 'This is for a scene where a woman who doesn't go out decides to visit a restaurant?' They never mentioned *Hello, Dolly!* to me again."

Herman's score crackles with infectious tunes all evening, little "Hello, Dolly!"'s—a series of prequels and aftershocks: bold declarations like "Before the Parade Passes By," "Put on Your Sunday Clothes," and "So Long Dearie," which sounds like "Hello, Dolly!" inside out, almost a rewrite of the title tune, a reprise that isn't a reprise but that slyly, almost inadvertently, echoes it.

We need to examine the number up close to see why it landed so totally. While a brigade of high-stepping waiters serenade Dolly upon her widow's return to her old haunt, the Harmonia Gardens, the Yonkers grand dame steps down a grand staircase wearing a garish plumed hat and a gaudy fili-greed red satin gown. She looks like Lillian Russell. What all those waiters are really serving up on a silver platter is a thick juicy porterhouse steak of a song for the audience to gobble up.

Carol Channing recalls that originally Champion "wanted the song to be little. Then he moved the waiters in, and the cooks, and everybody in the Harmonia Gardens, and it got bigger and bigger. Then he said, 'I think we should make the steps higher.' And he would run around to the back of the theater and say, 'Spread out more' and run back again. He would say, 'I can't get it big enough. These boys are too dinky—get bigger boys next to her.' It was getting mammoth, and then he realized, 'I haven't got an intimate show here.' That's how Gower found the show's level."

Like many of Herman's songs, "Hello, Dolly!" shimmers with vibrant DayGlo colors. It's no coincidence that the songwriter first studied at Parsons School of Design and enjoyed a second, profitable, little-known career between shows redecorating homes. He didn't just write songs—he upholstered them in posh silken fabrics and bold primary hues, like George M. Cohan and Herman's idol Irving Berlin before him. Many Herman songs are written in subtler pastels, even a few earth tones, but his best-known numbers, the showstoppers, are written in shimmering yellows and reds with purple polka dots.

Carol Channing announcing her exuberant return to life in "Hello, Dolly!"

"Hello, Dolly!" is her announcement to the world that she has returned to the land of the living—"back where she belongs," as Herman phrases it—and is ready to rejoin the parade. Not since John Philip Sousa has a songwriter written so many march-tempo songs, certainly not in musicals. It's no coincidence that Herman's first full score was titled *Parade*. About the only Broadway march that can match his own is "Seventy-Six Trombones."

Hello, Dolly! may have the deepest, or at least most entangled, roots of any musical since *The Threepenny Opera*, which began life in the eighteenth century as John Gay's *The Beggar's Opera*. *Hello, Dolly*'s ancestry stretches back two centuries, starting with an 1835 London play by John Oxenford, *A Day Well Spent* (itself based on the Viennese play *He Wants to Have a Lark*), which was adapted by Johannes Nestroy for the Austrian farce *He'll Have Himself a Good Time*, which Thornton Wilder turned into his 1938 comedy *The Merchant of Yonkers*, which was revised and retitled *The Matchmaker* by Tyrone Guthrie for a brief London production. Whew! *That* play was then done on Broadway with Ruth Gordon in the Dolly Levi role, which became a quirky little black-and-white 1955 movie *The Matchmaker*, with Shirley Booth, Paul Ford, and Tony Perkins. Enter, licking his chops, David Merrick.

Several phrases from *The Matchmaker* later pop up in *Hello, Dolly!* as lines and songs: "I'm a woman who arranges things," "put on your Sunday clothes," "ribbons down my back" (both song titles), and "Dolly is a damn exasperating woman!" The musical's original title was "A Damned Exasperating Woman," quickly changed once Louis Armstrong's growly version took off.

The title song arrives in the show after it's been carefully, cagily set up by an earlier number, "Before the Parade Passes By." In that song, Dolly Gallagher Levi—the busybody Yonkers yenta, a matchmaker who has emerged from widowhood to make her own match with a rich and grouchy feed-and-grain dealer—tells us that she wants to live again "before the parade passes by, / I'm gonna go and taste Saturday's high life; / Before the parade passes by, / I'm gonna get some life back into my life." The emotion in "Hello, Dolly!" behind Gower Champion's showy staging and Channing's declaration of independence is released because it was so artfully calculated. Herman and librettist Michael Stewart prepare us for the crucial "Hello, Dolly!" moment with "Before the Parade Passes By." Showstoppers are rarely lucky accidents. This pre–"Hello, Dolly!" scene setter is a shadow showstopper, a renewal song that, like the title tune it leads us to, declares that our heroine is determined to resume her life again. Of course the way that Channing (and others) play her, Dolly hardly seems the grieving widow in need of a peppy song to get her kicking up her heels again.

"Before the Parade Passes By" leads Dolly to the front porch of the Harmonia Gardens, but "Hello, Dolly!" is the forceful tune that swings open the doors and propels her inside and escorts her as she promenades down the restaurant staircase. That Harmonia Gardens door is as crucial to Dolly's liberation as the slammed door is to Nora in Ibsen's *A Doll's House*. Nora stalks out; Dolly sashays in.

The song starts slowly, quietly, inviting us in just as Dolly is inviting us to dine with her. Much of the song's zing is how carefully and cannily Herman builds the glee to bursting. When the number first arrived on the scene—that is, before it was the famous showstopper we now await—there was no way to know you would be enthralled by the pulsating life-enhancing spirit that the tune unleashes onstage and that overwhelms us as we watch Dolly welcomed back, a surefire theatrical payoff. You've been down, the song says, you've been crushed by life, but now you're back on your feet and, by god, you're ready to take on the world! It's a sentiment that reverberates down through the annals of musical theater, from "I Ain't Down Yet" in *The Unsinkable Molly Brown* and "I Hope I Get It" in *A Chorus Line* to "Defying Gravity" in *Wicked*.

Herman's song sneaks up on you, or did before it became a gigantic hit, as the waiters welcome Dolly to the restaurant she frequented with her late husband, Ephraim. The boys are so overjoyed to see her again that they commence a frenzied waiters' gallop, prancing giddily between tables, aprons flying, trays held precariously aloft, stacked with dishes. No matter how the chorus boys leap and strut, not a drop of soup is spilled. It's a goyish "Bottle Dance" from *Fiddler on the Roof*.

Herman had a hunch something important was about to happen once Champion mapped out "Hello, Dolly!" Everybody did. "Mike Stewart, who wrote the book, and I went down below the stage where we could be by ourselves to talk about it, and we said to each other, if nothing else, we have a great second-act number." Champion infused his dancing waiters with the spirit of Herman's prancing melody, which suffuses Dolly as she enters, welcomed by scores of waiters and warmed by their song, words, and music. Would that we all could be greeted so lavishly at our favorite restaurant after being away awhile. Dolly is home again, having made a triumphal return—not merely in her favorite restaurant but in the world.

Lyrically, "Hello, Dolly!" is a fairly ordinary song with a simple idea—"I feel the room swayin' / For the band's playin', / One of my old fav'rite songs from way back when. / So bridge that gap, fellas. / Find me an empty lap, fellas, / Dolly'll never go away again." It doesn't need a great lyric, because musically and choreographically the number erupts with energy, which

Champion dispenses in sunny and charming steps as Herman ramps up the melody and the festive mood, one key change at a time, his signature device. Champion's choreography for the show, indeed for this very number, set the stage for dance-crazed musicals that followed in the '70s and beyond, prefiguring the total takeover by choreographer-directors that began in 1957 with Jerome Robbins in *West Side Story*. Robbins was a ballet master slumming in musical comedy, but Champion was a field hand who, with *Hello, Dolly!*, became Broadway's song-and-dance overseer.

———

Looking back, Gower Champion's peppy dance partner and ex-wife, Marge, says, "I think Gower was more of a showman than he was a choreographer. He did things that were surprising and wonderful, but he had assistants to help him with tap dancing. We had done tap dancing in movies, but that was not our mother tongue. I think he came up with things that were suitable to making a great number, like the second number in *Bye Bye Birdie*, with all those kids up onstage in the cubicle set."

She adds, "He was known for fixing things on the road. When we were in Detroit with *Hello Dolly!* he had to make some enormous changes before it was ready to go to Washington. That's when he asked for a new song, and that's where he came up with 'Before the Parade Passes By.' He brought in Charles Strouse. Jerry Herman had only one produced show. He really came up with the song himself, but Charles Strouse and Bob Merrill gave him a couple of hints—but they never wrote any of the songs."

Strouse recalls, "Gower was thrilled. He said 'You solved it—go write the song.' Lee [Adams] and I wrote a song called 'Before the Parade Passes By.' It was not very good, but we put it in, and then Jerry wrote another song, which was very good, also called 'Before the Parade Passes By.' But we felt in a sense that we not only had contributed to it but had discovered the key to ending the first act. We had a big fight with Gower and [librettist] Mike Stewart, not with Jerry so much. We worked very hard for a week and wanted some recognition. The tune for 'Before the Parade Passes By' that I wrote, my version, ain't bad, but Jerry wrote a better version. They ended up paying us a weekly royalty and we own half of that song, but it is Jerry's song. That's the story behind it." Long after the show closed, a rumor persisted that Strouse and Adams had written the song, until Herman finally had to ask Strouse for a note attesting to Herman's sole authorship of the song, which he willingly provided.

It was Marge Champion who suggested Carol Channing for the show: "The first time I brought Carol to audition for Gower was out in California. She was in a little show called *Lend an Ear*. He already had two comedians and he wanted a third. I found her at Rodgers and Hammerstein's office in California. I asked the girl at the office if they had anybody they didn't need, like a comedienne. That's where I first saw Carol. I said to the woman, 'Would you mind if I took her over to where Gower and the director were auditioning?'" She adds, "Carol gives me credit for discovering her."

Gower, Marge goes on, "thought she was just right for the part. She was larger than life, and Dolly was larger than life. He really wanted her for it." Champion worked with her privately because producer David Merrick was not convinced Channing was so right. "She really wanted to do it. She was not the fastest study in the world. She had to have everything always exactly the same. She had very fixed ideas. It was hard to change her once she had learned a part." Like certain schtick? "Yeah. She always did the role exactly the same." Harvey Evans, who played Barnaby on tour with Channing, witnessed her robotic style that broke a cardinal acting rule—make each performance fresh. "She defied the rule, but it worked for her," says Evans.

In the song, Herman exploited his favorite theatrical theme—seize the moment!—that he repeats in many songs in other shows: "Open a New Window," "It's Today," and "We Need a Little Christmas," all from *Mame*; "Tap Your Troubles Away" from *Mack and Mabel*; "It Only Takes a Moment" from *Hello, Dolly!*; "The Best of Times" from *La Cage aux Folles*; "Kiss Her Now" from *Dear World*; and his lifelong credo, "Let's Not Waste a Moment" from his first Broadway show, *Milk and Honey*. But it was "Hello, Dolly!" that showed Jerry Herman what a showstopper can do and should do—a lesson in the art of whipping up audiences. Corny? Probably, but then life can be corny, and Herman never shied away from nutritious corn, willing to face a corn-inflected situation and give it its sophisticated due—elevating it, spinning gold out of wholesome kernels. Cohan was corny, god knows; Berlin's songs were corn-fed; and Rodgers and Hammerstein eagerly planted corn ("I'm as corny as Kansas in August," "the corn is as high as an elephant's eye"). Herman's songs often seem to say, *OK, maybe it's corny, but it works, theatrically and viscerally.* Lyricist Fred Ebb put it this way: "Jerry Herman shows embody American optimism. They're smart, they're accessible, they're melodic, they're lovable. You kinda want to reach out and hug whatever Jerry writes."

———

Jerry Herman has long pondered all of this and had seventy-five years to come up with a plausible theory on the art of the showstopper: "It's possible to explain what the songwriter *thinks* are the reasons, but there's always more to it," he told me. "There's an underpinning of emotions that creates a really huge showstopper. If you just do a brilliantly staged number and there's no heart or story behind it, it's just a moment of empty celebration."

He adds, "I would say 'Hello, Dolly!' is the most perfectly staged production number I've ever had in a show. It's gorgeously staged by Gower Champion. It does everything it's supposed to do and it constantly builds, another reason it gets the audience so excited. It starts very quietly, very charmingly, and it builds and builds, and I help the build by constantly changing keys, going to a new plateau, until it makes every person in the audience go 'Wow!'" Channing was the song's wow girl, its efficient delivery system, her first big show after breaking through fifteen years before in *Gentleman Prefer Blondes*. "Miss Channing's performance is impeccable, one of the greatest performances I've ever seen," coos Herman. "Her joy and all her skills as an artist are on that stage. It's a very accessible song that's easy to take to your heart. But putting all of that together still does not make a showstopper."

Herman explains that other crucial elements must be mixed in to create the total explosive result: "The costumes and sets are very important in the 'Hello, Dolly!' number. The poster colors, the sense of where we are in time, and of glamour and gaslights and red velvet curtains." Herman also acknowledges the importance of the show's signature spiral staircase. "It would not work without a staircase. Strutting down the staircase is a definitive theatrical look that I love. It makes stars regal, it makes them Ziegfeld girls. There's something ladylike about it. Carol just bathed in the joy of taking those steps. But even all of *that* added together would not make a showstopper if there weren't a woman's choice to stop her grieving period—which has been going on for decades—and making the decision to put that dress back on, and to come down those stairs as she did in the old days with Ephraim. There is something so heartrending about it that most people, seeing or remembering the number, don't know *why* they were moved by that. But that's the secret behind the whole thing."

Well, part of the secret anyway. When David Merrick asked Herman to write audition songs for *Hello, Dolly!*, he said they were fine but none he heard was the blockbuster he wanted. His initial faith in Herman ("Kid, the show is yours!" he said after hearing the audition songs) waned. Merrick told

Herman, "I'm not sure you're American enough for this project"—whatever that meant; no more all-American songwriter exists.

Late into rehearsals, Herman learned through the company grapevine that Merrick was considering other songwriters (Strouse and Adams), so—to save his career—he holed up in a hotel room all night and, fortified with candy bars, wrote "Before the Parade Passes By," which saved his career and maybe the show.

Merrick seriously threatened to bid good-bye to *Hello, Dolly!* in Detroit. Why did he lose faith in it so quickly? "Because he was a very mercurial man," says Herman. "One day he would have all the excitement and faith producers should have. The next day he would be gloomy about its prospects. We could not and did not know how to deal with that."

So as Herman explains, you need the backstory to make the showstopper combust: "At the end of act 1, she sings 'Before the Parade Passes By,' which tells us she's going to do something about locking herself away and fixing up everybody else in the world. We purposely gave the audience ten minutes to wait for her entrance. The *Dolly* number wasn't as effective originally. It was just a big brassy march, a declarative song—a wonderful combination telling of Dolly's transition. People don't realize it, but it's not intricately staged. It just makes Dolly the important focal point." Notes Herman, "When the entrance finally happens, it happens to everybody in that audience—you don't have to be a woman of sixty, you can be a twenty-one-year-old, but there's still an emotional power that you feel when she brushes the curtains aside and she makes that appearance and marches out on that ramp—I'm getting all excited now just telling you about it! The essence of that number is what Thornton Wilder was writing about in *The Matchmaker*. Every person who was connected to that number contributes—the designer, the chorus boys, the lighting; the lighting in that number builds along with the music. The audience is being swept into this moment, and people have cried at this very happy number. But what's behind it is the reason it's so special."

What was the title song meant to do? "Well, it was obviously written to be the climactic moment. And I wanted it to be accessible for everyone, and Gower made the staging ultratheatrical but at the same time quite simple and uncomplicated. And *we*, the audience, are all the other people in the Harmonia Gardens scene. There are no other people on the set. In the movie they had people all over the floor and it wasn't as effective."

Herman says he never thought "Hello, Dolly!" was destined to be a hit, let alone a milestone number. It was hardly Louis Armstrong's kind of song, but by then Satchmo had recorded just about anything, and he made the number his own. Herman's publisher suggested to Armstrong's manager that Armstrong might want to record it. By the mid-1960s, his popularity was fading, like jazz itself. The song revived his career and gave Herman's show a stamp of hip street cred. Herman was stunned by Armstrong's version: "In the show the melody and orchestrations are very 1890s. The first time I heard Louis Armstrong's record I was in shock. I couldn't believe he'd gotten that jazzy record out of my little period song," which musicals historian Mark Steyn notes "is a fifty-year-old song that was born sounding fifty years old." Broadway archivist Miles Kreuger adds, "The Louis Armstrong recording was the turning point in Jerry Herman's career."

Herman in his prime seemed almost incapable of writing a boring tune. He told Mark Steyn: "I write simple melodies, and critics don't understand simplicity. They're looking for the complicated, and they only understand simplicity in retrospect. When *Hello, Dolly!* opened in 1964, it was called a one-song show. On the twentieth anniversary revival, they called it one of the classic Broadway scores. I don't mind anymore. I write for the people." Herman says the ability to charm an audience is instinctive. "You need to be born with that. I had no formal training. Everything I do comes out of some place in me. I believe in genetics"—he inherited his mother's sunny philosophy—"but you don't necessarily have to emulate as a person the things you write about. I am a hopelessly romantic musical comedy nut who was taken to hear Ethel Merman sing those songs as a kid and something just touched me."

Herman's mother saw his potential when, at fifteen, he had memorized scores of classic songs besides writing several of his own pieces, and she arranged for him to meet Frank Loesser, a friend of one of her bridge partners. Loesser politely agreed to a brief meeting with the alleged prodigy but was so taken with the kid's songs that he asked to hear them all, then called his mother and told her Jerry should pursue a songwriting career. "The course of my life changed that day," says Herman.

Herman can't quite fathom why the desire to simply delight audiences has all but vanished, or become almost quaint. "The evolution of the musical theater went in the direction of very serious subject matter. The whole idea of a musical used to be just a silly book and a lot of girls and colorful costumes—and that was an evening's entertainment. Then it evolved into Richard Rodgers, God bless him. But even in *Oklahoma!* you had 'Pore Jud Is Daid.' Then we had *South Pacific*, a much more serious subject matter but still in the guise of entertainment. And the *Dolly*s and the *Mame*s stayed in that category." He goes on, "But then the musical theater was taken into darker territory and to less entertaining territory, by some of the most brilliant people we've ever had in the theater." (He doesn't mention Stephen Sondheim, clearly the brilliant person in question, or Andrew Lloyd Webber.) "And what they've done is extraordinary and I would never fault any of that—it's just a natural evolution to want to do something more significant."

Why did that drive to be more significant squelch Jerry Herman's kind of bright, cheery musical? *Hello, Dolly!* had something important to say about renewal, and *Mame* says something significant about family. "What has changed is a style of music. If I turn on a radio station today, I honestly can't listen to it. That's how divorced I am from the sound of music today." Herman insists a major part of the audience still craves his brand of upbeat show, even if today's songwriters seem to lack the gene that enables them to create one. "They don't aspire to write that kind of a show because they think it's old-fashioned, one of my favorite expressions. I'm sitting in a room right now looking at a French country table, one of my favorite possessions, and the older it gets the more beautiful it gets. You wouldn't call it anything but old-fashioned, but to me it has a great value."

Decades after *La Cage aux Folles*, Herman became a charming antique himself. "I think there's a fear now of being called old-fashioned. The whole style of music has changed so dramatically that it actually takes guts to write a song like 'The Best of Times.' It's defying today's convention." He adds, "People say New York is too cynical for my songs. I know many young composers, but I don't know anyone who would try to emulate my sound. They would feel they were of another time." He adds, "I don't think it's gone for good—I think there'll be a cycle. There's nothing now except *Hairspray* and *Wicked*, which are entertaining." He pronounces "entertaining" in a polite but unfelt tone. The king of the showstopper says of *The Phantom of the Opera*, *Les Misérables*, and *Into the Woods*: "They have melody and use all the theatrical arts. They're entertaining, exciting pieces of theater." He "admires" them, he says, but, again, with little enthusiasm in his voice.

New composers he hears at workshops have lost the gift for melody. "Maybe every art form must come to an end. I don't think we're there yet. I hope it's a cycle we're not at the end of. But I've not heard a new show tune that grabbed me in years. They don't know how to write 'em now. So many songwriters are trying to be so different that they've forgotten what first made musical theater popular. Young composers today are interested in being avant-garde. There's nothing wrong with getting away from tradition, but something is wrong when *everybody* is getting away from it."

•••••••••••••• BACKSTAGE DISH ••••••••••••••

+ Marge Champion seemed a good one to ask about David Merrick's terrorist tactics. "Gower knew how to handle him. He once told his stage manager in Detroit, 'When Mr. Mustache leaves, I will come back and do the rest of the show.' He went away for a couple of days." Josh Ellis, the publicist who worked with Merrick on *42nd Street*, recalls, "He just liked causing chaos. He had a good time doing it. He enjoyed the manipulation part of it. He had a persona, people knew who he was. He was a star." Ellis adds, "You were always on your toes. It's not that he was the only volatile person I was working with. David was a pro, and often you had to deal with amateur producers. I was thrilled to work with a pro. When I did *42nd Street* for eight and a half years, Merrick made me realize how much fun it was to work in the theater. Even when it was going horribly he was still having fun. He was a prankster."

+ Gower Champion, says Marge, chose not to direct the *Hello, Dolly!* movie once Barbra Streisand was cast. "He thought she was totally wrong because she was Jewish to begin with and this was a story of Dolly Gallagher, who is Irish" (her late husband Ephraim Levi was Jewish). "And she was too young. It didn't make any sense." Gene Kelly's $25 million 1969 expected blockbuster film, with Barbra Streisand as a cutesied-up young widow, opposite costar Walter Matthau (who couldn't stand her), was a financial failure and all-around disappointment, despite throwing in Louis Armstrong to reprise his unlikely hit that knocked the Beatles's "Can't Buy Me Love" off the number-one spot on the charts, what Mark Steyn calls "a charming moment in a film otherwise almost wholly bereft of charm." "She was part Mae West and part Barbra Streisand," says musicals historian Ken Bloom, dismissing the film. "They lost the heart of *Dolly* and it almost sank 20th Century Fox."

+ Herman was threatened with a lawsuit by songwriter Mack David (older brother of Burt Bacharach collaborator Hal David), who—in what sounds like a jealous pique—accused the song of plagiarizing the first four bars of the melody from a pop ditty he had written in 1948, "Sunflower," as in,

"She's my sunflower / She's my sunflower / From the sunflower state." A fragment of the tune has a similar lilt, but Herman claimed he had never heard of David's song and hoped to defend his reputation in court but took a $250,000 settlement so that the upcoming movie version wouldn't be delayed. Mack David, notes Mark Steyn, "[made] more money from those first four bars of 'Sunflower' than for any other song he ever wrote."

✦ "Hello, Dolly!" became iconic when Lyndon Johnson stole it for his 1964 campaign theme song, "Hello, Lyndon!"; Sinatra upgraded its status with a Count Basie recording. In time, Herman's song was lifted for any and all occasions: Bobby Darin recorded "Hello, Dolly!," tossing in a reference to his hit single "Mack the Knife," replacing "Look out, ol' Mackie is back" with "Look out, ol' Dolly is back," and at a British Tory party for Margaret Thatcher, she was serenaded with "Hello, Maggie!"

✦ Herman is so beloved for his ingratiating melodies that his lyrics are unfairly overshadowed, the reverse of Cole Porter songs more famous for their lyrics than their infectious tunes. Herman is too easily dismissed as a lyricist when, like Irving Berlin, he was capable of sharp, insightful lyrics in songs from *Hello, Dolly!* (such as Horace Vandergelder's engaging "A Penny in My Pocket," ruthlessly cut); his unduly trashed *Dear World* ("Just a Little Bit More," "Garbage," "One Person"); *Mack and Mable* ("I Won't Send Roses"); *The Grand Tour* ("I'll Be Here Tomorrow"); *A Day in Hollywood/A Night in the Ukraine* ("Just Go to the Movies"); and two witty songs from his last show, an unproduced Las Vegas musical, *Miss Spectacular*, with lyrics Porter or Sondheim would be proud to claim in "Miss What's Her Name" and, brilliantly, "Where in the World Is My Prince?"

✦ Ethel Merman was David Merrick's first choice to play Dolly, and Herman admits, "I also wanted Ethel, but she told Merrick that she didn't want to perform anymore. She was tired of having dinner in a dressing room. I became very fond of Ethel. We became pals." Instead, Merman was the last Dolly in the original Broadway run. To entice her back, Herman reinstated just for her two songs cut from the show, "World, Take Me Back" and "Love, Look in My Window." Herman says, "Carol Channing was ultimately the right choice because she was unique. But that was also how I also felt about Ethel doing *Dolly*. When she finally did it, everything I had ever imagined was on that stage."

FUNNY GIRL

◆ 1964 ◆

"Don't Rain on My Parade," "People"

When Barbra Streisand broke through on Broadway in 1962, she played a put-upon secretary named Miss Marmelstein, the title of the song that shot her to stardom in *I Can Get It for You Wholesale*, a musical about life in a Lower East Side dress-making firm that featured singer Lillian Roth and featured Streisand's husband-to-be Elliott Gould.

The show, a modest hit, was based on Jerome Weidman's bestseller about the colorful New York City Garment District, with its fast-talking low-rent Jewish wheeler-dealers. It only ran three hundred performances despite a strong creative team: score by Harold Rome, direction by Arthur Laurents, choreography by Herb Ross, and a solid supporting cast that included Harold Lang, Sheree North, and dancer Bambi Linn. Rome, who had written a 1937 hit revue for the Ladies' Garment Workers' Union, *Pins and Needles*, was a natural to stitch together a score about the garment game.

The show produced no big songs, just a megastar, and is now known mainly as the launching pad for Streisand, a studiously kooky actress who auditioned in a ratty ten-dollar used fur coat from the 1930s, singing a song that became one of her early Harold Arlen classics, "Sleepin' Bee" (lyrics by Truman Capote). As soon as she was cast, the role of Miss Marmelstein was enlarged to embrace Streisand's unbounded talents ("Somebody is that good," said Rome, "you try to use them as much as possible"), though "Miss Marmelstein" was a comedy song that gave no hint of the singer's vocal dynamism.

Streisand sang "Miss Marmelstein"—which got her a best supporting actress Tony nomination the first time out—while seated in a swivel chair that she rolled about the stage while lamenting her lowly role as much-ignored secretary whose first name nobody in the company knows. It's not a great, or even especially funny song, but Streisand made it into a showcase moment with her repertoire of mugging, inflections, and body language. It was your classic *42nd Street* example of going out there a Miss Nobody and coming back a Miss Marmelstein, a star; the song became the show's big number. Two months after the musical closed, Columbia Records' Goddard Lieberson signed Streisand for a debut LP (the label read "Barbara").

In the showbiz cosmos, she was quickly tagged a surefire star whose raves as a cabaret singer at the chic Bon Soir cabaret (plus kooky appearances with Mike Wallace on a late-night TV show called *PM East/PM West*) preceded her role in *Funny Girl*. But most people had never heard of Barbra Streisand when she was cast at twenty-two to play Fanny Brice, the perfect match of performer and part. She was Jewish, funny, and funny looking, with Picasso-like features, a comic singer and equally compelling balladeer born for the role. It's hard now to imagine anyone else doing the character, which she has never come close to equaling onstage or on screen, her first and final Broadway musical. Despite its show-stopping score, the show is rarely revived because Streisand put her stamp so indelibly on the role that few actresses have the nerve—or the talent—to take it on.

Not only was Streisand right for *Funny Girl*, it soon became clear that the funny girl depicted was far more Barbra than Fanny, whose actual identity was eclipsed in Streisand's persona, purposely so. The show became a star vehicle, not a real biography. By the time the musical began rehearsals, Streisand's quirky wise-guy public character was being shrewdly marketed. Arthur Laurents, her director in *I Can Get It for You Wholesale*, said, "They [Fanny and Barbra] needed to become the same thing, at least for promotional purposes." She quickly became the role model for every funny-looking girl. Wrote British critic Hugh Leonard of the most famous profile since John Barrymore, "The Nefertiti nose lends her the appearance of a disdainful eaglet. The face is that of an urchin, the nose too big for it, and emphasizes the fact that her eyes are hell-bent on joining forces in a Cyclopian manner.... She is, in a word, plain, and therefore a source of comfort to every un-bobbed nose in sight. Beauty is, after all, in the eyes of the ticket-holder." Streisand said she didn't fix her nose because she was afraid of the pain. Her nose was her future. Because of it, she said, "I knew I had to be a star or nothing. People tell me I'm beautiful this way. Well, they're wrong. Beautiful I'm not, and never will be."

Funny Girl, though ostensibly Fanny Brice's story, is your basic backstage musical: gawky girl from nowhere defies everyone to become a star because of her native quirky gifts that can't be ignored. *New York Times* critic Howard Taubman wrote that the show was a routine showbiz saga. He said its creators could "rarely untrack themselves from the hokum and schmaltz that show people consider standard operating procedure." Kevin Kelly in the *Boston Globe*, reviewing the show prior to Broadway, wrote, "The hard fact is that *Funny Girl* is meant to be more than the exploitation of a single talent."

Funny Girl was a presold smash. Audiences came to the show ready to love the unlikely star. Streisand admitted as much, telling reporters, "I'm not approaching it as a life story of anybody. I'm doing it as an actress doing another character." She even told AP, "This play is really about me. It simply happened to happen before to Fanny Brice." She thus deftly upstaged Fanny. As biographer William J. Mann writes, "Barbra wasn't about to share top billing with the woman she was playing." Mann adds, "In fact, the two women weren't as much alike as the *Funny Girl* team tried to insist. Fanny had let men run her career, and occasionally ruin it, about as far from Barbra as one could get." Even Streisand as a real-life "Second-Hand Rose" was a contrivance to woo her cult, a pose she went along with until she wearied of the scruffy gimmick, got a hair stylist, and began designing her own clothes—and image.

"I'm not a fan of that show," comments director Greg MacKellan. "It's written for and around Streisand. Merman's shows were like that too, but Streisand is playing a real person. So the reality of Fanny Brice takes a backseat to Streisand and her persona and her way of singing. I don't think 'People' should even be in the show. It's not right for Fanny. It has nothing to do with the show."

Even so, *Funny Girl*—first the show, then the film—created Streisand and it's still her main ticket to posterity. The score by Jule Styne and Bob Merrill was such a custom-made hit for her that, a few years later, she was able to wrest *Hello, Dolly!* away from Carol Channing's chokehold on the role in the film version, even though Streisand, at twenty-seven, was a generation too young for the part. Channing extracted early revenge when she won a Tony for *Hello, Dolly!*, beating out Streisand, who later tied for the 1968 Best Actress Oscar with Katharine Hepburn. When a radio reporter asked Streisand the eternal showbiz platitude, "In your wildest dreams, did you ever think this would happen?," Streisand shrugged, "Of course." She was not only "the greatest star" but also her greatest fan.

The disappointing fact is that, in her urgency to become a movie star, she threw away a great musical-comedy career on mediocre films and a pop idol pedestal. Streisand might have become another Ethel Merman, Mary Martin, Bernadette Peters, or Audra McDonald, but she quickly cashed in her Broadway diva's tiara for the gaudier crown of Hollywood star, bestowed upon her even after the failed *Hello, Dolly!* Streisand chased a movie career that never gelled (*What's Up, Doc?*, *Nuts*, *The Mirror Has Two Faces*). It was only as the idealistic lefty loudmouth in *The Way We Were* that she was authentically, memorably showcased.

All of *Funny Girl*'s showstoppers were locked up forever by Streisand, none more so than **"Don't Rain on My Parade,"** a character song that came to define Streisand's defiant—dare we say strident?—public persona. It's as two-fisted a declaration as "People" is warm and fuzzy; one is a battle cry, the other almost a prayer. Opening night the audience began applauding on the last line of "People"'s act 2 reprise, before she finished the song (like baseball fans drowning out the last line of "The Star-Spangled Banner"), leaping to their feet and shouting as the curtain fell.

"Don't Rain on My Parade" has the same get-outta-my-way-don't-mess-with-me message as "I'm the Greatest Star," but it's tougher and more insistent, a dukes-up dare: "I'm gonna live and live NOW! / Get what I want. I know how! / One roll for the whole shebang! / . . . One shot, one gun shot and bam! / Hey, Mr. Arnstein, here I am."

It's a classic Broadway showstopper in which the hero or heroine declares he or she won't be stopped, dammit—songs like "Some People," "Just You Wait," "Before the Parade Passes By," "I Ain't Down Yet," "The Impossible Dream (The Quest)," and "If My Friends Could See Me Now." "Don't Rain on My Parade" is a central tenet of backstage mythology, and of the American dream: if you have the talent, the drive, and the guts, you can make it. Nobody has been more responsible for propagating this shaggy showbiz fairy tale than Broadway lyricists; somehow luck and connections never figure in.

The show's mightiest number began when Jule Styne was sure he had a great tune for a song he called "Very Special Person," but Bob Merrill luckily talked him out of that, retitling it **"People"** and suggesting a possible opening line—"People, people who need people, are the luckiest people in the world." Merrill jotted down the rest of the lyrics as Styne played the melody until all the words were in place. Total elapsed time, reported Styne: thirty minutes. The stuff of legend.

Barbra Streisand owned "People" the moment she first sang it, as it zoomed up the charts. "People" was responsible for helping to turn *Funny Girl* into a colossal hit, just as "Don't Cry for Me Argentina" did for *Evita* and "Memory" did for *Cats*. "People" was released as a teaser single in January 1964 and *Funny Girl* opened in March, by which time audiences were applauding the tune, Streisand's first Top 40 song, during the overture, ready to proclaim the show a hit by curtain time.

Neither of *Funny Girl*'s first two in a parade of directors, Jerome Robbins and Bob Fosse, liked "People" when they first heard it, though the song was Styne and Merrill's favorite in the show. The musical's eventual director

Garson Kanin tried to dump it, saying it didn't fit in the script. Merrill was aghast: "I could not believe what was happening to us. The best song in the show was in danger."

Styne's biographer writes that the usually confident composer momentarily wondered about the song, ready to write a replacement tune; Styne, a melody machine, wrote fifty-six pieces of music for the show. The composer related, "Now we're hearing for the third time [that the song doesn't fit]. So I looked over at Bob Merrill and said, 'Maybe "People" just didn't belong in *Funny Girl*.' The show was the thing. We could write something else and shove 'People' into the trunk."

But then Styne dug in his heels. After he played "People" for Fosse, who was then the director, Fosse told the composer (relates Martin Gottfried in his Fosse biography): "Well, Jule, it's a very beautiful song, no doubt about it. But I'm afraid we can't use it." Styne: "What do you mean, 'We can't use it'?" Fosse: "It just doesn't make any dramatic sense for Fanny to sing this song." Styne: "Why the hell not?" Fosse: "Listen to the words. Fanny Brice isn't 'a person who needs people.' She's a great star in the *Follies* and she's surrounded by people—people onstage and people backstage. Then she has a family, she has a mother, and she has neighbors; she has all kinds of people at home. She doesn't need people anywhere, Jule, that's why the song doesn't make any dramatic sense. And that's why there's no point in her singing this song."

Styne replied in a quiet measured voice, "Listen, kid, I'll tell you what the point of singing this song is. Would you like to know what the reason is for Barbra Streisand to sing 'People'?" Fosse replied, "Yeah, what is the reason?" Styne: "The reason she is singing this song is *BECAUSE THIS SONG IS GOING TO BE NUMBER ONE ON THE HIT PARADE! THAT IS WHY SHE IS SINGING THIS FUCKING SONG!*" Fosse had to laugh, reports Gottfried, and he backed down, either out of fear of the combative composer or unable to counter Styne's logic. "OK, Jule, now I understand," he said. "People" almost got snipped out again during its LP recording session when it ran over four minutes, long for an LP cut in 1964.

Even Frank Sinatra trashed "People," riled that he hadn't been given first crack to record the song by Styne (his former house composer with Sammy Cahn and Jimmy Van Heusen). Styne said Sinatra told him at a party, "You blew it, Jule. You didn't know where to go on bar 16." In an earlier article in *Look* magazine Sinatra went out of his way to knock "People," writing that the song "fell apart in the release." After Styne confronted envious Ol' Green Eyes, the two didn't speak for three years.

In *Funny Girl*, Barbra Streisand is depicted discussing her need for "People."

The song doesn't fall apart in the sixteenth bar, as Prof. Sinatra contended—it's a pretty tune—but Merrill's gooey lyric does fall apart, better suited to a Hallmark verse. Examined closely, it's hard to figure out exactly what Merrill means by "people who need people" and why that makes them "the luckiest people in the world." It further declares: "Lovers are very special people, / They're the luckiest people in the world! / With one person, one very special person . . . No more hunger and thirst, / But first be a person who needs people." Hunger and thirst? Sounds more like a person who needs a rhyme for "first." Merrill was a polished lyricist, but "People" is treacle trying to sound profound, saved by Styne's soaring melody and, to be sure, by Streisand's sincere, compelling delivery.

It's a measure of Streisand's stage persona and vocal powers that she was able to make what is a lush but semi-incoherent song into a massive hit, a standard, a personal statement, indeed an anthem. You rarely hear it sung by anyone else; cover versions by Dionne Warwick, Nat Cole, and Aretha Franklin barely made a dent.

•••••••••••••• BACKSTAGE DISH ••••••••••••••

+ *Funny Girl* was rife with creative battles, dissension, firings, and bad blood all over the stage. Producer David Merrick pulled out (after contributing the show's title), as did Stephen Sondheim when Mary Martin was the leading candidate to star; Isobel Lennart had originally written the Brice story as a movie for Martin. "I don't want to do the life of Fanny Brice with Mary Martin," Sondheim said. "She's not Jewish. You need someone ethnic for the part. Fanny was a hokey comedian and Mary's terrific with characters, but this is East Side New York and she can't do it." Martin dropped out on her own. When Carol Burnett was offered the part, she agreed, "You need a Jewish girl." Anne Bancroft was Italian, close enough, though Styne wasn't convinced she could sing the "range-y" part. Merrill argued, "Anne Bancroft can't sing any of these songs." Bancroft didn't like Merrill so she withdrew on her own. Eydie Gormé was considered but insisted her husband Steve Lawrence play Nick Arnstein.

   Apart from Lennart, who confessed she didn't know anything about theater writing after a lifetime of screenplays, the company was a collection of difficult, contentious, willful characters, from Merrick on down. Nobody seems to have liked anybody, a classic pileup of artistic egos. Producer Ray Stark was lead villain, a mixture of polished manners and trash talk, so gruff he drove away even Broadway's favorite monster, David Merrick, who said, "Life is too short to deal with Ray Stark"; Stark reportedly bought out Merrick's share for $100,000. He refused to sign Streisand until she agreed to a four-movie deal with him. Stark played backstage backstab games, mainly between Streisand and her understudy Lainie Kazan, whom Stark was lusting after. When Robbins tried to fire Kazan, claiming she was too sexy for the role, Stark insisted she stay.

+ Jerome Robbins was Styne's wish to direct the show, but Robbins felt it wasn't his kind of musical, so Bob Fosse was brought in to direct. Fosse decided against it after two weeks, much to Streisand's relief; she much preferred Robbins. By then the company was in chaos. Eventually the quiet, efficient, undramatic Garson Kanin was brought in to stabilize things and get the show on its wobbly feet. Lainie Kazan recalls, "People were being fired and replaced left and right." But Streisand wasn't happy with Kanin either. She said he didn't take charge, kept mute, and was forever conferring with his wife, Ruth Gordon; Streisand wanted more direction. Kanin, not a combative man, gave in to many of the star's demands until Streisand brought her drama coach to rehearsals; Kanin banned him.

✦ Jule Styne had read a rave review of Streisand at the Bon Soir in Greenwich Village, went to see her, and returned several times, sure she was the real deal. Robbins was likewise infatuated: "The kook's looks are ravishing," he wrote in a letter, sounding like a man dangerously in love. "Her beauty astounds" he said, "composed of impossibly unconventional features. Her body is full of gawky angles and sensuous curves." He raved about her "El Greco hands" and called her "sexy." He wrote, "Her performances astound, arouse, fulfill. When she sings she is as honest and frighteningly direct with her feelings as if she was, or will be, in bed with you." All this from a gay man. Fran Stark, Brice's daughter, felt otherwise and vetoed Streisand after seeing her at the Bon Soir, vowing, "I'll never let that girl play my mother." The ever-tactful Merrick was even more loudly anti-Streisand, calling her a *meeskite* (ugly) and allegedly screaming at his casting director, "I want you to take her out and kill her!"

✦ Styne rejected the seemingly inspired notion of Dorothy Fields as lyricist, worried that a female star and female lyricist might gang up on him, though Fields, so good at describing the feminine psyche with wit, may have been a wiser choice. Styne, though an established pop songwriter, perhaps also felt he would be overshadowed by Fields's fancier movie musical credits with Jerome Kern. In any case, he had more rapport with Bob Merrill, who had never written a musical, but Stark wanted Fields. Styne told Merrill to write lyrics to five tunes on spec, and in three days he came up with "Don't Rain on My Parade," "Who Are You Now?," and "The Music That Makes Me Dance." Styne, a veteran deliverer of ultimatums, informed Stark that either Merrill was in or he was out.

✦ Streisand fought with everyone except costar Sydney Chaplin, with whom she had an affair while dating Elliott Gould. Robbins and Streisand were the only ones who seemed to get along—mutual adoration. Robbins wrote, "She tests you with childish stubbornness, impetuosity and conceit, concedes you are right without admission, and balances all with her generous artistry and grace." He might have been describing himself. Before Robbins stepped in, Streisand was all but running the show. Merrill called her "a know-it-all." Streisand and Merrill got into it over lyric interpretation, specifically a skirmish about the ballad "Who Are You Now?," when Merrill insisted she held the word "someone" too long in the line, "are you someone better?"

+ Nobody quite knows who directed what in *Funny Girl*. Kanin "staged" it, according to the credits, but he was replaced by Robbins out of town, whose credit reads "production supervised by Jerome Robbins"—who redid Fosse's and Kanin's direction and was responsible for the look of the show. Herb Ross staged a few of the numbers, yet the choreography is credited to Carol Haney, but Robbins also restaged Haney. As in *Fiddler on the Roof* and *Gypsy*, the cast was terrorized by Robbins's scorched-earth tactics. Robbins salvaged a weak song, Chaplin's solo "You Are Woman, I Am Man," turning it into a charming countermelody duet between Fanny and Nick. But Chaplin was peeved at losing his big solo. Styne recalls hearing Chaplin teasingly whisper to Streisand as she sang her part with him for the first time, "You're flat, you cunt."

+ New York notices were good to mixed, with only one all-out rave—Norman Nadel in the *World-Telegram & Sun*, who saluted the star, "Hail to thee, Barbra Streisand." Walter Kerr, in the *Herald Tribune*, called the show a tuneful, enjoyable jumble: "One feels that management is trying to cram an entire career into one show," adding, "inspiration wanes, and craft must make due in its place."

+ When Johnny Desmond first replaced Chaplin, after Streisand sang "Don't Rain on My Parade," her new costar, the casino-trained Desmond shouted to the audience, "Let's hear it for this little girl!" (Well, that's one way to stop a show.)

+ The movie version was a faithful imitation of the stage show, and just as problem-plagued, but Columbia wanted kook-at-large Shirley MacLaine to star in the film. Stark said he wouldn't allow the movie to be made without Streisand. Styne lobbied to get Frank Sinatra to play Nick Arnstein, but Sinatra demanded six new songs for himself. Stark thought Sinatra was too old (and as Jewish as Shirley MacLaine), and anyway Stark had Cary Grant in mind to play the Jewish gambler. Such an obvious choice. But the even less likely Omar Sharif, an Egyptian-born actor, won the part, largely because Streisand wanted him for her own offstage reasons. When the Six-Day War erupted, the Egyptian press demanded Sharif's citizenship be revoked if he starred opposite Streisand, who said, "You think the Egyptians are angry? You should see the letter I got from my Aunt Rose!" All the flirty scenes between Sharif and Streisand are hard to watch today, with

Sharif flashing his charming rogue grin as Streisand, as coy Jewish dumpling, melts. Roger Ebert thought Streisand had "the best timing since Mae West," but others felt her Fanny Brice had far too much Mae West in her.

+ When William Wyler, who had never directed a movie musical and was aging and hard of hearing, came in after Sidney Lumet departed over good old "creative differences," it was rumored Streisand did much of the directing. Styne complained that the orchestrations sounded more pop than show tune. Several songs were dropped, and the studio asked Styne and Merrill to write new ones; they refused. The movie instead added two classic Brice songs—"My Man" and "Second-Hand Rose." Styne said, "They didn't want to go with success. It was the old-fashioned MGM Hollywood way of doing a musical. They always change things to their way of vision, and they always do it wrong. But, of all my musicals they screwed up, *Funny Girl* came out the best." A 1975 sequel, *Funny Lady*, with James Caan as Fanny's next husband Billy Rose, had some good songs by John Kander and Fred Ebb, but the movie flopped anyway. By then, people were all Fanny-ed out.

FIDDLER ON THE ROOF

◆ 1964 ◆

"If I Were a Rich Man"

In a musical with a wagonload of woes, **"If I Were a Rich Man"** erupts from *Fiddler on the Roof*'s larger-and-louder-than-life lead character Tevye with great hopeful joy—*naches* in Yiddish.

The song suggests that, no matter how much angst befalls this little forgotten Russian village, all will be well in the end. Tevye's spirit is much too overflowing with life to be extinguished by a few Cossacks. Nobody as amusing as Tevye, when he confronts God, could possibly come to a bad end. "If I Were a Rich Man" must be the jaunty tune played by that happy-go-lucky fiddler prancing precariously on his roof.

The playful number by Sheldon Harnick and Jerry Bock sums up the wishful/wistful spirit of the entire show—and of Tevye, really. The song says

Tevye may as well dream big despite his troubles, because a poor, bedraggled milkman's fantasy is all he has left to spend.

Tevye doesn't curse God but gives him a nice sharp elbow in the ribs as if asking the Almighty, "Hey, Lord, would it ruin your day to make me richer? Surely you can spare a few thousand shekels for a decent man." It's a joshing taunt that only the defiant Tevye would make and hope to get away with, displaying a less-than-worshipful, indeed devilish, attitude. What gives Tevye guts, and makes us love him, is that he's a man of deep faith who nonetheless questions God's treatment of the Jews—and specifically him. But Tevye and the show are never preachy—he's antipreachy.

Harnick's impudent lyrics sum up Tevye's brash character but also something else—a gutsy Jewish attitude that says, we may be down and almost out, but we've not thrown in any towels yet; we have enough gall left to wish for wealth. The song is sung without self-pity but with a sarcastic shrug and a belligerent attitude of, *Take that, God!* Bock's merry tune makes you want to jump up and join Tevye in his little jig.

"If I Were a Rich Man" was inspired by a 1902 monologue by the Yiddish writer Sholem Aleichem, on whose short stories *Fiddler* was based, titled "Ven ikh bin Rothschild" ("If I Were a Rothschild"). The lyric is based in part on passages in Aleichem's story "The Bubble Bursts," one of the tales from his 1949 English-language collection, *Tevye's Daughters.*

The song is almost a chant, sung to a foot-stomping klezmer-like tune, with only a few simple buried rhymes richly embroidered by Harnick's flavorful nonsense sounds—"biddy-biddy-bum . . . deidle-diddle digguh-digguh-deedle-deidle-dum." Bock and Harnick make the song sound extemporaneous, like an authentic Yiddish folk tune, when of course it's a carefully crafted Broadway song that became an instant showstopper. As Alisa Solomon writes in *Wonder of Wonders,* her history of *Fiddler on the Roof,* "The ghosts of Tin Pan Alley were harmonizing with strains from the [Jewish] Pale: Bock fused his jaunty pop proficiency with a deeply absorbed feel for the thick harmonies and sweet-and-sour falling fourth notes of Russian folk music." She adds, "Bock didn't need to do any research to compose this score. He 'felt it was inside me.'"

Tevye laments his hard life as a dairyman that he could quit if he were just wealthy with "a big tall house with rooms by the dozen, right in the middle of the town," to display his nouveau riche lifestyle, including "one long staircase just going up, and one even longer coming down," and to allow his wife, Golde, to cook huge meals, put on airs, and scream at the servants all day. At the end

**Zero Mostel imagines life in a different tax bracket in
"If I Were a Rich Man" from *Fiddler on the Roof.***

of his urgent plea, when he's all out of reasons why he deserves to be rich, Tevye finally tries to bargain with God, telling him that more money would give him more time to pray in synagogue and become a learned man. He knows God isn't going to buy it, but he literally has nothing to lose. Throughout the show, the fearless Tevye respectfully challenges God, even baits him. "Send us the cure," he requests of the Lord. "We got the sickness already."

The song is an exasperated explosion by Tevye about his sorry plight, and whoever plays it can pretty much go for broke, as Zero Mostel did in the original 1964 production, whose deserved success was both because of and in spite of his performance. Others might (and did) play Tevye equally well, maybe better—Herschel Bernardi, Harry Goz, Theodore Bikel, Harvey Fierstein in the 2004 Broadway revival, plus Chaim Topol in the highly faithful Norman Jewison movie version, one of the few hit Broadway musicals to survive the transfer from stage to film intact. In ways, the latter is even richer, and Topol stays in character, unlike Mostel, who tried every trick up his raggedy sleeve to bring down the house. Mostel is still most identified with the role, because he so looked and acted its essence, squeezing out every drop of Tevye's comic juices—until he went so zany in the part that he was almost fired for overembellishing the character and turning *Fiddler on the Roof* into a one-man show, not the first time a star would upstage a musical and threaten to overwhelm it and spoil it.

Harnick says "Rich Man" became a big song because of Bock's klezmer-inflected melody and tells how the number came to be: "Jerry Bock and I, before we were in rehearsal, had gone downtown to a Hebrew Actors' Union benefit. We went mostly to see if there was anybody in the cast that would be right for us. And there was Zvee Scooler, the guy who played our innkeeper. He was playing the rabbi. At one point, a mother and a daughter came out and they sang a Hassidic chant. It was absolutely enchanting. Jerry Robbins was enthralled by it."

Harnick goes on: "Jerry [Bock] went home and worked all night with that chant in his ears, and he wrote the music for 'If I Were a Rich Man.' He called me early the next morning and said, 'Meet me at my publishers. There's something I have to play for you.' He played it, and it's a very catchy, ingratiating melody, and when he sang it, it was in all those Hassidic syllables. We thought, when I write the lyric let's leave in some of those Hassidic syllables. I didn't know how to spell them so I invented phrases like 'didle deedle' that sounded like them." One critic dubbed it Yiddish scat. "The other thing I borrowed very heavily from Sholem Aleichem. He has Teyve saying, 'Oh, if I were only a Rothschild, oh, what I could do with my life.' Then he mentions this and that. All of that, I thought, will make wonderful lyric material. The lyric is borrowed heavily from the genius of Sholem Aleichem." Harnick says he told Mostel, "Zero, I wrote 'Didle deedle' because I can't do that Hassidic chanting. He said, 'I can. I grew up with that,' and he did." The song instantly replaced an earlier song about Tevye's horse.

Harnick adds, "I wasn't conscious of it when I was doing it, but it has been pointed out to me that the song is constructed beautifully. The line that goes from the very first 'If I were a rich man,' to what kind of house he wants to live in, the kind of fowl he will have in his backyard, what he is doing with his wife when the other people in the village come to visit him, ending with the religious notion of wanting a seat by the Eastern Wall, and if he were rich he could go to synagogue and really listen to the wise men expounding the Talmud." The lyrics grew out of Joseph Stein's script, in which he describes "a large house with a tin roof right in the middle of the town" and "a rich man's wife, with a double chin," both of which became phrases in the song. "Knowing that it was Zero, I put in a line about ducks quacking that would let him cross his eyes. I knew what he was going to do with that line if it had animal noises he could make." Beyond all that, it's an idea that resonates with everybody: *If I were rich, what would I do?*

To his later great regret, director-choreographer Jerome Robbins gave Mostel a prop to play with—a big milk can for Tevye the dairyman, which Mostel turned into major shtick. Recalls Harnick, "At one point he raises his hands to heaven and sighs, he lowers his arm and by accident it goes into the milk can. He is supposed to take his sleeve out, which is dripping with milk, rinse out the milk as he looks at God, as though to say, 'And this *too* you do to me?'—and then go on with his song. Zero didn't do that. Within three days, what he did with that sleeve added about six minutes to the show. He took the milk, he dabbed his ears with it like perfume, he greased the wheels of his cart, he did this with it, he did that with it. It was just ruining the song."

The cagey Robbins came up with a solution to foil Mostel. Recounts Harnick, "One day Zero sang the song and raised his arms to heaven, lowered them, and then he took his arm right out of the milk can because there was no milk in it! Robbins had emptied out all the milk because that was the only way we could get him to do the song straight." For all his antics, the cast respected Mostel's gifts, experimentation, and skill at learning new material at a glance. Librettist Joseph Stein said, "He can do the same thing four ways and they all seem right." Frank Rich, then a young critic, told the show's chronicler Alisa Solomon that Mostel's Tevye is "the greatest performance I have ever seen in the musical theater." Howard Taubman in his *Times* review said Mostel and Tevye "were ordained to be one."

Mostel instantly loved "If I Were a Rich Man." Harnick says he didn't mind Mostel adding shtick if he "stayed within the confines of the song." He says, "It was that milk can and the wet sleeve that allowed him to start improvising. Otherwise, the song had to keep moving forward. He invented lovely stuff when he was feeding ducks and chickens. I don't know if it was his idea or Robbins' idea to give him the stuff he did in the song." Harnick credits Mostel with insisting he not cut a verse in which he fantasizes how, when rich, he will "discuss the Holy Books with the learned men seven hours every day / That would be the sweetest thing of all." Harnick thought it too serious, but Mostel argued, "If you change that you don't understand this man." Harnick kept it in and says, "He saved me from myself."

Many times, says Harnick, "we went to the stage manager and said, 'Please try to get Zero to stop doing it, it's too much.' But it was impossible to try to control him." Did Hal Prince ever try to fire Mostel if he wouldn't stop ad-libbing? "No, because Zero recognized that no matter what he did, the audience adored him. So it was very hard to say, 'Zero what you are doing is putting the audience off,' because that was not true. They adored him. But as writers and as a director, we thought this is too much."

The cast was not as pleased as the audience with Mostel's ad-lib monkey business, which threw the actors off. "When they turned to Zero to give him a line, they never knew where he was going to be. They appreciated his comic genius, but it was difficult to work with him. We gave a benefit performance for the other Broadway actors on a Sunday night when the audience was all actors; Zero behaved. He knew they would see what he was doing was unprofessional," recalls Harnick.

Keeping Mostel from building moments became a growing problem. Harnick recalls, "After the show opened, I asked Robbins, 'How often will you come around to keep the show tight?' He said, 'I don't do that. I like to go on to the next show. In this show in particular I do not want to see what Zero Mostel is doing to the role two months after it opens.' And he was right. Somebody sent us a review from a Lexington, Kentucky, newspaper. The critic had come to see the show and had written a review saying, *Fiddler on the Roof* is an adorable show and I urge you to go and see it, but wait until Zero Mostel is no longer in it because he is distorting the scenes he is in."

Prince read that and decided, "We have to speak to Zero about this. Actually, rather than speak to him, Hal wrote a letter. He sent it to Jerry Bock and me and Joe Stein to see if there were any criticisms we wanted to make. We thought it was the most diplomatic letter imaginable. In effect, it said, Zero, we know you are a genius and you are wonderful and the audience adores you, but every so often you do something that is a little more than we would like and at that time we would like permission to talk to you. Zero hit the ceiling. He said, 'Nobody tells me how to do a show!' He was furious, furious. He just loved to kid around onstage."

Luckily for the producer Hal Prince, Mostel only stayed in the show nine months, most likely to gain more bargaining power should the show become a smash hit. But Prince turned the tables, using the short-term contract to boot Mostel from the show after he made outrageous demands, such as demanding 10 percent of the gross to star in the London production. Prince instead cast Chaim Topol, who wound up taking the role away from Mostel not only in London but also in the movie version of *Fiddler*. God might not have answered Tevye's prayers, but he came to Bock, Harnick, and Prince's rescue.

··············· BACKSTAGE DISH ···············

✦ Rodgers and Hammerstein, who had created shows about almost every people—Oklahomans, Pacific Islanders, Siamese, Chinese, Austrians—but their own, Jews, considered making a musical out of the Sholem Aleichem stories but came to the same conclusion as librettist Joseph Stein, who loved the stories but said, "Who would be interested in producing a show about a shtetl?" One potential producer wondered, "What will we do when we've run out of Hadassah groups?"

But of course it's more than a show about a shtetl—it's about Tevye's problems with his daughters' modern ways, the universal theme that instantly made the show a hit in twenty-four countries. (Tokyo playgoers called it "so Japanese.") The show's great triumph is that it managed to make a deeply Jewish story available to all. As Alisa Solomon writes, *Fiddler* belonged to everyone—even Jews, the toughest of audiences, for whom the show became a "dignified, religiously correct self-portrait." She remarks that the show both "bewails and celebrates" Jewish life. Also, the time seemed ripe. Jewish was in, or at least had its foot in the stage door. Jerry Herman's hit show *Milk and Honey*, about Israel's founding, had opened and also a show about a Jewish wedding, *A Family Affair*. *I Can Get It for You Wholesale* had been a modest hit featuring an unknown named Barbra Streisand, who starred two years before *Fiddler* in *Funny Girl* as Fanny Brice.

✦ Director-choreographer Robbins was notoriously difficult to work with— demanding, prickly, remote, insulting, even cruel, flinging Joseph Stein's rewrites back at him, calling them embarrassing and amateurish. He told Austin Pendleton (Motel the tailor) that during the wedding scene, "I had to leave the theater. I couldn't bear the thought of that wonderful young woman being married to you." Pendleton didn't speak to Robbins for a week. Once, after an actress kept forgetting to reach for a cup in rehearsal, he hid the cup from her opening night. Robbins could be an equal opportunity creep, getting into "black moods" as opening night approached; everyone walked on eggshells around him during rehearsals. Ballet master Peter Martins said that, despite his authoritarian stance, "Jerry's insecurity was incredible." Deborah Jowitt, in her Robbins biography, says he "goaded his cast into extra rehearsals by telling them that they could either work a little more and maybe be part of a hit, or they could cry mercy and play to the congregations of synagogues." Genius or no, it's a wonder he found anyone who would hire him. Yet everyone invariably said that they would eagerly work with him again. The set designer Boris Aronson, who had his own run-ins with Robbins, proclaimed, after first seeing the Bottle Dance, "Any man who can do that, I forgive everything."

✦ Robbins steeped himself in shtetl life and vowed to avoid not just the sentimental but anything slick and "Broadway," fearful of turning the show into *The Goldbergs*, the radio and TV series of the era that he felt stereotyped Jews as sweet, cozy, lovable creatures, full of "pixie humor." He wanted more earthy reality and to avoid, as Solomon writes in her study, "making all the Jews understanding, philosophic, with hearts of gold, wry of expression and compassionate to the point of nausea."

Robbins also shied away from "lovable schnooks" and scenery-chewing "stage Jews" (like the wailing father in *The Jazz Singer*), with singsong inflections, rolling eyes, and flailing arms. He wanted actors who didn't "play Jewish"; Yiddish theater veterans and Borscht Belters need not apply. He rejected Stein's first script as "terribly anti-Gentile and Jewish self-loving," and he turned down Bock and Harnick's early songs, saying, "Though most of the songs are charming even the charm wears thin." The score wasn't "robust" or "virile" enough. "If every song is sweet, sentimental, sad, touching, and nostalgic, it will come off as Second Avenue" (the Broadway of Yiddish theater).

Robbins described the characters: "They are tough, working, resilient, tenacious; they fiercely live and hang onto their existence. . . . We are not to see them through the misty nostalgia of time past." Despite Robbins's campaign to make the show un-Broadway, a few critics found it just that; a Jewish scholar labeled Anatevka "the cutest shtetl we never had." *Herald Tribune* critic Walter Kerr wrote, "I think it might be an altogether charming musical if only the people of Anatevka did not pause every now and again to give their regards to Broadway."

✦ Zero Mostel was cast because he fit Robbins's notion of how Tevye should be played. Robbins envisioned the show as a stark play about a humble dairyman, not a splashy Broadway musical or a Zero Mostel vehicle. He didn't even consider *Fiddler* a "musical"; he called it "a combination opera, play, and ballet." He rejected actors who were too handsome, pretty, or "too American," his original take on Bea Arthur, but he later changed his mind and cast her as Yente.

Mostel was a modern-day New York Tevye (albeit a much richer man), who grew up in an Orthodox Jewish home and was steeped in, well, tradition—even if he was in fact a rebel in every way: politically, comically, personally, even ethnically (his children had no religious training). But he embodied Tevye, from his dumpy, rumpled, roly-poly shape to his don't-give-a-damn attitude and crude, clownish behavior; in a favorite bit I witnessed in a lunch interview, he buttered his sleeve. It all seemed to shout that he was the ideal Tevye. Zero was by then a certified Broadway star after *A Funny Thing Happened on the Way to the Forum* two years earlier—that didn't hurt his chances either; and in 1961 Mostel had played an enraged beast in *Rhinoceros*. He was a lock once Robbins saw Mostel in *The World of Sholom Aleichem* on TV, playing not Tevye but two other characters.

Harnick and Bock wanted Howard Da Silva in the role. They also had seen him in *The World of Sholom Aleichem*, but Robbins nixed Da Silva, a respected journeyman actor but not charismatic enough for Robbins, who wanted a more expansive Tevye. Lesser Mostels considered for the role included Danny Kaye, Eli Wallach, Joseph Schildkraut, and Rod Steiger. Mostel dallied about accepting the role, feeling that it sentimentalized Sholem Aleichem. When he didn't grab the offer, Robbins pleaded in a letter, "Dear Zee. Please don't make me do this without you. Please." He asked others, "Will somebody tell Zero that this show will be good for him?" The reason for Mostel's reluctance wasn't the role, it was Robbins, who had named names at the McCarthy hearings, including Mostel's leftist friends, such as Jack Gilford, his costar in *A Funny Thing*. Gilford's wife talked Mostel into taking the part, but Mostel told Hal Prince that, while he would work with Robbins, "You didn't say I had to have lunch with him."

Even so, Mostel and Robbins were on a collision course, or as Solomon puts it, "Mostel was an unstoppable force, Robbins an immovable object." Mostel would ridicule him—shake his rear end or flip him off behind his back and chew gum in defiance of Robbins's orders. It became a power struggle, with Mostel happily mocking the feared director, to the delight of a terrorized cast. Mostel once improvised kissing the mezuzah at the front door as he entered and Robbins asked him not to. So Mostel went inside and crossed himself. Robbins relented. The mezuzah gesture was left in. But Mostel made fun of everyone, once sending Bea Arthur offstage in tears. "Mostel likes to test you when you work together," Robbins said, soft-pedalling their battles to a reporter. "There was a certain amount of squaring off against each other, but we both felt some good healthy respect beneath it all." After Mostel left the show, Luther Adler replaced him and was a pussycat compared to the out-of-control Zero.

The Israeli actor Topol won over director Norman Jewison and snagged the movie role. Jewison (who was not Jewish) did not emerge from Broadway's *Fiddler* a Mostel fan. The director found him "too big, too American, and he pulled the viewer out of the play."

+ Robbins, as famous for his delays, dithering, and dictated rewrites as for his tantrums and genius, never felt a show was ready to open and demanded long rehearsals, inflating the budget; Prince threatened to sue Robbins for the $55,000 of his own money he would need to to pay for postponing rehearsals. Austin Pendleton (Motel the tailor) said Robbins restaged a table-setting scene twenty-five times before he was satisfied. He even changed numbers that were working perfectly, driving the cast crazy. Seven weeks into rehearsals, Robbins still had not staged the crucial opening number, "Tradition." The cast was near mutiny, but he staged it in two hours and renewed their spirits.

+ Stephen Sondheim recalled on PBS's *American Masters*, "Jerry was endlessly inventive, but that meant he was never satisfied and demanded endless revisions. But some of his inventiveness rubs off on you—so it's worth it." Critic Frank Rich comments that Robbins could never make up his mind. "He wouldn't take yes for an answer." Joseph Stein remembered how Robbins would say, "I like this scene [you've written] very much. Can you give me something else?" Robbins departed Broadway for good after three mighty hits—*West Side Story, Gypsy, Fiddler on the Roof*—because he found musicals too difficult. Ballets were easier, and he could control them more than a sprawling show with many collaborators to please. He could rule ballet totally.

+ In a familiar story, Robbins was unable to get a handle on *Fiddler on the Roof* until he could put his finger on precisely what it was about, which he felt the opener failed to state. Robbins needed a theme to give the show a vital, coherent through line. Harnick recalls, "The original song was just about the mama and the five daughters bustling around, called 'We've Never Missed a Sabbath Yet.' It was an up-tempo song about them getting ready for the Sabbath. It's a lovely song and Robbins loved it, but he said it does not set up what the show should be saying. After we had all those preproduction meetings, he finally realized the show really was about the preservation of some traditions and the replacing of other traditions. I remember his words. He said, 'It will be like a tapestry against which the rest of the material plays.'" Nobody remembers who came up with the magic word—*tradition*—to which Robbins said, simply, "Yes, *that's* the show." It all comes into focus when Tevye asks the audience, "And how do we keep our balance? That I can tell you in one word." The orchestra strikes the now telltale chord and Tevye shouts, "Tradition!"

* The show's most flamboyant showstopper has no lyrics—"The Bottle Dance," with the village men balancing wine bottles on their hats as they step through a complex dance at a wedding. Robbins asked Bock and Harnick to write a scene that would allow him to choreograph a second-act blockbuster, which became the acrobatic Bottle Dance. The dance invariably brings down the house but not the bottles. Robbins insisted it be real—no Velcro or glue holding bottles atop the hats. Recalls Harnick, "That's a showstopper that derived from Robbins during his research, when we went with him to Hassidic weddings. There was an entertainer, and all he did was walk around the room with a wine bottle on his head." Robbins wrote a friend, "The rough dominant force released by all this kinetic energy was overpowering." Mostel was unimpressed, scoffing, "A couple of weddings in Williamsburg [Brooklyn] and that putz thinks he understands Orthodox Jews!" Robbins felt that such moments exploded the myth of "weak" Jewish masculinity. Robbins (born Rabinowitz), not an especially observant Jew, began to grill his relatives about their Eastern European childhoods. As in *West Side Story*, Robbins wanted masculine dancers, not chorus boys, and he wanted the entire cast to dance, not just an ensemble. He devised "The Bottle Dance" out of town in a Detroit hotel room.

* Harnick explains how the show's most beloved song, "Sunrise, Sunset" came about: "Robbins told us in rehearsal, 'I don't want to cut it, but I don't know what to do with it.' Finally he decided how to use it at the wedding. Jerry wrote the music first. The rise and fall of the music suggested a sunrise and a sunset to me. Usually once he set a lyric to a tune, I would sing it over and over until the words felt comfortable in my mouth." "Anyway," he continued, "we invited Jerry's wife Patty to hear it. If she liked it, we thought, OK, we can set that one aside. I have learned over the years not to look at anybody when I audition a song. I look over their head. So at the end of the song, I looked at Patty, and to my astonishment she had tears in her eyes. Later I was in Bethesda, Maryland, where my sister lived and I played her the song. When I finished, I looked at her and *she* was crying. I thought, wow, I guess this song is special. I didn't know it had that kind of appeal." "Sunrise, Sunset" is now played, sung, and danced to at every bar/bat mitzvah in the known world.

+ Harnick says certain contemporary musicals want every number to be a showstopper by cranking up the tempo. "That's a songwriter who thinks that's what he needs to make the show successful. All audiences demand is to be entertained. They come in not knowing what to expect, or sometimes their expectations are foiled. They don't get what they expected, but if it is entertaining they got what they came for—an evening of enjoyment. They don't keep score when they are watching a show and say, 'Aha, there are not enough showstoppers.' If they're really engrossed from moment to moment, that's all one can hope for. Then it doesn't matter whether there are showstoppers as long as you are getting through to the audiences and keeping them interested and involved." He objects to the pop mentality that primes audience to whoop it up after every number. "I don't like all this whistling and screaming. We saw a show, *Rock of Ages*, and I was startled. During one number, two rows of young people sitting down front took out their cigarette lighters and lit them and were holding them and swaying as though they were candles. It was a rock concert!"

+ Harnick recalls a number in *Fiddler* that was such an audience pleaser that it triggered extended applause—the comic but endearing "Do You Love Me?" in act 2 between Teyve and Golde. "It was very hard to write. While we were in rehearsal, I thought it would be funny, given that society, if Teyve asked Golde, 'Do you love me?,' and she looks at him like, *Wha-a-t?* I thought it would be a nice way to begin a song, but I had no idea where to go from there." To resolve such problems, Harnick would often take long walks for hours. "At the end of the day, if I had four lines I was happy."

+ Bock and Harnick wrote only one more show after *Fiddler on the Roof—The Rothschilds*, a modest 1970 success that ran fourteen months but caused their breakup. Harnick didn't want to divulge the details of the split but said, "It was very ugly. It took thirty or forty years for Jerry and me to patch it up, but he never wanted to work with me again." Of their two final collaborations, Harnick said, "I was talking to somebody once about the difference between these two Jewish shows, *Fiddler* and *The Rothschilds*. The guy made an interesting observation. He said, *Fiddler* works because the Jews are victims. *The Rothschilds* doesn't work because the Jews are conquerers."

SWEET CHARITY

◆ 1964 ◆

"Big Spender," "If My Friends Could See Me Now"

Your basic hardworking, hip-thrusting Bob Fosse number, **"Big Spender"** is the *Sweet Charity* showstopper and later pop hit, sung onto the charts by Shirley Bassey and Peggy Lee. It's the breakout number in the 1966 show starring Gwen Verdon in full comeback mode, with a tough but touching score by Cy Coleman and Dorothy Fields, making her own comeback after a long layoff. Fields's savvy lyrics revealed that the author of such refined classics as "A Fine Romance," "The Way You Look Tonight," and "I Can't Give You Anything but Love" could still write great lyrics, in a more raw, streetwise '60s idiom than when she worked with gentlemanly Jerome Kern thirty years earlier.

When Coleman called her to join him on a new show, Fields was sixty, sitting around her apartment resting restlessly on her laurels from an earlier heyday spent writing standards with Jimmy McHugh and Astaire-Rogers movies with Kern. She was hungry to get back in the gritty Broadway game she had grown up in. Ethan Mordden, the Broadway historian, writes, "Dorothy Fields may be the only lyricist in musical-theater history who sounded more youthful as time ran on. Her first show had come along in 1928, when Cy Coleman was running around in a propeller beanie. Yet in *Sweet Charity*, Fields has the ear of a teenage prodigy." She was able to get into the head of a young taxi dancer who sprinkled her speech with "wow," "holy cow," and "riff raff."

"You must stay au courant," she told songwriter biographer Max Wilk. "I don't pull myself into a shell like a turtle and withdraw. I go to the theater. I listen to whatever's being played. I get a *feel* of what's around." Indeed. The same woman who wrote the tender "Don't Blame Me" was capable of a hard-boiled number that begins, "The minute you walked in the joint, / I could see you were a man of distinction, . . . / Good looking, so refined. . . . So, let me get right to the point, / I don't pop my cork for every guy I see. / Hey, big spender, spend a little time with me." In a few cork-popping lines, Fields captures the shabby come-on of sequined dance-hall hostesses/hookers plying their trade. Later in the number, the lyrics bat their false eyelashes in unfinished suggestive lines: "How's about a . . . (laugh)? / I could give you some . . . / Are you ready for . . . (fun)? . . . Let me show you a . . . (good time), / Hey, big spender."

Coleman, her jazzy junior partner by twenty-four years, revived Fields's fading career in their hit musical set to the comic/poignant Neil Simon book based on Fellini's *Nights of Cabiria* starring Giulietta Masina (plainly a prostitute in the film). It tells the fond, indeed dog-eared, whore-with-a-heart-of-gold story of a desperate, put-upon, insecure, vulnerable ten-cents-a-dance girl at the Fan-Dango Ballroom involved with a rich guy who buys her devotion—sort of a *Pretty Woman* with zippy songs. As Martin Gottfried writes in his Fosse biography, the dances in *Sweet Charity* are "really an insinuating series of moves, poses and stances, a writhing of women who are at once alluring and threatening." Helen Gallagher, one of those writhing women and Verdon's understudy, says, "It was as close as the show got to saying we were hookers."

Gwen Verdon, then forty-one, played innocent Charity Hope Valentine (that name tells you all you need to know about the show's terminal sentimentality), and the musical about her life is mainly a vehicle for Verdon to dance her way into our hearts, driven by flashy, fleshy Bob Fosse choreography. The show is equally a Bob Fosse vehicle, propelled by his trademark sexed-up razzamatazz dance numbers embodied by "Big Spender." Musicals archivist Ken Bloom says, "When Cy Coleman was writing *Sweet Charity*, he got really upset with Bob Fosse because the accent that Coleman put in the music Fosse wasn't using for the choreography. He would change the accent of Coleman's music to suit his choreography. Cy Coleman was furious about this, so he deliberately wrote 'Big Spender' where it is *all* accents. Coleman chortled, 'This is my revenge on Bob Fosse.'"

The song is a titillating come-on for big-shot high rollers to "spend a little time with me," a frank number for its time, set to a thumping stripper's beat. People who missed *Sweet Charity* may recall "Big Spender" as the background music for Edie Adams's seductive 1970s Muriel Cigars commercials, with a slight rewrite ("Spend a little *dime* with me"). Early in his career, Fosse worked in burlesque houses, so he knew from bumps and grinds, a heavy (maybe too heavy) influence on his style, especially in *Sweet Charity*, whose score also includes the bumpy (and carbon-dated) "Rich Man's Frug" and "The Rhythm of Life."

Fosse, a fabled womanizer, was always drawn to shows about bawdy women—Velma Kelly and Roxie Hart in *Chicago*, Sally Bowles in *Cabaret*,

Lola in *Damn Yankees*, Anna in *New Girl in Town*, and Charity. Most of his dances read like carnal dreams come to life onstage. His numbers rarely express much more than blatant come-hither urges, songs that ask, "Hey, mister, wanna party?" So "Big Spender" was very much the ultimate Bob Fosse statement. The musical was his idea, which he developed the same night he and Verdon saw *Nights of Cabiria*. "I just hated it," Verdon said later. "So depressing. But Bob just loved it. He couldn't sleep. So he woke up at 6 a.m. with a nine-page Americanization of it." The jazzy swinger Coleman and the older, refined Fields meshed musically, but Coleman told Charlotte Greenspan in her Fields biography, "We had terrible arguments about things," partly due to their sleep habits. Fields was up early, pencils sharpened, ready to collaborate with Coleman, a night owl who slept in late. "She'd say, 'You're still in bed?' She'd get this kind of funny imperious tone in her voice, and I would be *furious*."

"If My Friends Could See Me Now" and "I'm a Brass Band"—not to mention the overshadowed and underrated "I Love to Cry at Weddings"— are upbeat sides of the show's fragile, woebegone, self-obsessed heroine. All three songs are peppy show-stopping shouts of glee. Like the needy Charity, the numbers cry for attention, big whomping numbers hard to resist. "If My Friends Could See Me Now" is one of Fields's best lyrics, full of street slang she rendered with a perfect ear: "If they could see me now, / That little gang of mine, / I'm eating fancy chow and drinking fancy wine. / I'd like those stumble bums to see for a fact / The kind of top-drawer, first rate chums I attract." Only Frank Loesser equaled Fields at capturing low-rent characters with a few handpicked words—"fancy chow," "stumble bums," "top-drawer chums." And in the next few lines we hear, "Tonight I landed, pow!, right in a pot of jam. / What a setup! Holy cow! / They'd never believe it / If my friends could see me now." That's more than just a great comic song. It brings Charity alive in just the lingo she would use to talk to her dance hall girlfriends.

During the Philadelphia tryout, Fields and Coleman realized Verdon needed another big "I am" song, so they wrote her "I'm a Brass Band." "We wrote that in one morning," recalled Fields. "Here's what happened. I was living at the Barclay Hotel; Cy was at the Warwick. I went over to work with him, and I had the title in my head. I had the first line for it—'I'm a brass band, I'm a harpsichord.' We called Bobby Fosse, also at the Warwick. He came up and said, 'Fine, do it.' I wrote the lyric and Cy wrote the music almost simultaneously. We'd done that several times. I write very fast." Set to Coleman's brash music and Fosse's hard-driving dances, Fields's lyrics give heart and wit to Charity's impulsive, irrepressible, over-the-top spirit. "I'm the band from Macy's big parade, / A wild Count Basie blast! / I'm the bells from St. Peter's in Rome, / I'm tissue paper on a comb."

Debbie Allen starred in the hit 1986 revival of the show, Fosse's last bow as director-choreographer before his death, and a 2005 revival with Christina Applegate won three Tonys, but it wasn't movie star–proof. The 1969 film version starred Shirley MacLaine at her most dimpled and goony, an in-your-face, please-love-me heroine; on a big Broadway stage, the brassier and more believable Gwen Verdon got away with it. Not even Chita Rivera, Stubby Kaye, and Sammy Davis Jr. could save the movie from MacLaine's twinkly, tear-streaked excesses.

MAME

◆ 1966 ◆

"If He Walked into My Life"

Following *Hello, Dolly!*, the odds were stacked against Jerry Herman coming up with another megahit his next time out, but he did exactly that with *Mame*, as if to prove that *Hello, Dolly!* was no fluke and that he was on Broadway to stay. "I thought lightning was not about to strike twice," Herman said, but it zapped both shows with an electricity that helped light up Broadway from 1964 to 1970.

Mame began as a memoir by Patrick Dennis about his eccentric Auntie Mame, as the book and movie with Rosalind Russell were titled. Jerome Lawrence and Robert E. Lee turned *Auntie Mame* into a musical starring Angela Lansbury, a risky idea. Lansbury had mostly appeared in dramatic movie roles, but her triumph in *Mame* at forty led her to long runs in *Gypsy* in London and *Sweeney Todd* on Broadway. Herman, despite everyone's doubts, instantly believed Lansbury was an ideal Mame and coached her privately to learn the songs.

Mame and *Hello, Dolly!* are almost companion pieces, with much in common: both are what critic Ethan Mordden calls "big lady" musicals—lovable larger-than-life eccentrics, meddling unmarried middle-aged women who try to organize peoples' lives while trying to reorder their own. Both 1964's

Dolly! and 1966's *Mame* defined Broadway musicals of the '60s—feel-good extravaganzas performed with nonstop pizzazz, propelled by high-stepping title songs that became promotional ads for the shows. One difference: *Dolly!* is set in small-town New York, Yonkers at the turn of the twentieth century, whereas *Mame* is set in cosmopolitan Manhattan during the Depression. But both shows have a festive New York spirit, fueled with Herman's unquenchable and unapologetic optimism. He wrote the book on audience-friendly shows. "My greatest fear," Herman said, "is not being liked by everyone."

Jerry Herman was one of the last of a breed of Broadway songwriters who believed in happy endings, youthful romance, and—well, a belief that life is good and should be lived fully. It's an easy philosophy to mock, but Herman has the guts—and to be sure, the melodic and lyrical gifts—to make a convincing case for uplift in his most loved shows. Herman readily, defiantly admits, "I don't want to write shows that aren't uplifting"—as laid out in "I Don't Want to Know" from *Dear World*.

"He's an optimist," said Arthur Laurents, his collaborator on *La Cage aux Folles*, "and he believes it, that's why he's good. . . . It's so much easier to be cynical." Indeed, Herman's shows expressed an almost radical joy in an era when it was growing more fashionable to be brittle and sardonic. Musicals historian Miles Kreuger says, "Jerry's determined to make you feel better. If you had a fatal illness at the start of a show, you'd be cured when the show ended."

Although *Mame* wallows in exuberant showstoppers ("Gooch's Song" and the title number), the song that most moves the audience is the heart-stopping **"If He Walked into My Life,"** the only Herman ballad that became an unexpected pop hit. The song found a romantic future outside the show when Eydie Gormé recorded it as a torchy ballad in 1965. In the show, the song has a totally different meaning—a lament Mame sings about the nephew she brought up, with recriminations after he leaves home about how she raised him. It's a rare Broadway show tune with two separate lives, in the show and outside it, where it became a standard. When Gormé sang it as a love song about an affair gone awry, the lyrics took on an unexpectedly romantic, instead of a motherly, meaning: "Did he need a stronger hand? / Did he need a lighter touch? / Was I soft or was I tough? / Did I give enough, did I give too much? / At the moment when he needed me / Did I ever turn away? / Would I be there when he called if I walked into his life today?"

Herman's publisher E. H. Morris first realized "If He Walked into My Life" could be a love song and not just a madcap auntie's regrets. Morris told him, "You have a big future with that song." "She didn't change anything," Herman

Angela Lansbury, celebrating a new day in *Mame*.

says. "She just fell in love with it and went to her arranger Don Costa. All of a sudden I was beginning to hear that song on the radio. I was overwhelmed by how quickly it became a popular song. The timing was beautiful. It was right before the show opened." It was the exact lucky break that *Hello, Dolly!* got when Louis Armstrong recorded "Dolly" just before the show opened. A hit single is the best promotion any new show could pray for.

Herman, the leading living exponent of the showstopper, has never written one by mistake, but "If He Walked into My Life" came close. "I had written something I felt was missing in the novel *Auntie Mame* and in the play. I thought, if I really do my job well I will fill in a big empty area that everyone else forgot about—how does Mame really feel when she sees the boy she has so lovingly brought up turns into the kind of a bigot that she has fought against and despised all her life. That's a very very strong moment."

He goes on, "Here I am, without children, but I can still imagine how I would feel if my son or daughter disappointed me so totally, after I carefully taught them the right thing to do. And I knew I was filling in a very important missing piece of business. I wrote the song with great excitement because I thought I was really being a musical playwright and not just writing a number. And because of Angela Lansbury's heartfelt rendition, and also Eydie Gormé's hugely successful recording of it at the same time, it just went through the roof! And again, the audience was able to identify with that moment. I expected it to be a lovely moment, but it went a little beyond that."

Lansbury was Herman's favorite for the role from the start, but not everyone involved was so certain. "I had such great belief in her, because I wanted someone who was not just a singer or a glamorous woman." Herman always took it on faith that Lansbury could embody the songs, and when he heard her sing the first time he was sure of it. "She had that voice. When I taught her the songs, I suddenly heard the Angela that did the show. I made a date for the following day to have her sing those two songs for our producers. They were blown away. They had never thought of her that way. They were thinking of Lisa Kirk and other singing ladies. But once they heard Angela . . ."

One naysayer said he felt Lansbury had trouble "taking stage," that is, she lacked onstage authority. "Not for me," said Herman. "She had every qualification I was looking for. She was first and foremost a brilliant actor. When she appeared at my home, I opened my door and knew that she was Mame when she took off her coat. She was glamorous and yet not just a glamour girl. She was the combination of everything. I knew she could do it because I had seen all her work. I taught her two songs that afternoon. She was the first person who heard 'It's Today' and 'If He Walked into My Life.'"

Josh Ellis, the publicist for *Mame*, recalls, "I saw two versions of *Mame*, both with Angela Lansbury, the one who did it in Philadelphia and the one who did it on Broadway. The one in Philadelphia was a really fine actress. She hit all the dramatic points, but she was not a star. But once on Broadway she was absolutely in charge. She was not in charge in Philadelphia. It is the confidence you can only get by doing a show. It was the difference between a Broadway star and the person who does the national tour."

COMPANY

◆ 1970 ◆

"The Ladies Who Lunch," "You Could Drive a Person Crazy"

Songwriters, like everyone in show business, are easily and lazily stereotyped. Stephen Sondheim's reputation as a remote songwriter who can't, or refuses to, write songs that connect easily to audiences is a tired rap, a careless charge that at least four undeniable showstoppers from *Company* efficiently disprove. There are other songs in the score almost as ingratiating and memorable.

Yet Alan Jay Lerner told author Mark Steyn, "Steve has all the skills of Larry Hart or Ira Gershwin, but, unlike them, he doesn't reach out and touch." Steyn added, "Out there, in the rest of America, he means nothing." Not quite true, but one sometimes has the feeling that Sondheim isn't much interested in the rest of America.

Sondheim calls his work "caviar to the general," adding, "It's not that it's too good for people; it's just that it's too unexpected to sustain itself very firmly in the commercial theater." Jule Styne said, "The really clever thing is to write simple," which Sondheim has always resisted. *New Yorker* profiler Stephen Schiff wrote, "He wants to write music no one has ever heard before, and he succeeds, but at a price. . . . Sondheim's melodies often feel as though they were pinballing from synapse to synapse. . . . His melody lines work the way people do: they stammer, they hem and haw, they undercut themselves, they get assertive and then take it back, they entertain second thoughts, and third ones."

Steyn claims, "At a basic level, Sondheim lacks the courage to have his characters let rip with, 'I'm in love with a wonderful guy!'" True enough, but then if he did he wouldn't be Sondheim. One Oscar Hammerstein is plenty, just as one Sondheim will do nicely, as his many imitators have proved.

By now, however, it's hard to alter the old charge that Sondheim is a cold intellectual songwriter, even when in *Company* he's anything but; often he's downright jaunty. He dates his reputation as a "cold" songwriter from *Company*, which almost fifty years later exudes far more warmth that it did in 1970. In a *New Yorker* review of a 2010 Sondheim anthology, *Sondheim on Sondheim*, Hilton Als wrote of him, "In his most heart-wrenching work, from *Company* to *Into the Woods*, to *Passion* to *Assassins*, he is his own bogeyman: a romantic who attacks his own heart for needing to feel." Since Lorenz Hart, no songwriter's heart has ever been so subject to ultrasound readings.

Company is really a revue, a "concept" show more than a musical, with a strong, rich, vital theme but no plot per se; the theme (to be married or not to be married?) is the plot, and it's as complex as any traditional story line. Sondheim called the show a "twilight-zone revue." The idea appealed to him instantly for its uniqueness. "I knew from the beginning the score would have to be quite strange. I was pretty sure I could do something fresh with it."

Since (and because of) Rodgers and Hammerstein, plots in musicals have been vital, if overrated. Most plays need plots, but musicals are elastic enough to entertain and move people without a classic structure, one reason they're fun and open-ended. In the end, most people go to musicals for the songs, not the story; though conventional wisdom insists a show with a weak book is doomed, that's not always true. What kills shows isn't a weak book but a stale one. The weakest part of *Company* is its sketches, two of which, dealing with pot and karate, are lame and dated and need to be tossed out for fresh ones.

Company is a series of playlets about friends that engage us the way a formal plot does. Has anyone else ever written a musical about *friends*? (Sondheim, George Furth, and Hal Prince revisited the theme eleven years later in *Merrily We Roll Along*, which features the bracing "Old Friends.")

The show blurs formal musical boundaries, taking us to a different place, inside Bobby's uneasy single psyche. No show, notes Ethan Mordden, "was as misunderstood as *Company.*" *Company*'s director Hal Prince says, "The whole show was kind of abstract and impressionistic." Stephen Schiff observed, "What Sondheim brought to the American musical for the first time was subtext."

Sondheim says that, prior to *Company*, he can't think of any other "plotless musical that dealt with one set of characters from start to finish," but he thinks it influenced other plotless shows, like *A Chorus Line*, with its equally "thin thread of story line concerning one group of people. *Company* started that." *Company* may not have a traditional plot, but its wise and touching score is worth one hundred marriage books—songs like "Sorry-Grateful," "Marry Me a Little" (cut from *Company* but added to later revivals), and "Being Alive." It may be plotless, but it's not aimless, and it hinges on the compelling question of whether Bobby should, and will, ever marry.

In 1993, the only autobiographical song Sondheim would admit to is "Opening Doors" from *Merrily We Roll Along*. Leonard Bernstein said of Sondheim that he has a fear of being too straightforward, "because it's dangerous, because it reveals our real insides." In "Opening Doors," Sondheim neatly zings his critics when a producer in the show chastises the experimental composer character by saying there isn't one tune anybody can hum and asks if he could at least throw them a crumb. Sondheim, Bernstein added, fears being corny or platitudinous, but songs in shows like *Pacific Overtures*, *Assassins*, and *Sunday in the Park with George* veer dangerously close to art songs—more head than heart.

With *Cabaret* and *Company*, Hal Prince became a kind of auteur musical director, creating an aura, a world. *Company* was immediately recognized as a landmark groundbreaker that influenced musicals like *A Chorus Line* and *Chicago*. Asked if the show reflected or changed his own feelings about commitment, the unmarried Sondheim scoffed, "It didn't affect me at all. I just wrote it. It's just a show." Because he had always been single, to learn about marriage from the inside, Sondheim interviewed his friend composer Mary Rodgers (Richard's daughter) and took notes. The show questions the cliché, spoken by one of the husbands, "You're not complete until you're married." But a spouse who envies Bobby's single status says, "I have everything . . . except freedom." The show is a debate on the virtues of marriage versus friendship. It winds up a draw, perfectly expressed by "Sorry-Grateful," a husband's tender lament of, and ode to, marriage's mixed blessings in which a spouse swings from one mood to the next, regretting marriage one moment and embracing it the next. Such insights would impress any marital counselor.

There's also the rollicking "What Would We Do Without You?" mini-song nestled inside the warm and fuzzy "Side by Side by Side," two great ensemble numbers performed in old-fashioned musical chorus style. The show ends with an upbeat finale, "Being Alive," ordered by Hal Prince to replace Sondheim's original mordant closer "Happily Ever After" (an idea later pursued in *Into the Woods*). Since *Company* opened nearly half a century ago (it still feels contemporary, apart from those pot and karate sketches), some of the songs have become, well, "old friends," thanks to cabaret singers who have kept the numbers alive and given them time to reveal *Company*'s incisive gems.

The show didn't catch on beyond the theatrical cognoscenti, never had a sold-out week, and ran a moderately respectable twenty months (but made back its money). It didn't become a must-see show because it failed to come down on the side of marriage, which troubled audiences in 1970 and Prince knows why: "Some people are simply afraid to acknowledge the manifest difficulties of living together." Prince insists it's not antimarriage, quite the reverse: "*Company* says very clearly that to be emotionally committed to somebody is very difficult, but to be alone is impossible." *Company*, wrote Wendy Smith in *The American Scholar*, "painted with ferocious honesty feelings that were previously off-limits for a Broadway musical: the paralyzing fear of committing to another person; the frustrations and compromises inherent in any relationship; desperate loneliness, agonizing ambivalence."

Sondheim claims the show wasn't more of a hit because it lacks a happy ending, which Sondheim doesn't believe in. "Shows that run a long time tell the audience what they want to hear." Audiences like shows with defined endings, yet the finale, "Being Alive," makes a strong case for coupledom of some kind—because, as it states, "two is company, comfy and cozy." Bobby realizes he perhaps needs "Somebody [to] hold me too close / Somebody [to] hurt me too deep / Somebody [to] sit in my chair and ruin my sleep / And make me aware / Of being alive." That's not a bold yes to a show proposing marriage, but it's a pretty hopeful maybe. Sondheim is the poet of the uncommitted, who also deserve a spokesman and are lucky to have such a wise, sympathetic one.

"The Ladies Who Lunch," like "Everything's Coming Up Roses" in *Gypsy*, is a Sondheim phrase that has found its way into the language. The song, act 2's rousing 11 o'clock number, describes a certain sort of woman—still prevalent—whose days are comprised primarily of long lunches fueled with liquor, bitchy chatter, and secret remorse. These ladies are visible in any big city, dining at the fancier, trendier luncheon spots. Such women are usually rich and thin and loaded with more than liquor and money. They engage in catty banter; their theme song is a vodka stinger laced with bitters.

"The Ladies Who Lunch" would have stopped the show with almost anyone singing it, but it was written for Elaine Stritch, who so perfectly embodied the sardonic character. The song is really a set piece for Stritch, whose bitter toast suggests a ruthlessly honest if perhaps troubled, hard-drinking woman. As she revealed in her one-woman Broadway show, *Elaine Stritch: At Liberty*, she was a recovering alcoholic. You didn't have to hear it from Stritch. You could hear it in her scratchy whiskey-tinged voice, rich in innuendo and invective, which one critic compared to a car shifting gears without the clutch.

Even her name, Stritch, sounds like her voice, stretched and scratchy, fingernails on a blackboard; Dickens couldn't have devised a more suitable sounding name for her. She embodied the sensibility of nervy, smart-alecky New Yorkers, which the show so deftly depicts, with its assortment of Manhattan types residing in Boris Aronson's sterile steel and glass cubicles and dead-end elevators. The musical's signature sound—an insistent telephone busy signal—opens and defines the show.

Hal Prince said that not only was "The Ladies Who Lunch" written for Stritch but "the whole character was." Says Prince, "No one ever was as good as Stritch. There is only one Elaine Stritch. Elaine was just out there being Elaine Stritch—or Joanne, the character," a hard-bitten abrasive dame, by no stretch a "lady." "Here's to the ladies who lunch," the song begins on a cheery note, as Joanne stands to address the audience, but it's a mock toast, more of a roast. It goes from there to sarcastically sketch in these ladies who lunch, not missing a single zinger. Stritch was the queen of zingers, and few singers have been able to match her razor-edge delivery. Patti LuPone boldly managed it in a 2011 Broadway revival. Stritch sang it with just the acid tone; it's hard to match it, or revise it. The terminally acerbic song became Stritch's property.

She owned it and, though now gone, still does, the way Judy Garland forever locked up "Over the Rainbow."

The number is easy to overdo, and even Stritch in later renditions built it into too much of an angry diatribe, digging into the words with venomous hostility. It's wiser to underplay it and let the biting words leave the teeth marks. The song is a searing indictment of a whole lifestyle—wealthy idle wives who have nothing to live for except their lunches; it even includes the phrase, "Everybody dies!" Depressing? Maybe, but Stritch made it funny in her corrosive way, so you didn't pity Joanne but admired her for facing the truth and speaking it so pointedly. One of his lines nails the type exactly: "Lounging in their caftans / And planning a brunch / On their own behalf."

It's a long list of insults. "Another long exhausting day, / Another thousand dollars, / A matinee, a Pinter play, / Perhaps a piece of Mahler's." (Sondheim says Stritch first thought "a piece of Mahler's" referred to a brand of coffee cake.) The lyric must have left flesh wounds on some of the actual ladies who lunched, then rushed to see *Company*, but Sondheim offers an uplifting ending, a teasing apologia, as Joanne raises her glass one last time and sings: "A toast to that invincible bunch, / The dinosaurs surviving the crunch. / Let's hear it for the ladies who lunch— / Everybody rise!" At song's end, she cries, "Rise! Rise! Rise! Rise! Rise! Rise! Rise!" Sondheim confesses, "Privately, I had hoped that the number would be such a showstopper in Elaine's hands that the audience would actually get up on the 'Rise!' repetition and give her a standing ovation. It was a showstopper, all right, but not quite that big." Despite its strengths, author Ethan Mordden notes that the song really doesn't belong in the show: "It does not relate to the show's [singlehood vs. marriage] theme, as the other songs do. It's simply great music-making." Showstoppers are allowed to break all the rules.

Sondheim explained to Craig Zadan, author of *Sondheum & Co.*, how he wrote the song: "'The Ladies Who Lunch' is so packed that it exudes ferocity, mainly because I chose a fairly rigid form, full of inner rhymes and with the lines in the music almost square . . . very formed." He added, "The inner rhymes are hidden to give the lines a tautness so the audience would feel what the lady is feeling: 'Keeping house but clutching a copy of *Life* / Just to keep in touch.' The 'clutch' is hidden, there's no musical pause there, no way of pointing it up, but it's there to make the line terse, the way the character is."

Donna McKechnie, in the original cast, claims that Prince gave Stritch a brandy before each show, which Sondheim says is untrue—"It would have aided and abetted her drinking, something Hal would never have done." But McKechnie recalls, "She was insecure about that number, and on opening night out of town, she went up on her lyrics and [conductor] Hal Hastings was throwing her the lyrics. They were all scared of her. But with all of that—you never worried what was gonna happen with Elaine—she was so consistent. She never missed a show."

For pure energy and jubilance there is no livelier song by Sondheim, or anybody, than **"You Could Drive a Person Crazy,"** performed by a trio of girlfriends of the show's elusive hero, who have failed to snag him for matrimonial purposes. The song expresses their exasperation at Bobby's evasiveness in a jazzy, syncopated, tight harmony of accusations, calling him everything from crazy to troubled to a zombie to gay.

A school of thought has persisted that Bobby is really a closet case, a fairly far-fetched theory that undercuts the whole point of the show, which is about romantic and marital, not sexual, choice. The theory likely persists because Sondheim is gay, as were choreographer Michael Bennett and Tony Perkins, who was to have played Bobby originally and whom Ethan Mordden labels "the very model of a closeted gay man." When nongay Dean Jones suddenly

Susan Browning, Donna McKechnie, and Pamela Myers expressing their frustrations in "You Could Drive a Person Crazy" from *Company*.

quit the show after two weeks, the role was inherited by Larry Kert (whom Mordden called "the least closeted man in New York"). Jones's own marriage had recently collapsed, and the show depressed him. He later wrote in his autobiography: "It was a clever, bright show on the surface, but its underlying message declared that marriage was, at best, a vapid compromise, insoluble and finally destructive." Even so, Jones recorded the cast album, not Kert. The most traumatic moment for the *Company* company came when Jones left the show. Teri Ralston said, "Hal came to us and said Dean had hepatitis, but Dean just wanted out. We later had this talk [at a cast reunion show in the mid-'70s], and he explained, 'I was so unhappy. I was going through a divorce. They kept telling me it was pro-marriage, but it was everything that was going on in my marriage.'"

If Bobby is gay, he wouldn't be seducing stewardesses, as in the sexy comic song "Barcelona," or reflecting in another song on all the women he's known. It's fashionable to say, or was in 1970, well, obviously Bobby isn't married at thirty-five so he must be gay, and some productions imply as much. If so, then why write the show in the first place and surround him with women, including one or two wives who fancy him? (The brash Joanne even blurts out, "So, when are we going to make it?")

Company is as much about friendship as it is about marriage. Bobby has chosen affairs and friendships over marriage, an original and worthy theme that Sondheim and Furth (also gay) explore in depth in the show, hence the title. Many straight people who are neither gay nor zombies prefer romances and friendships over marriage, as perfectly expressed in "Marry Me a Little," one of Sondheim's most astute songs, dealing with romantic and marital indecision, which was cut from *Company*.

Prince's analysis: "Bobby was a single man, wanting to be a single man all his life. He would look at these couples and they would always be wrangling, a little edgy, always arguing with each other or whatever or competing. The minute he left and was away and they were left alone, you saw immediately they were very much in love and they were terrific married couples. What Bobby wanted to see was that they had problems, because it reinforced his sense that it is better being single."

"You Could Drive a Person Crazy"—sung originally by Susan Browning, Donna McKechnie, and Pamela Myers—has the exuberance and drive of Rodgers and Hart's "Sing for Your Supper," a knockout 1938 number from *The Boys from Syracuse* twittered by a trio of songbirds who express a less complex subject: that perky female singers will always be fed and well taken care of, though in fact it's really a sly, catchy metaphor for courtesans.

"Sing for Your Supper" was arranged by songwriter Hugh Martin when Rodgers, feeling he needed someone with a hipper, swingier style, hired Martin to turn the song into a zippy imitation Boswell Sisters number. "You Could Drive a Person Crazy" is sung in much the same jazzy style, with birdie-like "doo-doo doo-doo" trills. McKechnie recalls, "We did it to all of these flouncy '40s moves, it was hilarious. We were like the Andrews or McGuire Sisters, all smiley and bouncy. The song comes out of left field."

It begins, "You could drive a person crazy, / You could drive a person mad. / Doo-doo-doo-doo-doo. / First you make a person hazy, / So a person could be had. / Doo-doo-doo-doo-doo. / Then you leave a person dangling sadly / Outside your door, / Which it only makes a person gladly / Want you even more."

Prince calls "You Could Drive a Person Crazy" an undeniable showstopper. He told me, "It builds from the fact that you have a guy and you have three single girls he dates, and he is not serious about any of them. They finally turn on him. The three girls get together and sing, and it is very funny. It was marvelous where it was in the show. Those three girls were used terrifically because the rest of the people in the cast were married couples." Pamela Myers recalls the difficulty of staging the song: "It took a long time. It's a long song and complicated, with three harmonies. I had the melody. Michael Bennett would try stuff and set it I don't know how many times, so he could watch it. He wanted to see it over and over. It was very concisely staged. There were a lot of upper-body movements." Once heard, you can't ever get it out of your head.

• • • • • • • • • • • • • BACKSTAGE DISH • • • • • • • • • • • • •

+ *Company* began as a series of eleven linked playlets by George Furth, boiled down to three plus two new ones. Sondheim brought them to Prince on Furth's behalf to persuade him to produce them. Originally Kim Stanley was to have played all the women in the play, with two other actors playing all the men, but Prince cast a diverse assortment of actors to reflect New York—actors who looked like real people who sang a little, but with no dancers except Donna McKechnie. The show's episodic format is a sort of revue but with a strong through line and defined characters who relate to each other. The early run in Boston Prince felt was too dark, so he worked to lighten the show. Prince says that he borrowed a theatrical device favored by his old mentor, George Abbott, who believed that just throwing light on an actor helped get laughs, or at least literally lightened the mood.

+ "Being Alive" was an attempt to write a closer to replace the deeply cyni- cal "Happily Ever After," which was a replacement for "Marry Me a Little," a brilliantly insightful song about the appeal but also the confining nature of marriage. "Being Alive" gives *Company* a more upbeat if still inconclu- sive ending. "Happily Ever After" reads like a suicide note, with phrases about being bored to death, rare displays of feeling and scant love mak- ing. Sondheim recalls, "Hal persistently called it a 'downer.' He fervently urged me to write an 'up' song to replace it, but I argued that a sudden positive song, one without irony, would be unearned and pandering." Michael Bennett figured out how to make it an upbeat ending that fits into the ironic context, using spoken voices as in "Side by Side by Side," a warm, infectious number about the need for relationships (friends if not family), for "company," that, says Sondheim, "suggested to me a song which could progress from complaint to prayer. Thus, 'Being Alive'"—a solution that partially satisfied the show's creators if not all the critics. He told Craig Zadan in *Sondheim & Co.*, however, "In Boston, I wrote 'Being Alive' and, although I love the song, I feel that the ending of the show was a cop-out. When Bobby suddenly realizes that he shouldn't be alone at the end of the scene, it's too small a moment and you don't believe it."

+ Sondheim maintains he doesn't write showstoppers on purpose, but one of the most undeniable exhibits of same is "Getting Married Today," a showy tour de force (just like "The Ladies Who Lunch" and, indeed, "Another Hundred People"), in which Amy (Beth Howland in the original cast) has a meltdown before heading down the aisle, rattling off at warp speed all the neurotic reasons she *isn't* going to get married today: "Lis- ten everybody. I'm afraid you didn't hear, / Or do you want to see a crazy lady fall apart in front of you? . . . I telephoned my analyst about it / And he said to see him Monday, / But by Monday I'll be floating / In the Hud- son with the other garbage."

  "Getting Married Today" is a contrapuntal trio sung by an anxious bride, her proud groom ("Today is for Amy!," crooned like Dick Powell), and a female choir member who claims what a wondrous occasion it is, "a pinnacle of life, / Husband joined to wife. / The heart leaps up to behold / This golden day." If any song ever displayed Sondheim's complexity, this is it—it's funny, sweet, ironic, honest, and tormented all at once, a perfect example of Sondheim as the expert on romantic self-doubt, the theme of *Company*. "Sorry-Grateful," likewise, is simultaneously sad, wise, wry, and tender, sung by a longtime husband full of mixed feelings, not about getting but *being* married, a rueful voice of experience.

✦ *Company* produced critical reaction all over the map. Clive Barnes of the *New York Times* didn't get it or, if he got it, didn't want it. He trashed the characters—"trivial, shallow, worthless and horrid"—but grudgingly approved Sondheim's score for its technical virtuosity only to sneer at the end that "the result is slick, clever, obvious and eclectic rather than exciting. But I stress that I really believe a lot of people are going to love it." He then reminded readers he'd had reservations about *West Side Story*. *New York Times* Sunday critic Walter Kerr likewise admired the show's sophisticated craftsmanship but, even so, wasn't moved by it. "I left *Company* feeling rather cool and queasy. . . . At root, I didn't take to Mr. Jones' married friends any more than he did. I had difficulty—what do you call it?—empathizing." Richard Watts Jr. of the *New York Post* called it "surprisingly uningratiating." *Variety* wrote, "The songs are for the most part undistinguished. As it stands now, it's for ladies' matinees, homos and misogynists."

Two of the show's major critical cheerleaders were Jack Kroll of *Newsweek* and Ted Kalem of *Time*, who labeled it "a landmark." Henry Hewes in the *Saturday Review* said the show "remarkably distilled the essence of today's middle generation New York life," and John Lahr, late *New Yorker* theater critic, wrote that "thanks to the energy of Stephen Sondheim and Harold Prince, the genre is not yet a fossil."

One of the few critics who recognized the show for its genius and significance, John McCarten of the *New Yorker* was aware *Company* was something special: "An original piece of work that joyously breaks new ground. . . . What a pleasure it is when a work of art not only delights the eye but also astonishes it! . . . Mr. Sondheim's deservedly celebrated talents are at their wryest, driest, highest pitch of tunefulness and wit."

✦ *Company* got a new life in 2006 when British director John Doyle revived it on Broadway with everyone in the cast ludicrously playing a musical instrument, to just what end was unclear. It smells like a theatrical gimmick that says more about Doyle than the show, which most critics blithely accepted, not wanting to appear stodgy sticklers for the original, non-talent night version. The revival survived the musical instruments gimmick. It's not too hard to guess why Prince and Sondheim may have approved Doyle's wacky version: an ardent wish to give their 1970 show a second chance on Broadway, even if the cast was walking on their hands. A winning 2011 concert version was filmed and shown in selected movie houses with Neil Patrick Harris, Patti LuPone, and, yes, Stephen Colbert. A widely respected 1995 revival at the Roundabout Theater was directed by Scott Ellis, choreographed by Rob Marshall and featured Boyd Gaines as Bobby and Kate Burton, Debra Monk, Jane Krakowski, Charlotte d'Amboise, and Veanne Cox as the women in his life.

✦ Prince confessed to me he didn't love all the songs in *Company* instantly. When Steve handed me 'Barcelona' I said, 'Is this funny?' And he said, 'Yes, it is very funny, Hal.' I said, 'I don't get it.' He said, 'Hal, "Barcelona" is one of the funniest words in the English language. Why don't you try staging it?' So I staged it, and it became funny to me. I did funny things with the actors, and I suddenly realized, my god, Steve's right, this is really funny stuff." He adds, "Reading it off the page I didn't think it was funny. I'm very proud of it now. We never changed it. As I was staging it, I began to see, oh that's funny! I hadn't read it right. Here were two people in bed, and the guy's just made love and he wishes the girl in the bed would put on her uniform and go fly to Barcelona." But she changes her mind and decides to stay and suddenly he's stuck. Bobby just wanted a roll in the hay, nothing more lasting—that's Bobby for you, and it also says a lot in a few insightful lines about single life in the '70s, maybe any time.

• •

Teri Ralston, who in two or three years zoomed from San Francisco State College to *Company* and was quickly cast as Jenny, recalls, "I was just so young and naïve. I had just arrived in New York. It was just fun. It was my first Broadway show. I didn't know how much was at stake. They offered me a year's contract, and I thought, *a year*? I wouldn't sign it. I couldn't imagine doing anything for a year. My agent said, 'Teri, this is a big Broadway hit.' I kept saying no, but I ended up staying a year." Smart choice. The show gave her a career.

Ralston got along with everyone in the cast, even the combative Elaine Stritch. "I had a great relationship with Stritch. I was so young I didn't know any better, and I wasn't afraid of her. I stood up to her. We had a couple of confrontations. She was being really rude to the conductor—this was during her drinking days—and I said, 'Oh, Elaine, stop!' Elaine loved it when people stood up to her. There was another time when she was drinking and I got up and discretely left. She was loaded and it was too painful. Well, she heard about it. She was so mad at me. I said, 'I can't stand it, Elaine. It's just too hard.' I cared a lot for her, and to sit there onstage with her in that state was really difficult. We had a pretty good standoff because of that. Ultimately it made us very close."

Ralston hit it off with the very private Sondheim when she appeared in *A Little Night Music* right after *Company*. "We hung out, kinda. I was one of the lieder singers in *Night Music*. When I got back from *Company* in London, I would go over to Steve's house to rehearse the music. I was the first one to sing the score. That was quite an experience. You know what a perfectionist Steve is. Well, closing night of *Company* Steve came back and said, 'You now have a perfect performance'—on closing night!"

Appearing in two Sondheim shows right away quickly catapulted Ralston. "It gave me credibility for my entire life! I'm recorded. I'm in the history books. And it happened at such an early age. Because of the strong following for Sondheim, there's a following for all of us, particularly for *Company*. That was such a special show. It changed my life. To have been a part of that collaboration, I didn't even know what I was learning at the time. It taught me technique. I learned from everyone I worked with, like the simplicity of Larry Kert when he sang a song. I learned from Michael Bennett how hard it is to be creative and then have to change something—how do you just keep being creative? I learned the simplicity of choreography from Michael—that everything has a reason. His choreography was so specific. I learned clarity. I learned the need to trust your director's eye—that he knows what's right, helping you find your own way. But he's not gonna let you do it wrong. Hal and I got along great. He always said I was his favorite typical American girl. I'm just very American."

Ralston remembers the intense responses from *Company* fans: "Everyone felt it was about them. People were just passionate about it and came back again and again. Single people so related to not being ready to commit. There was always a debate about it being antimarriage, and Hal said, 'It's *not* antimarriage.' He just kept fighting it."

———

Much like Teri Ralston, Pamela Myers's biggest theatrical moment was her first on Broadway, chosen at age twenty-two to play Marta in *Company*, where she sang the hypnotic **"Another Hundred People,"** a pulsing showstopper, seated on a park bench ruminating on all the frenzied imported New Yorkers, just like her character—and indeed just like Myers herself, a small-town girl from Ohio.

Myers recalls the moment vividly: "It was a read-through. I remember reading through the script, and I can't imagine what they thought because I was so green." For her audition she sang "Shy" and "Little Green Apples."

"I sang onstage and they [Sondheim and Prince] were out there in the dark house and you couldn't see them. They both talked to me, Hal and Stephen. I don't remember what they said. And George Furth was there. They had me read Amy's part because they had not fashioned my part yet. They didn't have the script finished." As Sondheim recalls Myers's audition, "She strode in purposefully, belted out 'Shy' from *Once Upon a Mattress*, and broke us up laughing, then followed it with 'Little Green Apples' and broke us up crying. We knew we had a 'discovery' on our hands. The only problem was that she was blonde, looked like a 4-H poster girl, and was about as squeaky clean as . . . June Allyson." Yet she had a powerfully brassy, but heartfelt, voice just right for a song that captures the harshness of New York City life. The song combines the vibrancy of New York underscored with a depressing, ominous feeling.

Sondheim refers to writing the song as his *42nd Street* moment. "Hal swiveled to me and barked, 'Can you write a song for her, kid? Give her a real spot?' I could feel the cameras turning on me as I barked back, 'Of course!'" And so he did. Sondheim explains, "It was written for a performer instead of a character—which makes me no less pleased with it as a song. During rehearsals it clearly threatened to stop the show. . . . Even the critics who disliked the show loved Pam. It was a triumph of her attitude as much as her talent, exactly the way I had hoped. Ruby Keeler in *42nd Street*, with variations."

Myers goes on: "I think she was supposed to be a New Yorker, but then they geared the part much more to my persona. The part was written for me. Sondheim came up to me after the reading and told me, 'I wrote you a song.' Sondheim is the one genius I've met in my life. He's so articulate, but he's so poignant; he writes such passionate stuff. He is so smart and so feeling and brave and fearless. He has suffered for it."

"Another Hundred People," the only nonrelationship song in the show, except for "The Ladies Who Lunch," is a pointed New York number about the hordes of hustling outsiders descending hourly upon the city and trying in vain to connect. ("And they meet at parties / Through the friends of friends / Who they never know. / Will you pick me up / Or do I meet you there / Or shall we let it go?") The passage acutely sketches in a vivid, detailed picture of manic Manhattan, sung to the tune's relentless beat. In that line, Sondheim taps into three million New York telephone lines. The lyric keeps hammering, "And *another* hundred people just got off of the train . . . and *another* hundred people"—until you can see people clamoring out of the trains at Grand Central.

Paul Bendix, a writer and musicals maven, says, "It must be the best song ever written about New York, and the city isn't even mentioned. There's nothing self-adulatory about it [like the two "New York, New York"s]. The song pauses in the refrain and says, 'And every day, some go away.' The essential truth of the city is that its very inhospitable nature makes it exciting!"

At one point, it was decided to cut "Another Hundred People" because it wasn't about any of the people in the show but a song about New York, which in its way *is* a song about the characters, a cross-section of immigrant New Yorkers. Cut it and you cut out the heart of the show. Myers remembers, "Hal came to me first and said, 'We are going to have to cut your song. We have to cut it tonight because we are changing some things.' Then Stephen came over to me and he was very upset. He said, 'We are going to get it back in.' And [orchestrator] Jonathan Tunick told me that it was the favorite orchestration he had done for the show and he was also very upset. I didn't know what to think. The next night they had totally rewritten it and put it in the first act. I would sing part of it and each single girl would sing part of it."

Myers thinks the song connected because it was so much about her, still new to the city. "That part was really me, so I just went ahead and did it. I was young and green. I was guileless and I think that is why it worked." The song exactly captures the overwhelmed, breathless feelings of new arrivals to Manhattan as "a city of strangers." In the song, Sondheim masterfully triple rhymes "guarded parks" with "dusty trees" with "battered barks" and walls plastered with "crude remarks." Is there a more perfect New York City image?

Myers was feeling her way through a big Broadway show, learning as she went. "Completely! I thought they were going to fire me. It was a very difficult song to learn." She remembers audiences reacting to the song but mostly to the language in the dialogue. "I was stunned. We would get verbal reactions from the audience. People would gasp. I would hear the audience saying, 'Did you hear what she said?' We said 'bastard,' we said 'son of a bitch.' If you think of the time, it was pretty vulgar."

Myers told me rehearsals were, like the show itself, pressurized. "There was some tension. There was some anxiety. I did not know you could talk back to your director. We were very respectful then." Elaine Stritch talked back to Hal. "I learned a lot from Elaine. She was so natural. She was fascinating onstage and so real. I got along well with her. She was still drinking then. That was hard for her. She was so vulnerable. It didn't cause problems, but sometimes if she drank during the matinees it would prolong things; she was slower. It added a few minutes. But there was nobody like Elaine ever."

After *Company*, Myers was in a Broadway flop, *The Selling of the President*, and a revival of *Into the Woods*. She played in a regional production of *Sunday in the Park with George*, the revue *Sondheim on Sondheim*, and *Gypsy*, and gave a wondrous performance in "Snoopy!!!," among many shows. But Pam

Myers is still best, most fondly remembered for "Another Hundred People." It doesn't bother her. "I'm just thrilled to have done the song," she says.

FOLLIES

◆ 1971 ◆

"Broadway Baby," "I'm Still Here"

*F*ollies is a cavalcade of showstoppers—about half a dozen in a musical that methodically, melodically, and forever dispels the chronic charge that Stephen Sondheim can't write catchy songs—even blockbusters—when he wants to and the occasion demands it. Sondheim disdains the idea of showstoppers but proved himself a master of the art in nearly every *Follies* song. Let us zero in on two of the showiest. A musical that celebrates the end of a showbiz era and explores two damaged marriages against that glittering backdrop, *Follies* is among Sondheim's least revived shows and yet arguably his best—grandest anyway.

Follies lost money for its investors and is so lavish and calls for such a huge cast that few companies can afford to produce the show. It's always an event whenever it gets revived. *Follies* is the "Ring Cycle" of musicals that its fans are happy to travel long distances to see. The show overflows with smart, sunny songs and heartbreaking ballads as hummable as anything by Berlin or Kern. It's as if Sondheim was telling his detractors, OK, hum *this*, melody fiends! He even calls the show, *Hello, Follies!*

Sondheim, bristling, confronted the "unhummable" charge in 1976, when he told *People*'s Guy Flatley: "*Everything* is hummable. When they say my music is not, they're really saying it is not reminiscent of something else. Hummable is a meaningless word, and so is melodic. If a tune is heard often enough it becomes hummable. The hits from shows are the tunes that are played four or five times during the course of the evening. The reprises? Well, I don't like to use reprises, because the emotional situations themselves [in a show] do not recur. I've always thought reprises were fake." Only once did he reprise a song, "Send in the Clowns" in *A Little Night Music*—and bingo, a hit.

Follies has a flawed plot unsatisfyingly resolved, despite subsequent reworkings of its troubled ending by librettist James Goldman and Sondheim, who added new songs ("Ah, But Underneath") for a 1987 London revival. Yet *Follies* was an occasion for Sondheim to show off his consummate crowd-pleasing skills, writing pastiche songs in half a dozen traditional modes as the show flashes back to nostalgic eras of Broadway's glory days when catchy songs ruled. Apart from its sumptuous but ominous spectacle—shadowy showgirls in feathery headdresses floating across stage—*Follies* is a last gasp of the Broadway past that musicals lovers lament, as do the characters in the show. Critic Frank Rich called it a musical about the death of the musical.

The show, which deals with a favorite Sondheim theme of disenchantment, focuses on two couples, old friends in the Weismann (i.e., Ziegfeld) Follies, attending a reunion of showgirls where they confront their regrets, wrong choices, and mismatched marriages. The score's ballads come out of their real-life pasts—forlorn but unforgettable songs like "Too Many Mornings" and "Losing My Mind" and one bitterly hostile song, "Could I Leave You?," in which one of the wives, Phyllis (created by reborn film star Alexis Smith), brutally summarizes her marriage to a wealthy, equally distressed financier. In the song she expresses her resentment and threatens to leave.

Much of the show's brilliance began with director Hal Prince's inspired casting, which featured faded, forgotten, used-up Hollywood stars like Smith, a second-tier movie actress abandoned decades before; Dorothy Collins, the beloved girl-next-door star of radio and TV's *Your Hit Parade* in her pert Peter Pan collar; and Gene Nelson, the old movie hoofer who had never set foot on Broadway. The only lead character who wasn't reclaimed from Hollywood was Broadway's reliable John McMartin, who played Smith's philandering husband who Collins's character, Sally, loved in their youth; as a consolation prize, Sally married Martin's philandering pal Buddy.

The show is a metaphor for their crumbling marriages. It begins on such a sparkling (if later heartbreaking) note of bright hopes in double duets sung by their innocent young romantic selves in "You're Gonna Love Tomorrow" and "Love Will See Us Through," plus a nostalgic courtship number, "Waiting for the Girls Upstairs." The original peppy, endearing foursome were Marti Rolph (young Sally), Virginia Sandifur (young Phyllis), Harvey Evans (young Buddy) and Kurt Peterson (young Ben).

Beyond all that, *Follies* was filled with former authentic Broadway veterans like Fifi D'Orsay, Mary McCarty, and Ethel Shutta. Subsequent casts unearthed other neglected stars—Betty Garrett, Ann Miller, Gretchen Wyler, and Kaye Ballard.

Yvonne De Carlo, the other major old-timer in the original cast, plays a Hollywood relic whose number, "I'm Still Here," is one of the show's lasting showstoppers, matching "Broadway Baby," sung pretty much for all time by Ethel Shutta, then in her midseventies, a onetime real-life Follies girl who stopped the show every night. Ted Chapin, author of *Everything Was Possible*, a superbly detailed book about the show's creation (he worked on it as a gofer), says, "I don't think any other musical is as haunted by its original production as *Follies* is. It captured the romance of the theater that *Follies* was imbued with."

Shutta's dynamic performance of **"Broadway Baby"** was a major factor in the song becoming a Broadway standard, a textbook case of a singer who creates not just a showstopper but a song for all time by an unforgettable performance. Shutta ("shoe-tay") had appeared on Jack Benny's radio show, starred in the Eddie Cantor classic *Whoopee!*, and toured in vaudeville with her family, but most people never heard of her when she opened in *Follies* at seventy-four as Broadway veteran Hattie Walker in what became her career finale. She died a few years later but had left her mark in Broadway history well past her prime; the musical returned Shutta to her prime for a final bow, as it did the other beloved showbiz relics.

Sondheim reveals the reason the song worked so well: "Shutta's sly, unsentimental performance appropriately saved the song from any hint of self-pity." A gal this tough needs no pity; she's sure to land on Broadway with both feet. Much of the fun and the impact of Shutta's performance is partly because she *had* been forgotten. Her Hattie was an instantly embraced character when Shutta socked home "Broadway Baby." It was clear from the first rehearsal that the number was showstopper-bound. Hal Prince says, "Ethel knocked us off our feet. She sang so brilliantly and so excitedly and she was quite an old lady. No one will ever sing that song as well. It belongs to her."

Even so, she told Chapin, longtime head of the Rodgers and Hammerstein Organization but then a college boy, "Don't expect a grand voice from an old girl like me," warning everyone she hadn't sung in years. "I don't care if they let me go. If I'm fired, I'll look at the show and say, 'Goodbye,' because I did this show to prove to myself that I still had it, that I could still make people laugh and keep them entertained." Choreographer Michael Bennett wisely let Shutta do her old-timey thing and left in whatever still worked. At the end of each session she politely thanked Bennett for taking time to work with her, saying, "Hey, I didn't know acting could be so hard!" She became a company favorite. Paul Gemignani, the show's conductor, recalls stowing a bottle of booze for Shutta, who liked to take a nip now and again during rehearsals.

She might never have had a great voice, but she could sell a song with a trouper's vitality and conviction. Shutta, a stumpy dame with a determined look, took stage with a commanding bulldog presence. The song wasn't written for her, but it may as well have been. If ever singer and song were soul mates, "Broadway Baby" was it, but the number, with its insistent beat and by-God-I'm-gonna-make-it message, is so powerful and infectious that any number of actresses have put it across; I've never seen it done by a man, but there's no reason it couldn't be equally effective (if uncamped up).

"Broadway Baby" is a simple, straightforward song, what Sondheim calls "a genre pastiche," with no irony or subtext, just the dogged credo of everyone who ever vowed to make it on Broad-

Ethel Shutta, declaring her birthright as a true "Broadway Baby" in *Follies*.

way: "I'm just a Broadway baby, / Walking off my tired feet / Pounding 42nd Street, to be in a sho-o-ow." When Shutta sang it, you could feel her feet throbbing. She pleads, "I don't need a lot, / Just a tube of greasepaint / And a follow spot." It's hard to imagine it sung any way other than how Shutta presented it, though it's possible to oversell it, as Bernadette Peters did in a one-woman show in London, where she sexed up the number and turned it into a sultry striptease. That was a different approach, and pretty silly. It can't be vamped for laughs. Sondheim argues, "It wasn't silly. It was different."

Michael Bennett told Shutta after a preview, "You looked like you knew how funny you were last night." Shutta said, "Well, yes, I did." Bennett: "Please don't *tell* us—just *be* funny." She had begun adding shtick, such as ending it with a loud foot stomp. (YouTube has a scant record of Shutta in performance, but battered Broadway veteran Elaine Stritch, in her one-woman show, comes close, though she overdoes it a little.)

"Broadway Baby" instantly grabs you and defies you not to love the song, whoever belts out its spirited tune and gritty lyrics. Like many songs in the score, it's a Sondheim creation written in fond imitation of a famous songwriter or songwriting team. Sondheim's deep, detailed knowledge of Broadway styles past is astonishingly accurate, as is his skill at writing numbers that suggest but don't ridicule the originals, affectionate homages delighting us on their own terms.

"One More Kiss" is his take on Sigmund Romberg and Rudolf Friml; "The Story of Lucy and Jessie" and "Ah, Paris" are Cole Porter riffs; "You're Gonna Love Tomorrow/Love Will See Us Through" and "Loveland" are tributes to Jerome Kern and Burton Lane tunes with lyrics in the style of Ira Gershwin and E. Y. Harburg; "Beautiful Girls," the grandiose *Follies* opener, recalls Irving Berlin (within a Busby Berkeley montage); "The God-Why-Don't-You-Love-Me Blues" is a mock vaudeville number written in the manner of Lorenz Hart and Frank Loesser; "Losing My Mind" is his version of a George Gershwin tune with a Dorothy Fields lyric; and the mirror number "Who's That Woman" is a fond reflection of Porter and Rodgers and Hart. He deftly mimics each of their styles.

"Broadway Baby" is Sondheim's take on pre-Crash songs of the 1920s, he's pointed out. His model was the team of DeSylva, Brown, and Henderson, who wrote feel-good standards like "The Best Things in Life Are Free," "Button Up Your Overcoat," and "Life Is Just a Bowl of Cherries." Their songs, Sondheim writes, insisted that "happiness was in your own backyard and everybody could become a star."

In *Follies*, "Broadway Baby" is one of a trilogy of pastiche numbers with "Rain on the Roof" (a duet) and Fifi D'Orsay's "Ah, Paris!" Choreographer Michael Bennett moved Shutta's number to the last of the three. D'Orsay was not pleased and became a pain in the neck to Bennett and her costars, forgetting lyrics, moves, and cues. At one point Shutta bellowed (quite in character), "If that French bitch screws up once more, I'm going to go out there and sing 'Broadway Baby' in French!" When D'Orsay complained about standing around too long, Shutta cried, "Squattez-vous!"

With *Follies*, Sondheim let loose his inner Ziegfeld. The show gave him a chance to return to the Broadway era of his boyhood, then put behind him. *Follies* allowed him to display his musical dexterity, writing not just nostalgic songs but witty comedy songs that Cole Porter, Lorenz Hart, or Ira Gershwin would have envied.

A showstopper just as undeniable as "Broadway Baby," **"I'm Still Here"** is sung by a character who was also a Broadway baby, among many other things, all unreeled as she celebrates her showbiz longevity. The lyrics unsparingly but comically sum up an aging performer's career of another era. Sondheim claimed his model was Joan Crawford, not De Carlo. "Crawford's career was unique," says Sondheim.

As played by the still sexy if slightly blowzy Yvonne De Carlo—at forty-nine, not all that ancient a has-been when she landed the role of Carlotta Campion—"I'm Still Here" has entered the showbiz lexicon as shorthand for survivorhood, Diva Division. Any singer who performs it, in or out of the show (one of Sondheim's songs that has had a busy cabaret afterlife), is guaranteed an ovation. It connects with everyone, not just performers, reveling in the fact that we're all still here, maybe a bit shopworn but alive and singing, or at least applauding.

"I'm Still Here" replaced an earlier song for De Carlo, "Can That Boy Foxtrot!," which Sondheim figured would knock their socks off but soon realized was a one-joke song that was virtually over after you heard its risqué payoff—"But, oh, can that boy . . . *fff-ox* trot." The number had a brief cabaret reincarnation, but in the show's early previews it didn't have the intended impact. Hal Prince suggested something more serious was needed, so Sondheim sat down with De Carlo and discussed her checkered career. He wanted a song that said something about Carlotta's character and life, not just trigger an easy laugh. He came up with one of the most popular, long-lasting numbers in the show, indeed of his own six-decade career.

The idea—and title—occurred in a real-life replay of a classic songwriter movie. When Sondheim was in a meeting with librettist James Goldman, brainstorming about an idea for De Carlo's survivor song, Goldman blurted out, "You know, with everything she's been through, she's still around, she's still here." Sondheim said, "That was all I needed." He realized De Carlo had only twelve spoken lines in the show and deserved a number to dramatize her life that would justify a seven-minute song. He decided on what he calls "a potted social history of the USA between the Depression and the 1960s," a blend of E. Y. Harburg's sociopolitical style and Dorothy Fields's "introspective ruefulness infused with self-deprecatory humor and eventual optimism, reflected here by the song's progression from resignation to triumph at the end. In other words, a showstopper."

He says in his book of annotated songs, *Finishing the Hat*, "The true pastiche in this song is a musical one—one of my many homages throughout the years to Harold Arlen, whose music is always a thrill to hear and a pleasure to steal. His ability to extend a blues into an art song ('Stormy Weather,' 'Blues in the Night') without losing the simplicity of the first or the complexity of the second has always astounded me and seemed like the appropriate things to attempt here, Carlotta being a character who would see her life as a flamboyant, torchy ballad."

Like "Broadway Baby," "I'm Still Here" grabs our attention from the first line, as Carlotta (which neatly echoes "De Carlo") relates her life story in all its amusing, tawdry, sorry chapters that put her in a historical context, from down-and-out to up-and-coming to over-the-hill. It's a quick tour through fifty years of pop culture fads and events that reveals she's had a crazy quilt life but is part of a bigger crazy national picture. The song is packed with topical Porteresque touchstones—"I've been through Gandhi, Windsor and Wally's affair, / And I'm here. / Amos 'n' Andy, mah-jongg and platinum hair, / And I'm here. / I got through 'Abie's Irish Rose,' / Five Dionne babies, Major Bowes, / Had heebie-jeebies / For Beebe's Bathysphere, / I've lived through Brenda Frazier / And I'm here."

Between the newsreel shots, Carlotta reveals her personal history with disarming frankness, a minimemoir: "I've been through Reno, / I've been through Beverly Hills, / And I'm here / Reefers and vino, / Rest cures, religion and pills / And I'm here." She recalls how she was once called a "Pinko," should have gone to acting school but it didn't matter because people thought she was "sincere." And then a verse that sums up every aging bombshell performer's history: "I've gotten through, 'Hey, lady, aren't you whoozis? / Wow, what a looker you were' / Or better yet, 'Sorry, I thought you were whoozis / Whatever happened to her?'"

Prince said, "It's a very long song, but it's a very interesting and intelligent song"—maybe too intelligent for a showgirl who sings, "Then you career from career / To career." "We had already cast Yvonne," Prince told me. "We cast that show so that everybody is playing a character suspiciously close to who they were in real life. The idea for the show was James Goldman's, says Sondheim. He and Sondheim spent two years writing the musical before bringing it to Prince, who conceived of a set constructed of rubble. The vision in Prince's head was the famous *Life* magazine photo of Gloria Swanson standing in the rubble of the recently demolished Roxy Theater in New York City. Prince was inspired by *Sunset Boulevard*, "which I thought was a spectacular movie because Billy Wilder had the gall, or guts if you will, to cast Gloria Swanson in it. It's an old film star playing cards with her former self. I thought we must cast *Follies* this way." One problem was that De Carlo, like Fifi D'Orsay and other old-timers, "had trouble learning the lyrics. I don't think Yvonne ever sang all the lyrics 100 percent correct, including on the cast album. But she was good. She was glamorous and good."

Ted Chapin recalls in his show diary that "I'm Still Here" didn't stop the show when it first went in. "First, nobody knew what it was. In the world of *Follies* it is neither what Sondheim calls a pastiche song nor a modern-day song with a Sondheim feel to it. It is somewhere in the middle. Yvonne de Carlo—I want to be polite—was not the smartest performer. She had good instincts but messed up the lyrics constantly. I don't think she was a smart enough performer to understand that it was a showstopper, something subsequent actresses in that role realized. But she was the biggest name on that marquee."

•••••••••••••••• BACKSTAGE DISH ••••••••••••••••

+ For "Who's That Woman?," three offstage dancers tapped the same steps as the aging onstage dancers on a piece of Masonite, with a mic attached, to "sweeten" the clacking sound—a sort of tap track. The stage was so steeply raked that it was lethal for any dancer to tap on such a sharply angled surface, so taps were removed from some of the dancers' shoes. To further aid the easily winded singers, a few songs were enhanced with a tape of singers in the basement crooning along with the phantom tapsters.

+ Michael Bennett, worried that *Follies* was too much of a downer, wanted to hire Neil Simon to add some comedy lines (as he did to *A Chorus* Line), to lighten the bleak tone of James Goldman's script about two desperately unhappily married couples. Hal Prince quickly nixed the idea.

+ Marti Rolph, who played the young Sally Durant (Dorothy Collins) role on Broadway, says that early audiences were surprised and disappointed that the show wasn't all about the Ziegfeld Follies, even though it evokes a genuine old Ziegfeld show, minus gorgeous sets and costumes. *Follies* was Rolph's first (and only) Broadway show. She was in her midtwenties. "I was new to New York, new to everything, and I had a hard time learning my big tap number ["You're Gonna Love Tomorrow," Sondheim's favorite song in the score]. I was struggling, and one dancer said to me, 'No matter what, don't get upset in front of Michael [Bennett].' So one day I totally lost it and ran into the bathroom and was in the stall crying. In the next stall someone was also crying. We both came out. It was Dorothy [Collins]!" Yvonne De Carlo was not as fearful. "She was laughing at the two of us."

+ A big emotional number in *Follies*, a near showstopper, is "Could I Leave You?," in which Alexis Smith's character savages her husband with a barrage of bile. Prince told me, "That's Steve Sondheim at his most brilliant. It's just a brilliant, brilliant, brilliant number. Michael Bennett did most of the staging, but I ended up staging that number because I felt it should not look staged. It should just be that woman standing still and surprising us with the venom she feels after being rejected by her husband. All I wanted was the audience to listen to the lyric."

Bennett disagreed, wishing to choreograph it. Prince recalls, "Alexis asked Michael to stage it because she wanted the choreographer to do it. Then he did stage it and it was too much, so it was a slightly uncomfortable moment when I said, 'Michael, I want to do this. I don't think you guys are right.' Steve was very much behind me on that. I took the actors into a room and staged it in no time because it was *not* staged. It was felt." In brief, your classic director-choreographer battle. Choreographers tend to want more movement and directors often want less. Prince said, "You just have to prevail. It makes for momentary confrontations but never bad ones. I think there was enough respect flowing both ways. And I got an OK track record, so maybe I'm right."

A LITTLE NIGHT MUSIC

◆ 1973 ◆

"Send in the Clowns"

Before it became a hit with Judy Collins's 1975 recording, **"Send in the Clowns"** was in no way a showstopper—nor was it intended to be when *A Little Night Music* opened in 1973. The song was written by Stephen Sondheim at the last minute, like so many fabled show tunes batted out in a hurry in Boston or New Haven that go on to become legendary standards. In fact, it was written in New York near the end of rehearsal.

The song was written for Glynis Johns when director Hal Prince felt she needed a song to express her character Desiree's dismay, hurt, and bitterness at being spurned by her old lover Fredrik for a younger woman; when his marriage somehow can't be consummated with a virginal bride, he returns to Desiree. The show is an adaptation by Hugh Wheeler of Ingmar Bergman's cinematic romantic roundelay *Smiles of a Summer Night*, about bed-hopping lovers, disappointed and otherwise, circa 1900, a Chekhovian commentary on the whims, vagaries, poignancy, and craziness of love—in brief, right in Sondheim's creative wheelhouse.

The song came about late in rehearsals. According to Terri Roberts in *The Sondheim Review*—a quarterly devoted to all things Sondheim—when director Hal Prince felt that, as the star of the show, she needed a solo some-where in the second act. He called Sondheim to come over and watch the scene; it was 4:00 PM. At 10:00 the next morning, Sondheim sat down and sang "Send in the Clowns." "Len and I were standing by the piano," recalls Johns, "and he played the first half a dozen notes, and I had tears in my eyes; I could tell by the timbre of the chords, of those few bars, and I looked at Len and his eyes were full, too."

Johns never tired of the song, she said in 1990, nor of tearing up. "I did it for eighteen months in New York, and in Boston. And not once did I ever sing that song that I didn't time the tears." At first she was afraid of breaking into tears too soon in the song, but Sondheim instructed Johns not to cry—"Most of the performances she didn't," he says. Johns claims he told her, "'Sing it alone again and again, even if it's a thousand times. Sing it until you can control where those tears come, and if you want them. You must keep on and on and on.' He was right. I got to control it. I knew exactly when I would let the tears roll down and how long it took. I timed it with the orchestra." It's become the show's emotional high point, even though in his review the *New Yorker* critic Brendan Gill failed even to mention it.

After Judy Collins and others gave the song a new life, "Send in the Clowns" evolved into a quiet showstopper in revivals that audiences now wait for as eagerly as they do "Hello, Dolly!" It is Sondheim's only song to make the charts in his sixty-year, seventeen-show career, recorded by more than nine hundred singers after Collins's signature version, with a nice boost from Frank Sinatra's single that certified its pop standing. In her cabaret show, Collins proudly and rightly talks about "owning a piece of the property" and took pains to tell a San Francisco interviewer, "I'm the only one who had a hit with 'Send in the Clowns,' including Sinatra. Which sometimes people forget." She's making sure nobody forgets.

No singer has been able to resist the song. YouTube sends in scads of clowns, including Judy Collins on *The Muppet Show* with clowns capering behind her, and a master class with Sondheim carefully instructing student singers how to properly request those clowns. Sondheim says he has no idea why this particular forlorn ballad, of all his compelling ballads—many just as beautiful—was a hit, the 1975 Grammy Song of the Year. "The success of 'Send in the Clowns' is still a mystery to me."

Even though Sondheim had six major shows behind him by the time Collins discovered the song, the singer claims she had never even heard of Stephen Sondheim when a friend sent her a Sondheim album and insisted she listen to a haunting song on it about clowns. She sent the song into the world beyond Broadway, but it was a strange ballad for Judy Collins to record. The song was plaintive, like many of her folk songs, but it was a Broadway show tune, of all things. Four decades later, the song inspired a major career leap for Collins at seventy-five, a 2015 cabaret show called *Finding Sondheim*. She makes the audience wait for The Song, of course, the inevitable finale. It's odd that Collins, whose fame rests on her long career as an iconic folkie, should wind up with a Broadway song now a major part of her legacy.

The song was custom-built for Glynis Johns in the Broadway show. Johns was not a trained singer and had a narrow range and a slight but vulnerable voice—or as Sondheim has described it, "a small but silvery voice that was musical and smokily pure." He loves smoky voices. So the song needed to be written in short phrases—no extended notes—to allow Johns room to breathe, to make it easier for her to sing. He explains that he phrased the lines as questions to fit the short melodic phrases.

Sondheim wrote "Clowns" in one night, and he says it "sat so well in Glynis's voice" that she recorded it perfectly in one take, though she had never recorded a song before. He remarks, "I've heard it sung since by many fine singers (I'm happy to say), but to me her version is still the most satisfying." He says the first singer he hears singing his songs "tends to be the recording I want to live with. Deeply moving as Judi Dench's cello-voiced performance of this song was in the National Theater revival of the show, I'll always hear Glynis's flute."

The contemplative song was also just right for Johns's heartbroken character, delivered with wistful rue. It's a number about missed chances, bad timing, dumb luck, and longing—a bittersweet sigh of a song. Sondheim notes in the annotated collection of his lyrics, "I had tailored songs before to the talents and limitations of particular performers ('Everything's Coming Up Roses' for Merman, 'The Ladies Who Lunch' for Stritch), so writing one for Glynis was not difficult. . . . The breathiness I loved was, ironically, her liability as a singer."

Sondheim explains, "It was never meant to be a soaring ballad; it's a song of regret. And it's a song of a lady who is too upset and too angry to speak. She is furious, but she doesn't want to make a scene in front of Fredrik because she recognizes that his obsession with his eighteen-year-old wife is unbreakable. So she gives up." He says the lyric is flawed because in the last line, "Well, maybe next year," the melodic stress is on "year," but the dramatic emphasis should be on the word "next." Equally risky is the line, "Don't you love farce?," because it forces the performer to sing two "fricative" sounds, the "v" in love and the "f" in farce, which might be heard (by Brits anyway) as "don't you love arse?" In master classes, he makes sure that singers carefully enunciate the line "There ought to be clowns" with a tiny pause between "ought" and "to" so they don't run together.

Len Cariou, who played Fredrik opposite Johns, tells how he couldn't wait to hear the song Sondheim was working on that he assumed would be for him, but Sondheim was unable to come up with a song for Fredrik. Sondheim came in one morning, dark circles under his eyes from staying up all night to write it, and Cariou couldn't wait to hear it. Sondheim said, "I'm sorry, Len, you don't sing this song. It's for Desiree." Cariou's opinion is that Sondheim almost seemed worried the song might be too popular, ruining his reputation as a cult favorite.

Many people, including many singers, didn't understand why clowns were being sent into the room, but Sondheim's nostalgic, evocative tune expresses a mood of dismay that helped listeners get the point. The metaphor fits Desiree because she's an actress who would know the phrase "send in the clowns"—an old theatrical, circus, and rodeo expression unknown to the public. When a vaudeville show was going badly, they sent in the comics to salvage it—a perfect metaphor for Johns's desperate state of mind. Or if a trapeze artist falls, clowns are quickly summoned; at rodeos, when a bull or bronco rider gets into trouble, clowns are let loose to distract the animal.

The irony of a clown image adds to the song's appeal—a sorrowful ballad with jesters, very Sondheimesque. He says that he could have used "fools," but it doesn't have the same meaning or the right ring. Though Sondheim dislikes reprises, "Send in the Clowns" is sung again as a coda at the end of the show, with new lyrics, a love duet between Desiree and Fredrik that deepens the song's meaning.

The song has circus imagery beyond clowns, suggesting high-wire artists who can't quite connect: "Isn't it rich? / Are we a pair? / Me here at last on the ground, / You in mid-air. / Send in the clowns." The stage motif continues ("making my entrance again with my usual flair"). The song reads like an actor's nightmare, with two more theatrical lines—"Don't you love farce?" and "losing my timing this late / In my career."

When Barbra Streisand was making a new album in 1985, she asked Sondheim to add a stanza to the song just for her, to help listeners who might still be stumped by the lyrics. She felt the lyrics needed a transition between the two choruses, and Sondheim agreed that "there was indeed an emotional gap," which in the show is covered by a monologue. Such a request from the imperial Streisand amounted almost to a summons, so Sondheim—who might never entertain a suggestion to alter a lyric from anyone of less regal standing—agreed, explaining, "It seemed a logical request rather than the whim of a diva." He wrote a new stanza for her that says in part, "Who could foresee / I'd come to feel about you / What you felt about me?" It doesn't hurt the lyric and in fact clears it up, so Streisand's trademark chutzpah was here justified.

BACKSTAGE DISH

+ After two critical hits, *Company* and *Follies*, Harold Prince was banking on *A Little Night Music* to be a financial, as well as an aesthetic, success. The Bergman movie's theme of ill-fated romance is one of the elements that hooked Sondheim, whose idea it was to turn the film into a musical. Prince felt Sondheim's first few songs were *too* bleak, rather like Strindberg with show tunes, and Sondheim realized later he had written the score more with Bergman's movie in mind than Hugh Wheeler's fizzier seriocomic adaptation. Sondheim, Ilson reports, told orchestrator Jonathan Tunick he "wanted the orchestra to have the sense of perfume rising out of the orchestra pit."

+ Hermione Gingold was the first actor cast, as the dowager Madame Armfeldt, and she now seems so right for the role it's hard to imagine she wasn't a shoo-in. Prince thought Gingold wasn't at all right—thinking of her broader comic roles such as Madame Alvarez in *Gigi*. Gingold was sure she was perfect for the part and pestered Prince until he finally agreed to let her audition. She sniffed, "And *I* haven't auditioned in forty years!" She said she only knew one song, sang it again, and ten days later got the part, creating a template for the dry, austere dowager (think Maggie Smith in *Downton Abbey*) that all other later Madame Armfeldts are still measured against.

+ The show got lukewarm notices that praised the musical's concept, design, and artistic construction but felt that overall it lacked much soul, by then a familiar theme of critics of Sondheim shows. "It reveals the work of superior craftsmanship," said Douglas Watt in the *New York Daily News*, echoed by other reviewers. "But stunning as it is to gaze upon and as clever as its score is . . . it remains too literary and precious a work to stir the emotions." But Clive Barnes in the *New York Times* was ecstatic with praise, calling the show "heady, civilized, sophisticated and ingratiating.

It is Dom Perignon. It's supper at Laserre. It is a mixture of Cole Porter, Gustav Mahler, Antony Tudor, and just a little of Ingmar Bergman. . . . It is a remembrance of a few things past, and all to the tune of a waltz and the understanding smile of memory. Good God—an adult musical!"

To some critics, the musical has a chilly center, despite the intensity of the characters and the powerful theme of love gone awry. It has everything but heart and humor, and the plot plays out mechanically. Maybe all of those music-box waltzes give the show its slightly monochromatic tone. Even so, *Night Music* played six hundred performances and produced a touring company and a *Newsweek* cover story. Sondheim's theory as to why the show did well: "What I really think is that *whatever* the last show would have been they [audiences] would have liked it more than the first two [*Company* and *Follies*]. They're just getting used to our stuff. . . . I suppose I'm finally wearing them down." Prince himself was divided about the show. He called *Night Music* a stylish and intellectual musical but "felt it was too pale and romantic and not bloody or emotional enough." But the ultimate review came from Ingmar Bergman, who told Prince, "I was surprised that it was possible to eliminate the shadows of desperation, eroticism, and caprice without the whole story collapsing. At the moment, I forgot that this entertaining and witty musical had anything to do with my picture. I enjoyed it tremendously." "Bergman liked the score so much," Sondheim recalls, "that he asked me to collaborate with him on a movie musical," but it never got made.

A CHORUS LINE

◆ 1975 ◆

"One," "What I Did for Love"

"**O**ne," the glitzy high-kicking finale of *A Chorus Line* that falsely glamorizes the dancer's gritty life, is a number with all the dancers we've seen only in sweaty leotards who finally appear in gold satin costumes and top hats in a razzamatazz number that audiences adore. It's a showstopper from the show-within-a-show we never see and also ends the show we're witnessing; finales shouldn't count as showstoppers, but this is an exception. When we watch the number, we realize the blood, sweat, and tears that went into it for our momentary pleasure. After seeing *A Chorus Line*, it's hard to look at a chorus number in other musicals again with quite the same eyes.

Lyricist Edward Kleban told author Ken Mandelbaum in his book on Michael Bennett's shows, "'One' was a craft-technique challenge, in that it was a song that was supposed to have been 'written' by somebody. It's not like the show's other songs, with someone singing their true feelings. It's a something that some songwriter—the composer of the show for which they're audition-ing . . . has written, and yet it has to have a subtext about other things in the play." Tricky. "You have to keep it very plain, like it's almost a Jerry Herman song but it isn't quite. To say nothing is always harder than to say something."

Kleban's lyrics are obscured by Hamlisch's dynamic music and the daz-zling high-stepping chorus line in the show's climactic finale. You're looking at the glittering gilded costumes and the grinning faces, not listening to lyrics for a nonexistent show within a show. Almost nobody can quote the lyric beyond its famous opening line ("One singular sensation, / Ev'ry little step she takes") or likely even tell you what the song is about—a detailed portrait of a desirable woman you can't look away from: "One thrilling combination, / Ev'ry move that she makes." The words just give the chorus line something to mouth while they're executing their big dance number.

The vamp to "One" is almost as effective and famous as the song—"dum . . . da-da-dum . . . da-da-dum . . . da-da-dum." It's impossible to hear it without suddenly flashing on the finale—a powerful vamp, one of Broadway's most memorable opening notes; it bears a similarity to the equally famous vamp to "New York, New York." Donna McKechnie, the show's star, comments, "That vamp said everything. It's Las Vegas, but dissonant, not quite major or minor [chord]. It hits you in the solar plexus. It's a little jaded or melancholy." The original idea, said McKechnie, was to bring someone onstage from the audience and put them in the line, but it ruined the precision of the number, so they wisely ditched it. "We found we didn't need to make Everyman the One. Every person in that line was the One."

Stephen Sondheim analyzes "One" with his sharp showman's eye: "The finale is right out of the end of *Follies*, but that was right out of the tradi-tional Ziegfeld-style line in top hats and tails. It's also close to the Rockettes. Michael Bennett used the Rockettes [as a model] for the last two numbers in *Follies*. Ken Mandelbaum agrees: "As the dancers [in *A Chorus Line*] form a wedge and a circle, to the accompaniment of spontaneous applause from the audience, the number becomes a celebration of the mindless glitz and excitement of Broadway musicals . . . and the show literally never ends, the

**Dancers display their "One"-ness in the showstopper's
showstopper from *A Chorus Line*.**

lights fading on a still-kicking line, the music continuing as the houselights come up."

Mandelbaum adds, "Just as Broadway can never completely cease to exist, these dancers will never stop kicking. But the sad irony is that these dancers who we now know are special are kicking their way into musical-comedy oblivion. Bennett thus sums it all up by giving the audience the big obvious all-out rouser for which it has waited, but he undercuts it by once again depriving the cast of their hard-earned individuality. They are all 'one' again—that is, one anonymous mechanical unit." Bennett said, "The finale says everything the show says. And it fades on them kicking. That's the end of the show. There are no bows. I don't believe in bows, just fade-outs. That's what a dancer's life is."

The big flashy closer obscures this harsh point, because "One" is so dazzling and imitative of so many musicals before it. "One" looks like a feel-good finale, but in fact it's a kind of cruel parody.

In nearly every way, *A Chorus Line* was a different breed of musical cat—a show all about itself, a backstage musical in the grand tradition of Broadway shows but based on fact, on interviews with the actual dancers in the show. It's a show without stars, part of the point. The chorus line is the star, but the individual dancers remain anonymous.

The show, despite its being an early "concept" musical, has a kind of plot: a desperate aging lead dancer wants to resume her career in the chorus with a director she once had a fling with—but the essence of the book, the hook, is which dancers will make the show and which will take their resume and skulk out the stage door to the next audition.

The musical details the daily grind dancers go through, the grim scramble of their arduous profession and the bumpy emotional road to get there. Most of their tales are steeped in adolescent angst, relieved only by a few amusing moments. It's often heartrending, if at times self-pitying, docudrama. The book—based on the dancers' backstories told at a series of midnight workshops—is by James Kirkwood and Nicholas Dante (punched up with a few uncredited comic lines by Neil Simon). The score wasn't fully appreciated at the time, overshadowed by the dancers' minidramas.

The musical excited the critics, some of whom overpraised it a little, dazzled by its inventive concept, but one who underpraised it was crusty *New Yorker* dance critic Arlene Croce, who accused the musical of extolling "the banality of show business." She mocked the dancers' clichéd backstories: "I used to dance in front of the mirror. I put shows on in the garage. I got interested in my sister's dancing classes. My mother pushed me into it. I had to get out of Buffalo. I saw *The Red Shoes* . . . all fairly innocuous stuff by Broadway standards but mediocre stuff by any sterner standard." Even so, said Clive Barnes in the *New York Times*, "all the hokum works—because it is undisguised and unapologetic."

But Croce felt the show makes the dancers sound shallow, and she claimed we learn very little about dancers' real lives and work. She added, "The cast is a statistical sampling of ethnic and geographical origins, class divisions, and levels of professional experience. . . . Nearly everyone is over-earnest and strained or cute-tough." All true enough, but the show's cumulative power is more than the sum of its parts, or its legs. As even Croce concedes, the "powerful illusion" of the show, and its great appeal, is that the dancers are playing out their own lives. Bennett's staging builds to the show's most ingenious theatrical moment—when certain dancers are singled out and asked to step forward, only to be told they didn't get this job. You could almost hear the audience's shocked gasps.

One theory about why *A Chorus Line* became a smash is that the finale "One" brings back all the dancers who were told to go home and *didn't* get the job, and then the rejects all reappear in gold satin costumes with the others—"a symbolic resurrection," as one writer put it. Without that ending, the show collapses. That was assistant choreographer Bob Avian's masterstroke; Bennett had little to do with the finale, according to one history of the show.

Dancer Pam Blair recalled that, though she found the finale "boring," "that Rockettes number made the statement of the show. . . . It was the culmination of everything we've been saying all night long. It was as essential as *Chorus Line* itself." Hamlisch agreed: "Yeah, it's sort of a saving grace. Everyone picked their favorite dancer so there was something for everyone. Also, you're left with a feeling of not judging people too quickly. I don't remember anything I've ever seen that educated me like this show did." Contradicting Sondheim's theory that the finale is really an ironic ending, McKechnie adds, "This show says, 'You're not alone, we're all the same.' In the finale, we're all in hats and kicking. It's a fantastic metaphor. It's very powerful. It touches people beyond the rational, beyond the intellect. It hits people in their gut."

Hamlisch and Ed Kleban's big take-home number, **"What I Did for Love,"** was a made-to-order showstopper. Hamlisch felt that *A Chorus Line* needed a breakout tune that might have a shot at the charts, explaining, "At some point—and this is the commercial part of me, not the artistic part—I said, 'We don't have a song in the show that, when the *Ed Sullivan Show* asks us to do a number, what song do we do? We can't take 'One'—it's too long. We can't put 'Tits and Ass' on television. 'At the Ballet' is too long. What are we gonna do? We needed a song that is excisable. In the old days, excisable was a big thing. It meant you might have a hit song from the show. Today that's almost impossible—we're in the world of hip-hop. So I lobbied hard for 'What I Did for Love,' which I felt was the one number that had a chance to break out of the score. So that's the one I argued for." He later admitted, "That song was a real cheat." Hamlisch, who always had sharp promotional instincts, wrote it expressly as a PR tool, a pure commercial song.

"What I Did for Love" is the only song not directly connected to the show, yet it seems very much of a piece with the other numbers, both in style and its yearning message. It is, in fact, what the show is all about, even though the people who put the show together didn't realize it at the time. Hamlisch recalled, "Joe Papp said he wanted to cut it, because it felt stuck in. He was right—and I was right." Shubert executive Bernard Gersten told writer Michael Riedel in his book about the Shuberts, Papp "thought it was 'just a Broadway number.' It was pandering to the Broadway audience"—which of course it was. But Bennett wanted a tear-jerker in the show. "Fine," said Papp, and walked out.

Musicals essayist Mark Steyn reports that when Bette Midler came up to see the show, she told coauthor James Kirkwood, "It's such a pity. You almost had a hit. But that awful song—what was it? Something about what they did for love?—that threw the show right down the toilet. Oh, well." But that song came to represent the score and is the number most people remember. "Written for opportunistic reasons," notes Styne, "the song had become true and real." It's really the theme song of all artists, not just dancers: doing a painting, a novel, a show, not just for money but because you love doing it, and you must do it. Few singers can resist it and YouTube has a dozen on display—Eydie Gormé, Priscilla Lopez, Idina Menzel, Frank Sinatra, Judy Collins, an overwrought Barbra Streisand, but the most unexpectedly moving is Carol Burnett singing it, sans theatrics, on her TV show.

·············· BACKSTAGE DISH ··············

+ *A Chorus Line* had no stars when it opened, but it made stars of Bennett, Hamlisch, and McKechnie. Everyone else in the chorus line was pretty much forgotten except Priscilla Lopez. Few had any visible follow-up success, leaving some of the dancers bitter because their stories form the essence of the script but initially they got no royalties and—just as the show relates—returned to the life of faceless Broadway gypsies.

   People who saw the musical and recall its happy ending—in which everyone "gets this job" in the chorus line finale, "One"—are unaware that many of the original cast had decidedly mixed to miserable feelings about the whole experience. Some were disappointed their careers didn't take off, others were just happy to have been in a milestone musical, dead end or not. Some felt used and abused by Michael Bennett, who rode the show to global glory as they did not (McKechnie and Lopez excluded).

+ The dancers signed away any right to the show for a dollar, an our-way-or-the-highway moment. Most felt that if they didn't sign, they'd be out of a musical that would showcase them and make them, literally, footnotes to Broadway history. Lopez said, "I felt—and it was probably true—that Michael Bennett didn't need me to do this show. But I wanted to be a part of it, so I felt that if that was the price I had to pay, it was okay." From producer Joseph Papp's standpoint, giving all the dancers involved a royalty would have made the show financially unfeasible. Papp wound up a wounded hero.

   A year after the contested one-dollar buyout, a truce was reached in an agreement that gave the original performers in the 1974 workshops and recordings an undisclosed share in the current production that applied retroactively and in all future first-class productions of the show. Bishop, Lopez, McKechnie, and Robert LuPone took an active part in the talks.

McKechnie noted, "It was absurd that we signed our lives away for one dollar. I feel real stupid about that. But you have to recall the atmosphere at the time. We had a group of people who were working together on this show, and were made to feel it was designed for them." One of the dancers, Wayne Cilento, said that without the dancers' stories there would be no show—"I just think we were smacked in the face." Thommie Walsh, later Tommy Tune's assistant, recalls that the cast was casually asked to sign the release during a break and was told it was all just routine. Robert LuPone, who played Zack, the show's cold-blooded director, said he felt the cast was "being manipulated." They were told, recalled dancer Trish Garland, that "if you don't want to sign it then we just won't put you on the logo [i.e., the poster]. Well, we all wanted to be on that logo."

Dancer/choreographer Baayork Lee at one point tried to get everyone in the cast to pony up $2,000 apiece toward the T-shirts and lobby trinkets, recalled McKechnie. "Do you know how rich we'd all be? Well, not rich, but it would be a lot in our coffers. We all could've shared in that. I don't think Michael wanted us to have anything—it was about the show and he wanted us just to be onstage. He was very linked to the show, in an abnormal way maybe. He was up there every night although he never *got* up there. So he had this overly territorial feeling about all that." On an early tape of the workshop that Bennett put together, he told the assembled dancers, "I don't know whether anything will come of us, or whether there is anything interesting. I think we're all pretty interesting, all of you are pretty interesting, and I think maybe there is a show in there somewhere, which would be called *A Chorus Line*."

✦ *A Chorus Line* was among the first "concept musicals"—a show that has more of a theme than a story with a beginning, middle, and end. The dancers tell their dramatic—in many cases traumatic—stories at the make-believe audition we're watching, even though no audition was ever as heart-wrenching as the one in this show, each dancer spilling out his or her guts to a brutal director we never see, only hear. Zack is a chilling voice in the dark signifying the impersonal nature of open calls, arrogant director-choreographers, and the ruthlessness of Broadway itself. *A Chorus Line* is the shady side of *42nd Street*, the antibackstage musical. None of the characters goes out onstage a nobody and returns a star; everybody goes out there a nobody and returns a nobody.

So *A Chorus Line*'s showstoppers work only in the context of the rest of the score, and only one song, "What I Did for Love," broke free of the show to make good on its own. Just two other numbers have ever been heard from since: "Nothing" (a clever put-down of pretentious drama school exercises) and "Dance: Ten; Looks: Three," a.k.a. "Tits and Ass," about the harsh realities of female dancers judged for body parts other than their feet.

✦ The movie version of *A Chorus Line* was soundly and deservedly trashed and mercifully vanished quickly. *A Chorus Line*, more than most musicals, is a total theater piece that can't truly be translated into cinematic terms. None of the original members of the Broadway show were in it, though many auditioned. The director, Richard Attenborough, argued that the original cast was too old for the film and revealed his ignorance of the show's theme when he explained why he didn't use any original actors. "Those people are all in their late thirties now, maybe their forties. This show is about kids breaking into show business."

Kelly Bishop, Sheila in the original cast, almost kicked in the TV set when she heard Attenborough's comment: "Breaking into show business! *Breaking into show business!* It's not about that!" Bishop's husband noted, "It's odd: the stage version is more cinematic than the movie." Attenborough had never directed a book movie musical (apart from *Oh, What a Lovely War!*, a 1969 filmed revue) and was as strange a choice as John Huston directing the movie *Annie*. Attenborough had no feel for the original, and it's interminable to sit through. Attenborough turned "What I Did for Love" into a love song, again missing the point. He did away with Bennett's landmark choreography, claiming it was too seventies. Bishop seethed, "It's amazing. Millions of people have seen the show and understood it. The two people who did not get it are the director and choreographer of the film. It was a skeleton of *A Chorus Line*. There was nothing there—no flavor, no taste, no beauty. Just bones. They just ruined it."

• •

Marvin Hamlisch, who began at nineteen as a rehearsal pianist for *Funny Girl* in 1963 and never looked back, was a lifelong wunderkind until his death in 2013 at a still boyish sixty-eight. Because of his other lives—film scoring, conducting, touring with Liza Minnelli and his own one-man shows—he wrote too few musicals, the most memorable other two being *They're Playing Our Song*, based on his romance with lyricist Carole Bayer Sager, and *Smile*, an underrated musical version of Michael Ritchie's film about a small-town beauty pageant, a sharply observed look at a now nearly extinct American ritual. While mulling over *A Chorus Line*, Michael Bennett knew about Hamlisch and put him together with lyricist Ed Kleban, and they jelled. I spoke with Hamlisch over brunch, just months before his death.

Did you and Ed Kleban have any creative battles?
No, not even arguments, just discussions. I've heard about Gilbert and Sullivan, who couldn't stand each other. If it comes to that, I want out. That's not my style. You come to some sort of agreement. Life is too short.

***A Chorus Line* is peppered with ministoppers, like the funny "Dance: Ten; Looks: Three," but the biggest number is its closer, "One," which would stop the show anywhere in the evening.**
We all love that moment in a show when everything stops, but the problem with writing showstoppers is that somehow they still have to be authentic and indigenous to the book—that's in today's world. Fifty years ago we didn't have to worry about that. Fifty years ago the book wasn't that important. In the old days, musicals were almost like revues, where they had a clothesline you just hung songs on. Today it's a little more difficult. You can have great scores today in shows that last a day and a half. I don't believe anymore that a musical score is as important as much as finding numbers indigenous to the book.

I'll also tell you that sometimes showstoppers are bad in a way, because they literally stop everything and you get away from the book. You've lost your train of thought, and that can be very bad. There are two types of shows now: we have shows that are critical hits and shows that are not critical hits, and both shows can run as long as the other. Just look around. In New York right now there are about six shows that got panned that are gonna run for ten years. *Spider-Man: Turn Off the Dark* is a perfect example of the critic-proof show. In that world, showstoppers are very easy to create because that's what the producer really wants. He thinks that will be the answer to it all and make his money back. I am still of the old school in trying to write something meaningful, so that when you come out of the theater to get some Chinese food, you at least talk about what you just saw.

Does a showstopper ensure a hit?
To be frank, a showstopper in no way guarantees success. There have been shows this year [2012] packed with showstoppers and the critics didn't like them. You have to be careful about that; I myself have to be careful about that. There are shows packed with gratuitous big numbers that are a dime a dozen, like in *George M!*, where they're all Yankee Doodle Dandy–type songs. Or when in doubt, go to a black singer and soup it up. It's wonderful, but it's often a number that you can hear any Sunday in a black church. What you have to do is find a number that is so peculiar to that show that *that's* what makes it great.

In *A Chorus Line* I didn't try to write hummable ditties. I wrote for what the show needed. I think it's amazing that a song like "One" has had its own life. It is catchy, but at the time no one thought it was catchy. [Certain songs become catchy after the *show* catches on, like "Send in the Clowns" in *A Little Night Music* or "I'm Still Here" in *Follies*—decent enough songs when first heard in a show, which gradually achieve a life of their own beyond the show.]

Any thoughts on contemporary musicals that rev up numbers into wannabe showstoppers?

I think it's more hard and fast now than it ever used to be. I don't think Lerner and Loewe ever knew that "Get Me to the Church on Time" was going to be a great showstopper. But a showstopper is made up of a lot of things. You can see Barbra Streisand in *Funny Girl* sing "People" and it stops the show, and then you see it somewhere else and it's just a nice song. It's just such a delicate thing. But you know what? Shows today are being created more for the road and for the people who come into New York. So the local audience can only hold a show open for three or four months, which is all New Yorkers. Then you need those buses that come in from wherever. I try to have a really funny showstopper in shows, but you need to be lucky enough to have a situation like "Hello, Dolly!," with six waiters coming downstairs. That's what you're looking for—a situation that can allow you to write a showstopper.

Can you write a showstopper on demand?

Just because the situation is there doesn't necessarily mean you can still write it. One of the biggest problems with shows is, sometimes writers pick the wrong place for the songs. There are just so many variables. Just deciding, where are we going to do a song? You could write a showstopper and it doesn't stop the show. It happens all the time. You don't know what you've got until you put it up there. Once you put it up there the audience tells you what you've got. Everyone can love it at the table, but it can die in front of an audience.

So it's a fragile entity. "Dance: Ten; Looks: Three," the show's only comic song amid all the suffering, when a female dancer named Val zeroes in on the stark truth of auditioning—where sex appeal is as crucial as experience or talent—was almost ruined by its original title.

When we opened the show, it didn't get a laugh in previews, and I'll tell you why: in the program it said "Tits and Ass," and we had to change it so audiences wouldn't see that line coming. It was changed in the program to "Dance:

Ten; Looks: Three," and then all of a sudden there it was! It has to surprise the audience. And it has to be unique. Sometimes you're so close to a showstopper, *so close*, and you don't see it. That's how close you can be. I always say, it's like having a 35-mm camera out of focus, and you go one-hundredth of an inch to the left and suddenly it comes into focus. That's how dangerous shows are. If you're off by one-hundredth of an inch, you're way off.

Great as the "Hello, Dolly!" number is, what makes it even greater is that Gower Champion had the dancers come out over the orchestra pit. They had a walkway that made the song even better than in the movie. In the movie, you can construct it, but it won't ever have the same feeling [which is the main reason movie versions of Broadway shows often look deflated on screen—the visceral human factor is missing, which no zillion-dollar budget or digital pizzazz can replace].

Sometimes a show can turn on a dime due to one crucial choice.
Five days before we were previewing *A Chorus Line*, the show did very well, but it was not yet there. Marsha Mason came in and told Michael Bennett, "I know what's wrong." What? She said Cassie [McKechnie's character] did not get the job and the audience rebelled against that because they felt she was the main person up there. [Bennett originally had Zack fire Cassie, as McKechnie explains: "He was trying to be real, and in real life he said, 'I wouldn't hire her, because I wouldn't want her around.'"] But the audience was so depressed after that. Nobody had hope and I symbolized hope. Marsha's bringing it to his attention made sense to him. So the next night all he had to do was give her the job—and there it was.

How did Michael Bennett help shape certain songs?
The whole opening number, "I Hope I Get It," was shaped by him. Look— if you're working with someone who's considered a genius, you're gonna do what he tells you to do. I see the director as the captain of the ship who is gonna get us there in one piece. When I was hired to do the show there was no show—it was just an idea. It was like, let's just see where this takes us. There was no book, just a transcript of the dancers' stories. I worked from that and from the scenes that were being worked on in the workshop. I like to write to a title. A lot of lyrics in "Hello Twelve, Hello Thirteen, Hello Love" come from the transcripts—totally. "At the Ballet" is my favorite. Donna McKechnie said that when that song was brought in, it was the soul of *A Chorus Line*, and I think she was right.

CHICAGO

◆ 1975 ◆

"Razzle Dazzle," "We Both Reached for the Gun,"
"Mr. Cellophane"

Chicago opened to only modest success in 1975, even with Gwen Verdon and Chita Rivera starring, and the consensus now is that audiences just weren't ready for the show's cynical look at criminal celebrities. O. J. Simpson, the Menendez brothers, the Zodiac killer, and various mass slayers somehow changed all that. Maybe, except that celebrity murderers have been around since Lizzie Borden, Bonnie and Clyde, Al Capone, and Leopold and Loeb, to name just a handful that creep to mind.

The 1920s doted on tabloid evildoers like Harry Thaw and Fatty Arbuckle, but what made the difference when *Chicago* returned in 1996 to blockbuster Broadway success was the bloodthirsty tabloid TV culture in full flower. By '96, America feasted on flamboyant murder, the grislier the better. Suddenly crime was a branch of showbiz and as lavishly exploited as any new *Die Hard* movie. This is what *Chicago* is all about: the art of the hype, reality-show division. The musical celebrates and crucifies the idea of celebrity madness.

In 1975, even critics who admired *Chicago*'s craftsmanship were turned off by its sardonic, corrosive style. Douglas Watt in the *New York Daily News* labeled it "a luridly effective spectacle" and praised Bob Fosse's staging but dismissed the songs as "serviceable" (that most damning of critical praise). A week later, Watt wrote a follow-up review headlined, "Not My Kind of Show, 'Chicago' Is," in which he called the musical "strangely unaffecting" and songwriters John Kander and Fred Ebb "a good second-rate team" whose songs "are merely good hack work." Watt added, "Our ready grins are continually turned sour by the show's esthetic." He summed up the show as "a brilliantly empty affair." Clive Barnes wrote in his 1975 *New York Times* review, headlined "'Chicago,' Musical, Disappoints," that the show was too stylistically reminiscent of *Pippin* and *Cabaret*. Another critic said, "The ingenuity of stylization keeps the characters unreal and remote, more like puppets than people and impossible to care about."

Chicago was custom-built for Fosse's footprint—for, in one critic's description, his "spider walk dances, tipped derbies, hiked shoulders and bent knees." Jack Kroll in *Newsweek* warned that "'Chicago' has an astringency and a clenched tightness that will put some people off." Martin Gottfried in the *New York Post* led off his 1975 rave by declaring unequivocally, "'Chicago' is as dazzling a demonstration of the craft of musical theater as you're ever going to see on a Broadway stage." Of the '96 revival, the *Times's* Ben Brantley declared, "Every number (and most of them are showstoppers) buzzes with an implicit, irresistible declaration: watch me. What I'm going to do is going to be terrific, and you're going to love every second of it."

In the heyday of vaudeville, celebrities of every kind were trotted out to perform, or at least sing a song, say hello, and take a bow, so-called "freak acts." Babe Ruth had an act, as did Helen Keller and boxer Jack Johnson—anybody who was exploitable; Paris Hilton, the *Duck Dynasty* family, and the Kardashians are all part of a hallowed showbiz tradition.

The Kander and Ebb score is a musical tour of American vaudeville—the original 1975 subtitle was *A Musical Vaudeville*—a pastiche in which almost every song is a subtle salute to a different fabled headliner. The score includes rag, Dixieland, jazz, and soft-shoe. Velma Kelly (Chita Rivera) and her song "All That Jazz," said Kander and Ebb, is inspired by Texas Guinan (the "Hello, sucker!" gal); Roxie Hart (Gwen Verdon) and her song "Funny Honey" are based on torch singer Helen Morgan; lawyer Billy Flynn's phony heartfelt plea "All I Care About (Is Love)" is meant to recall Ted ("Is *ev*-rybody happy?") Lewis; Mama Morton's "When You're Good to Mama" is clearly channeling Sophie Tucker, that last red-hot mama; "Me and My Baby" is pure Eddie Cantor, a veritable rewrite of Cantor's "My Blue Heaven"; and "Mr. Cellophane" is an homage to Bert Williams's forlorn "Nobody." This comes as news to most people who see the show (it did me) but makes it even more fun if you can envision (or are old enough to remember) the phantom showbiz personalities behind certain numbers. The 1996 revival deleted "vaudeville" from the subtitle, the producers no doubt fearing it would sound too old or that most young ticket buyers have no idea what vaudeville was.

Chicago is one of a handful of musicals with multiple showstoppers. It's impossible to choose just one or two and move on, an elite club that includes *Show Boat, South Pacific, Annie Get Your Gun, Babes in Arms, Cabaret,* and *Les Misérables.* Wherever it lands, *Chicago* has proved to have great legs (make that gams): 936 performances in its first production; fifteen-plus years in revival (finally outrunning the hard-breathing *Cats*); and longest-running American musical in Broadway history (and second longest-running show overall, still chasing the immovable *Phantom of the Opera,* another musical about misguided love). It won six Tonys, more than any revival in Broadway history.

After the sizzling opener, "All That Jazz," in which we meet the two lead characters Roxie Hart and Velma Kelly, it would seem as if the score has nowhere to go but down, and yet the wonder of *Chicago* is that it maintains that same level of sizzle, right to the end—"Nowadays"/"Keep It Hot." Gwen Verdon and Chita Rivera kept things hot for two hours in the 1975 run, and Bebe Neuwirth and Ann Reinking relit their torch in the equally torrid '96 revival—all four slinky seductresses conning their way into our hearts.

"Razzle Dazzle" is much of what *Chicago* is all about, a number sung by the slick flim-flamming attorney Billy Flynn (the ever ingratiating Jerry Orbach in the original, a cunning James Naughton in the revival), who has three of the show's most dazzling songs. From El Gallo and Mack the Knife to Billy Flynn, has there ever been as lovably sinister a guy on or off Broadway as Jerry Orbach?

In "Razzle Dazzle," Billy reveals his defense attorney's courtroom con. The number was perfectly tailored for a song-and-dance smoothie like Orbach, a charmer who glided through the number as he did in every show, from Macheath in the 1960s long-run landmark off-Broadway *Threepenny Opera* revival, to his final major stage role as the hard-boiled director in *42nd Street*. In each of his roguish roles Orbach seemed as amused by the character as we were, his lizard eyes and crooked grin just a mask for the wry guy inside. He exuded the fun of pure performance that made him the definitive Broadway musical leading man. Orbach had effortless style and authority and never overdid it. Alas, most people knew him only as the gritty cop on TV's *Law and Order*, a fraction of his talent.

"Razzle Dazzle" has a gentle soft-shoe tempo at odds with Ebb's acerbic lyrics that celebrate the razzamatazz tactics of high-profile lawyers like Billy Flynn: "Give 'em the old razzle dazzle / Razzle dazzle 'em . . . Give 'em the old hocus pocus / Bead and feather 'em / How can they see with sequins in their eyes?" Later: "Throw 'em a fake and a finagle / They'll never know you're just a bagel," and finally, "Give 'em the old double whammy, / Daze and dizzy 'em, / Back since the days of old Methuselah, / Everyone loves the big bambooz-a-lah." The song not only describes Flynn's showbiz brassiness but also Kander and Ebb's trademark songwriting handiwork. No team has ever been as adept at speaking basic Broadway showbizese.

A major crisis occurred when Fosse decided to restage "Razzle Dazzle" and asked the actors to improvise lines during the song, deleting lyrics that Ebb had carefully crafted. (Making the show as vulgar as possible, Fosse had performers screwing on the courthouse steps below a statue of a woman holding

**Jerry Orbach lays out his "Razzle Dazzle" defense
tactics to Gwen Verdon in *Chicago*.**

scales of justice.) Ebb said, "The musical was just an entertainment. It had
something to say about celebrity, celebrating killers. But you didn't need people screwing on the stairs under the scales of justice to make that clear. The
fact that Roxie and Velma were now in vaudeville was quite enough." Added
dancer Tony Stephens, "The fun was going out of the show. Bob wanted it to
be dirty and mean." Ebb confronted Fosse: "We all love dirty jokes, but we
don't put them onstage." Fosse never shed his early training as a dirty dancer
in Chicago grind houses. "Among mostly gay choreographers," notes Mark
Steyn, "Fosse was thrustingly heterosexual, reveling in erotic exhibitionism."

Finally, Jerry Orbach, trying to sing the number in the midst of all the distracting courthouse coupling, objected to Fosse's staging. Orbach, a seasoned,
highly regarded member of the ensemble, tried to reason with Fosse, who
told him, patronizingly, "I thank you for your interest." But Fosse respected
Orbach and backed down. The next day he told the cast, "You know, let's cut
all that crap on the stairs and all the fucking. Get rid of that shit. We need to
pay more attention to the story."

Just to tolerate Fosse, Kander and Ebb resorted to game-playing tactics.
Fosse asked them to write a new finale for Velma and Roxie's cabaret act,
to replace two songs ("It" and "Loopin' the Loop") that Fosse had staged so

crudely the songwriters were embarrassed by it. Ebb: "It was like he gave us a vacation in Florida." They wrote the song "Nowadays" in about an hour but took the day off so Fosse would realize how much grueling work went into writing a new song. Two days later, before demonstrating "Razzle Dazzle" for Fosse, Ebb told Kander, "Try adding a few finger snaps to it. Bobby will love that." Fosse fell for it. "As soon as he heard the finger snaps he loved the song," said Kander.

Another razzle dazzler, **"We Both Reached for the Gun,"** is as jaw-droppingly inventive as anything in the musical (or any musical), conceived and executed with stunning showbiz know-how. It's the sort of number that elevates a musical to art, that makes it forever memorable and that people talk about on their way home. It's tricky to describe—it's so visual, a sensory overload in the best sense. When Roxie encounters reporters on the courthouse steps, flinging questions at her, she's overwhelmed and takes refuge on Billy Flynn's lap. She tries to field the questions, but all her answers are spoken by the lawyer as her mouth flaps open and closed while he delivers her defense and she mimes his words like a dummy. Onstage you marvel at how deftly it's performed, whereas in the movie, with Renee Zellweger perched on Richard Gere's lap, it becomes mainly a flashy cinematic circus of sharp cuts that undermines its beauty as pure theatrical invention—Bob Fosse at his most wildly creative.

Billy (as Roxie): "He came toward me" . . . Reporters: "With a pistol?" . . . Billy (as Roxie): "From my bureau" . . . Reporters: "Did you fight him?" . . . Billy (as Roxie): "Like a tiger" . . . It goes on like that, rapid-fire, for five minutes, gaining speed and getting ever more frenetic. In the movie, Roxie's body also becomes a jerky marionette manipulated by strings, confusing the image. In any case, it's just an astonishing set piece, fun both to watch and listen to, requiring precise timing and miming, while making a devastating point at the same time.

Flynn's near showstopper, "All I Care About (Is Love)," is a phony plea about his heartfelt earnestness and love of justice. He croons it, Bing Crosby style, with little "ba-ba-ba-boos" tossed in, surrounded by a chorus of sexy showgirls fanning him. Fosse's approach to numbers like this is summed up by his instruction to the original cast: "Dare the audience to look at you, and then look back at them with murder in your eyes." Orbach's dark good looks and gimlet eyes gave him a head start as he slyly eased into the song, oozing sleaze, as he is introduced by an announcer: "Ladies and gentlemen, presenting the silver-tongued prince of the courtroom!"

Flynn, the ultimate sharpie courtroom charmer—see Johnnie Cochran, Mark Geragos, or F. Lee Bailey—performs the soft-shoe smoking a cigar as he matter-of-factly strips down to his shorts and undershirt while pledging his love of the law and desire to help his fellow man, tossing in an offhand, "And physical love ain't so bad either." He warbles, "I don't care about expensive things. / Cashmere coats, diamond rings / Don't mean a thing . . . I don't care for wearin' silk cravats, / Ruby studs, satin spats / Don't mean a thing. / All I care about is love." The girls coo, "That's what he's here for." And that's what we're here for.

The musical's quiet showstopper, "**Mr. Cellophane**," is in studied contrast to the rock-'em sock-'em flamboyance of all the other songs in the score. The number comes out of nowhere, a breather that changes the frenetic pace of the show for ten minutes. It's easily the most laid-back song in the show (almost any show), a solo by Roxie's schlemiel husband, Amos, whom everyone ignores. All the other characters in *Chicago* are over-the-top personalities with egos run amok. Amos has no discernible ego, or personality, to speak of. But he *does* speak of it in this confiding little solo, his brief moment in the spotlight, hoping to explain himself—or simply announce himself, letting us know he exists even if nobody sees him, as he sings, ever so politely:

"If someone stood up in a crowd / And raised their voice up way out loud / And waved their arm and shook his leg, you'd notice him . . . unless, of course, that personage should be / Invisible, inconsequential me . . . Cellophane, Mr. Cellophane, shoulda been / My name / Mr. Cellophane, 'cause you can look right through me, / Walk right by me and never know I'm there."

Amos (Barney Martin originally and, more indelibly, Joel Grey, in white gloves, in the 1996 revival) is a neglected bystander amid the crazy headline-shouting goings-on all around him. Roxie and cellmate Velma are both accused of murder, but Amos wouldn't swat a fly. He seems to have stumbled into the wrong show, and in "Mr. Cellophane" he mumbles a shy hello and then tiptoes offstage, with a perfect exit line to delighted applause: "Hope I didn't take up too much of your time." "Mr. Cellophane" is an almost performer-proof piece, sadly funny and effective, whether sung by a big bruising guy like Barney Martin (who finally got noticed himself, years later, as Jerry Seinfeld's bumptious dad on *Seinfeld*) or by pixie Joel Grey in the revival. Grey owned the see-through part of Amos Hart the moment he slipped onstage and, minutes later, slunk off.

Grey says he didn't want to do "Mr. Cellophane," Roxie's cypher of a husband. "It was originally done by a 6-foot tall, 200-pound guy, and the show depended on him being dumb or naïve, and not seeing how he's being cuck-olded. I thought that number was ridiculous. When they called me, I said, this guy was a giant dumb mechanic. He did that wonderfully. I do not fault the performance. But I thought he was too sad sacky, too feel-sorry-for-me. So I said no, no, no, no, no, and then [director] Walter Bobbie and [chore-ographer] Ann Reinking decided that the reason that he let Roxie do what she did, or turned his eyes away from whatever cheating she did, was that he loved her so much. But I could be vulnerable and show he would do anything for love. Amos was not a pathetic character—he was a guy who followed his heart. When you're in love, you're blind. He was in love and could not see the downside. That's what we ended up doing." Once Grey found the motivation, "I realized it was a wonderful piece of material. That point of view was very specific to me."

It was Grey's idea for Amos to wear white gloves, but not in homage to black performer Bert Williams, whom "Mr. Cellophane" was meant to recall. "We never thought about it that way," says Grey. "We were just thinking about the reality of the character." The number's vaudeville style somehow suggested white gloves, and the song is right in Grey's vaudeville comfort zone. "It came easy, once I made that acting adjustment. The rest was inevita-ble." One critic said "Mr. Cellophane" is the one song with genuine emotion. "I think that's true," agrees Grey. "He's the only person with a heart."

•••••••••••••• BACKSTAGE DISH ••••••••••••••

+ *Chicago* has a theatrical pedigree that dates to a 1926 play, *Chicago*, by Maurine Dallas Watkins, a crime reporter whose drama satirized the city's corrupt justice system. The plot came out of stories she wrote for the *Chicago Tribune* about two accused female murderers, Belva Gaertner and Beulah Annan, who became celebrities. In the actual cases, both women, one a cabaret singer and society divorcee, were acquitted—mainly because they were women, then as now rarely executed—and sexy dames at that. (The cases recall a line in comedian Don Adams's movie courtroom parody, "Ladies and gentlemen of the jury, I ask you: are these the legs of a homicidal maniac?") It provided a hot, sexy, irresistible plot for a 1942 movie (*Roxie Hart*, with Ginger Rogers) and a 1927 silent film directed by Cecil B. DeMille. As Gwen Verdon sensed when she first read the play in the 1960s and suggested to her then husband Fosse that it might make a musical, *Chicago* had Fosse's name all over it.

+ Rehearsals for the original production were fraught with more than the usual troubles. For starters, Fosse had a severe heart attack and bypass soon after work on the show began in 1974. He didn't return for three months, a changed man—depressed, depleted, and abusive, drained of the humor, confidence, and ebullience he was known for. He gave everyone a hard time, none more than Fred Ebb, his coauthor on the libretto. When he returned to rehearsals, he was convinced that some in the company had hoped he would die or that he would be replaced by Hal Prince. Prince didn't even like *Chicago*, indeed resented it. Ebb says, "He thought we had ripped off *Cabaret*. He wrote us a note saying that." The note said, "Tell Bob Fosse that Chicago in the late 1920s is not Berlin." No, but there are strong decadent similarities.

+ As depicted in the film *All That Jazz*, Fosse was an obsessive compulsive man, self-destructive emotionally and physically (cigarettes, liquor, women). He once told Ebb he picked on him "because you were vulnerable, and vulnerable people drive me crazy." Kander says in his and Ebb's dual theater biography, "Bobby was a terrific man with a dark side. Once we got into rehearsal things became very unpleasant. . . . The atmosphere was not good, and he and Gwen were having a difficult time, too. At one point I remember she said, 'They can pack his heart in sawdust as far as I'm concerned.'" Kander adds, "When he came back after his heart attack, he got really dark." Ebb referred to Fosse as "the Prince of Darkness." It didn't help that, during rehearsals, negative reviews of Fosse's film *Lenny* came out.

Kander goes on, "Bobby was much more fun when we first knew him. I think he had gone through a great deal with his heart bypass operation, and that affected the show, which became more cynical and biting than it had started out to be." Kander adds, "I was concerned that *Chicago* might be another piece that we were writing where show business would be a metaphor for life." Fosse could be thoughtlessly insulting. One day he threateningly told Kander. "I'd like [composer] Cy Coleman to hear this score." Fosse, a notorious womanizer, "was hitting on most of the girls in the show," said costume designer Patricia Zipprodt, who recalled that, in front of the cast (and Verdon), he told one of the dancers, "Don't think you're gonna have special treatment just because of last night."

Meanwhile, Chita Rivera was fretting because Fosse didn't let her dance more in a duet and she felt he was favoring Verdon ("I don't have the 'moment' in the show that I want," she complained). Excuses were made for Fosse's cruel behavior, that he was "a perfectionist," usually a showbiz code word for monster. Kander says, "Isn't that a wonderful word? Most bullies will try to justify their behavior that way." The atmosphere got so bleak that Kander, reflecting on Fosse's heart attack, told Ebb, "This isn't worth dying for. Let's go home."

Echoing feelings about other dictatorial choreographer-directors Jerome Robbins and Michael Bennett, Ebb said, "For all the difficulty working with him, and that was enormous, I always thought it was worth it. It's a very complicated issue. There you are working with a man who in your opinion is a bona fide genius. But at the same time he shows signs of being a detestable bully." Even Fosse's close friends, playwrights Paddy Chayefsky and Herb Gardner, called him "an arrogant son of a bitch." Producer Manny Azenberg, working with Robbins on *Jerome Robbins' Broadway*, said, "He'd scream and shout and humiliate you. He was a horrible man."

✦ The milestone 1996 *Chicago* concert version for Encores! didn't set out to be a full-blown Broadway revival, just a nostalgic revisit by Encores!, the New York City company that brings back old shows for weeklong revivals. Ebb: "What happened that night was astonishing. It was like we had invited everyone in the audience." Kander: "Like a rock concert." Ebb: "What was different was the presentation. It was stripped down . . . so the songs were sort of in your face. Most of the performers came down center stage and sang to you." Kander: "Reviews for the original production were very mixed and critics who hadn't liked it suddenly liked the revival." Ebb: "The audience finally caught up with the show, and history has been a great friend to us. We were helped enormously by the O. J. Simpson case, presidential adultery, and similar stories that had our sort of jaundiced worldview in the headlines."

Kander: "I guess it proves, much to our delight, that corruption never goes out of fashion. . . . The success of *Chicago* is a little bit like the history of *Pal Joey*, which was originally considered just too mean in spirit. Then it was revived [twenty years later] and was a big hit." Ebb: "What we hear most often about *Chicago* is that it was ahead of its time." Overnight it became the hottest ticket in town and earned back its money quicker than any show in history, partly because it kept the stripped-down look of the Encores! revival and still remains an elaborate concert. Robert Brustein, critic and director, in a 1997 review in the *New Republic*, said not since *The Threepenny Opera* had a musical "chronicled the weaknesses of humankind with such engaging sangfroid and sardonic shrugs."

✦ The 2002 film version was as huge and unexpected a hit as the Broadway revival, but it was just a version, only great if you never saw the original. It was a rare movie musical hit at a time when screen musicals had gone the way of westerns. The genre, once a staple in Hollywood that grounded them out almost once a week, had long been declared passé, played out. Somehow movie musicals fell on hard times and never recovered, though many hoped that after *Chicago* made such a splash in 2002 it might mean a return of film musicals. It was a false hope.

Chicago the movie was a surprise blockbuster that won many Oscars with a cast of unlikely singers and dancers who had never been in any Hollywood or Broadway musicals, stars cast solely for box office appeal—Renee Zellweger and Catherine Zeta-Jones as Roxie and Velma, with Richard Gere as Billy Flynn. The movie, like most modern Broadway musical screen adaptations, was a series of fragmented camera shtick—quick cuts, odd angles, reaction shots, and other devices that sabotage the songs with directorial pizzazz. Hollywood didn't trust *Chicago* not to do that. Anthony Lane said in the *New Yorker* that director Rob Marshall "edits his way out of trouble, cutting away furiously during not only each song but almost every line of each song, as though not daring to presume that younger viewers will stomach more than four and a half seconds of inviolate music." Lane called the movie "a pack of theatrical tricks."

Marshall decided to set the movie musical numbers *inside* Roxie's head, for commercial rather than cinematic reasons: movie audiences, contemporary wisdom insists, will no longer accept people breaking into song and dance (tell it to Fred Astaire, Ginger Rogers, Judy Garland, and Gene Kelly), so the only way to make the songs credible for today's moviegoers was to make them fantasies. On Broadway, each number emerged from the Hart-Kelly saga, which seemed already a kind of fantasy, as they are in any stage show—an accepted theatrical contrivance. The movie, to justify presenting the songs, turned the story into an incoherent montage of set pieces—returning the show, ironically, to its original concert form, but audiences and critics were so razzled and dazzled by *Chicago* the movie that nobody really cared or even noticed.

ANNIE

◆ 1977 ◆

"Tomorrow"

That all-time gutsy can-do showstopper from Annie, **"Tomorrow,"** is a sunny vow of belief sung by one of pop culture's most beloved urchins, but the classic number fell flat in the show's early version at the Goodspeed Opera House when Annie was played by an actress too fragile for the role. Not until she was replaced by feisty Andrea McArdle did the song—indeed the show itself—soar into hallowed "Over the Rainbow" country.

Once McArdle took over the part, the 1977 show was retrofitted to suit her yearning yet determined voice and gritty persona. McArdle's belting plea gave "Tomorrow" the resonance that sold the song and still brings down any house. "Andrea is the armature around which this entire show was built," the show's creator, lyricist, and director Martin Charnin told me. "It's not even a question of best—Andrea was the original, Andrea was *it*! Nobody has ever been able to duplicate her, nobody's been able to make the score happen as she did. You're never going to eliminate the ghost of Andrea."

McArdle was the centerpiece of the entire *Annie* saga. It was her vivid, earnest, and appealing portrayal of the title character that exhumed Little Orphan Annie from the graveyard of forgotten comic strips and breathed life into the peppy musical when she opened her mouth to sing its twin ballads of hope, first "Maybe" and then "Tomorrow," a one-two show-stopping punch.

In his search for believable orphans, Charnin nixed young stars and slick child actors. "We were looking for 'unfinished' children, not totally complete as performers." He wanted to shape them. "We were looking for kids with rough edges"—like the Jets in *West Side Story* (one of whom was originally played by Charnin) or the guys in *Guys and Dolls*. When McArdle turned up to audition for *Annie* in 1976 at the Bellevue-Plaza Hotel in her hometown of Philadelphia, she was immediately cast as one of the six backup orphans. Andrea was the second child Charnin saw and the first he hired. "She instantly impressed us because she was streetwise beyond belief, super-conscientious, and had a great sense of humor. She also had a wonderful athletic body. She was tight, built like a gymnast, the reason we first cast her as the toughest orphan, Pepper."

The lead, however, went to the more angelic Kristen Vigard, the first choice of composer Charles Strouse, smitten by Vigard's plaintive voice. But after a preview week at Goodspeed, it was clear that Kristen was too soft and innocent for the role, not at all the brash street-smart ragamuffin the comic strip's creator Harold Gray had in mind. Andrea was clearly the better choice, so Charnin was forced to dismiss Kristen (as well as her mother, who was in the chorus). "I was the only one you could hear in the back of the house," McArdle told

Andrea McArdle, looking forward to a sunnier "Tomorrow" in *Annie*.

me. "They cast Oliver and what they really needed was the Artful Dodger. Physically and vocally she couldn't have survived on the street—she'd be eaten alive in a New York minute."

Tom Meehan, for whom *Annie* was his first musical (he went on to write librettos for *The Producers* and *Hairspray*), told me, "The first Annie was a beautiful blonde angel, but it was a mistake for Annie to be a beautiful girl. Annie's got a mug face in the comic strip, and standing right behind our beautiful blonde girl was Andrea McArdle, whose face was the map of Ireland and who had this incredible Ethel Merman voice. Firing Kristen was tough. She and her mother got in the car and left in tears." (Semihappy ending: Kristen returned to the show as McArdle's understudy when the show opened on Broadway.)

Charnin recalls, "I had never fired anyone in my entire life. How do you fire a thirteen-year-old child? But it had to be done. Her vulnerability, an asset in the beginning, was seriously hurting the playing of all the streetwise scenes. I was demolished by the whole thing, but I had no choice. She just didn't have the grit the character needed. But the minute we made the change, everything fell into place. The difference between the first performance and one a week later was mind-boggling. We realized that's where the gold ore of the show resided. We rolled up our sleeves and began working in that direction."

Phyllis McArdle assured Charnin that her daughter, who had been in a Cheerios commercial and only one musical before *Annie*, could handle the role, so after a Sunday show Charnin sat Andrea down on his knee. As he tells it, "She seemed very, very small. I had my arms around her, holding her in a way that I have held my own daughter so many times. I said to her, 'Andrea, I want you to take over the part. I want you to be Little Orphan Annie.' She started to cry, and then asked about the young actress she would be replacing." They began work that night after dinner. The cast took the change in stride. Vigard left after Sunday's show, and Tuesday night McArdle walked onstage and nailed the part—"letter perfect," says Charnin.

In his memoir of the show, Charnin writes, "Andrea, who is tough stuff, was put into the role and the audience's entire attitude changed." Once she took over, the character became feistier. McArdle's persona shaped the character, indeed the show itself. "We needed a rugged kid, and Annie was not little Lord Fauntleroy. Annie was Mickey Rooney in a dress."

When McArdle sang "Johnny One-Note" at her audition, Meehan remembers his jaw dropping and thinking, *Wow!* Meehan adds, "She just walked out on a Broadway stage and took command. She was a little Merman, with great presence. She never had anything approaching stage fright." When McArdle sang her audition song, Charnin thought, *Where did* this *little girl come from?* From the first notes of the wistful opener, "Maybe," Andrea totally inhabited the part—physically with her jut-jawed look, vocally with her powerhouse voice, and temperamentally with her innate Annie-like spirit that allowed her to learn the entire role in two days.

Charnin says that of the thousands of Annies he's seen and the scores of girls he's cast in various companies, McArdle is still the best he's ever found. He adds, "Andrea was extremely bright. She had real instincts as an actor and impeccable instincts as a singer. When I'd ask her to invent something she never disappointed me. She was able to make a lot of stuff happen that I don't think would have happened with somebody else in the part. That's an invaluable difference."

What McArdle (not a *Little Orphan Annie* fan—"I never understood the comic strip when I was younger; it seemed so weird to me") most remembers about the rehearsals were "the excessive rewrites and reconceptualizing. I've never in my life seen that amount of rewrites every day. To have to adapt to that as an adult would probably have flipped me out, but I have a photographic memory. It didn't throw me. But when you're a kid you have nothing else to worry about—career, family, etc. Your mind is free and clear to retain things. As a kid, you can't get in your own way, so that saves you."

What McArdle brought to the role was a rare cuddly tomboy quality, blending two seemingly opposite traits, plus her mature voice, a belt but not a bray, with a vulnerable edge. Many actresses in the part tend to be either hyper robo-Annies or too precious. Whenever they cast Annie in other companies, subconsciously or not, they're still trying to duplicate the McArdle brand. (YouTube comes up with half a dozen Annies, but none as authentic as McArdle in a 1977 clip from the show—or indeed, the grown-up, glamorous McArdle singing it on a TV special.)

Tom Meehan still fondly recalls the pint-sized heroine: "Andrea liked to goof around—she was a little rascal—but I loved that kid. She was full of life and just so real and so perky. She never got a big head about being on Broadway." When McArdle was nominated for a Tony Award, she was the youngest performer ever nominated for Best Lead Actress in a Musical, but she didn't win. Otherwise a model performer, McArdle was addicted to stage pranks, like the time she and her mother were ejected from a Howard Johnson's hotel on Eighth Avenue during the early days of *Annie* when she dropped water balloons on passersby below. She once grabbed Daddy Warbucks's (Reid Shelton) hand during a tender moment in the show, her palm filled with Silly Putty.

"Tomorrow," composed by Charles Strouse to Charnin's chin-up lyrics, might easily have come across as sappy, but McArdle gave it a reality that carried over to the entire show, beyond sentimentality. You liked her, believed in her, and wanted very much for Annie to find a home beyond the orphanage. Charnin comments, "What was vitally important was to retain the sense of optimism, spunk, and energy that was rampant throughout the entire piece. In all of her comic strip adventures, Annie never lost her good humor and optimistic spirit that everything was gonna turn out OK." The number instantly became the show's enduring emblematic theme.

Says Charnin, "The song got its pedigree along with the show. It has become part of the show's identification. It's the glue. If you say *Annie* the first thing you think of is 'Tomorrow.' I don't know if there is another song and show that are as intimately connected as *Annie* and 'Tomorrow.' 'Tomorrow' represents a philosophy. She knows things are going to get better. That's a reason why the show and the song are as wrapped up with one another."

"Tomorrow" was no stroke of inspiration, *Annie* composer Charles Strouse explained, and in fact began life as a jingle for a TV commercial. "It has a very modest beginning," he told me. "I was working in advertising. I did a commercial for Arrow Shirts. They were interested in a more youthful rather than staid old-fashioned image. I used a choral group, five singers. I wrote some things that would sound hip for the shirts."

Strouse says the Arrow Shirt tune revisited him when he was casting about for a hopeful song for Annie. "I was reminded of it because one of the men in the background group for the jingle was Billy Crystal, who later told me, 'We sang "Tomorrow" first!' It was just a melodic phrase that caught my ear and that kept coming to mind. It was not an old-time show song. It was just that one phrase"—"The sun'll come out, tomorrow."

Strouse recalls, "We wrote 'Tomorrow' together, but Martin wrote most of the lyric by himself. I remember arguing very intensely against the phrase 'Bet your bottom dollar.' I said we'll never get a single recording with 'Bet your bottom dollar' in it." Strouse lost the argument after Charnin insisted it was a phrase from the Depression era, when Annie is set. "When we first brought the song to a Columbia Records man, he said no black guys will sing 'bet your bottom dollar.' That's why I thought it would kill any commercial possibilities. I argued against it. Martin won. Of course, it was exactly the right phrase. And my argument had been very superficial."

Charnin and Strouse generally worked easily together. "He would play something and I would say, 'That's awful,' and I would say a line and he would say, 'That's awful.' We were honest with each other. In many songs we had major disagreements. When we fought, it really had to be worth fighting for. We were not battling arbitrarily or for ego reasons. It only had to do with making the show work."

Originally "Tomorrow" was just a throwaway tune to cover a complex four-minute cinematic scene change that moved the locale from the street to inside the orphanage. "The set change got a great hand. They said, 'Oh, isn't that clever?' They didn't know that it was partly because of that song." The number, Strouse says, "is vital to the show because it's a song of hope during the Depression."

The song is a collection of by-golly-I'll-lick-'em clichés: "Just thinkin' about tomorrow / Clears away the cobwebs and the sorrow . . . The sun'll come out tomorrow / So ya gotta hang on / till tomorrow, / Come what may! / Tomorrow, tomorrow, / I love ya, tomorrow, / You're always a day away." But the combination of Strouse's compelling melody and Annie's defiant feet-planted resolve rises above blatant sentimentality. Its very simplicity seems to work in its favor; urchins don't think in sophisticated terms.

What most grabs people about Annie, Strouse goes on, isn't its most famous song. "I would say it's Tom Meehan's book. It has a fairy tale aspect, about a little orphan girl who meets the rich prince. Through it all we wanted to keep it very Dickensian. Tom captured it in the script." Like *Oliver!* the show never gets cutesy-pie, despite a gang of adorable orphans; it's always gritty and raggedy, like Annie herself.

Musicals authority Ethan Mordden calls *Annie* a "solidly capable fifties musical." The score is stuffed with engaging songs, not a dud in the lot, from the infectious "N.Y.C." and "I Don't Need Anything but You" to the supermean "Little Girls," Miss Hannigan's gleefully nasty turn. You walked into *Annie* thinking, *This show can't possibly be as good as they say*, only to find out it was much better. It surprised every cynic, each one converted by the finale, just like Daddy Warbucks.

But before it charmed everyone, *Annie* had to survive a crushing early *New York Times* review by its powerful theater critic Walter Kerr, who journeyed two and a half hours to East Haddam, Connecticut, to see a show at the Goodspeed Opera House he'd heard good things about; Kerr's word was gospel. Nearly all the New England reviewers that covered Goodspeed, a lovingly restored landmark opera house on the Connecticut River, gave the show raves, including Boston's hardheaded Elliot Norton, who called it "innocently beguiling and charming most of the time."

The first act ran an hour and forty minutes but eventually was cut to seventy-five minutes. They took out a big number set in a diner with the staff singing "We Love Annie" while dancing on the countertop. "As we kept cutting and replacing we could feel audience reaction going up," says Meehan. Early in the run, though, a man came up to Meehan at intermission and, spotting him scribbling on a notepad, asked, "Have you anything to do with this show?" "Yes," said Meehan, smiling proudly. "Well, it stinks!"

After Kerr's pan, there were major changes in the show's early version, moving songs around. "It was devastating," says Strouse. "I remember his review and the headline was, 'T'ain't Funny, Boys.'" The next morning the *Annie* trio sat down at breakfast and went over Kerr's review, line by wounding line, parsing every word, searching for a key to fix the show. "We were like rabbis deciphering the Talmud," notes Charnin. They finally decided that Kerr was an FDR liberal who lived through the Crash and perhaps felt the show made the Depression seem overly cheery and inconsequential, turned Roosevelt into a clown, and made Warbucks too liberal and Annie too saccharine. The writers turned FDR from a caricature into a sympathetic go-between who helps Annie find her parents. FDR even gets to reprise "Tomorrow," his cabinet singing backup, a brilliant touch.

The authors had tinkered with every facet of the show until the audience was responding with standing ovations. Even though the show was selling out, it looked as if East Haddam would be the first and last stop. *Annie* was nearing the end of its extended out-of-town run when Mike Nichols warily went to see it. When he was told, "You gotta come up and see this show!" Nichols moaned, "No, no! No way!" Playwright Jay Presson Allen, a hardnosed theater woman, called him and commanded, "Mike, I'm up here at Goodspeed and there's a show I think you should see. I don't care if your wife is having a baby. Get your ass up here!" Nichols told Charnin he was too busy producing the TV series *Family* to get involved, but the next day at 7:00 AM, Charnin says, "My phone rang and it was Mike, telling me he had been up all night, talked to his partner Lew Allen, and had decided they were going to produce it."

After the show Nichols told Charnin, Meehan, and Strouse, "You're sitting on a million dollars here." He was off by about a billion. Ten days later, Sam Cohn, Nichols's agent, called to say Nichols wanted to put up the money to produce it. Charnin says, "It was a thrilling moment. At that time he was the king of Broadway. *Annie* wasn't anything close to what he'd done before." Nichols instinctively realized it was a smash. Meehan says it took Nichols about twenty minutes on the phone in Sam Cohn's office to raise the money for a Washington, DC, opening.

When *Annie* finally landed on Broadway, Kerr had changed his tune, purring, "An old legend is made into a new one. . . . We're forthrightly invited to lose our minds at the Alvin, and that—reluctantly at first, then helplessly—is what we do." Kerr said the show had resolved its confused politics and praised Mike Nichols for not turning the show into anything satirical, or even camp (Dorothy Loudon's snarling Miss Hannigan aside). Kerr: "It doesn't even push for a calculated charm, which probably spares it from coyness. At heart it's straight . . . open, expansive, opulent, innocent." Kerr not only wrote a rave but, says Strouse, even sent the creative team an apology for his earlier hostile notice.

Annie opened at the Alvin Theatre on April 21, 1977, and by the following morning twelve-year-old Andrea McArdle—singing her scrappy little heart out as Annie—was a junior megastar. An instant and constant hit that ran five years on Broadway, *Annie* is endlessly revived (often at Christmastime), with a caravan of road companies touring the country since 1978. It still resonates powerfully with anyone who saw it, was in it, or whose daughter played in it.

Unlike Hollywood, it's almost unheard of for Broadway to deliver a child star, let alone one with the glow McArdle radiated. The child leads of Broadway hits like *Once on This Island, Beauty and the Beast, Billy Elliot, Newsies,* and *Matilda* remain anonymous; the young stars of *Oliver!* onstage and on screen are arcane trivia questions.

Annie holds a cherished place in the hearts of millions of little girls (now big girls, indeed grandmas) who formed its core audience, including the thousands of girls who appeared in the show in high school or community theater, where it's among the top ten musicals revived in the United States. A spokesman at MTI, the show's licenser, verifies, "It's definitely one of our top shows, with *Guys and Dolls*, *Fiddler on the Roof*, and *Disney's High School Musical*." At nearly forty, *Annie* has kept many a small theater company solvent, boasts Charnin: "Whenever a regional theater has a season and October comes around and they look at their books and say, 'We've had a pretty crappy season doing God knows what,' they book *Annie* from November to January and save their season."

For many kids, *Annie* was the first musical they ever saw. So the show made musical theater history, and not just in America. It was a global smash in some eighteen countries and was translated into twenty-four languages. "*Annie* came along at just the right time," says Charnin, during a downtime in the country's mood.

Annie was indeed a phenomenon, an unlikely out-of-the-blue musical smash that everyone, even devout cynics and tough-guy critics, took to heart—including famously hard-hearted John Simon, who was disarmed, writing, "You may acknowledge the show's unabashed sentimentality, but it's hard not to succumb to the show's innate charm, the result of some unusually deft theatrical craftsmanship." Everyone liked the show except for a few cranky critics who objected to a musical with kids and who thought it was, says Charnin, "too apple pie, too American, too obvious." A few condescending headlines called it "Nostalgic Fun" and "A Nice Clever Little Show." Charnin says, "We always tried very hard to avoid making it cloying. There were reviewers that said they thought they were going to be cloyed to death and then discovered universal truths, and those are sentimental truths."

Despite its glowing reviews, Charnin says, "There was a weird kind of reluctance," early on among audiences, to see it. "People thought it was a kids' musical. But the decision we made that is responsible for why it's so successful is that it's *not* a musical for children. It's a family show"—indeed, *the* family show. Producer-director Hal Prince had sagely advised Strouse during rehearsals, "Write a children's show that kids can bring their parents to, and you may be OK. But write a grown-up show that parents can bring their children to, and you've got a smash hit."

·············· BACKSTAGE DISH ···············

◆ Both Strouse and Meehan first thought *Annie* was a lousy idea for a musical. "When Martin said musical, I was thinking *Gypsy* and *My Fair Lady*," says Meehan, "and this seemed too trivial. I thought, oh, it's just another cartoony two-dimensional thing. I didn't like *Li'l Abner*. But when Martin told me he'd lined up Charles Strouse, who had won two Tonys [for *Bye Bye Birdie* and *Applause*], I thought, who am I to tell them to take a walk? I'd better get involved in this." Meehan plowed through thirty years of *Little Orphan Annie* strips at the *New York Daily News*. "I'd read a lot of Dickens, and I thought, let me see what I can do with this." He realized it was an American *Oliver Twist*. John Simon, in his original hostile review of the show, called it "'Oliver' in drag." "I took that as a compliment," says Meehan; Simon later recanted, writing of a later *Annie* revival, "What cannot be denied is that the songs are wonderfully varied, highly original, and uniformly pleasurable."

◆ After the Broadway-bound musical premiered in Washington, DC, critics were eager to see what Mike Nichols & Co. had wrought from a moldy cartoon character. When word first spread that Nichols was involved, Broadway agents perked up, two of whom suggested casting Bernadette Peters or Bette Midler as Annie (wearing training bras), even though Peters, albeit baby-faced and doll-voiced, was thirty years old.

◆ The first Miss Hannigan was replaced by a funnier, nastier Dorothy Loudon, whose "Little Girls" was an antidote to the show's high sugar content; in real life, said a cast member, Loudon really did hate little girls, little actresses most of all. She once told McArdle, "If you make one move on any of my laugh lines, you will not live to see the curtain call." The show began to find its footing, but it lacked a star or a star director. Strouse felt Charnin was a good director but not a big name and tried to persuade him to step aside. Not until Loudon joined the show on Broadway did the show have even a quasi-marquee name.

◆ The great irony of the show—and maybe its most inspired idea—is that the plot's politics are liberal, in stark contrast to right-wing cartoonist Harold Gray. The musical redeemed Warbucks and turned Gray's bald, blustering munitions-making conservative tycoon into a pussycat who is saved by the love of a good woman—Annie. As Charnin explains the switch from comic strip history to theatrical fairy tale, "When Roosevelt became president, Warbucks realized he had to work with him in order to survive." In

the musical they become mutual admirers. Warbucks, the rugged capitalist, helps inspire the New Deal after FDR meets Annie, is infected by her
sunny spirit, and in return enlists J. Edgar Hoover to find her lost parents.
Somehow Meehan and Charnin made it all seem perfectly logical—and
musically endearing. The show's most singularly charming moments are
when Warbucks and Annie sing their duet, "I Don't Need Anything but
You" and when the waifs pipe, "You're Never Fully Dressed without a
Smile" (meant to mimic chin-up tunes of the period and notated "Tempo
di Ted Lewis"), a companion song to Strouse and Lee Adams's "Put on a
Happy Face."

✦ *Annie* did not exactly cry out for a sequel, but there were two anyway,
both of which failed to beguile critics or audiences. The first, in 1989, was
a disastrous *Annie 2*, subtitled "Miss Hannigan's Revenge," mainly about
Hannigan, not Annie, a fatal mistake. It closed at the Kennedy Center
after thirty-six performances. *Variety* wrote, "Almost every ingredient
that made 'Annie' such a delight for both children and adults is missing"
from this "fancily dressed but greatly irritating show." One critic noted,
"The [original] was so flawless and complete that it made successful
sequels unnecessary." The *Annie* brain trust, unchastened, later retooled
Annie 2 at Goodspeed and turned it into a new, warmer 1993 show, *Annie
Warbucks*, about the further adventures of Annie (salvaging some songs
from *Annie 2*), which had a perfunctory six-month off-Broadway run. The
first show was about Annie finding a father, Daddy Warbucks, and *Annie
Warbucks* is about Annie finding a mother, Warbucks's secretary Grace
Farrell. Both *Annie 2* and *Annie Warbucks* LPs are now online hits, collec-
tor's items going for upwards of $100.

✦ The flat flop 1982 film version was directed by John Huston, "the incom-
parable master of the film musical," in Ethan Mordden's crack. The original Annie team was banned from the set, says Strouse. Huston had never
directed a musical. Not even stars like Albert Finney (Warbucks), Carol
Burnett (Miss Hannigan), Bernadette Peters, Tim Curry, Ann Reinking, and
Edward Herrmann (FDR, of course) could salvage the movie. But even the
dismal, charmless Hollywood two-hour version, which cut six songs, failed
to tarnish the stage show's reputation or allure. "It was wrong-headed
from the beginning," says Charnin. "John Huston had no right to direct it.
It wasn't *Treasure of the Sierra Madre*. He was old and infirm and only did
one more movie after that. I have no idea why they chose him. We sold
it for 9.5 million bucks and that was our mistake. Because of the money,
we gave up total artistic control of the piece and turned it over to people

who didn't know how to do it. It happens all the time. Hollywood always thinks they can do it better than the people who created it." Like nearly everyone, McArdle disliked the movie's Annie: "The girl who got the lead, Aileen Quinn, was Shirley Temple, which is exactly what Annie isn't! They needed someone scruffy, and Quinn had none of that. She was all outwardly affected, and she had no vibrato but was a great little dancer."

✦ A much livelier 1999 TV movie version was directed and choreographed by Rob Marshall with Kathy Bates, Alan Cumming, Victor Garber, Audra McDonald, Kristin Chenoweth, and Alicia Morton as a sweet but believable Annie with a more subdued urchin authenticity. It was everything the movie should have been. McArdle makes a special appearance, bursting on screen out of nowhere singing a rousing chorus of "N.Y.C." in her effortless belt that makes it clear she could easily hold her own in any movie musical, were there any today.

✦ Andrea McArdle's own zigzag saga rivals Annie's. McArdle finished school and was planning to go to NYU when a revue of Jerry Herman songs, Jerry's Girls, came along. She toured in it at nineteen in 1984, her first major stage role after Annie, and more than held her own alongside Carol Channing and Leslie Uggams. But when the revue reached Broadway, despite out-of-town raves, McArdle was replaced by Chita Rivera; the recast version had a very brief run.

McArdle once complained to Channing that she didn't want to be saddled forever with "Tomorrow." "I wanted to be cool," she said, and dissed "Tomorrow" with her pals, but, ever the canny veteran, Channing told her to thank God for a signature theme: "Leslie is still waiting for a song like that. What do they play when Leslie walks out on the Tony Awards?"

McArdle has only rosy recollections of her child star days. "I was thirteen and wanting to be sixteen like any other thirteen-year-old girl. I was incredibly embarrassed by Broadway. Had I only known it was cool to be on Broadway. I wanted to be a pop star. To me and my peers, Broadway seemed like opera."

All was bubbling along nicely for McArdle in Annie until the Attack of the Killer Cherries. For eight years, from the age of sixteen until her daughter was born, McArdle suffered from alcoholism. She was hooked from her very first drink—a concoction called "killer cherries" created by a security guard at Studio 54 up the street from the theater. "We had these giant cast parties under the orchestra catwalk, and I had like four of these killer cherries, and mind you I was so tiny, like sixty pounds."

She did her share of partying at Studio 54 with her fellow stage orphans, even though she was well underage. "But that was New York in the '70s. If you walked up to a bar in the '70s and looked even a little Irish, I was never turned down. We used to do it as a joke." She adds, "It's a family hereditary thing—my grandfather was alcoholic. I have the Irish disease. We have the gene. I worked alongside Elaine Stritch and Dorothy Loudon, so I saw it up close. It's ugly and especially ugly on women when they're older with physical problems."

For McArdle, *Annie* was a mixed blessing. She struggled for decades to shed an indelible image in order to strut her considerable stuff. The title of her cabaret act was "You Don't Know Me," almost a cry for help. A shapely, alluring, auburn-haired middle-aged woman, McArdle, with a magnetic stage presence, can still pretty much outbelt anybody in the room.

The central frustration of her adult career remains: Why isn't she as big a grownup star at fifty as she was at fifteen? Part of the answer is plain show biz luck—the right new role hasn't come along; but a more maddening part of the answer is that McArdle is still shadowed by—"shackled to" in Charnin's phrase—*Annie*. Because of *Annie*, McArdle became a kind of Broadway orphan, never called upon in forty years to open a new musical. But no need to pity her—McArdle has worked steadily, starring in a national touring company of *Cabaret*, playing Belle in *Beauty and the Beast* on Broadway for two and a half years, longer than any other actress in the show, and starring in major diva roles in regional theaters, from Momma Rose, Mame, and Peter Pan to Fantine and Eva Peron; she says *Evita* lyricist Tim Rice told her she was the best Evita he'd ever seen in America.

She was stuck in a classic awkward age for child actors, the midteens. "I wasn't old enough yet. I didn't look desirable. You couldn't put me any place. They didn't have the Disney Channel yet and there was no 'Tween Generation so my timing was totally off." She sounds hurt that none of the *Annie* creative team ever called her to audition for anything else. "They seemed so averse to casting me even though I helped send their kids to college and bought their houses in Westport." She adds, "In 35 years, Mike Nichols, Martin Charnin, Tom Meehan, and Charles Strouse have never given me a paying job—not one thing. I go up to the Vineyard and hang out with these people, so we're social—but they can't see me in anything else."

Seth Rudetsky, a Broadway pianist who hosts Serius XM's "Broadway" channel and a YouTube show called *Seth Rudetsky Deconstructs* (show tunes and singers) and who was McArdle's accompanist for her cabaret show, is equally puzzled by McArdle's frustrated career. He points out, "There are a lot of extremely talented people not working on Broadway. Talent is not all you need. It's very unfortunate. As good as she was in *Beauty and the Beast* it's not a marker of how talented she is. People are always shocked when they hear her sing and see how gorgeous she is. They can't believe it! People need to see her again and go, 'Oh, my God!' They also need to hear that she can also sing sweetly. She could have done *Gypsy* or *Mamma Mia* or *Annie Get Your Gun*. Her Fantine in *Les Miz* should have shown people what she's capable of. It's one of those mysteries, and it's very frustrating. People still just go, 'Oh, she's that girl from *Annie*."

THE PRODUCERS

◆ 2001 ◆

"Springtime for Hitler"

Much of the reason for the unstoppable success of *The Producers* had less to do with the intrinsic value of the show than with something historic. The 2001 musical signaled for many New Yorkers, and for older playgoers generally, a return from British and French extravaganzas that brought a rude end to the musical comedy dominion that Broadway regards as its God-given birthright.

Whooped screenwriter William Goldman in *Variety*, "The Mel Brooks musical is the final nail in the coffin of the shit that has been flooding the theater for 20 years. It is, if you will, finally and blessedly, the death of Andrew Lloyd Webber. Because what Mel Brooks has done is bring flat-out entertainment back to the musical theater." Broadway could hold up its head again. John Lahr in the *New Yorker* said the show had returned the element of "joy" to American musical theater—"a vivacious theatrical form, which for a generation has been hijacked by the forces of high art and lumbered with more heavy intellectual furniture than it can carry." (Lahr likely had in mind the sort of musical farces that starred his father, Bert Lahr.)

The Producers was seen by the theater establishment as the very embodiment of all that had been lost in musical comedies since *Cats* and *The Phantom of the Opera*; New York playgoers reacted to Lloyd Webber like poison in the water supply. *The Producers* was much more than a smash hit; it unloosed decades of pent-up revenge. Critics, New York audiences, local media, and most of all Broadway welcomed *The Producers* with a big sloppy kiss as the second coming of the New York–style musical; the show became symbolic of all that, a return to traditional Broadway values. Mel Brooks was the aging personification of a noisy blockbuster mentality. Yes, shouted the *New York Daily News*, "It's a cast-iron, super-duper mammoth old-time Broadway hit!" The show proclaimed, "Broadway is back! *The Producers* has saved the musical!" For New Yorkers, it seemed a cultural turnaround for a city whose leading heavy industry is musicals, which it exports to the rest of America.

The Producers was exactly how they used to make 'em, a joke-laden musical full of comic songs with nothing to prove, no urgent messages or mawkish sentimentality, and moreover it was a show about Broadway itself, in all of its glitzy glory and manic behavior. With *The Producers*, Brooks revitalized Broadway and reclaimed it as the capital of the kingdom of showbiz. Brooks and his show reigned over Broadway—and it was indeed *very* good to be the king. Howard Kissel in the *New York Daily News* insisted that Brooks must run for mayor. Kissel loved the show's "inescapably New York energy. . . . No new musical in ages has offered so much imagination, so much sheer pleasure. If we make Brooks our mayor, we'll laugh and sing and dance for eight years." Almost: the show ran six years and won a record-setting twelve Tonys, recouping its $10.5 million investment in less than eight months. New York audiences loved, and identified with, the chutzpah embodied by Max Bialystock, a stand-in for Mel Brooks, who might as well have played him. Brooks, a son of New York and a Broadway stepchild, is one showstopper of a guy.

"'Producers' Is Best Show Ever!" cried the *New York Observer*, whose theater critic John Heilpern declared that the show "is, quite simply, the best time you ever could wish for at the theater. The laughs might leave you literally rolling in the aisles. Susan Stroman's production succeeds joyfully at every conceivable level, spiraling traditional musical comedy to delirious new heights. . . . 'The Producers' makes us kvell because it brings to such joyful life that great, lost tradition, the all-American *show*." The musical mocked not just Hitler and Naziism but gays, the elderly and infirm, women, and Jews; Brooks, being Brooks, got away with everything, no matter how politically incorrect or flamboyantly crude, his calling card. He has always gleefully operated beyond courteous PC borders.

The musical was really a nostalgia trip to the Catskills. *Los Angeles Times* critic Reed Johnson called the show's routines belabored and "strip-mined from Brook's own *oeuvre*, right down to Marty Feldman's immortal 'walk this way' from *Young Frankenstein*" (in fact, from vaudeville). Johnson noted that the show was "a fondly remembered but rapidly fading style of comic theater fabricated by hyperbolic Jewish humor and Broadway in-jokes." He dismissed the show as "a Times Square darling." Terry Teachout in the *Wall Street Journal* said, "It occurred to me that what I was witnessing was . . . the last gasp of a dying comic language. 'The Producers' is nothing more (or less) than a virtuoso reminiscence of the lapel-grabbing, kill-for-a-laugh schtickery on which so much of the stand-up comedy of my youth was based."

"'The Producers,'" wrote one critic, "was a love letter from Broadway to itself, told with the sort of theatrical panache that doesn't exist anymore." Another said the show "is designed for showbiz-savvy literates" but guessed that "two-thirds of the show sails entirely over the heads of the audience." All of which explains its blockbuster status in New York. The musical didn't play that well in London, where *Observer* critic Matt Wolf sniped that its success in New York was "the ultimate showbiz love-in in a city that thrives on precisely that." *The Producers* was in fact a modestly amusing show, but its loudly trumpeted success by the media, thanks to the show's own noisy advance man Mel Brooks, and his ruthless marketing, created an irresistible force, which quickly collapsed when Nathan Lane and Matthew Broderick left the show and it was forced to exist on its own merits.

In fact, neither actor was really as right for his role as Zero Mostel and Gene Wilder in the film—Broderick especially, who has never seemed a persuasive schnook, like Wilder, but more of an actor playing a schnook, ever so cutely. Lane was likable but mechanical, without the innate, effortless, manic exuberance Mostel brought to the part. The role requires a crude Jewish vulgarian, and Lane tends to read civilized, gentile, and gay; he lacked Mostel's larger than life bluster and sheer physicality. When Lane and Broderick returned to the show, the news got second-coming treatment—further evidence of New Yorkers rolling over for a show once it has been certified a Colossal Hit. And if maybe it isn't all that colossal, New Yorkers vowed, then, by God, we'll make it one!

Brooks's score is really just an excuse to mock—no, not Hitler so much as over-the-top Broadway production numbers. Easily the best reason to see *The Producers* was **"Springtime for Hitler,"** a fabulous showstopper parody and the climactic moment of a crafty scheme by hustler Max Bialystock to write a blockbuster failure and make off with all of his little old lady investors' money. It's the title number of his show within a show about the glories of Nazi Germany—a peppy salute to der Führer. *New York Times* critic Ben

Brantley called the show "above all a celebration of theater, wallowing happily in every showbiz cliché it sends up . . . a big Broadway book musical that is so ecstatically drunk on its power to entertain that it leaves you delirious, too."

In the musical, director-choreographer Susan Stroman matched Brooks's zaniness, shtick for shtick and, in her trademark style, let out all the stops (and props)—like the number in which Max's wealthy old dowager backers become a chorus line with walkers. Brooks devised some amusing songs—"I Wanna Be a Producer," "Keep It Gay," "That Face"—but "Springtime for Hitler" is the centerpiece that audiences waited to see, Mel Brooks at his most gleefully irreverent. For some, though, the titillation and excitement slid downhill after the crazy Nazi number. Gary Beach was the original high-stepping Herr Hitler who salutes himself ("Heil to me!"), surrounded by gorgeous chorus girls in brown shirts, like fascist Rockettes. In the number's showstopper moment, they form a rotating swastika, with goose-stepping chorines, mimicking a Busby Berkeley routine.

The goofier Stroman's choreography got, the better, as Brooks's lyrics pay homage ostensibly to the Third Reich but, in reality, to *42nd Street*, to Gower Champion, Bob Fosse, Michael Bennett, and Broadway itself. Brooks, a show tune fanatic, knows his musicals, and the song perfectly mirrors the extravagant spirit of musicals past: "Springtime for Hitler and Germany, / Deutschland is happy and gay!" the lead storm trooper warbles. "We're marching to a faster pace, / Look out, here comes the master race!" At one point, a recording of Brooks's gravelly voice cries out, "Don't be stupid, be a smarty, come and join the Nazi party!" A few stanzas later Hitler sings, "I was just a paper hanger, / No one more obscurer, / Got a phone call from the Reichstag, / Told me I was Fuhrer."

In the original nonmusical movie *The Producers*, "Springtime for Hitler" was staged by Alan Johnson, but in the Broadway version Stroman made the number hers: "The whole point of the musical is to produce the worst show ever written in order to get all the investment money—so it had to have some moments in it that would be quite shocking. One of them is Hitler coming and sitting on the edge of the stage like Judy Garland. I turned that story into a huge production number, *as if* I were Roger de Bris [the flouncing director-choreographer character] doing a number. I had to put myself in his shoes. How would *he* do that?"

Nothing in the score measures up to the epic nonsense of "Springtime for Hitler," and only a couple of numbers even approach it—the tap-dancing old ladies with walkers, a routine with showgirls popping out of filing cabinets in Leo Bloom's fantasy of a producer's life. Otherwise, it's a festive but fairly ordinary score that the costars' manic antics and Stroman's inspired staging neatly obscures. When you listen to the cast recording, the naked score minus the visual pizzazz lacks much lasting charm or verbal wit.

When I first saw the show, the audience entered giggling and howled at set-up lines, in stitches over easy jokes, at every pop-eyed grimace and screech by Broderick, at every bellow and leer by Lane. This happens when allegedly seasoned playgoers lose their collective marbles over a show they've been programmed to love. *The Producers* was largely a PR smash that refused to be denied. New York had made up its mind. You couldn't hear the jokes for the hysteria. Audiences became a live laugh track, as if intent upon proving that their wildly sought-after tickets, bought at astronomical prices, somehow confirmed the show's stupendousness. To admit otherwise might be to concede that perhaps they had bought a lemon.

BACKSTAGE DISH

+ The 1968 movie *The Producers*, which had only two songs, was originally called *Springtime for Hitler* until *its* producer, Joseph E. Levine, persuaded Brooks to change it to something less provocative. It was an idea Brooks said he had first imagined as a *Your Show of Shows* sketch, with Sid Caesar as Max Bialystock, but it never saw the light of TV; he also envisioned it as a novel. Critic J. Hoberman said that "no movie has ever succeeded so well in reducing Totalitarianism to travesty" in "one tawdry show biz episode." (Chaplin's *The Great Dictator* might also make that claim.) *The Producers* movie is now considered a cult classic, but it was only a mild success, dismissed by Pauline Kael as "a violently mixed bag" and by Renata Adler in the *New York Times* as "shoddy and gross and cruel." Music to Mel Brooks's ears.

+ Brooks claims he based Bialystock on an actual unnamed producer he once worked for "who made love to a different little old lady investor every afternoon on a leather couch in his office." *Time* magazine guessed that Max was likely based on Broadway's ultimate conniving rascal, David Merrick. But an identical idea—a Broadway producer making a windfall out of a flop—was also the plot of a 1932 Moss Hart–Irving Berlin musical, *Face the Music*.

+ It was not Mel Brooks but David Geffen, the movie mogul, who supposedly got Brooks to turn the film into a Broadway musical. "Everything about the movie spoke to me that this had the potential to be a terrific musical comedy," said Geffen, who pledged to back the show. "It's a classic structure. The movie has music in it already. It was conceived as a play and turned into a movie, so it had that kind of structure." Geffen wasn't the first producer to suggest making a musical of the movie, but Brooks said no until Geffen allegedly wore him down, though it's hard to imagine Brooks resisting an idea so squarely in his crosshairs. Geffen later pulled out of the deal, forcing Brooks and cowriter Thomas Meehan to scramble for investors. In the end, so many would-be investors wanted in that three hundred names had to be drawn from a hat.

✦ Brooks's first choice to write the score was Jerry Herman, who told him that the obvious guy to write the songs was Mel Brooks. What surprised people was how Brooks suddenly emerged out of nowhere as a songwriter; skeptics wondered if he had actually written the music himself. Brooks said his late wife Anne Bancroft had suggested he compose the score: "You're musical, you're a good singer, and you've been talking my head off ever since I met you about how much you want to be a songwriter. So take a pad, a pencil, go into the next room, and I bet within an hour you'll come out with a very nice song." It took him an hour and a month to come up with a super nice song, "Springtime for Hitler," which he composed, as he did all his songs, by humming tunes into a tape recorder that an arranger, Glen Kelly, transcribed into notes on a page; Kelly turned Brooks's primitive tunes into playable songs. He told Richard Christiansen of the *Chicago Tribune*, "Don't forget. I wrote a lot of songs on *Your Show of Shows*. I wanted to write the score for this musical, but nobody was sure I could write music. They knew I could write lyrics." He adds, "Once I started writing them, I couldn't stop."

✦ The show was a victim of its own hype machine. Attempts to replace Nathan Lane with British actor Henry Goodman, unceremoniously canned, and then with Brad Oscar, revealed that the show's success was tied to its original costars. Many playgoers and summer tourists, eager to shell out $100 or more (dirt cheap these days), might have been disappointed to find a just OK musical encased in the protective Bubble Wrap of PR packaging.

✦ The show sabotaged its built-in goodwill when producer Rocco Landesman, Brooks, and their cohorts grew as greedy as Max Bialystock and decided to go toe-to-toe with scalpers, charging $480 a ticket for "premium seating," nearly five times the 2001 high of $100 a ticket. It was institutionalized scalping. Landesman defended the price gouging by saying, in effect, that rather than unscrupulous scalpers, unscrupulous producers deserved to profit. Few people were convinced, and the beloved Brooks was labeled an opportunistic money-grubber. Suddenly Mel Brooks was no longer Broadway's lovable happy warrior.

The legal heist unleashed weeks of bad press in New York and outraged letters to the editor from ordinary ticket buyers forced to settle for second-rate seats. Even Lane accused his producers of "a new kind of greediness." The show was selling out (one day, it sold more than $1 million in tickets). Critic John Heilpern, one of the show's biggest enthusiasts, turned against it, calling it "the most laughably unacceptable example of greed in the history of beautiful Broadway." The New York State attorney general, Eliot Spitzer, applauded the move as a way to stop scalping, but it just moved the practice indoors, into the box office. Max Bialystock could not have cooked up a cannier con job.

WICKED

(2003)

"Popular," "Defying Gravity"

Wicked has a real story buried under all of its hokey special effects, but it's hard to find, and almost as hard to care much about—unless you're a fifteen-year-old girl with identity problems. The musical, yet another revisionist *Wizard of Oz*, is ingeniously engineered to bowl you over with spectacle—literal smoke and mirrors that blind you to an emotional connection with the main characters. The songs by Stephen Schwartz, with a couple of endearing exceptions, are long, loud, and lyrically incomprehensible to the naked ear (mine anyway). Almost every spoken line, not just the lyrics, is screamed.

Like many musicals today, the show's guiding principle behind each song seems to be, if it's shouted loudly enough it must be a sensational showstopper. The lyrics may be brilliant if you can catch them, but somehow I doubt it. In any case, nobody who loves *Wicked* much cares, mainly adolescent girls who identify with the need to fit in, like Elphaba, the witchy outcast with the green face.

Many young girls have seen the show more than once, as if hoping its fairy dust will rub off on them. *Wicked* is a kind of phenomenon—a worldwide hit that has also become a rite of passage for female playgoers seeking empowerment. Nobody goes to *The King and I* or *Chicago* to be cleansed, but adolescent girls return to *Wicked* as if journeying to Lourdes. Noted Jason Zinoman in a *New York Times* piece, "Its popularity among teenage girls borders on the religious." The credit for much of this goes to book writer Winnie Holzman, who created the 1990s TV series *My So-Called Life* (*Wicked* is its second so-called life), which also wallowed in teenage angst and self-loathing. It was a cult TV show and went on to become a novel, memoir, and movie cliché. The musical covers all the familiar adolescent bases—love lost, bullying, insecurity, or in the words of one writer "the painful beauty and the beast of teenage despair." *New York Times* critic Ben Brantley referred to such shows as "shameless emotional button-pushers" that "come rushing at you head-on, all but screaming, 'Love me! Love me!'"

Beyond its presumed healing powers, *Wicked* is mainly out to dazzle you by employing every theatrical effect in director Joe Mantello's bag of staging tricks, hoping to mow us down or wear us out. The show is a concert stuffed with garish, no longer so special effects—monsters and gargoyles galore (a fire-breathing dragon, kids!), flashing lights, and thumping theatrics, sound and fury signifying, well, sound and fury. Theater reporter Jesse Green, in a 2009 *New York Times* piece titled "The Triumph of Bombast," wrote about "a new baseline of 'theatricality' that even top directors and performers seem powerless to resist," specifically "blockbuster entertainments geared to ADHD teenagers . . . [that are] desperately trying to attain the condition (and thus the audience) of summer films."

It's all about a good-hearted grounded girl who befriends an unfairly maligned, messed-up "bad" girl. The fairy tale plays off, exploits, and demolishes *The Wizard of Oz*, by now an exhausted source. It taps into the most gaudy aspects of modern pop culture: Las Vegas, *Star Wars*, and the Harry Potter/Hobbit books of wizards, gnomes, and goblins. The show is a festival of amusement park shtick amid the wailing songs, known as "power ballads" (translation: *LOUD!*). The overall effect, said one critic, is "the to-the-barricades sound of *Les Misérables* anthems." Schwartz's relentlessly upbeat score, wrote a critic, is filled with "bland anthems written in an easy-listening Broadway pop mode."

Wicked is a bad-taste extravaganza, so maybe it's no wonder the show is a monster hit with the easily entertained *Cats/Cirque du Soleil* crowd that really wants to see a circus, not a genuine musical, one complete with flying monkeys. The show is efficiently engineered to dazzle out-of-towners. Since it opened in 2003, *Wicked* has become not just a must-see musical but a tourist attraction for playgoers taking selfies under the Gershwin Theater marquee to show the folks back in Topeka. The lobby is a boutique of pricey *Wicked* mementos.

So millions of people have adored *Wicked*, if not many critics, but one wicked playgoing naysayer, JRombold, e-mailed the *New York Times* online in 2014: "I mostly remember thinking, *What's wrong with me?* Everyone else in the theater was laughing, crying and singing along. My only tears were from boredom." Assaulted by the musical's insistent razzle-dazzle, I too found it hard to stay interested, let alone involved in what was happening in Wickedland. The musical trades on the 1939 movie's treasured name but doesn't enhance it, musically, magically, or otherwise.

The show's two lead characters—thrown-together college roommates Glinda and Elphaba, an aggressive, sharp-tongued witch who secretly yearns to be as beloved as her peppy, spoiled, pink and blonde counterpart—bear scant resemblance to recognizable people. But even as metaphors they don't really register unless you're a pubescent girl who feels like a wretched witch.

The actresses who originated the two witches skipped up the yellow brick road to fame—Kristin Chenoweth as the sugary, bubbly, snobby Glinda (a funny airhead parody) and Idina Menzel in the star-making role of misunderstood Elphaba. Menzel's "metallic voice," wrote critic Charles Isherwood, "cuts through the synthesizer-heavy orchestrations with an ease and electricity that inspires shivers." Elphaba's evildoing, we learn, is really a 911 call. That pretty much sums up the musical's feel-good mind-set in what is a two-hour class in self-realization set to music, promoting the chronic all-American self-help myth that a woebegone girl can be changed and restored and achieve bliss overnight, especially after seeing a smash musical.

In a bizarre comparison, *Wicked* is your basic *My Fair Lady* makeover story about a miserable, unhappy girl who, through the powers of love, or redemption, or something, is turned into a cheery, self-confident, appealing woman; it all began with that darn ugly duckling who turned into a lovely well-adjusted swan. One seasoned playgoer called the show "a *Fantasticks* for little women." See also *Frozen*. Go girl power!

People forget that when *Wicked* first opened on Broadway, it was met with nearly universal critical disdain. "An overproduced, overblown, confusingly dark and laboriously ambitious jumble," scoffed a *Newsday* critic.

The convoluted plot is a thicket of entangled story lines, themes, and characters, but you *will* learn why the wicked witch is green and hangs out with flying monkeys. The *New Yorker* reviewer similarly sneered, "The show's 22 songs were written by Stephen Schwartz, and not one of them is memorable." *Variety*'s Isherwood called the show "a strenuous effort to be all things to all people," which "weighs down this lumbering, overstuffed production . . . stridently earnest one minute, self-mocking the next; a fantastical allegory about the perils of fascism in one scene, a Nickelodeon special about the importance of inner beauty in another."

On the show's tenth anniversary, Isherwood (by then at the *New York Times*) returned to *Wicked* and liked it even less, saying that the performance he attended "teemed with bopping tweens and their families. Many of the girls clearly knew the show's score already, greeting Mr. Schwartz's polished Broadway-pop confections and throat-searing ballads with the physical equivalent of a half-dozen smiley-faced emoticons." He observed how "female empowerment has become a snow-balling trend" in shows. Ben Brantley closed his opening-night review on a sour note: "*Wicked* does not, alas, speak hopefully for the future of the Broadway musical."

Indeed, shows like *Wicked* have little future themselves. The spectacle that makes them a hit is too expensive for later revivals. Likewise, shows such as *The Lion King*, *The Phantom of the Opera*, and *Cats*, which have had endless runs on Broadway, but you're unlikely to ever see them at your local community theater. But after thirteen years, forty million plus playgoers, and more than $3 billion in ticket sales, *Wicked* has no plans to go away any time soon.

The musical is based on a 1995 novel by Gregory Maguire about an earlier trip down that well-traveled yellow path, but before Dorothy lands in Oz, which one critic called "a windy exercise in literary subversion." It's both a prequel and a sequel (but a long way from an equal) to the original *Oz*. Kevin Fallon, in *New York* magazine, blamed the show for the "backstory" fad, which gave rise to prequels that suck the lifeblood from classic tales to pump into presold new versions—*Gone with the Wind* from Mammy's point of view, the real story behind *The Great Gatsby*. Coming soon: *Moby-Dick* told from the whale's perspective. Fallon pointed out the show's mishmash of "earnestness, irony and activism," with "preachy messages about equal rights and animal cruelty." In *Wicked*, every righteous button gets pushed before it ends with the two former rivals embracing, as unloved Elphaba finally wins her halo. But film director John Waters was distraught: "I didn't like *Wicked*. They made my hero Margaret Hamilton [MGM's wicked witch] into an ingénue!"

The show is part of what Fallon called "the race for each new [Broadway] show to out-spectacle the one before," all of which started in the 1980s with *Cats* and continued with *Miss Saigon, The Phantom of the Opera, The Lion King*, and *Beauty and the Beast*, a succession of light shows, fireworks, stunts, and stuff hurtling from the ceiling, culminating in *Spider-Man: Turn Off the Dark*. Audiences—ever since Mary Martin's Peter Pan—love to see actors dangling overhead. "Bombast was trumping originality and critics were at the end of their ropes with it," wrote Fallon. Well, not quite—it's the critics who should be blamed for praising the pyrotechnics. But in shows like *Cats* and *Phantom*, canny marketing and the Internet have made theater critics impotent and superfluous.

Many a major critic dumped on *Wicked*, like Brantley, who wrote about a "bloated production that [spent] close to three hours flapping its over-sized wings without taking off." Even so, Brantley and others went gaga over the female leads, which was sufficient for the show to take off, indeed soar. In his book about *Wicked*, Paul R. Laird notes how many critics failed to appreciate the show's qualities or anticipate its great success. In a 2008 essay in *Theater Journal*, Ellen Wolf claims that the relationship between Glinda and Elphaba is actually "a queer and feminist romance." How did I ever miss that?

The best song in the show, **"Popular,"** is a clever and appealing comic number out of an earlier Broadway tradition. It would have been right at home in *Bye Bye Birdie* or *Grease*. This is Stephen Schwartz wearing his bright Broadway hat, not his rock concert baseball cap. The chirpy ode to popularity was first sung by the sparkly, ever-spunky Chenoweth in what one critic called her "bright bugle of a voice." Schwartz based Glinda on high school cheerleaders—"the most popular girl at school who always went with the captain of the football team. She was always the homecoming queen, blonde with a perky nose." Schwartz compared "Popular" to the film *Clueless*, but Glinda seems closer to the ruthlessly perky Reese Witherspoon in *Legally Blonde*, possibly crossed, suggested a critic, with dithery film actress Billie Burke.

Schwartz, who wrote the number with Chenoweth in mind, described the bubblegum song as "empty calories," but the lyrics are funny and pointed, Schwartz at his best, most clever, and least overblown; Glinda tells Elphaba that her heart truly goes out to anyone less popular than she, especially such a needy case who cries out for a makeover. Glinda says she knows exactly how to fix Elphaba's flaws by teaching her all the tricks to use with boys, how to flirt, arrange her hair—everything that matters. She'll instruct her in how to understand sports, learn the right slang, and emerge as really popular—"just not quite as popular as me!" "Popular" is so good it deserves to be in a better show. It's a wicked little dig at shallow "popularity." Glinda amusingly lays out all the girly tricks of surefire popularity to Elphaba and how she has mastered each ploy. It's one of Stephen Schwartz's wittiest, most insightful songs, and you catch Chenoweth delivering the number with consummate savvy and charm.

Whenever Glinda pipes the word "popular," she gives it a hiccuppy spin, almost a yodel ("popu-oo-lar"), first delivered by Chenoweth in her baby doll bleat. Ben Brantley (who christened Chenoweth's career with his ecstatic review of her as Sally in a 1999 Broadway revival of *You're a Good Man, Charlie Brown*) gave the actress another big hug in his review of *Wicked*, writing that Chenoweth "is giving jaw-dropping demonstrations of the science of show-biz aeronautics in *Wicked.*"

Brantley slammed the musical itself as a "technicolored sermon of a musical . . . an arch and earnest show," but Glinda could do no wrong: "Ms. Chenoweth must put across jokes and sight gags that could make angels fall. Never for a second, though, does she threaten to crash to earth . . . proving that in the perilous skies of Broadway, nothing can top undiluted star power as aviation fuel." He was plainly still in love, a stage crush that critics declare in public mash notes. (I'm equally guilty, having written open love letters to Karen Ziemba, Lee Remick, Florence Henderson, and Gilda Radner, among others. It's an occupational hazard.)

Brantley's show-stopping review of Chenoweth might well be what got *Wicked* airborne. He damned with faint praise Idina Menzel's performance as Elphaba, writing that "she opens up her voice in flashy ways that should be required study for all future contestants on 'American Idol.' . . . But even such committed intensity is no match for Ms. Chenoweth's variety. . . . It's amazing how she keeps metamorphosing before your eyes and ears." He said she "evokes everyone from Jeanette MacDonald to Cameron Diaz, from Mary Martin to Madonna" and notes that she's so good it throws the show out of whack, because we're not supposed to root for her but for the underdog Elphaba. "What Ms. Chenoweth manages to do with the lyrics of a song of self-admiration called 'Popular' is a master class in musical phrasing." He blatantly swoons, "I was so blissed out whenever Glinda was onstage that I never felt I was wasting my time at *Wicked*. I just kept smiling in anticipation of her return when she wasn't around." Get this man a cold compress.

Brantley hit the nail on the head when he wrote that Menzel will "dazzle audience members whose taste runs to soft-rock stations. But for aficionados of the American musical, it's Ms. Chenoweth who's the real thing, melding decades of performing tradition into something shiny and new." Schwartz, who, since *Pippin*, has kept one foot in Broadway past and the other in Broadway present, tries to have it both ways in this score, offsetting the light comic "Popular" with the dark cry of "Defying Gravity."

"Wonderful," the other more traditional, catchy number in the show, rarely gets mentioned, maybe because it seems like it's also from a different, earlier musical. It's almost a throwaway number, but Joel Grey never throws anything away. "Wonderful" very much embodied Grey's vaudeville style; he even added a little dance.

As with "Mr. Cellophane" in *Chicago*, Grey turned down the Wizard role at first. "It didn't sound to me like there was a character there," he says. "The only way I would do it is to know who that person is in the song. I figured that the character always wanted to be a good father. It makes him an innocent of sorts and not a bad guy." Grey gave "Wonderful" the same low-key treatment and charm he brought to "Mr. Cellophane." *Wicked* doesn't seem a Joel Grey kind of show, but it is. "I loved it. I thought it was great, different from anything anybody had ever done. It became like a rock concert, with all those kids loving it so much." Just like Mr. Cellophane, his own presence in *Wicked* was all but passed over.

"Defying Gravity" is the show's emotional high point (literally), as Elphaba, reborn, rises Christlike to the ceiling, suddenly weightless as she rids herself of her demons and announces the new improved and empowered Elphaba, singing that she accepts her limitations but that, "defying gravity," nobody can keep her down.

Schwartz wrote meaningful lyrics to "Defying Gravity," but you need a song sheet to follow them above a pounding orchestra and Idina Menzel in rip-your-heart-out pop diva mode. Stephen Holden, reviewing Menzel's cabaret act, noted that she "is in the slightly absurd position of being a 43-year-old symbol of tween girl power." At the end, Glinda joins Elphaba in a duet, vowing their mutual affection and sisterhood. All join hands. Menzel rode the number to showbiz glory, and good for her, but mainly it's an exercise in mechanical showbiz chicanery.

●●●●●●●●●●●●●● BACKSTAGE DISH ●●●●●●●●●●●●●●

+ As an inside musical joke, in what he calls a tribute to composer Harold Arlen, Stephen Schwartz incorporated the first seven notes of "Over the Rainbow" into the song "Unlimited." Schwartz deftly dodged a lawsuit by the Arlen estate by not including an eighth note, which he says is where the copyright law kicks in. He disguised his good-humored theft by changing the tune's rhythm and reharmonizing it.

✦ More *Wicked* trivia to impress your friends: the wicked witch has no name in the original L. Frank Baum book, so Maguire devised one for her by using Baum's initials: LFB.

✦ According to New York writer David Sheward and author Paul R. Laird, the reigning authority on the show, the electronics in *Wicked* generate enough power to supply twelve homes, using five miles of cables, and it takes 250 pounds of dry ice to create the smokey effects onstage. The show's single most electrifying effect, at the close of act 1, is when Elphaba rises from the Wizard's palace and ascends high above the stage—without wires. The trick is done by having the actress run across the stage to a hidden deck that rises, operated by the actress. Tech production manager Jake Bell explains the illusion: "When Elphaba steps into the device, it locks, she's standing in a steel plate, and the whole thing lifts her off the ground and it looks like her skirt is extending and she's flying." Thus far no actresses have been squashed in the making of this number.

• •

Stephen Schwartz is an unlikely looking songwriter, a compact man of sixty-seven with a wrestler's taut muscled torso who is an easy conversationalist. We spoke in his hotel room in San Francisco, then segued to lunch.

You were a transition between traditional Broadway show tunes and today's Broadway pop sound.
I think I was one of the first, along with a couple of contemporaries. I would cite Andrew Lloyd Webber and Alan Menken also. We are all more or less the same age. We were the first in musical theater that brought in rock or pop music into musical theater, starting in the late sixties, which came into prominence in the seventies. For a while we encountered quite a good deal of resistance from people writing about musical theater. The theory was that you couldn't actually write theater songs in a pop style and you couldn't use that style to portray characters. Obviously it is not true. Contemporary musical theater now is virtually nothing but pop music.

At the time there was a lot of critical opinion that it was basically anathema to the business of musical theater. I think the critics were bothered by it, but I think in addition to that, they genuinely felt if you tried to portray a character, he or she simply couldn't sing in that style and be believable as a character. Obviously that has been proven to be nonsense. The New York critics saw a show that was visually spectacular, that had big sets and lavish costumes, and they felt that it couldn't be a show that had a serious content. They were completely wrong, of course. When they went back to see it, they saw beyond the spectacle, which is exactly what most audiences feel the first time. They appreciated that there was content there.

After *Hair*, people thought there would be more shows like that. There weren't any until yours—*Pippin* and *Godspell*—came along four years later. Would you say that *Hair* was a breakthrough?

Unquestionably! *Hair* opened the door for me to have a career. I feel the success of *Hair* and the interest of audiences at the time hearing the kind of music they heard on the radio in the theater made producers look for people who could write like that. Most of us were young and we were able to get a foothold in the Broadway theater at a much younger age than might otherwise have been possible. When pop music became more interesting with the advent of the Beatles, and even Burt Bacharach and the Motown sound, my writing style incorporated that sound and transferred from a more traditional Broadway style.

A friend of mine says that *Wicked* is not just for teenage girls. He says he even knows women his age, in their seventies, who love it because it connects so powerfully with their being young, horny, thoroughly smart, and not knowing what to do with it all.

I love that. I think that is very accurate. I like that very much. The producers of *Wicked* get extremely annoyed when people say it is successful because it's popular with teenage girls. You can't run a show ten years in New York or all over the world if the audience consists entirely of teenage girls.

But it is a young woman's show.

It connects very strongly to women of all ages, but our audiences are not dominated entirely by women. What happened was, a few New York critics that didn't like the show were surprised it became such a huge success despite them, so they invented this myth that it's just for teenage girls.

Many people say *Wicked* is a basic coming-of-age story.

I don't think it is about coming of age. It is about two characters coming into their *own*, reaching a certain kind of empowerment by accepting and embracing who they are. They happen to be women. I know the show is extremely popular with gay men, and particularly young gay men who also find the story about the outsider Elphaba who embraces who she is and becomes powerful that way. I think they find that inspiring. So I don't think it is only for women.

Are there misconceptions people have about your shows and you particularly?

I don't think people always understand that I'm interested in content but also trying to make the show entertaining and diverting for an audience. I do like numbers to land big. Some people don't see the content within all that. I have never been a critic's darling. Maybe they misunderstand my intentions, or they just might not like my work very much. I am not a big fan of musicals that are just there to entertain. That's not my kind of show. It doesn't matter how well done it is. I don't enjoy musicals that are all about tap dancing.

JERSEY BOYS

♦ 2005 ♦

"Can't Take My Eyes Off You," "Sherry"

Purists will argue that *Jersey Boys*, the 2005 show about Frankie Valli and the Four Seasons, has no legitimate business in a book about landmark musical theater showstoppers, because all of the show's songs were leftover hits from the 1950s and '60s. They may be right, but *Jersey Boys* vibrates with its own heartbeat. It's the most successful show of its kind since *Smokey Joe's Cafe* in 1995, featuring songs by Jerry Leiber and Mike Stoller, the first jukebox musical to crack Broadway's charts.

Jersey Boys earns its way onto our Broadway showstopper hit parade because, whereas the show might easily have been just another Top 40 rewind, a makeshift anthology of ancient pop classics, the show, artfully crafted by Marshall Brickman and Rick Elice, is far more than a checklist of re-doo-wop oldies. *Jersey Boys* is an original musical in how it's pieced together, weaving four stories in and out among the songs, a fresh look at how a real pop group was formed, endured internal stresses, and survived, at the same time coloring in background details of the evolving '50s/'60s pop music scene.

The Four Seasons represented the East Coast New York–New Jersey pop aesthetic. There was a cultural basis for their success. In the 1950s, the white pop music world was led by Italian crooners. The Four Seasons—the only pop group ever named for a hotel—represented Italian New Jersey street life, just as the Beach Boys were poster boys for the Southern California sand and surf culture. The groups were archetypes of polar—and bicoastal—opposites, both using falsetto leads and sharing overlapping hits. Before the Beatles wiped them both out, the Four Seasons and the Beach Boys were leaders of their respective packs.

"They were one of the first groups to have three consecutive hits," says *San Francisco Chronicle* senior pop music critic Joel Selvin. "A rock group was good for one hit, then a follow-up might go halfway up the charts and by the third song they were gone. There was no sense of career. Those were just kids that could sing and there were busloads of 'em—the Capris, the Crests, the Del-Vikings, who were integrated, and the black groups were all over the charts—the Coasters and the Platters, who were TV-ready." The Four Seasons was radio-ready. "Those records stood out on the radio at the time," observes Selvin. "They were snappy, there was an appealing texture to them. It was definitely something special. The sound had a sharp stinging attack good for radio, ideally suited for that highly rhythmic pop music."

Part of the musical's appeal, beyond the show and the music itself, is that it was a monster comeback for a nearly forgotten group whose last hit was "December, 1963 (Oh, What a Night)" in 1975. But Valli and the Four Seasons always had a steely survivor instinct. By '75, explains Selvin, "they were done, they were dead. They had a second life with 'Who Loves You,' No. 3 in 1975, and 'Oh, What a Night' got to No. 1. That's astonishing in and of itself, that any pop group could come back after nine years of being dead. These guys had more going on than you think. They didn't exhaust their run, they managed to figure out how to get back on the charts. So there's some cunning there beyond the ordinary." Much of the cunning was Bob Gaudio's, their songwriting muse, described by Selvin as "so smart he's practically disqualified as a musician."

Gaudio's collaborator on all Four Seasons songs, Bob Crewe, was a Philadelphia songwriter who caught the quartet in a club and was blown away when Valli did a Carmen Miranda impression in falsetto. Crewe instantly had them cut an album with a falsetto lead on "Sherry," took the recording to a DJ convention, and made a deal with the R&B Vee Jay label, which issued their first single with a falsetto, followed up by "Walk Like a Man" and "Big Girls Don't Cry," both monster number-one hits.

Selvin, author of books on Ricky Nelson and the Monterey Pop Festival, says *Jersey Boys* got their story just about right: "It was very authentic, not bowdlerized in any respect. They didn't Broadway-up the music—they just gave you the Four Seasons. Some parts were musicalized, but for the most part it's nitty-gritty." He says *Jersey Boys* is not just your standard nostalgia trip. "The ending of the first act is about as perfect a piece of stagecraft as a Broadway musical could be—where they make their TV debut on *The Ed Sullivan Show* with their big hit records and the TV set is behind them with their backs to the audience. That's like the showstopper of all showstoppers, singing 'Sherry.'" He raves, "'Jersey Boys' was such a brilliant invention that nobody will ever be able to do it again. Like the Beach Boys won't be able to do this now. 'Jersey Boys' cracked a nut that's pretty hard to crack."

Even if *Jersey Boys* resembles a jukebox job on the surface, Brickman and Elice's script burrows deeply inside the jukebox to dig out the Four Seasons' roots. It's as much about that era as it is about the singers and their songs. *Jersey Boys* tells a complex tale of the foursome, a journey as worthy of study as *Dreamgirls*, the quasi-fictional version of the Supremes. *Jersey Boys* isn't just a thinly disguised pop concert built for Las Vegas after an out-of-town Broadway tryout, although the show is a tourist stop on the Vegas strip where a Jersey Boys theater was even erected to enshrine the show.

Jersey Boys has the emotions, characters, and layered plot of any good musical. "That's why it is not one of those diluted jukebox musicals but is actually a real story that just happened to have some real songs ready to go," comments John Lloyd Young, who played Frankie Valli on Broadway and in London for two years. "The songs were ready to go, but they were placed in their proper places in the story" to evoke a dramatic response. "If you look structurally at *Jersey Boys* you can say that it doesn't fit like other book musicals, but actually it is *exactly* like other book musicals. They just have put the songs in the places they put showstoppers in dramatic scenes of traditional shows. When the Four Seasons got together to sing 'Sherry' on *The Ed Sullivan Show*, that moment is what made the band famous, so you are witnessing a dramatization of a real event. In this case, many events of the play are the musical moments. Characters in other shows succeed because they get the girl or they succeed in business without really trying. These characters succeeded with music. How could they not use the songs that they were famous for?"

As with *Dreamgirls*, audiences want to learn how four street corner guys became a group and how they coexisted. Young further embellishes his staunch defense of *Jersey Boys* as a dramatic entity:

"You know that the Four Seasons will become the Four Seasons, but you're watching a show about how it happened. They have various humiliations, and it looks as if they are never going to make it. But you see them have the success that you're hoping they'll have because you are invested in them. And then they have the success right in front of you with 'Sherry,' which you only knew from the radio. Suddenly, because of the circumstances of the script and the way the show is built, the song is imbued with the same electric emotional energy that a showstopper has in any other musical with a song written for a certain moment. It has exactly the same structure."

Young goes on, "In 'Can't Take My Eyes Off You' in act 2, everything in Frankie Valli's life has fallen apart when his band has broken up. He needs something to bring him back. That song ['Sherry'] brings him back. The audience sees the character coming back." Young compares it to "the emotional tidal wave" of "Rose's Turn" in *Gypsy*, "when the character sings this song and the emotion just washes out into the audience, and that's why it is such an impactful song." Except that "Rose's Turn," like most musical turning points, furthered the plot, whereas "Sherry" and the other hits don't really do that.

Young's own career plot is fairly dramatic: He was ushering at the same theater, the St. James, a year before he opened there at twenty-eight in *Jersey Boys* in 2005. He was also working days for the same producers at Dodger Theatrical Productions, which wound up producing *Jersey Boys*. "I was an intern at their office and knew them all for years. They were much too busy to know who I was until I starred in their show." He auditioned knowing nothing about Frankie Valli, two lifetimes ahead of his own.

At the time, Young was a serious dramatic actor uninterested in what looked like another jerry-built jukebox musical—what I call "popsicals." "A lot of them were just excuses for stringing songs together from a pop catalog," he says, "so when I got the *Jersey Boys* script I just lumped it into that category and did not go in expecting anything great. By the time I read some scenes, I realized it had real integrity and that there was work for an actor to do and not just as a cheerleader." He was initially turned down but tried out again a year later.

Young fell easily into the role because he is half Italian on his mother's side and drew on his grandfather for male Italian attitudes. "I was not exactly aware of who Frankie Valli was, but I had a good reference of working-class Italian Americans from that area because my grandfather was an Italian from Brooklyn. And Frankie Valli was training to be a hairdresser, another working-class type." Young describes that type: "The scrappy working-class desire to succeed and pushing your way through regardless. There is also a quick temper, which is stereotypical of that kind of person. Also, holding a grudge forever and never letting go, and the petty rivalries."

His major challenge was fusing his persona with that of Valli, whom he came to know after the show opened. Valli and Bob Gaudio, who first got the idea for a Broadway show, stepped aside to let Brickman and Elice fashion the musical their own way. "Because I had not had much exposure to Valli I had to draw from my own imagination of him. I was making my Broadway debut as an unknown, but I was playing somebody who was known already. You have to play your part with integrity and honesty, the way it's written, but you also want to introduce yourself through that part."

Young talks about the subtleties of inhabiting a real person: "On Broadway, the force of personality of a performer is deeply important to how the role is going over. Lots of men played the king in the *King and I*, but the force of personality of Yul Brynner is indelible. When you are in the position to make an impact because you are the first person in a show that's becoming a hit, you want to make sure that your personality is coming through."

Adding to its integrity, *Jersey Boys*, unlike other jukebox showcases, didn't resort to smuggling in pop stars to pump up the musical and keep it running. Playgoers wondered if the distinctive Valli falsetto was Young's true voice. "You can't play Frankie Valli without being able to sing those notes. Mine is a true falsetto that overlapped with the notes that he sang on his recordings. I had to be able to really sing them. A potentially torturous score like this had never been attempted by a singer on a Broadway stage. There was some adrenaline involved, too, because I knew if I didn't step up to the plate in this big show, a multimillion-dollar enterprise could have crumbled and failed. Especially since the show is essentially about the lead singer." The strain of singing falsetto eight times a week, twenty-four songs per performance, often left him, unsurprisingly, with a scratchy voice.

Jersey Boys is a pop showstopper cavalcade but pulls audiences to their feet for "Sherry" at the end of act 1 and "Can't Take My Eyes Off You" in act 2. "Sometimes I would get a standing ovation before I was even done with 'Sherry.' I didn't know that was going to happen." When Young came into the cast for the Broadway run, he was the outsider—unlike the three others who had been in the preview La Jolla Playhouse run. Young says 'Can't Take My Eyes Off You' is a showstopper because of where it lands in the show, not just for the number itself: "I don't think Frankie Valli had rousing standing ovations just for singing 'Can't Take My Eyes Off You.'"

Neither showstopper would be mistaken for Cole Porter songs. Both are standard issue doo-wop tunes with mindless lyrics. **"Can't Take My Eyes Off You"** begins, "You're just too good to be true, / Can't take my eyes off you, / You'd be like heaven to touch, / I want to hold you so much." But it's the dynamic release that sends the song surging and yanks people out of their seats: "I love you, ba-by, and if it's quite all right / I need you, ba-by, to warm the lonely nights. . . . Oh pretty ba-by, now that I found you, sta-ay, / And let me love you, ba-by, let me love you." It's not about the lyrics, baby, it's about the arrangement and imploring melody. Explains Joel Selvin, "It's called a sub-bridge that sets up the final chords rather beautifully."

"Can't Take My Eyes Off You," famous as a background track for a crucial scene in *The Deer Hunter*, is "post rock lounge-pop," in Selvin's niche description. "It finds a middle ground between rock and roll and what we could call adult pop at that time. It's produced and decorated in ways that a Frank Sinatra record wouldn't be, with instrumentation that Tony Bennett would turn up his nose at. The melody and adult sophistication of the lyrics are right in tune with that kind of grown-up song. A huge radio hit in those days. It was played on stations that wouldn't play rock and roll and wouldn't play 'Sherry.' It's graduated from rock and roll. It's a beautiful record."

"Sherry" is even more lyrically banal, with "Sherry, baby" repeated endlessly, but all of those repeated "Sherry baby"s make it as much a power ballad, in its teenybopper way, as anything in *Wicked*. "Sherry" is a simple three-chord progression that, notes Selvin, "was absolutely hand-crafted by Crewe and Gaudio for that purpose, a fairly typical doo-wop song. It's all on the top end, with very little fleshing out."

Jersey Boys didn't trigger standing ovations during the show's preview run on Broadway, Young recalls. "New York can be a hard place. The first few days of previews we had crossed arms and stone faces. These were the real theater insiders, the ones ready to take a shot. When the critics came, the success was deafening. By the first or second week people were coming because they had heard how great it was, and they were ecstatic. When we got to 'Sherry' the arms were not crossed and the faces had turned into amused wonder." The show literally stopped after "Sherry" before they could move to the next scene. "We would be standing there for five minutes before we could move on because they were standing and cheering. The same thing happened after 'Can't Take My Eyes Off You.'"

The 2014 movie version, directed by Clint Eastwood and starring Young, got no standing ovations from the critics or at the box office. Eastwood opened up a stage show that didn't need much opening up or deep background. But Young defends the film: "I think it translates to a film, but you have to watch it as a film. You cannot watch it and want it to be the Broadway show. If you do that you will be confused. There are a million people who didn't see the Broadway show, and for them the *movie* is 'Jersey Boys.'"

PART III:

O SAY CAN YOU HEAR—
BROADWAY ANTHEMS

A version of the rousing showstopper is the soul-stirring anthem for which one feels obliged to fall to one's knees—or to make a hasty retreat. Some are drenched in gooey or maudlin sentimentality. The best can move you into battle, romantic or otherwise, without turning weepy or worshipful. Most of them, good and bad, are cultural touchstones embedded in our brain whether we like it or not.

Musical theater's hardest-working songs are its anthems—usually protest cries or cries for help. Some are powerful expressions of resolve, such as "I Am What I Am" (*La Cage aux Folles*), or rebellion, such as "Do You Hear the People Sing?" (*Les Misérables*), or just the belief in a brighter tomorrow, like "Climb Ev'ry Mountain" (*The Sound of Music*) and "You'll Never Walk Alone" (*Carousel*).

Anthems are urgent pleas from the heart—"Don't Cry for Me Argentina" (*Evita*), "The Impossible Dream (The Quest)" (*Man of La Mancha*); but they are often so weighted with importance they topple over into devotional melodrama—"The Music of the Night" (*The Phantom of the Opera*), "Memory" (*Cats*)—laboring ever so earnestly to be heart-wrenching "experiences." The soggier anthems don't so much stop a show as grind it to a halt while the audience is asked to bow its head and, if possible, shed a tear. The most inspired Broadway anthems can lead you into battle ("One Day More" from *Les Misérables*), proclaim a passionate resolve ("I Am What I Am"), or summon profound, genuine feelings ("Ol' Man River" from *Show Boat*).

SHOW BOAT

◆ 1927 ◆

"Ol' Man River"

The grandfather of Broadway anthems, **"Ol' Man River,"** is perhaps the most powerful number of Oscar Hammerstein and Jerome Kern's long collaboration. It doesn't quite launch *Show Boat* ("Cotton Blossom" is the far cheerier opening), but the next song is clearly its thematic and emotional opener. The moving semispiritual sung by the imposing black stevedore, Joe, establishes the somber mood of the show that told audiences in 1927: this is not your usual perky musical.

Show Boat is really a pageant, with a huge cast (thirty-three speaking parts), a panorama of America and American show business that covers half a century, or tries to, from minstrels and vaudeville to jazz and movies. It even incorporates two old standards in early scenes, "After the Ball" and "Goodbye, My Lady Love," Tin Pan Alley musical snapshots added to lend the show a quasi-documentary feeling.

Show Boat is now recognized as Broadway's most important breakthrough musical (not *Oklahoma!* in 1943, the usual mistaken marker), a musical comedy/tragedy that first integrated music, story, and characters into a unified dramatic play with songs. Unless, of course, you count *Porgy and Bess*, a major challenger, as much opera as musical—a debate that still rages.

The musical's most operatic moment is "Ol' Man River," but other aria contenders include "Mis'ry's Comin' Aroun'," "You Are Love," "Make Believe," and "Bill," whose lyrics by P. G. Wodehouse were for a 1918 musical comedy *Oh, Lady! Lady!!* (cut from the show), which Hammerstein altered for *Show Boat* but gave Wodehouse full credit for.

Integration of course is central to *Show Boat*, with a plot based on the bestselling 1926 novel by Edna Ferber. That in itself was unusual; musicals then were rarely based on books. It deals with miscegenation between a light-skinned black woman, Julie, a mixed-race performer, and her secret illegal marriage to a white man. The ostensible plot is a traditional romance between Magnolia—daughter of cheery *Cotton Blossom* boss Cap'n Andy and his battle-ax wife, Parthy—and Gaylord Ravenal, the definitive riverboat gambler. But what drives the show is a forbidden affair between Julie, a mixed-race child, first played in the show by famed torch singer Helen Morgan (its only 1927 star), and an actor, Steve.

Show Boat was Broadway's first grown-up, socially aware musical, widely praised by theater critics weary of the form's slapdash story lines and farcical sensibility—the sitcoms of their day. Robert Coleman, in the *New York Daily Mirror,* said the show "realized the tremendous possibilities of the musical comedy as an art form."

It was Kern who read the Ferber novel and realized its tremendous musical possibilities, as Ethan Mordden relates in his overview of 1920s musicals, *Make Believe*: Kern called Hammerstein and said, "I haven't finished it yet, but get a copy and read it right away. This is a story in a million. It's a big show, too, grand and touching and really special." Hammerstein asked, "Is Ziegfeld enthusiastic?" Kern laughed and said, "He doesn't know anything about it yet." Ziegfeld's daughter later revealed that the impresario's first choice to write the show was Irving Berlin, but the bottom-line-minded songwriter turned it down as having no commercial potential.

In act 2, the show becomes a hodgepodge of operetta, vaudeville, night-clubs, and Broadway musical, as the sprawling plot spans showbiz between the 1880s and the 1920s, covering too much ground to quite absorb in its jammed second act—but then it *is* a show boat. Even so, producer Florenz Ziegfeld, though moved by the emotional musical, predicted it would be a disaster—"It's just plain suicide for me."

The shrewd old showman was fooled this time: *Show Boat,* sans florid sets and leggy showgirls, became the biggest hit of his career. Music historian Will Friedwald reports that when the show had its first out-of-town preview at the National Theatre in Washington, DC, on November 15, 1927, it ran about four hours. Ziegfeld suggested cutting "Ol' Man River," one of the last songs added to the score. A famous backer of the show, Evalyn Walsh McLean, owner of the Hope Diamond, vigorously objected and told Ziegfeld that if the song was not the show's hit she would hand over her favorite bauble. Two months later, *Show Boat* opened to raves and Evalyn McLean still had her diamond.

The original three-hour show is so packed with songs—even great secondary numbers like "Why Do I Love You?," "I Might Fall Back on You," "Hey, Feller"—that the entire score is rarely done, but Francesco Zambello produced a rare complete landmark version in 2012, the first time a virtually complete score of *Show Boat* was performed in major opera houses and on radio. In 2015, *Great Performances* performed a semistaged concert; John

McGlinn produced a superb CD, with Frederica Von Stade, Jerry Hadley, and Karla Burns, that captures the show's sumptuous bounty. Hal Prince produced the last Broadway revival in 1994, with a captivating cast—Rebecca Luker, Lonette McKee, Robert Morse, and Elaine Stritch.

"Ol' Man River" gets deeper and more moving the older you get. When I first heard it, in my twenties, it struck me as a tedious dirge, and I found the river metaphor a little corny. A lifetime later, I finally got it. Kern's music has the ageless cadences of the Mississippi, evoking the unchanging nature of a river that has silently witnessed the nation's troubled history and human upheaval that Hammerstein's somber lyric expresses with almost biblical simplicity.

The words have such authentic feeling that many who first heard the song assumed it was an old Negro spiritual instead of, in author Mark Steyn's phrase, just "a show tune cooked up in 1927 by two guys who needed something for a spot in the first act." The show, by two white men, feels as aware of popular song's black roots as *Porgy and Bess* (also the work of white writers) because of the presence of Joe and his woman Queenie. Indeed, a song that reveals Julie's heritage, "Can't Help Lovin' Dat Man," sounds as if it were cut

Paul Robeson, contemplating "Ol' Man River" in the 1936 film version of *Show Boat*.

from *Porgy and Bess*; the play that musical is based on, *Porgy*, opened just two months before *Show Boat*.

The first word in the song, "niggers," in the most charged opening line of any Broadway song ("Niggers all work on de Mississippi"), caused endless controversy, and has been changed to everything from "darkies" to "black folks" to, after World War II, "colored folks" (the most recently accepted version). In Frank Sinatra's version the line was totally bleached out—"Here we all work 'long the Mississippi." Al Jolson—in whiteface!—made it "lots of folks."

The movie version changed "niggers" to "darkies." Bing Crosby had a hit recording with Paul Whiteman's orchestra, sung in an up-tempo rhythm. Few women have sung it, but Judy Garland recorded it. Song parodist Stan Freberg weighed in with his politically and grammatically correct version, "Elderly Man River" ("You and I, we perspire and strain"). Nearly every pop singer, some unwisely, has been unable to resist the song, from Sam Cooke and Bo Diddley to Rosemary Clooney and Cher.

Jules Bledsoe first sang it in the '27 Broadway show, but it's become identified forever with Paul Robeson, who performed the powerful definitive version in the landmark 1936 black-and-white movie of the show, his rumbling voice rolling along like the river. Robeson had to turn down the offer to introduce the song in the Broadway show because of European concerts; even before *Show Boat* he was in demand after appearing in Eugene O'Neill's *The Emperor Jones* and *All God's Chillun Got Wings*. Kern said it was Robeson's speaking voice, first heard in a play called *Black Boy*, that inspired him.

Bledsoe's rendition was more intensely dramatic than Robeson's effective ruminative version, sung offhand as he sits on the dock whittling a stick. "Robeson took a no-frills approach" to the song, writes Todd Decker in *Who Should Sing Ol' Man River?*, an exhaustive deconstruction of the song and its history. Robeson gave the song a grandeur and dignity that elevated its stature and fills out Joe's character in the show; in the Ferber novel he's a minor figure. Robeson later sang the song onstage, in London in 1928, on Broadway in 1932, and in Los Angeles in 1940.

Robeson altered the lyrics and dialect over the years in concerts and rallies, switching "Dere's an old man called de Mississippi, / Dat's de ol man that I'd like to be" to "There's an old man called the Mississippi. / That's the old man I don't like to be." Rather than "tote dat barge! / Lif' dat bale! / Git a little drunk / An' you land in jail," Robeson made it "Tote that barge and lift that bale! / You show a little grit / And you land in jail." And in place of "Ah gits weary / An' sick of tryin'; / Ah'm tired of livin' an' skeered of dyin',"

Robeson sang, "But I keeps laffin' / Instead of cryin'; / I must keep fightin' / Until I'm dyin'." Robeson's delivery was subtler than Bledsoe's, observes Will Friedwald; Robeson dispensed with Bledsoe's operatic histrionics.

Robeson, a rebel, communist, and black activist, had his reasons for the changes—he hoped to make the number seem less self-pitying—but Hammerstein pretty much got it right the first time. Robeson wished to make it a defiant statement, but it changes Joe from a resigned black man with no hope of bettering himself to a man of fierce determination, not at all what Hammerstein had in mind. The changes may make a noble political statement, but they also make the lyrics false to the period when the show is set. Changing "niggers" for modern sensitivities dilutes the impact of the forlorn song, meant to describe the black man's lowly status and plight at the time. The change is as well-meaning but wrongheaded as banning *The Adventures of Huckleberry Finn* from schools because Mark Twain uses "nigger"—but ironically, to reveal the built-in brutality of the word in contrast to the gentle nature of Jim, Huck's fatherly mentor on the raft.

Duke Ellington also objected to the dialect of such songs, which he labeled "lampblack Negroisms" ("Dere's an old man," "He don' say nothin'"), today regarded as highly politically incorrect, even if the language attempted to approximate the vernacular of impoverished Southern blacks in the late 1800s. A major black Baltimore newspaper told readers to switch radio stations that played the song (also "Old Black Joe" and "Old Folks at Home"). Blacks are always "old" in these songs, maybe to render them harmless?

Hammerstein never intended "Ol' Man River" to be a protest song, even if some choose to read it that way, and a few singers have so delivered it. He meant for it to reflect the dreary, unrelenting reality of the black man's life. Hammerstein said, years later, that the song could be taken as a civil rights protest (especially the phrase "de land ain't free"), but he "wasn't conscious of writing that at the time," and commented, "I put the song into the throat of a character who is a rugged and untutored philosopher. It's a song of resignation with an implied protest."

Hammerstein wasn't in a protest mood when he wrote it, but its mournful message comes through clearly, all the more so because the lyricist isn't giving us a moral lesson, as in Hammerstein's "You've Got to Be Carefully Taught." Its timeless theme, trying to find meaning in a harsh, silent, relentless universe, almost transcends race: "Ah gits weary / An' sick of tryin'; Ah'm tired of livin' / An' skeered of dyin'." The song's epic sweep includes everyone who sweats and strains, day in and day out, and wonders what the point of it all is.

A rarely sung second verse more directly goes to the heart of slave life: "Don' look up / And don' look down—You don' dast make / De white boss frown. / Bend your knees / An' bow your head, / An' pull dat rope / Until yo' dead."

By virtue of Robeson singing it at civil rights events, the song slowly became politicized. Writes Friedwald, "By now, Robeson [was] no longer singing as Joe, riverboat laborer and rugged philosopher; he's singing as Paul Robeson, freedom fighter." Friedwald adds, "When a well-grounded basso like Paul Robeson belts it out, the attitude conveyed is not one of complaint but of overwhelming strength, which could be interpreted as representing the solidarity of the black race. . . . No matter which angle you view it from, 'Ol' Man River' is, more than anything, a heroic song."

This is a good spot to repeat an oft-told story of a party attended by Kern's and Hammerstein's wives where the hostess introduced them to the other guests. "This is Mrs. Jerome Kern," she said proudly. "Her husband wrote 'Ol' Man River.'" "Not true," said Dorothy Hammerstein, standing nearby. "Mrs. Kern's husband wrote *dum-dum-dee-dah. My* husband wrote "Ol' Man River.'"

Edna Ferber recalls in her memoir when Kern and Hammerstein first played her "Ol' Man River" to get her reaction: "The music mounted and mounted and mounted and I give you my word, my hair stood on end, tears came to my eyes. I knew this wasn't just a musical comedy number. This was a great song. This was a song that would outlast Kern and Hammerstein's day and my day and your day." And so it has. Hugh Fordin says in his Hammerstein biography that the lyricist wanted to find a theme that would help tie together the plot's many elements, and he found his unifying idea in the Mississippi River. Hammerstein later admitted he had never set eyes on the Mississippi when he wrote the song.

The lyrics are expressed in conversational style, with few rhymes, more sorrowful soliloquy than song. Hammerstein notes in his lyrics collection, "There should not be too many rhymes. Rhyme should be unassertive, never standing out too noticeably, for if a listener is made too rhyme conscious, his interest may be diverted from the story of a song." Rhyme implies a level of literacy that a poor unschooled laborer like Joe lacks.

Hammerstein's lyric was likely inspired by Ferber's last line in her novel: "Isn't she splendid!," Magnolia's daughter Kim says of of her mother sailing away on the *Cotton Blossom*. "There's something about her that's eternal and unconquerable—like the River." Years later, Hammerstein found a Tennyson poem, "The Brook," that echoes the theme ("For men may come and men may go / But I go on forever"). Part of the melody was created when Hammerstein suggested to Kern that he might take one of the banjo passages from the opener, "Cotton Blossom," and slow it down for a ballad. Kern took his advice. The first four notes of "Ol' Man Riv-er" are an inversion of "Cot-ton Bloss-om."

Oddly, the song had its first wave of popularity as an up-tempo fox-trot recorded in 1928 by twenty-four-year-old Bing Crosby with Paul Whiteman's band; it's one of Crosby's first recorded solos, sung in what Friedwald describes as a "peppy vocal." Dance bands played it as a number to dance to. Says Friedwald, "Crosby is brimming with *brio*, and far from sounding forlorn when he gets to the part about getting drunk and landing in jail, he sounds as if he might enjoy it." Two months later, Whiteman recorded the song with Robeson the way most people now recognize it, as a thoughtful soliloquy.

Even so, "Ol' Man River" went largely ignored until its 1932 revival, when it became a swing band and jazz band staple, performed in every tempo by any and all comers, from Glen Gray and Victor Young to Bix Beiderbecke and Martha Raye, who actually scats it (in her version, old man river is "truckin' on down"). The Ravens did a 1947 doo-wop version, and a female singer, Jerry Kruger, sang "Ol' Man River" in jive ("Smoke a little tea-o and sing 'O Sole Mio.'"). Ray Charles also messes with the lyrics, much like the swinging mid-'50s Sinatra, "And if you drink a little scotch / I want you to know you're gonna land in jail." Bobby Rydell whitened it up, singing, "Get a little out of hand and you land in jail."

But in fact it was Sinatra, of all unlikely singers, who gave "Ol' Man River" renewed popularity when he sang (and later recorded) it in 1943 at the Paramount Theatre, part of his effort to be regarded as more than a bobby sox heartthrob. Even if, like Crosby, he hardly seemed the most apt performer to croon what sounds like a black hymn, Sinatra gave the song a heartfelt reading that reveals a more serious performer (as he did in his Oscar-winning 1945 short, *The House I Live In*, a plea for racial and religious tolerance). Sinatra felt the song gave him credibility beyond his signature dreamy ballads, allowing him to sing a song, says Decker, with "grown-up emotions and experiences." By that time, notes Todd Decker, "Ol' Man River" had become "primarily a show piece for baritones with big voices," and few of Sinatra's hits had used his lower register; the song, adds Decker, "was very different than anything in his repertoire." Young blue eyes wanted to sit at the adults table.

Sinatra was always undaunted when he wanted to record a song, no matter who might have first sung it to hit status (like Liza Minnelli's "New York,

New York," which Sinatra now owns). He even managed to give "Ol' Man River" (and himself) purpose in the slick, overblown MGM Jerome Kern biopic *Till the Clouds Roll By*, in which Sinatra sings the song in a white tuxedo standing on a white pillar on a white set with an all-white orchestra all wearing white tuxes. But *Life* magazine trashed him for singing it, calling it "the worst single moment" in that year's films. "MGM stifles the music with an opulence [and] struck a high note of bad taste."

There have been three screen versions of *Show Boat*. The first was in 1929, released as both a silent and sound film, and the last was the glossy Technicolor 1951 MGM version with William Warfield, Ava Gardner, Howard Keel, Kathryn Grayson, Joe E. Brown, and Marge and Gower Champion. The color version pales next to the far warmer, richer 1936 black-and-white *Show Boat* directed by James Whale. "Ol' Man River" anchors the '36 *Show Boat* the moment Robeson's rolling magisterial voice intones the words, a perfect merger of singer and song. As he sits on the dock, musing as much as singing, we're drawn to Robeson's physical presence, orotund voice, and ruminative rendition. He gives the song a humanity and a resolve that launched *Show Boat* on its voyage into musical theater history.

CAROUSEL

◆ 1945 ◆

"You'll Never Walk Alone"

"You'll Never Walk Alone" is the lachrymose aria Nettie Fowler, cousin of the female lead Julie Jordan (Jan Clayton on Broadway, Shirley Jones on screen), sings to console Julie after her troubled carnival barker lover Billy Bigelow (John Raitt in his first Broadway show, on screen by Gordon MacRae) accidentally stabs himself in a knife fight rather than face prison for attempted robbery and murder. (The Bigelow role, says critic John Lahr, was originally conceived for Gene Kelly.)

So, OK, here goes: "When you walk through a storm / Hold your head up high / And don't be afraid of the dark. / At the end of the storm / Is a golden sky / And the sweet, silver song of a lark." This is directly followed by a variation on the US postal carrier creed: "Walk on through the wind, / Walk on through the rain, / Tho' your dreams be tossed and blown. Walk on, walk on / With hope in your heart / And you'll never walk alone."

The song was heard each Labor Day weekend for decades at Jerry Lewis's telethon for muscular dystrophy. "You'll Never Walk Alone" sounds like it was taken from a psalm. Indeed, Irving Berlin considered it Hammerstein's greatest song when he first heard it at a funeral; Berlin said it had as much impact on him as Psalm 23. Admittedly, the moment in the show that it's heard can be moving in the context of the story, but it's not one of Hammerstein's most divinely inspired lyrics. *Carousel* was Rodgers's favorite show, and the otherwise impressive and moving score survives its most lofty number.

If once isn't enough, the song is reprised at the end of the show at Billy's daughter Louise's graduation ceremony as Billy watches her from afar—heaven, actually. Billy is granted a one-day furlough to return to earth while a chorus of fellow graduates and presumably angels sings backup. And just to sock the sentiment home, in the final chorus Louise joins in as theatergoers en masse reach for their hankies. It's sort of an *Our Town* moment, with a heavenly choir providing harmony.

If that fails to make you wince, in the original version Hammerstein placed heaven in a parlor with, yes, "Mr. and Mrs. God"; Mr. G strummed a harmonium. Hammerstein wisely thought better of that idea, which Rodgers hated and talked him out of, and transported heaven to a ladder, where a guy called the Starkeeper polishes stars. It's not quite as bad as God and his missus but very close. Billy is led to the Starkeeper hanging strars on a celestial line. Later, the Starkeeper takes Billy to watch his daughter's "deam ballet." As Meryle Secrest writes in her Rodgers biography, "It was perhaps the only faltering of tone in an otherwise flawless work." Even geniuses have off-days.

The number is now hauled out on state occasions: Renée Fleming performed "You'll Never Walk Alone" at the Concert for America on the first anniversary of the 9/11 disaster and again at Barack Obama's 2009 inaugural. It's an even bigger song in England, where it's the official anthem of the Liverpool Football Club, sung by fans before every game; all over England it's played or sung before countless football games, like "God Bless America" in the seventh inning at many American ballparks. During Queen Elizabeth's Golden Jubilee in 2002, 750,000 Britons gathered in front of Buckingham Palace and sang "You'll Never Walk Alone." And in September 1997, the night before Princess Diana's funeral, hundreds of Londoners broke into a quiet chorus of the song.

Hammerstein, in his defense of uplift, once said, "I see plays and read books that emphasize the seamy side of life, and the frenetic and the tragic side, and I don't deny the existence of the tragic and the frenetic. But I say that somebody has to keep saying that that isn't all that there is to life." In this song and others with similar watercolor sentiments, Hammerstein was indeed the ultimate, indefatigable "cockeyed optimist."

THE SOUND OF MUSIC

◆ 1959 ◆

"Climb Ev'ry Mountain"

Almost a rewrite of their earlier never-walk-alone sermon from *Carousel*, **"Climb Ev'ry Mountain"** again finds Oscar Hammerstein at his most determinedly inspirational. Indeed, the lyrics sound like something the Reverend Norman Vincent Peale might have knocked out for a Sunday sermon before thinking better of it.

The dirgelike song arrives in *The Sound of Music* at the end of act 1 when the Mother Abbess sings it to the mixed-up would-be-nun Maria von Trapp, offering her a directive to "climb ev'ry mountain / Ford ev'ry stream / Follow ev'ry rainbow / Till you find your dream." Will do. This line is repeated three times, alternating with "A dream that will need / All the love you can give, / Every day of your life / For as long as you live." Hammerstein had a thing for hills and mountains—"There's a Hill Beyond a Hill," "The Folks Who Live on the Hill," and of course all those singing hills alive with the sound of music— or "the sound of mucus," as Christopher Plummer, Captain von Trapp in the movie, liked to call it.

Hallmark versifiers could not say it any sappier, yet many people are genuinely moved by the song, and Patricia Neway won a Tony for singing it in the original 1959 production. It has since become the theme of heartrending telethons. It's hard to imagine "Climb Ev'ry Mountain" was written by the same lyricist who came up with "I Cain't Say No" and "A Puzzlement." But the big lug also wrote "The Highest Judge of All," "My Favorite Things" ("raindrops on roses and whiskers on kittens"), and two obscure songs actually titled "Prayer."

Even the lyric usually cited as Hammerstein at his most preachy, "You've Got to Be Taught," his antibigotry lecture from *South Pacific*, has authentic feeling and a couple of sardonic phrases ("It's got to be drummed / In your dear little ear / You've got to be carefully taught . . . to hate all the people your relatives hate").

Hammerstein was capable of writing incredibly moving lyrics with honest sentiment—"When the Children Are Asleep," "Why Was I Born?," "The Last Time I Saw Paris," "The Folks Who Live on the Hill," "Ol' Man River," and "Make Believe." But for all his talent and finely tuned poetic sensibility, he was also capable of wrapping songs in holy vestments. He had flowery roots from his operetta youth, writing lyrics for shows with Sigmund Romberg (*The Desert Song, The New Moon*) and Rudolf Friml (*Rose-Marie*). A lot of lyrics in *The Sound of Music* are ponderous or precious—"Do-Re-Mi," "My Favorite Things," even "Maria."

For "Climb Ev'ry Mountain," Hammerstein had a coconspirator in Sister Gregory, the head of the Drama Department at Rosary College in Illinois, who wrote letters to Hammerstein and the show's lead, Mary Martin, pointing out the parallels between choosing a spiritual life and making life choices—something you might expect a woman of the cloth to say but not a seasoned, sophisticated Broadway lyricist. It isn't the idea that's so bad, it's those overloaded lyrics. Sister Gregory wrote to Mary Martin that, much as she liked Richard Rodgers's music, "it was the lyrics that sent me to the Chapel (Relax, chums, I'm sure it will not affect your audiences in the same way). Mr. Hammerstein's lyrics seem perfectly yet effortlessly to express what we ordinary souls feel but cannot communicate."

Adding to the treacle factor is Rodgers's mournful melody, weighted down with chords of doom, a song that early audiences may have figured was an actual old hymn. The song had "such a comfortable air of familiarity," writes Hugh Fordin in his biography of Hammerstein, that it soon became "such an established favorite at weddings, funerals and graduations that many people forget it was written for a Broadway show in the 1940s." The actual Maria von Trapp, a devout Catholic but no softie, was so moved by Hammerstein and his lyrics for the show that she called him "a living saint. It just emanated from him, and I'm sure he didn't know it himself."

Hammerstein's first working title for the song was "Face Life," and he scribbled a few notes to himself about the theme of climbing a hill, "which doesn't bring you much closer to the moon, but closer to the next hill, which you must also climb." Hammerstein then wrote a cautionary footnote to himself, "Don't let it be too obviously a 'philosophical number.'" He didn't take his own advice. Though a huge Hammerstein admirer, Stephen Sondheim says, "There's a fervent lack of surprise in Hammerstein's thoughts, made manifest by his need to spell things out with plodding insistence."

In the screen version of *The Sound of Music*, "Climb Ev'ry Mountain" was moved from the last song of act 1 to much later in the story. Peggy Wood, playing the Mother Abbess, felt the lyrics were so "pretentious" she requested to be photographed in silhouette, not face-front so everyone could see her as the anthem was heard. The song wasn't even sung by Wood, unable to climb the scale to the top notes, so it was dubbed by Margery McKay, wife of the movie's rehearsal pianist.

In *The Sound of Music*, Mary Martin listens dutifully as Patricia Neway advises her to "Climb Ev'ry Mountain."

Another backstage whisper, via Bruce Pomahac of the Rodgers and Hammerstein Organization: as the Mother Superior is singing the last line, "Till you find your dream," Mary Martin, on the word "dream," would snatch off her hat so everyone's attention switched to her, a canny star's felonious way of stealing the moment.

The Sound of Music has the most performances in a given year of any Rodgers and Hammerstein show, regularly trotted out by high schools, community theaters, and major regional companies. For all that, it has had only one major Broadway revival—it's not a critical darling—whereas *The King and I* has been revived four times. *Oklahoma!* is the second most revived Rodgers and Hammerstein show, but Ted Chapin of the Rodgers and Hammerstein Organization admits, "*The Sound of Music* is our calling card." He concedes, "I don't think Rodgers and Hammerstein shows are considered the hippest shows around, but they are certainly the best constructed."

Rebecca Luker, the go-to gal for classic Broadway revivals, played Maria in the 1998 Broadway revival and didn't see her at all as one-dimensional. "My favorite characters are those that are delightfully flawed," she says. "Maria is the perfect example of that. She's a good person at heart but has to work through something—those qualities make the most interesting characters. They have to fight for something and change something in their lives—that's how I look at Maria. It was just a great thrill to come out onstage and sing that opening number! Julie Andrews is forever in our brains. I did steal stuff from her, of course, because, well, why not? Mostly it was certain inflections that we so have in our heads—Julie in *Sound of Music*, Barbara Cook in *Music Man*."

Stephen Sondheim, explaining why *The Sound of Music* beat out *Gypsy* for a 1960 Tony Award, said that Maria von Trapp ended up a lot happier than Momma Rose: "She gets to be faithful to the cloth *and* lose her virginity *and* marry the richest man in town *and* escape the Nazis and *then* become successful in show business." Or as Ethel Merman put it, upon losing the Tony to Mary Martin, "How are you going to buck a nun?"

MAN OF LA MANCHA

◆ 1965 ◆

"The Impossible Dream (The Quest)"

Without **"The Impossible Dream (The Quest),"** the mighty showstopper from *Man of La Mancha*, the 1965 musical about Don Quixote's idealistic search to revive chivalry might never have become a megahit. The score—music by Mitch Leigh and lyrics by Joe Darion—has its moments, but rarely has one song virtually *created* a colossal hit, making it impossible for any other song in the score to get noticed. It totally overshadowed the rest of the show.

"The Impossible Dream" is as guaranteed a head-bowed anthem as "God Bless America," and many performers have eagerly rolled it out as their

In *Man of La Mancha*, Richard Kiley embarks on his "Impossible Dream."

concert finale. Not to stand and cheer the singer performing it is almost sub-versive. It was Robert and Ted Kennedy's favorite song.

"To dream the impossible dream / To fight the unbeatable foe / To bear with unbearable sorrow . . . / To right the unrightable wrong / To love pure and chaste from afar / To try when your arms are too weary / To reach the unreachable star." Then the song ratchets up an octave or so for the climactic, soul-thumping stanza: "This is my quest, to follow that star / No matter how hopeless, no matter how far / To fight for the right, without question or pause / To be willing to march into Hell for a heavenly cause." Many Broadway anthems sound as if they were written by the same lyricist with a somewhat limited vocabulary—lots of dreams, stars, hopes, following your heart, keeping your chin up.

Man of La Mancha, which ran 2,328 performances and quickly went global, in languages from Icelandic to Swahili, and made an instant star of Richard Kiley, has had four Broadway revivals (twice with Kiley, then Raúl Juliá and Brian Stokes Mitchell), and "The Impossible Dream" was recorded by nearly every major singer (Frank Sinatra, Elvis Presley, Andy Williams, Plácido Domingo, Jim Nabors). The musical debuted (like *Annie*) at the Goodspeed Opera House in Connecticut. Rex Harrison was considered for the lead—a truly impossible dream. *My Fair Lady* had sorely taxed Harrison's minimal vocal skills. He would have collapsed by the fifth line as the tune surges heavenward ("To right the unrightable wrong . . .").

The original lyricist of *Man of La Mancha* was, yes, W. H. Auden, whose lyrics were rejected, deemed too dark and acerbic for the musical's insistent message of hope against all odds. The lyricist who replaced Auden, Joe Darion, was an obscure songwriter whose best-known song before "The Impossible Dream" was Red Buttons's goofy "The Ho Ho Song." Composer Mitch Leigh was a former Madison Avenue jingle writer whose score was arranged for an orchestra with only one stringed instrument, a double bass. In Leigh's 2014 obituary, the *New York Times* recalled a 2002 review of the show that called the song "one of the most pervasive anthems of uplift in showbiz history and a song that will presumably wail on for as long as there are piano bars." The anthem has had many half-lives since Broadway, from the Boston Red Sox 1967 pennant-winning season known as "The Impossible Dream" to the background theme of a 2005 Honda commercial.

The show began as a nonmusical teleplay by Dale Wasserman called *Man of La Mancha*, but the sponsor, DuPont, correctly worried that viewers would have no clue what "La Mancha" referred to; "I, Don Quixote" survived as a hearty declaration in the score. The musical is really a show within a show that takes place in author Miguel de Cervantes's jail cell during the Spanish Inquisition, where he devises the play as his defense, which you tend to forget as the show unfolds in real time; the musical opens with Cervantes putting on his Quixote makeup.

The 1972 movie was a major wreck, with off-camera problems and a movie star cast that got in the way—nonsinger Peter O'Toole as Cervantes/

Quixote (his songs were dubbed) and Sophia Loren as his female quest, Dulcinea; James Coco was Sancho Panza. Both Kiley and Joan Diener (Dulcinea on Broadway) had flunked their screen test and were booted when the musical's original director, movie newcomer Albert Marre, was fired and British director Peter Glenville brought in. Glenville was also fired, so reliable Hollywood hand Arthur Hiller finished the job, but the film never approached the phenomenal success of the show.

Man of La Mancha has operatic ambitions, an almost sung-through score with a dozen more songs than the average Broadway musical. "The Impossible Dream" is a daunting Broadway aria, one of the first, breaking ground for songs like "Memory" and "The Music of the Night." Leigh's resounding melodic line defies you to ignore it, and Darion's right-makes-right lyrics are meant to melt the most cynical playgoer. The song is reprised four times in the show, just to make sure nobody misses the point.

EVITA

◆ 1979 ◆

"Don't Cry for Me Argentina"

No anthem better epitomizes a showstopper than Andrew Lloyd Webber and Tim Rice's aria from *Evita*, **"Don't Cry for Me Argentina,"** the imploring plea from a fascist dictator's dying wife. The bravura tear-jerker is red meat for any diva who sinks her teeth into the role of Eva Perón (first Elaine Paige in London, then Patti LuPone on Broadway). Curiously, the song became a showstopper only *after* it was a certified hit. Now audiences greet it with cheers before it's even sung, in the overture. And lest we miss its significance, the tune is also used as funeral music, sung by a grieving choir and by a ghostly Evita. It's a masterful bit of song-plugging that insures earworm hummability before we even get to the actual number in the second act.

"Argentina" is a throbbing, demanding number in which Evita wrings her heart out as she proclaims both her innocence ("Don't cry for me Argentina / The truth is I never left you / All through my wild days / My mad existence / I kept my promise / Don't keep your distance") and her devotion ("I love you and hope you love me"—every sleazy politician's pitch). It's a song that manages to be simultaneously angry, tender, and self-pitying. Shortly after the second-act scene, when she belts the song from a hotel balcony, Evita dies, expiring as theatrically as she lived.

The hypocrisy in the song is that Perón in fact *wants* all of Argentina to weep for her—her maudlin farewell political act. Although introduced in the West End by Paige, the song was already, by its opening night, a huge hit in England and Europe, thanks to an earlier "concept album," one of the first. As sung by Julie Covington in 1977, the tune sold nearly a million copies and became a major marketing tool for the 1978 musical that had people lining up outside the Prince Edward Theatre just to hear Paige deliver it onstage, even if audiences were stymied about what it actually meant.

Lyricist Tim Rice concedes, "The song in itself almost doesn't make sense. It's meant to be a string of political clichés, sounding pretty, and not really saying very much. But it kind of worked, bizarrely." Director Greg MacKellan clears up the confusion: "It took me the longest time to understand what that song was about. She's not saying don't cry tears for me. She's saying don't cry *out* for me. Don't call for me because I'm here, I never left you. I got that interpretation from a friend of Tim Rice's."

Whatever it means, "Don't Cry for Me Argentina" was a guaranteed star-maker—first for Paige in London in '78 and then for LuPone on Broadway a year later. The show also made a star of Mandy Patinkin, whose Che equaled LuPone's urgent performance with his peculiar, showy falsetto. Theatrically they're a matched set, each as intense onstage as the other.

The show got mixed reviews, but LuPone was beloved by the critics, though she revealed in a 2007 interview in the *New York Times*, "'Evita' was the worst experience of my life. I was screaming my way through the part. And I had no support from the producers, who wanted a star performance onstage but treated me as an unknown backstage. It was like Beirut, and I fought like a banshee." Even so, LuPone won her first Tony Award and never looked back.

The song's strange title did not originate with either Lloyd Webber or Tim Rice, who says it comes from Eva Perón's grave in La Recoleta Cemetery in Buenos Aires, where the plaques include a tribute from the city's taxi drivers' union. One of her epitaphs, roughly translated, reads, "Don't cry for me Argentina, I remain quite near to you." Evita was loved by the lower classes for her rise from poverty as an illegitimate child and possibly legit prostitute to radio star and actress. Yet she was despised by the wealthy, who considered her crass, crude, and Machiavellian, a conniving white-trash tyrant, a Hispanic Lady Macbeth—not to mention a Nazi sympathizer. But columnist Joe

Queenan deftly put it in a piece about the song in the *Guardian*, "Eva was too politically unsophisticated to know the difference between a Commie and a Nazi, as she was basically a lounge act."

Rice said in an online interview that the song's title was written late and "caused a lot of problems. When you get a bad title, it kills the song. It had some terrible titles, like 'It's Only Your Lover Returning' and also 'My Wild Days.' In the end, the line 'Don't Cry for Me Argentina' was used elsewhere in the show very early on, and everybody thought that was a nice line, so we made that the title of the song."

Patti LuPone asserts her blonde ambitions in *Evita*.

The idea for the musical album began when Rice heard a radio play about Eva Perón in 1973. He tried the idea out on Lloyd Webber. Evita's appeal—a *puta* with a heart of steel—was undeniable: "A glamorous sexy super-bitch who swayed the fortunes of an entire nation," to quote Lloyd Webber biographer Gerald McKnight. Evita was a sexier, needier Margaret Thatcher. At the time, there was a miner's strike in England that paralyzed the country, and Lloyd Webber said, "Things were getting pretty ugly and we found a kind of parallel in the story of Eva Perón . . . a cautionary tale of how a liberal democracy is a fragile flower that can be overturned by an extremist."

Rice's interest in Evita was more basic: "She was extremely attractive. She dolled herself up to speak to crowds"—as when she sings "Argentina" from a balcony in an evening gown with a sleek upswept blonde hairdo. Some critics thought she was portrayed too much as a red carpet sex bomb and not enough as a Fascist dictator's power-mad mate. Her opposing qualities— crude and genteel, naïve and clever, brutish and suave—made Eva Perón a natural appealing theatrical figure.

Yet Lloyd Webber was reluctant at first, saying he didn't want to do another show about a nobody who rises to fame at thirty-three and dies tragically, as he had just done with an earlier pop superstar, Jesus Christ. Rice persisted, so obsessed with the idea that he and his wife named their daughter Eva-Jane. Lloyd Webber finally caved in, unable to deny the semiheroic schizoid figure and self-created legend. As he told his biographer, "She was easily the most unpleasant character [he'd ever considered]." Noted Queenan in the *Guardian*, "Webber and Rice were less interested in Evita the Politician than in Eva the Diva. This is no more offensive than writing a musical called *Attila's Last Girlfriend* or *Franco's Main Squeeze*." Critics accused the show of being too sympathetic to Perón, and the *Village Voice* said she was presented as a "Cinderella Fascist."

Hal Prince heard a tape of the songs before they were recorded and sent Rice and Lloyd Webber a 3,000-word memo about doing a show. They wrote back that a musical would conflict with their album of the score, not yet released. When it became the number-one LP in Europe, Prince finally heard from the songwriters, but by then Prince had other commitments and had to delay directing *Evita* by eighteen months.

The score is nearly sung-through, then an innovative form, for which Rice had the elusive task of writing lyrics to a score without a libretto. Critic Walter Kerr said the score sounded as if Max Steiner had arranged it for Carmen Miranda. "It's very hard to get the story over when they're singing everything," he noted. Lloyd Webber and Rice had calculated that if they first produced a recording, with all their songs engraved in vinyl, it would keep a director from imposing his own vision on the plot. Ever the control freak, Lloyd Webber confessed, "Through-composing allows me to be in the driver's seat."

He hadn't counted on Hal Prince's spectacular staging that threatened to upstage the score. Prince built a legendary show atop the original 1977 hit recording, staging *Evita* with grandiose operatic sets—billowing curtains, balconies, flashing lights, stark backgrounds—mirroring his similar effects in his staging of *Cabaret* and *Sweeney Todd*. When it finally opened at the Prince Edward Theatre on June 21, 1978, *Evita* was little changed from the original recording and was met with near unanimous raves. One newspaper headline cried, "Don't Cry for Eva—Argentina's a Hit!" Prince's wife Judy said, "Hal took this LP of *Evita* and made it into a religious experience!"

Prince's dazzling theatrics can persuade you it's a powerful saga, but Brendan Gill of the *New Yorker* was not persuaded, calling *Evita* "a calculated muddle of half-truths and balderdash. As history, *Evita* is a radically irresponsible piece of work; as entertainment, it boasts one surefire sentimental song, 'Don't Cry for Me Argentina.' I am at a loss to understand what prompted the devisers of *Evita* to devote their extraordinary talents to the present trifle." He said the "sunny simple-mindedness with which the show addresses itself to its grim subject matter" reminded him of "Springtime for Hitler."

———

When I talked with Patti LuPone at a San Francisco coffeehouse, she said "Don't Cry for Me Argentina" wasn't a showstopper originally. The role had a big impact on her stage persona. She says playgoers didn't make a distinction between Perón and LuPone (whose names even sound similar). She believes that her tough-cookie reputation—enhanced years later after she snatched a smartphone out of a playgoer's hands—is largely due to playing Evita, whom she reluctantly tried out for when Kevin Kline, then her boyfriend, talked her into going for it.

If it wasn't a showstopper at first, how did the song assume megashowstopper status?
I don't know how "Argentina" became legendary and is perceived as a showstopper—I guess because it is the most recognizable song in the show. It now gets the most applause, but it didn't at the time. You couldn't stop the show then with that. People applaud the song now—because they're waiting for it—but in the beginning, no.

Did you comprehend the lyrics at first?

It didn't make any sense to me, even inside the show. Why is she saying, "Don't cry for me Argentina; I never left you"? I didn't get it. Where does "don't cry" come in? Because they're not crying. They're shouting, "Evita, Evita, Evita!" There was never anybody onstage going, "Boo-hoo, she left us." It took a *long* time for me to figure it out. It's a manipulation. After she sings the first verse I didn't know what she was trying to accomplish, what was going on. The lyric is a little vague.

Indeed: "You won't believe me / All you will see / Is a girl you once knew / Although she's dressed up to the nines / At sixes and sevens with you." Translation, anyone?

When I first heard the score I just hated it, and I thought Andrew Lloyd Webber hated women. I was raised on Rodgers and Hammerstein and Jule Styne shows. This wasn't a musical! It was very rock inflected, the first of the industrial musicals of the 1980s and '90s—*Cats*, *Sweeney Todd*, *Les Misérables*, *Miss Saigon*, *The Phantom of the Opera*.

How did you sing a famous song you didn't even understand?

[*laughs*] Well, you do your best. But you really can't fail because of the staging. It's a shocking exit—the music continues and the plot continues, and I give the Italian salute and just walk off the stage. It's a spectacular visual image, with the catwalk and all. I went with the song anyway even though I didn't understand it emotionally or intellectually. You take it moment by moment. I have really good instincts about audiences, and they weren't as confused as I was. It was very tricky.

What effect did such a spectacular role have on your career at the time?

Nothing. I got one offer when I left *Evita*—Lady Macbeth at Lincoln Center.

So it wasn't really a star-making role for you?

No, because Evita was a nasty woman. It's not like *Hello, Dolly!* or *Funny Girl*. Evita was a Nazi, and there was a natural hatred toward her before the show even opened. Audiences were ambivalent about me.

Hal Prince wanted the song sung just as Elaine Paige had sung it in London, but you resisted.

I didn't want it to be a retread of the London version. But they don't allow the actors in a British hit to add anything on Broadway. They always want a carbon copy of the original performance, a cookie-cutter mold. Everyone said, "Oh, it's such a different production for American audiences, so different from the London version." *Nothing* was changed in the Broadway production! Even the costume was the same, but it was too short for me—it was designed for Elaine Paige. Some people in the chorus of the London show tried to tell me what Elaine Paige did. I turned around and I said, "Stop it—right now!" The first thing I'm not gonna do is what Elaine did. Let me discover the role on my own.

You told Eddie Shapiro in his book on Broadway divas, *Nothing Like a Dame*, that Webber and Rice came in at the end [of rehearsal] and gave you notes.

Tim Rice told me to do what Elaine Paige did, and I was like, "Shut the fuck up! I'm not imitating anyone. That's not the way I was trained. I'm a living, breathing actor, if you don't mind." He [Rice] and Elaine were close at the time. And Andrew was in everybody's space, to the detriment of the production. Listen, I knew I could act the shit out of that part. You're given material, you make it work. I wrung a laugh out of the first act, and I made them cry in the second. I knew exactly what I was doing. But every day, I went onstage in absolute terror, even after the Tony Award. That's why I call it the worst experience of my life.

You say Prince's staging kept you in a straitjacket on Broadway but eventually you changed the character to suit you?

I did it the way I wanted to do it. I was unsuccessful in Hal's interpretation, because it didn't fit my body. I decided to smile, which I hadn't been allowed to do on Broadway originally. It was a wink to the audience. The smile said, *Can you believe this woman?*

It was so dissonant and so high and I'm going *yiiiiiii!* Now it's a powerful song, but then . . . well, it wasn't "Oh, What a Beautiful Mornin.'" It was totally avant-garde. If you didn't read the synopsis in the program you couldn't follow the story. So by the time I get to "Argentina" there was no stopping the show with that because nobody knew what the hell was going on! Now when they revive it people know, especially because of the movie with Madonna.

But despite your confusion over the lyrics, you were able to perform the song.

That was the least of my worries in that show. The song is not that difficult. The first thing is to believe it. The way to hook an audience is that you're telling them a story. An actor is a storyteller. "I want to tell this to you, and I'm going to do everything I can to get your attention." So it becomes about that as opposed to individual technical things. There are no tricks. If you sing with total conviction, if you dare an audience, you will get a standing ovation. Look, I'm up there for a reason—I know what I'm doing. That's my territory. The audience knows that. They want me to relax. They love me. They don't want to see a bad show. They don't buy tickets to waste their time. They *want* me to stop the show.

CATS

◆ 1982 ◆

"Memory"

"**M**emory," like "The Impossible Dream," "Hello, Dolly!," "Some Enchanted Evening," "People," and "Tomorrow," is the rare song that made its show a must-see hit. When I climbed into a taxi in London in 1981, the cabbie kept gabbing about a super new show he had just seen called *Cats*. Can anybody even name another song from *Cats*? I didn't think so. "Memory" is the whole ball of string. It made stars of Betty Buckley and Andrew Lloyd Webber while turning humble tabbies into ultracool cats.

Unlike some of the other anthems mentioned here, "Memory" has vivid imagery and earnest emotion, however overripe, a song about fading youth sung by an aging, once gorgeous cat: "Memory / All alone in the moonlight / I can smile at the old days / I was beautiful then . . . / The stale, cold smell of morning / The streetlamp dies, another night is over / Another day is dawning." Lloyd Webber's haunting melody (he cornered the 1980s market on haunting melodies) somehow turns the words into warmed-over mush.

This anthem of the feline world is performed twice in the musical—briefly, to close the first act and whet our appetites, and more fully near the end of the show, pushing the show over the top. The score itself is almost sung-through, with little dialogue or even a discernible story. The overwrought "Memory" lyrics are by the show's director Trevor Nunn—not by Lloyd Webber's usual collaborators Tim Rice or Don Black, both of whom's lyrics to "Memory" were rejected by Lloyd Webber (and presumably Nunn); Richard Stilgoe is credited with "additional lyrics."

The musical's lyrics were inspired by that old Broadway versifier, Tom (T. S.) Eliot. His poems "Preludes" and "Rhapsody on a Windy Night" gave rise to "Memory," sung to glory by Elaine Paige in the original 1981 West End run. Judi Dench was first cast in the role but snapped her Achilles tendon in rehearsals and had to withdraw, delaying her global stardom a few years. Paige went on instead, and the song remains her claim to fame. Lloyd Webber first planned to use the "Memory" melody as a ballad for Juan Perón in *Evita* and then later, in an early draft of *Sunset Boulevard*, as a solo for Max, Norma Desmond's over-the-hill silent-screen director turned devoted butler. It fits best in *Cats*.

The long-running show is based on Eliot's children's classic, *Old Possum's Book of Practical Cats*, a collection of wry verses about sundry cats and their problems, principle among them Grizabella, the washed-up "glamour cat" who sings of her dreams of a new life on the massive junkyard set designed by John Napier that became the show's most-talked-about element—a show-stopper of a set.

Cats has little plot or dialogue, just preening felines—actors with whiskers and face-painted pusses prowling through Napier's glorious mound of garbage and, when their close-up moment arrives, warbling a solo. Frank Rich astutely predicted in the *New York Times*, "The reason why people will hunger to see 'Cats' [is that] it's a musical that transports the audience into a compete fantasy world that could only exist in the theater, and yet, these days, only rarely does." Gillian Lynne's choreography herded a stageful of cats into a cohesive unit, but Bernard Jacobs of the Shubert organization insisted that Michael Bennett should take over the dances, or movement, or whatever, when it moved to Broadway. Bennett flew to London, took a look at the show and said, sagely, "Sure, I might come in with a few better steps. But I'd never come up with a better show."

The British musical got the backs up of the old Broadway establishment, many of whom hissed *Cats*'s immense success, which, wrote critic Rebecca Fowler in the London *Independent*, "buried the conviction that Britain could not take on the Americans at their own game; and one song, 'Memory,' was etched on the national consciousness, sung by everyone from street buskers to opera singers." She noted that "the melody tends to hover yearningly around a very few notes, while the harmony drifts sadly and restlessly from major to minor and back again." Fowler added that Lloyd Webber's critics accused him of "dragging theater down to the lowest common denominator. . . . The public fell in love with the Lycra and the crashing chords of 'Memory.'"

Importing Trevor Nunn from the Royal Shakespeare Company to direct, along with RSC designer John Napier, gave the show a veneer of upscale legitimacy—not to mention its original source, T. S. Eliot, whose distinguished, shadowy presence one critic said "was probably more significant than a single note of the musical." Eliot's name gave the show a classical gloss that made it hard to dismiss *Cats* as just a cheesy thrill ride. Even so, Lloyd Webber called the show a high-risk venture: "We knew we would either come up with something very extraordinary or a total turkey. I had forgotten how close we came to calling the whole thing off."

Producer Cameron Macintosh, trying to raise $500,000 to mount the show, was told by one of his regular backers, "Cameron, I love you. But I'm not investing in this one. It will never work. England is a nation of dog lovers." American critics were equally skeptical, if not downright hostile. Kevin Kelly of the *Boston Globe* wrote, "'Cats' is a dog," and Michael Feingold of the *Village Voice* sniped, "To sit through [the show] is to realize that something has just peed on your pants leg." No wonder producer Jacobs refused for years to quote any critics in ads, using just those spooky gleaming yellow cats eyes and the unforgettable line "Now and Forever," which was devised by publicist Nancy Coyne, which she remembered from the title of a 1934 Shirley Temple movie.

Lloyd Webber had figured *Cats* would become a children's classic, like *Peter and the Wolf* or maybe *The Carnival of the Animals*. Michael Riedel relates that Lloyd Webber invited Eliot's widow Valerie to a gathering at his country home in Sydmonton in 1980, hoping to entice her on board. She loved his tunes and, indeed, brought him some unpublished cat-related material that included a letter Eliot had written outlining a possible play based on his poems, with a verse about Grizabella that he had cut from his collection, fearing it was too depressing for kids.

Cats became as much a marketing as a theatrical phenomenon. The show was franchised, said critic Fowler, "in much the same way as McDonald's has franchised its method of making and selling hamburgers." The Winter Garden Theatre was gutted to carve out the gigantic junkyard set, and the theater lobby was turned into a boutique peddling *Cats* trinkets of every kind—coffee mugs, T-shirts, key chains, anklets, masks—making the show not just a hit musical but a kind of "experience." Playgoers had to purchase a gewgaw to show everyone that they had actually visited the famous *Cats*-land theme park.

Cats also broke the elitist barrier between well-turned-out West End and Broadway playgoers and the hoi polloi—or what Trevor Nunn delicately labeled "a populist audience." People trekked to see *Cats* as they did *Star Wars*. It was perhaps the first Broadway show that people attended in sneakers, sweatshirts, and baseball caps. British opera director Raymond Gubbay said that in time Lloyd Webber would be seen as the Puccini of his day, a composer also sneered at by the upper class when he became a hero of the masses.

Fittingly, Lloyd Webber was accused of filching from Puccini. Gubbay added, "There is no doubt that songs like 'Memory' will be around for decades and decades to come. Maybe it does offend the snobs, but if it's a beast that touches people's hearts, and it does, why not? It's just a bloody good tune." Virtually every singer has taken a crack at "Memory." There is no showier showstopper in Broadway history.

As lead cat Grizabella, Betty Buckley stayed with *Cats* eighteen months before padding off to a long career. Buckley has never quite shed "Memory," which she's sick of talking about to interviewers but will dutifully sing in her cabaret show if begged.

When Buckley sang "Memory" at an audition for *Cats*, Nunn and Lloyd Webber told her agent, "She radiates health and well-being, and we're looking for someone who radiates death and dying." Buckley sniffed, "They'll be back. I just had this feeling about it. I know who my colleagues were in the business, the girl singers who could act. There were only a handful of us. Even Cher wanted to do it."

Six months later they did in fact call Buckley back. Trevor Nunn had her sing "Memory" three times, she recalled, "and each time he would say, 'More suicidal!' By the third time I just felt my whole insides were turned inside out. He still looked like he wasn't sure. I said, 'Mr. Nunn, apparently you think I'm not physically right for this part, but I'm a good actress. If you want me to lose weight, I'll lose weight. If you want me to look smaller, I'll look smaller. But let me tell you this: nobody can do it better—and it's my turn!" Nunn laughed and Buckley thought, "*Uh-oh, what did I just do?* This is the kind of outspoken stuff I used to get in trouble for. Sometimes they look at me like I'm nuts. But this time I got the part."

There was never a more calculated showstopper than "Memory." As Buckley recalled to Eddie Shapiro in his book on musical leading ladies, "In *Cats* the job expectation was, 'Stop the show! We know the show can be stopped with this song.' I was not stopping the show during previews. They panicked so they started calling special rehearsals for me. In one hour of rehearsal, Andrew Lloyd Webber played 'Memory' over and over and over again while I sang. He said to me, 'Placido Domingo saw the show last night and he said,

"Tell the girl to just sing the song."' And I thought, 'But I *am* just singing the song. What are you talking about?'"

Nunn told her to think of *The Winter's Tale*, confusing Buckley even more. "I had no idea how *The Winter's Tale* applies to 'Memory.'" She then called director James Lapine, who advised her, "You're doing everything fine, but I don't know what you feel about it all." This further bewildered Buckley. Next she called an old voice teacher, who told her to get down on her knees and sock a pillow. Reluctantly she began hitting the pillow until she ended in a crazed pillow-busting rage, but that didn't work either.

Her next step was to follow homeless people. "I think Trevor created Grizabella to reflect his feeling about the problem of homelessness," she says. A few performances before opening night, it all came together for her. "It was out of the desire of my heart to connect, to really touch. It came from the dignity I had witnessed on the streets. Then finally I sang 'Memory' and it became a cry of the heart. I finished the song and it was . . . breathless, stunned silence, and then everyone went insane." Show stopped! Nunn came backstage and said, "That's what I was talking about."

Buckley reflects, "I learned big ol' lessons. I learned how to deconstruct a song, to take it apart and put it back together." Stanislavski goes Broadway. Buckley says she never tires of the song, though others may: "No, I love it. It's a beautiful piece of poetry with gorgeous music. Grizabella is one of my great teachers. It took me so long to find her. She's like my soul mate. She's not me; she's herself, and I get to lend my soul to her."

Even Lloyd Webber, well aware of earlier accusations, confessed that indeed the melody to "Memory" sounded too much like a specific Puccini flute solo. When he asked his musician father what he thought, the senior Lloyd Webber said, "It sounds like a million dollars." He was off by about a billion. *Cats* went worldwide and ran eighteen years at the Winter Garden Theatre in New York, the second longest running show on Broadway. In 1998, it arrived belatedly and benumbingly on PBS's *Great Performances*, with Elaine Paige as a disheveled Grizabella. The show, with songs sloppily lip-synced, looked like a cross between a Halloween party for alley cats and a Jazzercise class.

LA CAGE AUX FOLLES

◆ 1983 ◆

"I Am What I Am"

One critic called **"I Am What I Am"** the "Rose's Turn" of *La Cage aux Folles*. The defiant Jerry Herman showstopper became a gay anthem when it arrived in 1983, during the height of the early AIDS epidemic and the first wave of coming-out declarations. It was to gay men what "Secret Love" was for closeted lesbians in the Doris Day movie *Calamity Jane*.

The song is sung by the drag queen Albin when he announces that, yes, dammit, he's queer and proud of it. George Hearn, who played Albin, notes, "It's good it came along just before everything turned bad and we began losing people, about half the men in the cast. The zeitgeist changed and then people were at the barricades." "I Am What I Am" is a textbook Jerry Herman number set to a surging tempo with muscular, defiant, chin-out lyrics, but it's also a catchy tune that changes keys nearly every chorus, Herman's trademark. It's a protest song of a kind that challenges anyone to deny its charac-ter's humanity and individualism. As anthems go, it's one of the most genuinely moving, not just in the show but on its own.

Herman's lyrics spell out a gay manifesto that pretty much says it all, without apology: "I am what I am / I am my own special creation. / So come take a look, / Give me the hook or the ovation . . . / Life's not worth a damn, / 'Til you can say, 'Hey world, I am what I am.'" The song manages to be fierce and fiery without being confrontational. It's persuasive in the best way—by grabbing not your lapel but your heart.

"I had no delusions that this would not be a big moment," Herman told

George Hearn unequivocally declares "I Am What I Am" in *La Cage aux Folles.*

me. "I wrote it to end the act—and to be an emotional thing. But it *absolutely* transcended the showstoppers in every other show I've ever done. And it was just one person alone on a stage. There was a power on that stage that just knocked *me* out when I finally saw it all put together." He continues, "That song is a good example of everything being right—the right artist to sing it, the direction, which was so simple. . . . But the whole idea came from the opening number, 'We Are What We Are,' that Albin later twists into 'I Am What I Am' because he's so hurt. That gave it an emotional quality that topped the 'Dolly' and the 'Mame' numbers. What surprised me was that one man alone onstage, with the right song, orchestration, and director—it made people stand up. I'd never seen *that* before."

For Herman, an early uncloseted gay, it's the song he's most proud of writing. It honestly and deservedly stops the show, even surrounded by minishowstoppers like "The Best of Times," "A Little More Mascara," and "Song on the Sand." Brendan Gill, in his 1983 *New Yorker* review, was less enchanted, writing that "the big song that brings down the curtain on the first act is called 'I Am What I Am,' and I feel obliged to report that, despite my sympathy for Albin, the song put me in mind of nothing so much as the celebrated chant of Popeye the Sailor Man" ("I yam what I yam, an' that's ALL that I yam"). Gill noted that the oath could be uttered with equal fervor by St. Francis of Assisi or Genghis Khan.

Herman recalls that the idea for the song, and the title, was born when the show's book writer, Harvey Fierstein, arrived one day with an impassioned scene to end act 1 that included the phrase, "I am what I am." Herman asked Fierstein if he could steal the phrase and promised to have a song by the next morning. He delivered it, but instead of making the lyrics overly didactic, Herman purposely created a mainstream song that just might become a hit, a song that, like the show itself, not just gays would respond to but also straight mid-American audiences.

Of the show itself, he says he hoped to create, rather than a polemic, a "charming, colorful, great-looking musical comedy—an old-fashioned piece of entertainment." The show revitalized Herman after three respectable but resounding flops, *Dear World*, *The Grand Tour*, and *Mack and Mabel*. Leading up to *La Cage*, Herman had written three dark failures and was hungry for another jolly mainstream hit. "I thought the days for my kind of score were numbered," he remarks. Not quite, not yet.

Frank Rich, in his *New York Times* review, responded, "The show at the Palace is the schmaltziest, most old-fashioned major musical comedy

Broadway has seen since 'Annie.'" But Rich had hoped for more: "The glitz, showmanship, good cheer and almost unflagging tunefulness of 'La Cage aux Folles' are all highly enjoyable and welcome, but in its eagerness to please all comers, this musical is sometimes as shamelessly calculating as a candidate for public office." But glitz, showmanship, good cheer, and unflagging tunefulness pretty much sum up Jerry Herman's entire career, and *La Cage* is no more shamelessly calculating than *Hello, Dolly!* or *Mame*. It purposely avoids being a war cry. The show, wrote Hilton Als in the *New Yorker*, "is not the heterosexual's fantasia of gay life; it's something real, felt, and deep." Without any strain, the song works both as a traditional showstopper and a gay statement.

Herman explains why it's powerful: "The first chorus is done very slowly, with very little orchestra, and he revs himself up to this anger that he feels. The second chorus has a strong beat. When he finishes the second chorus, the orchestra goes wild in 2/4 time and he's able to just yell out his feelings. That's not a trick. There was a reason for it. It's very much a part of how the song was written. It has to be organic and germane. I did the number at my backers' audition exactly as it's done in the show."

Arthur Laurents, who wrote the libretto, said, "'La Cage' brought out the best in Jerry—his strongest work." Herman's openly gay sensibility fit the show perfectly and was an ideal match of show and songwriter; he has said that being gay was never a big self-acceptance issue for him. The musical took the Broadway smart money by surprise when it crossed over to become a hit with nongays. The fervor of Herman's songs overcame audience doubts. By the time "I Am What I Am" ends act 1, most straight playgoers relaxed their defenses, felt the emotion, and just enjoyed the show.

The musical's second most moving number, "The Best of Times"—the finale—likewise earns its sentimental medals, a twist on those-were-the-days-my-friend nostalgia; *these* are the days, the song proclaims, Herman yet again insisting on seizing the day, as the chorus belts, "So hold this moment fast, and live and love as hard as you know how." George Hearn says, "We should tell ourselves that every day." The number is a wide-open, misty-eyed, beer-garden finale, of which Herman says, "'The Best of Times' was written as a very simple song that the audience felt was an old friend—that was its purpose." Playgoers assume "The Best of Times" is an old beer hall sing-along number. Herman adds, "It very, very sneakily changes key and rises—that's not because of any emotional thing, but just to create an excitement, and it causes people to clap along"—a classic audience-grabbing device in such numbers as "Seventy-Six Trombones," "Once in Love with Amy," and "Master of the House."

Herman comments, "The secret of *La Cage* for me is that it's wholesome, it's a family show. It wasn't camped up or militant. I didn't write 'I Am What I Am' to make a political statement." A few critics, like Rich, felt Herman dodged tougher gay issues to make the show accessible and commercial, but George Hearn observes, "If it was a message show it would have run two weeks, not four and a half years. It was more than a play—it was a social moment in America. The show didn't need to make a statement to make an impact. It wasn't militant, it was entertainment. Theater can do things that you can't legislate."

LES MISÉRABLES

◆ 1987 ◆

"I Dreamed a Dream"

*L*es Misérables is at least as overpowering as *Cats* or *The Phantom of the Opera*, but it isn't a simple-minded fantasy. It tells Victor Hugo's multi-layered morality tale with lifelike characters whose desperate lives are dramatized against a historical mural of the Paris uprisings following the failure of the French Revolution and the Napoleonic Wars. It's a theatrical novel and the *War and Peace* of musicals.

Les Miz and its sumptuous score resist crumbling under their own dramatic weight by the intense stories that the urgent songs inhabit. It's been called syrupy, bombastic, excessive, illogical, and overwrought—all true, yet it's rescued from hokey melodrama by a majestic score and Trevor Nunn's and John Caird's life-size staging. You're moved by the show in spite of yourself, even at times in spite of *itself*. A woman I took to the show turned to me during the overture and said, "I'm already crying."

As Broadway spectacles go, *Les Misérables* has never been equaled in more than thirty-five years, seen by some sixty million people, as much of an operatic epic as *Porgy and Bess*, *Sweeney Todd*, or, for that matter, *Madame Butterfly*. A third Broadway revival opened in 2014 to rave reviews. Like Javert, *Les Miz* refuses to go away for good. It's just a ripping good yarn, as the Brits say, filled with compelling characters and incidents, about a noble Frenchman imprisoned for stealing a loaf of bread who (in case you didn't finish the novel in high school) spends his life fleeing a ruthless inspector. It's *The Fugitive* with great songs.

Les Misérables is almost a nonstop anthem, a steadily stirring musical in the vein of—but far more accomplished and complicated than—*Godspell*, *Pippin*, *Hair*, or *Rent*. The songs echo each other, weave in and out of the show, are often recycled as ironic motifs, and, movie-like, underscore many scenes.

The orchestrations include harpsichord and synthesizer, madrigals and rock 'n' roll, and evoke Bizet and Weill. The 1980 operatic musical is based on a Victor Hugo world classic, which doesn't hurt, but many musicals based on world classics crash on takeoff, too inflated for their own good—*Anna Karenina*, *Doctor Zhivago*, *A Tale of Two Cities*, *Gone with the Wind*. *Les Miz* is overblown, to be sure, as stuffed with sentimentality, coincidence, and melodrama as any Dickens novel, but somehow it never blows up in your face. The show hangs together, unlike, say, Frank Wildhorn's wannabe epics (*The Scarlet Pimpernel*, *Jekyll & Hyde*). A critic observed that *Les Misérables* "has everything to do with the electrifying showmanship of the twentieth century musical," but it's managed to move people with tenderness and taste, unlike, say, the jolts that surge through *Wicked*.

"I Dreamed a Dream" is about the best-known of *Les Misérables*'s half dozen heart-wrenchers, each as compelling and powerful an anthem as the next. In its first Broadway incarnation, critic Frank Rich said Randy Graff's Fantine sang this "go-for-the-throat" number "like a Broadway belter handed a showstopper rather than a pathetic woman in ruins." Fantine, forced to become a whore, sings "I Dreamed a Dream" as she recalls rosier times before losing her job and being cast into the Paris streets. Patti LuPone sang the role in the 1985 British version, Graff in 1987 on Broadway.

"I Dreamed a Dream" had an unexpected revival when plain, heavyset, fuzzy-browed Susan Boyle, who looked like a woman from the show's streets, sang it on *Britain's Got Talent*, tore viewers' hearts out (also the judges'), and went viral the next day. Boyle, partly thanks to a major makeover, rode the song to overnight stardom and a career that proved her rendering wasn't a fluke.

"I Dreamed a Dream" encourages singers to sing their guts out, but it doesn't cause retching thanks to Claude-Michel Schönberg's propulsive music and Alain Boublil's sensitive lyrics (English translation by Herbert Kretzmer) and, to be sure, by Fantine's dismal plight, in which she contrasts the mellow innocence of her girlhood when all was good and she was young and fearless to her present hellish plight, and how life had murdered her early hopes and dreams. The song has a crushingly beautiful melody, like so many of the tunes in the score.

In the belated 2012 less-than-compelling movie starring Hugh Jackman as Valjean and Russell Crowe as Javert, Anne Hathaway portrays the tragic Fantine, whose rendition of "I Dreamed a Dream" gives the film its most powerful moment and gave Hathaway an Oscar.

The song was among the first composed for the show, in 1978, when Schönberg sat down at a small white piano and wished for "a sparkle of light." It arrived in a line from the 1862 novel, which emerged from a phrase he kept singing to himself, "J'avais rêvé d'une autre vue." He later explained, "That's one of the worst feelings you can have, that your life has not been what you thought it was going to be. That's what I wanted to express through a song." A young singer, Rose Laurens, sang the song on a concept album, followed by a three-month live version of *Les Misérables* at Paris's Palais des Sports that launched the theatrical juggernaut.

The first English-language Fantine, Patti LuPone, found her way into the song's emotion after being dumped by a boyfriend. "I was dating some guy in New York who broke up with me over the phone," LuPone told Rob Brunner of *Entertainment Weekly*. "Well, what do you think informed the song for the rest of my run? My broken heart." That plus a bronchial cough tore the emotion to tatters when she sang the song. "Every night when I went onstage I felt like I did have tuberculosis and my heart was broken. I'll tell you what, it isn't easy. You have to sing through tears. You get to that point in the song and you're tearing your heart out." Britain's Ruthie Henshall, who sang it at a tenth anniversary concert, said, "It's so rich for an actress because it's not just a one-note song. It has the colors of the rainbow in it."

Randy Graff as Broadway's Fantine relates "I Dreamed a Dream" in *Les Misérables*.

Not to be outdone by LuPone or Henshall, Hathaway had her own searing memories of recording the song for the film, which took eight hours of retakes that left her spent. "As a human being, I am devastated that Fantine exists, that people on this planet go through that. So getting closer to that emotion just kept getting darker and darker. With each take, my rage took a quantum leap forward. I just had this tempest inside of me. I wish I could say that I was inside of it and loving every second, but I really wasn't." Afterward, she says, "I just went home and crawled into my husband's arms."

THE PHANTOM OF THE OPERA
(1988)
"The Music of the Night"

The musical that had even more lives than *Cats*, and still refuses to die, is of course *The Phantom of the Opera*, which will be running long after most of us have stopped walking.

The 1986 Andrew Lloyd Webber musical (which worldwide has earned a record $6 billion and counting, the McDonald's of musicals) produced the morose, show-stopping, histrionic anthem **"The Music of the Night,"** which the creepy masked Phantom (Michael Crawford originally) croons to his pretty prey, Christine Daaé. She is the naive beauty to his beastly abductor who takes her to his lair below the Paris opera house, there to be seduced by the song. To cite Noël Coward—extraordinary how potent cheap music is.

Lloyd Webber didn't really represent the musical theater future, as often described, but was, in fact, a throwback to its distant past—to the passionate operettas of Rudolf Friml, Victor Herbert, and Otto Harbach. Like their works, *Phantom* was drenched in flowery romance and melodrama. Critic Charles Isherwood called the overambitious score "mock-operatic."

The backstory, according to Sarah Brightman (the original Christine, also the composer's former wife), is that Lloyd Webber wrote the song for her just after he met her, but it had different lyrics than the famous version and was called "Married Man." Their own marriage didn't survive the show, but the song was stamped on Brightman for life, inspiring her later lavish overproduced concerts. Despite Brightman's impressive talent, she has never quite escaped the Phantom's clutches.

"The Music of the Night" is the acknowledged showstopper, but it isn't the best song in *Phantom*—"All I Ask of You" is a prettier, truer, more moving ballad, the score's most romantic number. "The Music of the Night" led to accusations that Lloyd Webber lifted the tune from Puccini's *Girl of the Golden West*. The Puccini estate even sued Lloyd Webber for plagiarism, but it was settled out of court, sealed from suspicious eyes.

Critic Steven Winn wrote about a revival that played San Francisco in 2015, "Give Lloyd Webber his due on this: As simplistic and sometimes insipid as they may seem on closer analysis, 'Think of Me,' 'All I Ask of You,' 'Wishing You Were Somehow Here Again' and the Puccini-assisted 'Music of the Night' cast an emotional spell, even on first hearing. That, as many other envious composers might concede, represents a certain kind of emotional promised land." He added, "The Phantom represents a kind of submission. He is mentor and mendicant to her, abductor and love-struck captive. It's all, perhaps, more for female than male audiences—potent, sexy, subliminal stuff."

The lyrics, credited to both Charles Hart and Richard Stilgoe, are not just syrupy but close to incomprehensible—something about surrendering to the fantasies of the night, whatever that might mean. The song is supposed to be romantic and erotic, but it's really theme music for an abduction: just lie back and relax, my dear, submit to the music of the night and think pretty thoughts while I ravish you. It's a standard male (maybe even female) fantasy, and a familiar ploy, but many women do indeed swoon at the song, swept away by the pounding orchestrations and the Phantom's hypnotic wiles: "Close your eyes and surrender to your darkest dreams / Purge your thoughts of the life you knew before / Close your eyes, let your spirit start to soar / And you'll live as you've never lived before." Oh, yes, yes, Mr. Phantom! Whatever you say.

Rebecca Luker followed Sarah Brightman into *Phantom* on Broadway. She had understudied the role and groomed for it, playing Christine for eighteen months, her first Broadway part at twenty-seven. Nine months in, they finally threw Luker onstage one night with Michael Crawford. "That went very well, so they started looking at me with more serious eyes," she recalls. The only hitch was that she didn't quite fit into Brightman's hallowed shoes. "Hal Prince really wanted it played a certain way. I'm not at all like Sarah Brightman, but there was a *Phantom* formula for the role." Luker adds, "I

Michael Crawford puts a fond choke hold on Sarah Brightman in "The Music of the Night" from *The Phantom of the Opera*.

tried to bring my own self to it. I wouldn't say it was stifling, but you did feel a little confined. If I could do it again I would try to make her more real. She's a bit larger than life character, a caricature I would want to flesh out a little more now."

Luker goes on, "It was a magical show when it opened, with a mysterious quality about it, especially back in 1988 when it opened. The score was so different for that time—a sexy rock electronic sound, mixed with this wonderful story that is very intriguing to a lot of people. I love horror, and the show mixes it in with romance. The show sort of had it all. And it was gorgeous to look at." Barbra Streisand recorded the song as a duet with Michael Crawford on her blockbuster 1993 album *Back to Broadway*, even though she hadn't been back to Broadway since *Funny Girl* in 1964. The album was recorded in a Broadway theater to lend the title its dubious credibility.

After it opened, *The Phantom of the Opera* was such a monolithic hit that it crushed everything in its path and even threatened a megahit across the street, *42nd Street*. But the phantom of Broadway, David Merrick, fearless producer of *42nd Street*, found a way to capitalize on the British interloper and to hijack its obsessed ticket buyers. Merrick moved the *42nd Street* curtain ahead to 8:15 so that playgoers unable to get into *Phantom* at 8:00 PM could scamper across the street to see *42nd Street*, which Merrick advertised as "Broadway's *Latest* Hit!"

CURTAIN

ACKNOWLEDGMENTS

I've been lucky and grateful to have a strong supporting cast to help get this little show on the road and turn a lifelong idea for a book on musicals into reality. Take a bow, guys: Harry Haun of *Playbill*, for his massive Rolodex that helped put me in touch with many of the major Broadway figures in the book; Carla Ruff, for helping get me to Tommy Tune; Greg MacKellan, for his keen insights into musicals; Michael Kerker at ASCAP, for lending a hand on copyright permissions; Amy Rennert, for her early efforts on behalf of the book; my agent Andy Ross, for quickly landing a publisher; Marilyn Levinson, for leading me to Chita Rivera; Paul Gilger, for putting me in touch with Jerry Herman; Randy Poe, for his ideas about, and enthusiasm for, musicals and for his input into the introduction; pals Mike Johnson, Morrie Bobrow, Maggie Berke, Rita Abrams, and Al Negrin, for patiently and politely listening to my fascinating tales of putting the book together, and to Mike for added wise editorial counsel; Kathy Philis, for her encouraging responses to excerpts from the book, and for her passion for, knowledge of, and insights into musicals, and for her demon and efficient fact-checking skills; Ted Chapin, Bert Fink, and Bruce Pomahac at the Rodgers and Hammerstein Organization, for sharing their views and for helping get me to several Broadway figures; Lisa Lombardi at Williamson Music, for expediting several last-minute song permissions; Nilda Rivera and Dollie Banner, for digging up two hard-to-find photos; Klea Blackhurst, for her savvy ideas about Ethel Merman; Lotte Lundell, for serving as faithful and efficient researcher, transcriber, and Scrabble opponent; Nick Carlin for his insights into intellectual law; Bill Lanese, for getting me to Patricia Morison; Kevin Kojack, for putting up with many e-mail requests to locate this or that performer; unflappable computer wizard Mel Margolis, for his skill at getting me out of countless cyberscrapes; Rick Simas, for his ideas about shows and songs; Norm Hershey for lending a sympathetic ear and hand to an early version of the book; Dore Brown, for graciously editing the introduction; keen-eyed Julie Brand, for her editing suggestions, tea, and sympathy; project editor Ellen Hornor and copyeditor

Mark Bast for smoothing out many a clunky sentence and saving me from various grammatical and factual embarrassments; Rebecca Lown, for her inviting cover design; Jonathan Hahn, for his handsome and inventive interior page design; and to my editor, Yuval Taylor, for saying yes to the idea and for his yeoman efforts on behalf of the book and for his patience with an anxious author.

PERMISSIONS

Williamson Music owner of publication and allied rights throughout the world
International copyright secured

Chicago

"All That Jazz," "Razzle Dazzle," "We Both Reached for the Gun," "Mister Cellophane"
Music by John Kander. Words by Fred Ebb.
© 1975 (renewed) Unichappell Music, Inc. and Kander & Ebb, Inc.
All rights administered by Unichappell Music, Inc.

Company

"Ladies Who Lunch," "You Could Drive a Person Crazy," "Getting Married Today"
Written by Stephen Sondheim.
Used by permission of Herald Square Music, Inc. on behalf of Range Road Music, Inc., Jerry Leiber Music, Silver Seahorse Music LLC, Burthen Music Company, Inc. and Rilting Music, Inc.

A Connecticut Yankee

"Thou Swell"
Music by Richard Rodgers. Words by Lorenz Hart.
© 1927 (renewed) WB Music and Williamson Music Co.

"To Keep My Love Alive"
Music by Richard Rodgers. Words by Lorenz Hart.
© 1944 (renewed) Warner Bros. Inc. and Williamson Music, Inc.

Follies

"Broadway Baby," "I'm Still Here"
Written by Stephen Sondheim.
Used by permission of Herald Square Music, Inc. on behalf of Range Road Music, Inc., Jerry Leiber Music, Silver Seahorse Music LLC, Burthen Music Company, Inc. and Rilting Music, Inc.

Funny Girl

"Don't Rain on My Parade"
Music by Jule Styne. Words by Bob Merrill.
© 1963, 1964 (copyrights renewed) by Bob Merrill and Jule Styne

Publication and allied rights assigned to Wonderful Music, Inc. and Chappell-Styne, Inc. and administered by Chappell & Co., Inc.

"People"
Music by Jule Styne. Words by Bob Merrill.
© 1963, 1964 (copyrights renewed) Wonderful Music, Inc. and Chappell-Styne, Inc.
All rights administered by Chappell & Co., Inc.

Garrick Gaeities

"Manhattan"
Music by Richard Rodgers. Lyrics by Lorenz Hart.
Copyright © 1925 Edward B. Marks Music Company
Copyright renewed. Copyright assigned to Williamson Music and Piedmont Music for the United States, Canada, and the British Reversionary Territories. International copyright secured. All rights reserved.

"Mountain Greenery"
Music by Richard Rodgers. Lyrics by Lorenz Hart.
Copyright © 1926 Harms, Inc.
Copyright renewed. Copyright assigned to Williamson Music and WB Music Corp. for the extended renewal period of copyright in the USA. International copyright secured. All rights reserved.

Girl Crazy

"I Got Rhythm"
Music by George Gershwin. Words by Ira Gershwin.
© 1930 (renewed) WB Music Corp. and Ira Gershwin Music
All rights administered by WB Music Corp.

Gypsy

"Everything's Coming Up Roses," "Rose's Turn," "Some People"
Music by Jule Styne. Lyrics by Stephen Sondheim.
© 1959 (renewed) Stratford Music Corporation and Williamson Music Co.
All rights administered by Chappell & Co., Inc.

"You Gotta Get a Gimmick"
Music by Stephen Sondheim. Words by Jule Styne.

The King and I

"Shall We Dance?"

Kiss Me, Kate

"Always True to You in My Fashion," "Brush Up Your Shakespeare"
Words and music by Cole Porter.

Lady in the Dark

"Tschaikowsky (and Other Russians)"
Music by Kurt Weill. Words by Ira Gershwin.

Mammy

"Let Me Sing and I'm Happy"

My Fair Lady

"Get Me to the Church on Time," "The Rain in Spain"
Music by Frederick Loewe. Lyrics by Alan Jay Lerner.

Oklahoma!

"I Cain't Say No"

Paris

"Let's Do It (Let's Fall In Love)"
Words and music by Cole Porter.

The Sound of Music

"Climb Ev'ry Mountain"

South Pacific

"Some Enchanted Evening"
"There Is Nothin' Like a Dame"

BIBLIOGRAPHY

Books

Bach, Steven. *Dazzler: The Life and Times of Moss Hart*. New York: Alfred A. Knopf, 2001.

Berson, Misha. *Something's Coming, Something Good: "West Side Story" and the American Imagination*. Montclair, NJ: Applause Theater and Cinema Books, 2011.

Block, Geoffrey. *Enchanted Evenings: The Broadway Musical from "Show Boat" to Sondheim and Lloyd Webber*. New York: Oxford University Press, 1997.

———. *The Richard Rodgers Reader*. New York: Oxford University Press, 2002.

Bordman, Gerald. *American Musical Comedy: From "Adonis" to "Dreamgirls."* New York: Oxford University Press, 1982.

Brahms, Carol, and Ned Sherrin. *Song by Song: 14 Great Lyric Writers*. Ross Anderson Publications, 1984.

Brooks, Mel, and Tom Meehan. *"The Producers": The Book, Lyrics, and Story Behind the Biggest Hit in Broadway History! How We Did It*. New York: Hyperion Books, 2001.

Burrow, Abe. *Honest, Abe: Is There Really No Business Like Show Business?* New York: Little, Brown, 1980.

Chapin, Ted. *Everything Was Possible: The Birth of the Musical "Follies."* New York: Alfred A. Knopf, 2003.

Charnin, Martin. *"Annie": A Theatre Memoir*. London: E. P. Dutton, 1971.

Citron, Stephen. *Jerry Herman: Poet of the Showtune*. New Haven: Yale University Press, 2004.

———. *The Musical from the Inside Out*. Lanham, MD: Ivan R. Dee, 1991.

Engel, Lehman. *The American Musical Theater*. New York: Collier Books, 1975.

———. *Their Words Are Music: The Great Theatre Lyricists and Their Lyrics*. New York: Crown, 1975.

Flinn, Caryl. *Brass Diva: The Life and Legends of Ethel Merman*. Oakland: University of California Press, 2007.

Flinn, Denny Martin. *Musical! A Grand Tour*. New York: Schirmer Books, 1997.

Fordin, Hugh. *Getting to Know Him: A Biography of Oscar Hammerstein II*. New York: Random House, 1977.

Friedwald, Will. *Stardust Melodies: A Biography of Twelve of America's Most Popular Songs*. New York: Pantheon Books, 2002.

Furia, Philip, and Michael Lasser. *America's Songs: The Stories Behind the Songs of Broadway, Hollywood and Tin Pan Alley*. New York: Routledge, 2006.

Furia, Philip. *Ira Gershwin: The Art of the Lyricist*. New York: Oxford University Press, 1996.

———. *Irving Berlin: A Life in Song*. New York: Schirmer Trade Books, 1998.

Garebian, Keith. *The Making of "Cabaret."* New York: Oxford University Press, 2011.

———. *The Making of "Guys and Dolls."* Oakville, Ontario: Mosaic, 2002.

———. *The Making of "Gypsy."* Oakville, Ontario: Mosaic, 1995.

———. *The Making of "My Fair Lady."* Oakville, Ontario: Mosaic, 1995.

———. *The Making of "West Side Story."* Oakville, Ontario: Mosaic, 1995.

Garrett, Betty. *Betty Garrett and Other Songs: A Life on Stage and Screen*. New York: Madison Books, 1998.

Gershwin, Ira. *Lyrics on Several Occasions*. Elm Tree Books/Hamlisch Hamilton, 1977.

Gilvey, John Anthony. *Before the Parade Passes By: Gower Champion and the Glorious American Musical*. New York: St. Martin's, 2005.

Goldstein, Malcolm. *George S. Kaufman: His Life, His Theater*. New York: Oxford University Press, 1979.

Gottfried, Martin. *All His Jazz: The Life and Death of Bob Fosse*. New York: Bantam Books, 1990.

Gottlieb, Robert, and Robert Kimball. *Reading Lyrics*. New York: Pantheon Books, 2000.

Green, Benny. *A Hymn to Him: The Lyrics of Alan Jay Lerner*. Milwaukee: Limelight Editions, 1997.

Green, Stanley. *Broadway Musicals, Show by Show*. Milwaukee: Hal Leonard Books, 1985.

———. *The World of Musical Comedy*. New York: A. S. Barnes, 1985.

Greenspan, Charlotte. *Pick Yourself Up: Dorothy Fields and the American Musical*. New York: Oxford University Press, 2010.

Gregg, Hubert. *Thanks for the Memory: A Personal Spotlight on Special People in Entertainment*. London: Victor Gollancz, 1983

Hay, Peter. *Broadway Anecdotes*. New York: Oxford University Press, 1989.

Herman, Jerry. *Showtune: A Memoir*. London: Dutton Adult, 1986.

Hischak, Thomas S. *The American Musical Theater Song Encyclopedia*. Santa Barbara, CA: Greenwood, 1995.

———. *The Oxford Companion to the American Musical: Theater, Film and Television*. New York: Oxford University Press, 2008.

———. *Word Crazy: Broadway Lyricists from Cohan to Sondheim*. Santa Barbara, CA: Praeger, 1991.

Ilson, Carol. *Harold Prince: From "Pajama Game" to "Phantom of the Opera."* Ann Arbor, MI: UMI Research Press, 1989.

Jowitt, Deborah. *Jerome Robbins: His Life, His Theater, His Dance*. New York: Simon & Schuster, 2004.

Kander, John, and Fred Ebb. *Colored Lights: Forty Years of Words and Music, Show Biz, Collaboration and All That Jazz*. London: Faber & Faber, 2003.

Kasha, Al, and Joel Hirschhorn. *Notes on Broadway: Intimate Conversations with Broadway's Greatest Songwriters*. Contemporary Books, 1985.

Kellow, Brian. *Ethel Merman: A Life*. New York: Viking, 2007.

Kissel, Howard. *David Merrick—The Abominable Showman: The Unauthorized Biography*. New York: Applause Books, 2000.

Lamb, Andrew. *150 Years of Popular Musical Theater*. New Haven: Yale University Press, 2000.

Laurents, Arthur. *Original Story By: A Memory of Broadway and Hollywood*. New York: Alfred A. Knopf, 2000.

Lees, Gene. *The Musical Worlds of Lerner and Loewe*. London: Robson Books, 1991.

Leopold, David. *Irving Berlin's Show Business: Broadway, Hollywood, America*. New York: Harry N. Abrams, 2005.

Loesser, Susan. *A Most Remarkable Fella: Frank Loesser and the Guys and Dolls in His Life; A Portrait by His Daughter*. London: Donald I. Fine Books, 1993.

Logan, Josh. *Josh: My Up and Down, In and Out Life*. New York: Delacorte, 1976.

Mandelbaum, Ken. *"A Chorus Line" and the Musicals of Michael Bennett*. New York: St. Martin's, 1989.

Mann, William J. *Hello, Gorgeous: Becoming Barbra Streisand*. Boston: Houghton Mifflin Harcourt, 2012.

Marmorstein, Gary. *A Ship Without a Sail: The Life of Lorenz Hart*. New York: Simon & Schuster, 2012.

Maslon, Lawrence. *The "South Pacific" Companion*. New York: Touchstone, 2008.

Mast, Gerald. *Can't Help Singin': The American Musical on Stage and Screen*. New York: Overlook, 1987.

McBrien, William. *Cole Porter: A Biography*. New York: Alfred A. Knopf, 1998.

McGovern, Dennis, and Deborah Grace Winer. *Sing Out, Louise!: 150 Stars of the Musical Theater Remember 50 Years on Broadway.* New York: Schirmer Books, 1993.

McKnight, Gerald. *Andrew Lloyd Webber: A Biography.* New York: St. Martin's, 1984.

Merman, Ethel. *Don't Call Me Madam: An Autobiography in Neon.* London: W. H. Allen, 1955.

Miller, Scott. *Deconstructing Harold Hill: An Insider's Guide to Musical Theatre.* London: Heinemann, 2000.

Mordden, Ethan. *Beautiful Mornin': The Broadway Musical in the 1940s.* New York: Oxford University Press, 1999.

———. *Coming Up Roses: The Broadway Musical in the 1950s.* New York: Oxford University Press, 2000.

———. *Make Believe: The Broadway Musical in the 1920s.* New York: Oxford University Press, 1997.

———. *On Sondheim: An Opinionated Guide.* New York: Oxford University Press, 2016.

———. *One More Kiss: The Broadway Musical in the 1970s.* London: Palgrave, 2003.

———. *Rodgers & Hammerstein.* New York: Harry M. Abrams, 1992.

Nolan, Frederick. *The Sound of Their Music: The Story of Rodgers and Hammerstein.* London: Walker, 1978.

Prince, Hal. *Contradictions: Notes on Twenty-Six Years in the Theatre.* New York: Dodd, Mead, 1974.

Rich, Frank. *Hot Seat: Theater Criticism for the "New York Times," 1980–1993.* Random House, 1998.

Rodgers, Richard. *Musical Stages.* New York: Random House, 1975.

Secrest, Meryle. *Somewhere for Me: A Biography of Richard Rodgers.* Monclair, NJ: Applause Theater and Cinema Books, 2001.

———. *Stephen Sondheim: A Life.* New York: Alfred A. Knopf, 1998.

Shapiro, Eddie. *Nothing Like a Dame: Conversations with the Great Women of Musical Theater.* New York: Oxford University Press, 2014.

Sheed, Wilfrid. *The House That George Built: With a Little Help from Irving, Cole and a Crew of About Fifty.* New York: Random House, 2007.

Simon, John. *John Simon on Theater: Criticism 1974–2003.* Montclair, NJ: Applause Books, 2005.

Solomon, Alisa. *Wonder of Wonders: A Cultural History of "Fiddler on the Roof."* New York: Metropolitan Books, 2013.

Sondheim, Stephen. *Finishing the Hat.* New York: Alfred A. Knopf, 2010.

Steyn, Mark. *Broadway Babies Say Goodnight: Musicals Then and Now.* New York: Routledge, 1999.

Strouse, Charles. *Put on a Happy Face: A Broadway Memoir.* New York: Union Square Press, 2008.

Suskin, Steven. *Opening Night on Broadway: A Critical Quotebook of the Golden Era of the Musical Theater; "Oklahoma!" to "Fiddler on the Roof."* New York: Schirmer Books, 1990.

———. *Show Tunes, 1905–1985: The Songs, the Shows, and Careers of Broadway's Major Composers.* New York: Dodd, Mead, 1986.

Taylor, Theodore. *Jule: The Story of Composer Jule Styne.* New York: Random House, 1979.

Thomas, Bob. *I Got Rhythm: The Ethel Merman Story.* New York: G. P. Putnam's Sons, 1985.

Tune, Tommy. *Footnotes.* New York: Simon & Schuster, 1997.

Vaill, Amanda. *Somewhere: The Life of Jerome Robbins.* New York: Broadway Books, 2006.

Viagas, Robert, Baayork Lee, and Thommie Walsh. *On the Line: The Creation of "A Chorus Line."* New York: William Morrow, 1990.

Wilk, Max. *OK! The Story of "Oklahoma!": A Celebration of America's Most Beloved Musical.* Milwaukee: Applause Theater and Cinema Books, 2002.

———. *They're Playing Our Song: The Truth Behind the Words and Music of Three Generations.* New York: Moyer Bell, 1991.

Zinsser, William. *Easy to Remember: The Great American Songwriters and Their Songs.* Boston: David R. Godine, 2001.

Interviews

Adams, Edie (3/24/04)
Barbeau, Adrienne (4/18/15)
Blackhurst, Klea (2/27/14)
Bloom, Ken (5/8/15)
Champion, Marge (2/18/14)
Chapin, Ted (5/14/15)
Charnin, Martin (3/26/14, 11/1/14)
Church, Sandra (2/5/14)
Ellis, Josh (5/7/15)
Evans, Harvey (6/3/14)
Fink, Bert (2/19/04)
Gardner, Rita (4/30/14)
Garrett, Betty (3/24/04)
Gemignani, Paul (10/11/12)
Grey, Joel (10/12/12, 9/8/15)
Hamlisch, Marvin (5/6/12)
Harnick, Sheldon (10/9/12)
Herman, Jerry (1/19/04, 2/13/15)
Holm, Celeste (3/4/04)
Irving, George S. (1/6/15)
Jones, Tom (3/23/14)
Kander, John (10/16/12)
Kreuger, Miles (4/8/14)
Lahm, David (10/1/14)
Lee, Sondra (2/28/15)
Luker, Rebecca (6/17/15)

LuPone, Patti (5/24/04)
MacKellan, Greg (3/9/04, 8/13/15)
Martin, Hugh (3/11/04)
McArdle, Andrea (10/10/12)
McKechnie, Donna (3/23/04)
Morison, Patricia (2/20/04, 2/10/14)
Myers, Pamela (6/13/14)
Neuwirth, Bebe (4/3/15)
Prince, Faith (5/8/14)
Prince, Harold (9/18/12)
Raitt, John (3/22/04)
Ralston, Teri (3/26/04)
Reams, Lee Roy (6/12/14)
Rivera, Chita (6/13/14)
Rolph, Marti (8/6/14)
Schwartz, Stephen (3/25/14)
Selvin, Joel (8/18/15)
Small, Mews (7/11/15)
Stroman, Susan (6/15/12)
Strouse, Charles (2/8/14)
Sullivan Loesser, Jo (10/2/14)
Suzuki, Pat (7/29/14)
Tune, Tommy (10/10/12)
Van Dyke, Dick (3/20/13)
Watson, Susan (3/1/04)
Young, John Lloyd (7/23/15)
Ziemba, Karen (6/4/15, 7/11/15)

INDEX